Clarissa Percival

This book belongs to:

Alicia Vianne Paine

ON THE TRAIL OF THE TRUTH

A PLACE IN THE SUN

MICHAEL PHILLIPS
JUDITH PELLA

BETHANY HOUSE PUBLISHERS
MINNEAPOLIS, MINNESOTA 55438

Cover illustration by Dan Thornberg
Bethany House Publishers staff artist.

Copyright © 1991
Michael Phillips/Judith Pella
All Rights Reserved

Published by Bethany House Publishers
A Ministry of Bethany Fellowship,Inc.
6820 Auto Club Road, Minneapolis, Minnesota 55438

Printed in the United States of America
First combined hardcover edition for
Christian Herald Family Bookshelf: 1992

Library of Congress Cataloging-in-Publication Data

Phillips,Michael R., 1946–
      On the trail of truth/ Michael Phillips and Judith Pella.
        p. cm.   (The Journals of Corrie Belle Hollister; bk. 3)

       I. Pella, Judith. II Title. III. Series: Phillips, Michael R., 1946–
Journals of Corrie Belle Hollister ; 3.
PS3566.H49205 1991
813'.54—dc20   91–6660
ISBN 1–55661–106–4   CIP

The Authors

The PHILLIPS/PELLA writing team had its beginning in the longstanding friendship of Michael and Judy Phillips with Judith Pella. Michael Phillips, with a number of nonfiction books to his credit, had been writing for several years. During a Bible study at Pella's home he chanced upon a half-completed sheet of paper sticking out of a typewriter. His author's instincts aroused, he inspected it more closely, and asked their friend, "Do you write?" A discussion followed, common interests were explored, and it was not long before the Phillips invited Pella to their home for dinner to discuss collaboration on a proposed series of novels. Thus, the best-selling "Stonewycke" books were born, which led in turn to "The Highland Collection," and the "Journals of Corrie Belle Hollister."

Judith Pella holds a nursing degree and B.A. in Social Sciences. Her background as a writer stems from her avid reading and researching in historical, adventure, and geographical venues. Pella, with her two sons, resides in Eureka, California. Michael Phillips, who holds a degree from Humboldt State University and continues his post-graduate studies in history, owns and operates Christian bookstores on the West Coast. He is the editor of the best-selling George MacDonald Classic Reprint Series and is also MacDonald's biographer. The Phillips also live in Eureka with their three sons.

Books by the Phillips/Pella Writing Team

The Journals of Corrie Belle Hollister

My Father's World
Daughter of Grace
On the Trail of the Truth
A Place in the Sun

The Stonewycke Trilogy

The Heather Hills of Stonewycke
Flight from Stonewycke
Lady of Stonewycke

The Stonewycke Legacy

Stranger at Stonewycke
Shadows over Stonewycke
Treasure of Stonewycke

The Highland Collection

Jamie MacLeod: Highland Lass
Robbie Taggart: Highland Sailor

The Russians

The Crown and the Crucible

ON THE TRAIL OF THE TRUTH

ON THE TRAIL OF THE TRUTH

MICHAEL PHILLIPS
JUDITH PELLA

BETHANY HOUSE PUBLISHERS
MINNEAPOLIS, MINNESOTA 55438

Cover illustration by Dan Thornberg,
Bethany House Publishers staff artist.

Copyright © 1991
Michael Phillips/Judith Pella
All Rights Reserved

Published by Bethany House Publishers
A Ministry of Bethany Fellowship, Inc.
6820 Auto Club Road, Minneapolis, Minnesota 55438

Printed in the United States of America

Library of Congress Cataloging-in-Publication Data

Phillips, Michael R. , 1946–
    On the trail of the truth / Michael Phillips and Judith Pella.
        p.   cm.   (The Journals of Corrie Belle Hollister ; bk. 3)

    I. Pella, Judith. II. Title. III. Series: Phillips, Michael R. , 1946–
Journals of Corrie Belle Hollister ; 3.
PS3566.H49205   1991
813'.54—dc20   91–6660
ISBN 1–55661–106–4   CIP

To
Gregory Erich Phillips

EMIGRATION TO
CALIFORNIA !

Do you want to go to California ! If so, go and join the Company who intend going out the middle of March, or 1st of April next, under the charge of the California Emigration Society, in a first-rate Clipper Ship. The Society agreeing to find places for all those who wish it upon their arrival in San Francisco. The voyage will probably be made in a few months. Price of passage will be in the vicinity of

ONE HUNDRED DOLLARS !
CHILDREN IN PROPORTION.

A number of families have already engaged passage. A suitable Female Nurse has been provided, who will take charge of Young Ladies and Children. Good Physicians, both male and female go in the Ship. It is hoped a large number of females will go, as Females are getting almost as good wages as males.

FEMALE NURSES get 25 dollars per week and board. SCHOOL TEACHERS 100 dollars per month. GARDNERS 60 dollars per month and board. LABORERS 4 to 5 dollars per day. BRICKLAYERS 6 dollars per day. HOUSEKEEPERS 40 dollars per month. FARMERS 5 dollars per day. SHOEMAKERS 4 dollars per day. Men and Women COOKS 40 to 60 dollars per month and board. MINERS are making from 3 to 12 dollars per day. FEMALE SERVANTS 30 to 50 dollars per month and board. Washing 3 dollars per dozen. MASONS 6 dollars per day. CARPENTERS 5 dollars per day. ENGINEERS 100 dollars per month, and as the quartz Crushing Mills are getting into operation all through the country, Engineers are very scarce. BLACKSMITHS 90 and 100 dollars per month and board.

The above prices are copied from late papers printed in San Francisco, which can be seen at my office. Having views of some 30 Cities throughout the State of California, I shall be happy to see all who will call at the office of the Society, 28 JOY'S BUILDING, WASHINGTON ST., BOSTON, and examine them. Parties residing out of the City, by enclosing a stamp and sending to the office, will receive a circular giving all the particulars of the voyage.

An Agents are wanted in every town and city of the New England States, Postmasters or Merchants acting as such will be allowed a certain commission on every person they get to join the Company. Good reference required. For further particulars correspond or call at the

SOCIETY'S OFFICE,
28 Joy's Building, Washington St., Boston, Mass.

Propeller Job Press, 143 Washington Street, Boston.

CONTENTS

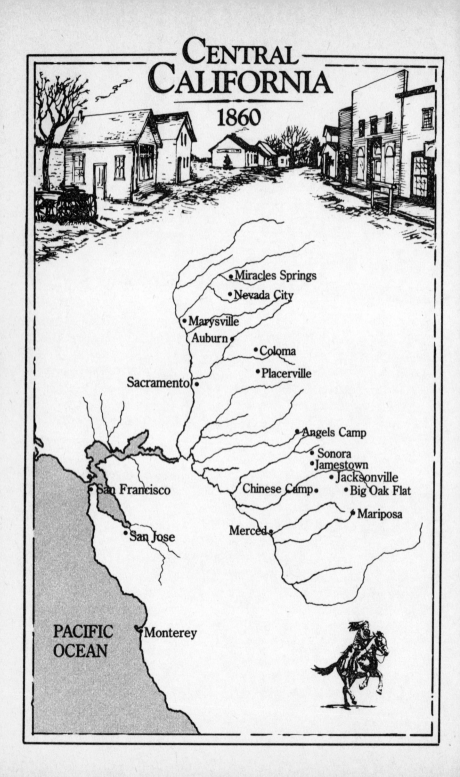

CENTRAL CALIFORNIA
1860

- Miracles Springs
- Nevada City
- Marysville
- Auburn
- Coloma
- Placerville
- Sacramento
- Angels Camp
- Sonora
- Jamestown
- Jacksonville
- Chinese Camp
- Big Oak Flat
- Mariposa
- Merced
- San Francisco
- San Jose
- Monterey

PACIFIC
OCEAN

CHAPTER 1

REFLECTIONS

I remember the last time I was here listening to Miss Stansberry play the wedding march on the church piano. Two months ago, back in June, I was sitting down in the front row waiting for what I thought was going to be my pa's wedding to Katie Morgan.

But that wedding never happened. Uncle Nick crashed in, shouting that Katie should marry *him*, not my pa, and to my amazement, Pa agreed. I was filled with a lot of feelings that seemed to be fighting inside my head. I wanted Pa to be happy, but down inside I just didn't feel right about him and Katie. Right from the beginning they somehow didn't seem like the kind of man and woman that were meant to be together. Not married, at least. Not when I thought of Ma. An hour later, I was there again—only this time sitting *next* to Pa, watching Katie becoming Mrs. Nicholas Belle. Instead of marrying Pa, Katie had ended up married to Uncle Nick.

So this day in the second week of August 1854, I felt a heap different than I had the last time I heard the wedding march. No seventeen-year-old girl could have been happier than I was standing up there in front of the church alongside Mrs. Parrish. Uncle Nick stood on the other side next to Pa, with Rev. Rutledge in between. It was the perfect ending to the last eight or nine months, since that day toward the end of last year when Pa announced to us kids that he was planning to get married again. For weeks—ever since Nick and Katie's wedding, ever since I saw Pa and Mrs. Parrish walking quietly away from the church after Uncle Nick had busted in—I'd been so happy and distracted, I hadn't been able to think straight. And on the big day, even standing there in front of the church, I couldn't keep my mind focused on what was going on. All of a sudden I realized the music had stopped and Rev. Rutledge was talking and telling folks about what the wedding vows were supposed to mean. By the time I started listening in earnest, he was already getting on with the business of what we were all doing here! As he said the words, my brain was racing, remembering so many things. I had to stand there, straight and quiet next to Mrs. Parrish, smiling and acting calm. But inside I was anything but calm.

"Do you, Drummond . . ."

When I thought back to the first day I heard that name, and how Pa and Mrs. Parrish squared off on the street in front of the Gold Nugget, I just wanted to laugh. He was *Mr.* Drum then. None of us knew who he was or what was to come from that day. He and Mrs. Parrish sure didn't like each other much at first!

"So, Mr. Drum, what might be your intentions now?" I could still hear her stern voice, her glaring eyes bearing down on Pa's bewildered face.

And he roared back, "I reckon it ain't none of your dad-blamed business!"

Mrs. Parrish said she aimed to *make* us kids her business and told him he ought to be ashamed of himself. Pa said he had no intention of having a woman tell him what to do, and then he rode off through the middle of town.

What a beginning that had been! Who'd have ever figured it would come to this?

"Take this woman to be your wedded wife . . ."

Wife . . . his *wife*! My first thought was of Ma. But instead of showing sadness or regret or sorrow when her face came into my memory, she was smiling. I knew she understood and was watching with pleasure, glad that the Lord had sent such a good woman to this man and his kids.

At first Pa was looking mostly at Rev. Rutledge, but now he glanced over toward me and Mrs. Parrish. He wasn't looking at me but her, and he looked right into her eyes. I couldn't see her face looking back at him, but from the look of love in Pa's eyes, I didn't see how he could possibly concentrate on what the minister was saying. Pa's eyes were so full it must have taken all his concentration just to fill them with that look. I don't think I'd ever seen such a look in his eyes before.

I couldn't help remembering the meeting of their eyes on that day he and Katie were supposed to be married, after Uncle Nick had run in and the uproar had started. Pa had a sheepish, embarrassed look on his face as he stood next to where Mrs. Parrish was sitting, and she looked back at him sort of half-crying.

That memory sent me back further, to a day when Pa and I were talking in the barn. He told me that when he looked into Katie's eyes, it just wasn't the same as it used to be with Ma.

Now as I saw Pa and Mrs. Parrish looking at each other, everything seemed to be coming right after a long time of wondering how it would all turn out. No one would ever replace Ma, but you could sure tell there was something pretty special for both Pa and Mrs. Parrish.

" . . . to have and to hold from this day forward, for better, for worse, for richer, for poorer, in sickness and in health . . ."

During the last few weeks, getting ready for the wedding, I often found myself wondering when Pa actually started thinking differently about Mrs. Parrish. I thought back to that day of the first church service in Miracle Springs, when there wasn't even a church yet, when he stuck up for the minister. I wondered if he had done that for her, maybe without even knowing it himself. Or that first Christmas dinner at Mrs. Parrish's house, when Pa got mad and we all left early. I wondered if they really liked each other back then, if some of their arguments were just to cover up feelings that might have been sneaking up on them from behind. I guess that's something I'll *never* know!

> *". . . to love and to cherish, till death do you part, according to God's holy ordinance?"*

I asked Pa about three weeks before the wedding, "When did you first notice Mrs. Parrish?" He looked at me as if to say *What are you talking about, girl?* But he knew well enough what I was driving at. "When did you look at her different than just another woman, Pa? You know what I mean."

He kept eyeing me, serious as could be, then a little grin broke out on his lips. Once he got to talking about it, I think he enjoyed the memories. We talked about the meetings for the school committee, and he sheepishly admitted that we had gone early a couple of times so he'd be able to see Mrs. Parrish before the minister got there, just like I figured. "And you got all cleaned up and shaved and smelling good too, didn't you, Pa?" I asked. "And that was on account of her, wasn't it?"

"I reckon," he answered. "But don't tell no one."

"Everyone knows by now, Pa," I laughed. "There ain't nothing more to hide!"

He blustered a bit after I said that, but in a little while he started talking again, and this time it was about Katie. He said almost the minute she got to California, he realized he'd made a mistake, but he didn't know what to do about fixing it.

"Why didn't you just call the whole thing off?" I asked.

He said he could see it all perfectly clear now and couldn't imagine he could have been such a fool, thinking it might work if he just went ahead and didn't say anything. "But by then, Corrie," he said, "my head was so blamed full of that Parrish woman I couldn't even think straight. I was so muddled I pretty near got myself hitched to the wrong woman, just like Nick said. I was just a downright nincompoop 'bout the whole thing!"

"It's a good thing Uncle Nick came when he did," I said.

"Tarnation, you're right there, girl! Yes, sir, Nick saved my hide but good! And that more'n made up for all the times I hauled him outta his share of the scrapes we got ourselves into. Yep, I figure we're about even now."

It was quiet for a minute, then I asked Pa, "How come you wrote off for Katie in the first place, Pa?"

Pa thought a minute, scratched his head, and finally said, "I don't know, Corrie . . . I just don't know. I been wonderin' that same thing myself for quite a spell."

"Maybe for Uncle Nick," I suggested with a grin.

"Yeah, probably," said Pa. "But you know, Corrie, folks sometimes say there's times a man's just gotta do what he's gotta do—which is just another way of saying that a man is sometimes determined to go his own fool-headed way no matter how stupid it might be. And I reckon that's how it was with me back then. I was already startin' to feel something inside for the Parrish lady, and I reckon it scared me a little. At the same time, I wasn't sure if I even liked her, 'cause she could sure be ornery sometimes. So maybe I figured gettin' me a bride like Katie would put a stop to the crazy thoughts I was havin'. But it didn't work at all! The minute Katie got here I found myself thinkin' of Almeda all the more."

I smiled, and that was the end of my conversation with Pa.

Whatever his mistakes and uncertainties back then, he sure wasn't making one now. And he wasn't having any more second thoughts. For when the words *I do* came out of his mouth, the whole church heard them, and I couldn't keep from crying.

Then the minister and all the eyes of the people turned toward Mrs. Parrish.

Do you, Almeda . . .

Poor Rev. Rutledge! It must have been hard for him to utter those words. Mrs. Parrish had brought him here, and they had been together so much the whole first year. It was hardly any secret that he was sweet on her. Everybody in town figured they were going to get married one day. And now he was having to marry her to somebody *else!* But ever since Rev. Rutledge came to Miracle Springs, folks have been surprised at what a fine man he turned out to be—building the church, pitching in with all the rest of the men when anything needed to be done, helping folks, going to visit anybody who was sick. I think he'd earned the respect of just about everybody in the whole community. And now he was marrying Mrs. Parrish to Drummond Hollister with his head high and being a real man about how things had turned out.

" . . . take this man to be your wedded husband . . ."

Only about a week before the wedding, one Sunday afternoon Mrs. Parrish came out to our house for dinner. Of course she'd been spending a lot of time with us, but she wouldn't come there to live till after the wedding. She was there, along with Katie and Nick and everybody else, and the talk was getting lively and everybody was laughing. Katie asked the question, but I'd wondered about it too, just like I had with Pa.

"Now tell us, Almeda," she said, "when did you first fall in love with this cantankerous gold miner?"

Mrs. Parrish laughed, and Uncle Nick chimed in, "Yeah, that's somethin' I'd like to know! How any woman in her right mind could think o' marryin' a coot like him, I can't figure it!"

"Aw, keep your no-good opinions to yourself, Nick!" Pa shot back, but neither of them were serious.

When it quieted down a bit, Mrs. Parrish told about how much she'd admired him when he stood up in church, and even when he'd stomped out after Christmas dinner that time. She said part of her was angry with him for ruining her nice dinner, but at the same time she couldn't help respecting him for wanting to stand up for what he thought was right, and for not wanting things said about him that he didn't think were true. "But I suppose the very first time my heart thought about fluttering must have been that day, not long after the children and I had gone on a picnic out in the country, when I was getting ready to leave on a business trip. Drum rode up in a great flurry of dust and noise, jumped off his horse, and came striding up to me so determined-looking I didn't know what he was about to do! But when he took me aside and told me he was the children's father, and then apologized for not coming forward sooner—well, right then I think something began telling me this was an unusual man."

"No, you were already after me sooner'n that!" said Pa seriously, but with a twinkle in his eye.

"What do you mean, I was *after* you?"

"You know perfectly well what I mean. You always were a mighty headstrong woman, and you—"

"Headstrong! Drummond Hollister, I ought to—"

"You know well and good you're headstrong. And you know you were out to get me right from the start."

"There is no truth in that whatsoever."

"Come on, Almeda, don't lie in front o' the children." Pa threw a wink at us. "Do you deny you went out on that picnic intentionally to get near to my place here?"

"I simply said that—"

"There! You can't deny it! Right from the start you were trying to weasel in closer toward me."

"It was only for the sake of the children. I've told you that before."

Pa laughed. "I don't believe that for a minute. You had your sights set long ago. Once you took a look at me, you couldn't help yourself. Go on, tell Katie the truth."

By now everybody was laughing at their good-natured argument. Mrs. Parrish didn't say anything for a minute. I was beginning to wonder if Pa'd hurt her feelings. But I guess she was just trying to think up some good way to get the best of him. Finally she burst out:

"Well, it worked, didn't it? I got you in the end!"

" *. . . to have and to hold from this day forward, for better, for worse, for richer, for poorer, in sickness and in health. . . .*"

I suppose after the incident with Becky's kidnapping by Buck Krebbs and the thing with Royce and the ransom money, there could hardly be any doubt that Mrs. Parrish was prepared and willing to give everything she had for Pa and us kids, even if it meant she *would* be poor from then on. After what she did that day, the minister hardly needed to ask if she was pledged to Pa for better or worse and richer or poorer. She'd proved that already!

Pa didn't realize what she'd done right at first. He didn't know how she'd twisted Royce's arm to give her the money. If I hadn't seen her go into the bank with that parcel of papers, and then seen that horrible look on Mr. Royce's face later when she left, none of us might have ever known, because Pa and Uncle Nick had already gone to the sheriff's.

But later that night when I told Pa what I'd seen, he jumped up and, hurt as he was, rode into town right then to get the money back to her. And almost as quickly, she lit off out of town for Royce's home, even though it was past banking hours.

Pa told us later that she'd signed over the deeds to all her property, her business, her home and office, and all her supplies and equipment as collateral against the $50,000. If she hadn't gotten the full amount of money back to Royce within twenty-four hours, everything she owned would have become his! That was how much she cared about Becky's safety, and how much she trusted Pa!

The minute Pa learned what she'd done, he must have known that their lives were made to be intertwined together somehow. After that, his future could have no one in it besides her—not after all they'd already been through together, and how close it had brought them toward each other.

That's when, he told me later, he suddenly realized he loved Mrs. Parrish *himself*, and not just because she was nice to us kids.

So when Mrs. Parrish answered the minister's question, every single person in that church knew the depth of love behind the vows.

". . . to love, to cherish, and to obey till death do you part according to God's holy ordinance?"

And with eyes brimming full of tears, and a radiant smile

of love and thanksgiving spread all across her face, Mrs. Parrish answered: *"I do."*

Ten minutes later, as I walked back down the aisle in time to Miss Stansberry's playing, my hand on Uncle Nick's arm, I was following my pa and my brand-new mother!

CHAPTER 2

RICE, BOUQUETS, AND GARTERS

As Pa and Mrs. Parrish walked through the front door of the church and outside, I heard shouts and yells, followed by Pa's loud voice and then Mrs. Parrish's laughing.

Uncle Nick and I were right behind. As the sunlight hit our faces, there were six or eight of the saloon girls gathered around, tossing handfuls of rice in the air at them. The whole rest of the church was right on our heels, and within a minute or two they were all getting into the act. Katie had made sure everyone in Miracle Springs under the age of fifteen—and a lot of those older, too!—had a good supply of rice. And before you knew it the whole town was after them, whooping and hollering.

Mrs. Parrish could hardly move fast enough to get away in her beautiful white wedding dress, the same one as she'd worn in Boston and which she had packed away all this time. Most of the folks weren't after her at all. Pa had by far the worst time of it with the rice! But I knew he loved every second, yelling and running and pretending to be trying to get away, while at the same time letting Tad and Becky and the other kids get him good a few times. When it was all done, and people were laughing and panting and hand shaking and back slapping, Pa's hair and black broadcloth suit looked as if he'd walked out in the middle of a hailstorm.

There'd been a big afternoon of festivities planned. Pa had

22

fussed about it ahead of time. "Let's just get the thing done, and then slip outta town, Almeda," he'd said. "There don't need to be a big to-do on our account."

Pa still didn't understand. Mrs. Parrish took me aside and said, "Your father, bless him, is so humble he has no idea how folks around here look up to him!"

She was right! If people around Miracle Springs were interested in Pa's getting married before, *now* with him marrying Mrs. Parrish—and almost two months after Nick and Katie's wedding for word to spread about it—why, folks had hardly been talking of anything else! The little church was packed, with people standing up all around the outside walls. Lots of folks from the hills and neighboring towns knew there'd be no room inside, so they just came and waited around outside for the festivities afterward. Rev. Rutledge had made sure the doors and all the windows were open, and so folks peered in however they could. Then afterwards the tables were set up and filled with food, with the big wedding cake in the middle. When everyone started gathering around, I reckon there were more people than would have filled the church three or four times over, and a lot of faces I'd never seen. Mrs. Parrish herself was a pretty well-known woman, so no doubt lots of people were there on account of her.

It's not often a man gets married with his kids right there with him. Pa had the five of us—me and Zack and Emily and Becky and Tad—come stand beside him and Mrs. Parrish. It was such a proud, happy moment! We were a *whole* family again! Uncle Nick stood right there in front of us with his arm around Katie. Zack's best friend, Little Wolf, was there, as well as Miss Stansberry and her brother and Rev. Rutledge and all the other folks that we'd come to know. I hardly know how to describe what I was feeling—complete, I reckon. None of the pieces were out of place or missing anymore.

Then Mrs. Parrish took Pa's hand and together they began to cut the cake. Uncle Nick and Alkali Jones kept the men stirred up with their catcalls and poking fun at Pa, and there was plenty of laughter to go around, with Pa getting in his share of jibes back at his two friends. Then they handed out slices of the cake, first to the kids and then to everybody else, and there was more handshaking and well-wishing and congratulations offered to the bride and groom. A few of the women cried again, but most of the tears, mine included, had come and gone in the church. By now everybody's spirits were pretty high.

"Time to throw the bouquet!" someone called out.

I glanced up, but couldn't see who it was. It had been a woman's voice—probably someone wanting to get it herself! Mrs. Parrish had told us earlier about the custom of the bride throwing the bouquet over her shoulder to the women of her wedding party and family and whoever else wanted to join in. "And whoever catches it," she said, and eleven-year-old Becky's eyes were big and wide listening to every word, "that woman's going to be the *next* one to get married."

"Really?" said Becky slowly, full of wonder.

"That's what they say," answered Mrs. Parrish.

"Then *I'm* going to catch it!" said Becky, more as if she was speaking fact than hope.

Emily didn't say anything. She was thirteen, and turning into a pretty young lady. It wouldn't be long before fellas would be turning their heads to look at her twice. And I couldn't help wondering what *she* was thinking about the bouquet. Flowers or not, I had no doubts she'd have half a dozen handsome young men courting and sweet-talking her before *anybody* threw a second look toward me. Maybe that's why I had the feeling that Mrs. Parrish would try to toss her bouquet in my direction.

"All right . . . all right," she answered to the call, coming out from behind the cake table. "Ladies, girls—all of you gather round right over here in front of me!"

A scurry and bustle followed. All the little girls came running, some of the saloon girls, laughing to themselves but wanting to join in the fun and maybe hoping for a chance to grab at the bouquet, the three of us Hollister girls, and the few unmarried women that were there.

"Are you all ready?" she said, and as she did her eyes caught mine. I wasn't sure I *wanted* to catch it.

A chorus of high-pitched shouts went up.

Mrs. Parrish turned around, her back to us, picked up her bouquet from the table, and gave it a mighty heave up in the air back over her head.

I was right; it did come in my direction—but not nearly close enough that I could even have jumped up and touched it. The bouquet went sailing over my head!

Becky cried out in disappointment. Sounds of *oohs* and *aahs* and various cheers went up. I spun around to see a red-faced Miss Stansberry, standing far toward the rear, holding Mrs. Parrish's flowers with a look of shock and surprise in her eyes.

We all clamored around her, while the men clapped and cheered, and a few winked and kidded each other with knowing expressions of significance on their faces.

"And now, Drummond, it's time for you to throw my garter," said Mrs. Parrish.

"Yeah, Drum!" several called out. "The garter . . . throw it to me!"

Now the men *really* erupted with shouts and yells and laughter. Above it all I could hear Mr. Jones's *hee, hee, hee*! and Uncle Nick's whooping. All the men were having a good time trying to make Pa feel as uncomfortable as they could!

Mrs. Parrish pulled up the corner of her dress to the knee, and now all the yelling changed to whistling, while the women tried to shush up their husbands. But nobody was going to be denied making sport of anything they could on this day. Mrs. Parrish took her time, throwing Pa a smile as she slowly slipped the garter down over her calf and ankle.

"Here, Drum, will you help me a moment?" she said coyly. Pa stepped up and lent a steadying hand to her free arm to keep her balanced.

"No, Drum," she said. "I want *you* to slip the garter over my shoe."

A red flush crept over his face. Pa stooped down to one

knee and began the process, while the whistling and calling out doubled in volume.

When he finally stood up, the garter in hand, he shouted, "Cut out all your hollerin', you pack of baboons! Can't you see there's ladies present!"

But the men just fired off more teasing and jesting at Pa all the louder.

"All right, then, you loco varmints!" shouted Pa back. "Any of you characters who's fool enough to want to get yourself hitched come up here and get yourselves ready, 'cause I'm about to give this little thing the heave-ho."

All the boys hustled forward, nine-year-old Tad right in the front.

"Throw it to me, Pa!" he cried.

"You gotta fight for it with everyone else, boy," Pa answered. "Get in there, Zack . . . Little Wolf . . . come on, all of you get ready."

Not nearly so many men gathered around as women, even though there were twenty times more men available for marrying than women.

Pa turned his back to them and threw the garter in the air behind him. Zack made a halfhearted reach for it, Tad leaped up in the air, but neither was even close. Like the bouquet, the garter flew over the top of them, and I saw it hit Rev. Rutledge on the back of the head. He'd been talking to Patrick Shaw and wasn't even paying attention to what was going on behind him.

The minute it hit his head, the minister's hand unconsciously shot up to investigate the disturbance he'd felt. He then turned around to see every face upon him, the garter hanging from two of his fingers, a bewildered expression on his face.

When the truth of what happened dawned on him, a broad grin spread over his face, followed by an embarrassed laugh.

"Well, Reverend," called out Uncle Nick, "I reckon you're next!"

"No, no, not me," insisted the minister. "Here, this souvenir ought to be your pa's," he said, leaning down and handing

the garter to Tad, who had scampered through legs and bodies
and now stood next to Rev. Rutledge.

"Yes, sir!" exclaimed Tad, taking it from him, a happy
smile on his face. He ran back to Pa and held it out to him.

"No, boy, you keep it," said Pa. "Who knows? Maybe you
will be next—with the Reverend there performing the ceremony!"

Everyone laughed again, and then settled down to the serious business of consuming the cake and other food people
had brought.

CHAPTER 3

A GLIMPSE AHEAD

Pa's marriage to Mrs. Parrish was just about the happiest day of my life.

By the time we all got to bed that night, I was exhausted, and I think everyone else was too. Being too happy for too long at one stretch can wear a body out just as much as hard work.

But as I lay in my bed on that warm August evening, even though I was so tired I didn't think I could have kept on my feet another minute, sleep didn't come for a long time. Once my feet and hands quit being so active, my brain figured it had to get some exercise. The instant my head rested against the pillow, my mind raced off and I had no choice but to follow.

This day wasn't just the first day of Pa's and Mrs. Parrish's life together as husband and wife, I thought. It was also *my* first day, I guess you'd say, as a grown-up.

I *wasn't* grown up yet, of course. And it's ridiculous to say that all of a sudden, on a *certain* day, you just up and become an adult. I was only seventeen, and plenty of seventeen-year-olds *did* have to fend for themselves and were a lot closer to full grown and independent than I was. But I knew on the day of the wedding that a lot of things were going to be changing for me real soon.

I'd been so busy the last two years since Ma died, acting like a mother to the other kids, helping Pa with the chores and the cooking and cleaning. Suddenly I realized time was passing quickly and I was getting older in a hurry. Ma had been right about the prospects of my marrying. And even if I did have any prospects—which I didn't—I don't think I'd have relished the idea anyhow. If I ever did get married one day, it'd have to be the Lord who saw to that part of my life, because there was a heap of living I wanted to do, things I wanted to see, places I dreamed of going.

It began to dawn on me that maybe now I *could* do some of those things, go to some of those places. Now that Pa was married, Mrs. Parrish would be taking care of everything that I'd been doing—all those housekeeping and wife and mothering things I'd sorta done because there was nobody else to do them.

Pretty soon I'd *have* to figure out something to do besides just being underfoot around the house. I was pretty close to being past schooling age, and I suppose I could study to be a teacher someplace else, like Miss Stansberry. Pa and Mrs. Parrish would have kept me at home till I was fifty—that's just how wonderful they both were. But somehow I wasn't sure that'd be exactly right—or if it was what I wanted.

Something inside me started stirring that night. Ma and Uncle Nick and Pa—they all used to talk about the "Belle blood," as if when your name was Belle, you had no choice but to get ornery and stubborn and independent every so often. I didn't think I ever got too much that way, but once in a while when I'd get riled or headstrong over something, Pa'd mutter about the Belle blood.

Maybe it was my Belle blood stirring. I started thinking about going off alone to some strange new place just to see what it was like, thinking about meeting new people, about being a grown-up who had to take care of herself because she didn't have to tend to her Pa and brothers and sisters anymore. I found myself wondering what Los Angeles was like, and thinking about the Oregon territory folks were talking about. I wanted to know more about the mountains and the miners and Indians and trappers who lived in them and what kind of people they were.

Even a month earlier I would have been afraid at the prospect of going someplace by myself, of being away from Pa and the others, of having a job of my own somewhere besides Miracle Springs. But it didn't frighten me now. It was kind of exciting, adventurous.

Maybe that was what the Belle blood did to folks. Maybe that's why Uncle Nick was always in trouble and then came out here—that adventurous spirit in his blood.

So when I say it was my first day as a grown-up, I don't mean that anything really *changed* all at once. But my thoughts and my outlook toward things began to change—no longer a little girl way of viewing. I began to think, *This is my life, and I'm getting older. Pretty soon I'm going to be out doing things and going places because I decide to, not because my ma and pa decide for me.*

Maybe that's what growing up is more than anything else— being on your own, relying on *yourself* to decide what's going to become of you instead of looking to somebody else like you've always done. And as I lay there that night, that was the question that kept coming to me: *What AM I going to do with myself now?*

It wasn't as if I needed to decide anything before I got up the next morning. With Uncle Nick and Aunt Katie still there in the cabin with us, and with Pa and Mrs. Parrish off to Sacramento and San Francisco for a week, for a while it'd be just like the last six months. School would be starting up again in a few weeks, and I had already agreed to help Miss Stansberry again this year.

But Uncle Nick was already building a new cabin for him and Katie up past the mine in a little clearing in the woods, about five or six hundred yards from ours. Zack was now fifteen and had been growing like a weed. He was still quiet, but his voice had deepened and he was apt to be as tall as Pa in another six months. He'd be thinking man-thoughts before long.

Mrs. Parrish and I'd already laughed several times over what I should call her. She told me, "I would be honored, Corrie, to have you call me *Mother,* but only when you feel comfortable doing so. And you must never call me what you called your real mother."

"I called her *Ma*," I said.

"Then you call me whatever you like." She smiled and put her arm around me. "I will always call you just Corrie. But I want you to know that I do think of you as a very special daughter—a spiritual daughter, a daughter whom the Lord gave me first as a friend . . . a daughter of grace."

"Thank you," I replied. "But I'm afraid you will keep being *Mrs. Parrish* for a while yet."

She laughed, that laugh that always seemed to have music at the back of it. "Oh, I do love you, Corrie Belle! I will be as happy as can be to keep being *Mrs. Parrish* to you forever!"

I gave her a tight squeeze. I loved her too—differently, but I think by now probably just as much as I loved Ma and Pa. I couldn't believe how good it was of God to bring together the two people I loved most in the world.

Just then some of Ma's last words came back to me. It had been two years, but I could almost hear her voice saying them like it had been yesterday.

You turned out to be a right decent-looking girl, she said. *You're gonna get along just fine, Corrie. I know you'll make me and your pa proud.*

I cried thinking about her. It was still the happiest day of my life, but sometimes happiness and sadness get all mixed up in a girl's heart, and then tears come out and you don't quite know why.

Then Ma's words about women getting on in the world came to my mind, her telling me—as she did more than once—to be strong and have courage and to try things.

"Don't be afraid to go out and do things, Corrie. And never worry what folks'll say or think. How else is a woman gonna get on in the world if she don't try?" That wasn't the kind of thing you heard most women talking about. But I guess Ma had plenty of the Belle blood in her too!

When I finally began to get drowsy, the last thought I can remember was praying that God would make me strong and

would give me the courage to go out and do whatever it was he
might want me to.

But I don't think my prayers were completely finished when
I fell asleep.

CHAPTER 4

POSSIBILITIES

That next week I found myself wondering even more about what my future held. Katie and I took care of things, the kids played, Uncle Nick worked on his new cabin, but most of the time I kept thinking about Pa and Mrs. Parrish getting back home. Now that they were married, it didn't seem *right* with them not here.

But their being gone did give me and Katie a good chance to get to know each other better. I reckon with it all settled between Pa and Mrs. Parrish, I found myself able to see a lot in Aunt Katie that I hadn't seen before when my feelings were getting in the way placing her up alongside Mrs. Parrish and comparing the two. Now, Katie was . . . just Katie! And I discovered I really liked her a lot more than I ever thought I would. We talked about many things, and she told me about growing up in the East, and even some about her and Uncle Nick. She treated me like a friend, and I found myself thinking about her as mine too.

But she also had an annoying side. Now that she and Uncle Nick and Pa and Mrs. Parrish were married, she seemed to figure it was *my* turn. That whole week whenever we'd get to talking, she'd make little comments how I needed to be practical and look ahead to the time when I'd be starting my *own* family, and how I oughtn't wait as long as either of them. According to Katie, it was high time I either got a job or got married.

"There's that new young fellow up the pass, Corrie," she reminded me more than once, "not much older than you, and a nice young man. He's going to be looking to settle down with a wife before long."

She just didn't understand that I wasn't interested in marriage yet. Maybe I would be later, maybe I wouldn't. I didn't know. But right now there were other things I wanted to think about. Still, Katie kept whispering these kinds of things in my ear. She was determined to be practical, a realist, while Mrs. Parrish had always encouraged me to think about my dreams.

As much as I missed Pa and Mrs. Parrish, the time without them helped me to see this difference between Katie and Mrs. Parrish, and to think more about myself too. Mrs. Parrish was always telling me that *everything* has a good side, if you know how to look for it and find it, and I reckon this was one of those times.

Mrs. Parrish had asked me to go into town once or twice while they were gone to check in at the Freight Company, just to make sure everything was in order. I thought it a mite strange—she'd gone on lots of trips before without anyone having to check up on the business. But I wouldn't find out why she'd asked me to do that until a few days after they got back.

In the meantime, I did ride into Miracle Springs one afternoon. When I walked into the Parrish Mine and Freight Company office, Mr. Ashton immediately stood up from the desk where he was sitting and gave me a very pleasant, though awfully formal, greeting.

"Good morning, Miss Hollister," he said.

Miss Hollister! I thought. *It's only me, Mr. Ashton—Corrie Belle!*

But instead of saying what came into my mind, I just answered, "Howdy, Mr. Ashton. Mrs. Parrish said I should come in to see you while they were gone and see how you were doing."

"Everything is smooth as can be, Miss Hollister," he replied, still in a stiff but friendly voice. "Marcus loaded up the

Jefferson order this morning and is off to Nevada City with it. And the invoices for the shipment of tools and that sample for the new kind of sluice box came—" He picked up some papers off his desk as he spoke and held them up to show me. "So I have no doubt the merchandise will be arriving in the next day or two. Several of the men are anxious to see the new box."

I hardly had a notion what he was talking about, but when he was done he kept looking at me like he was expecting me to say something.

I gave a halfway sort of nod. "Uh . . . so Marcus Weber's not here today?" I said. I had intended to say hi to him too.

"That's right, Miss. On his way to Nevada City. When do you expect Mrs. Parr—"

Mr. Ashton caught himself and smiled with an embarrassed grin.

"When do you expect Mrs. *Hollister* back, I should say, shouldn't I, Miss Hollister!"

"Takes a heap of getting used to the idea, doesn't it, Mr. Ashton?" I said. "I don't know what to call her either."

"Yes, indeed! Many changes, indeed."

"I don't know exactly, Mr. Ashton," I said, finally answering his question. "I figured it'd be about a week, like maybe we'd see them back on Sunday or Monday."

"Yes, yes, that's what I thought, too. I only wondered if you, now that you and Mrs.—Mrs.—*Hollister*—now that you are family, you know—I thought perhaps you might have heard something differently. But yes, Sunday or Monday . . . I'm sure that's about right."

As I left the office I couldn't ever recollect seeing Mr. Ashton act so strangely. He was talking to me like a perfect stranger! And I was at a loss to figure how Mrs. Parrish marrying Pa would make him behave so downright peculiar to me.

But it started to come a little more clear after she and Pa got back from their honeymoon trip.

On Thursday, after they got back to Miracle on Tuesday, Mrs. Parrish said, "Corrie, it's time you and I had a talk."

"Woman to woman?" I said, smiling. I loved the chances

we had to be alone and talk for a long time, especially about living as a Christian and thinking more about God in the things that went on every day. I wanted to be a woman like Mrs. Parrish, a godly woman who was different than other folks. I had already learned so much from her, but there was still a lot I didn't understand. She was teaching me to find out answers for myself by praying and searching in the Bible. So I was expecting another talk like that when she took me aside.

"Yes, woman to woman," she replied. "But perhaps even more . . . mother to daughter," she added.

"I like the sound of that," I said.

"So do I." But from the look on her face and the serious tone of her voice I could tell something different was coming than the kind of things we'd talked about before.

There was a long pause. A knot twisted in my stomach, as if something bad was about to come, although Mrs. Parrish had never said or done anything to make me afraid. Finally she spoke up.

"This is very difficult for me, Corrie," she said, then paused again. "You know how much I love you—both your father and I?"

"Yes, ma'am—of course," I said.

"Well then, Corrie, you must take what I'm about to say as coming from a heart that loves you very much."

I nodded.

"Well, Corrie," she went on, "I have to be honest with you and say that I've been thinking a great deal about you—about your future. Both your father and I have. And we have discussed what some of the possibilities might be for you—alternatives, things you might do."

I didn't like the sound of her words. Was she going to start getting like Katie and try to marry me off? Had she and Pa spent their week away planning out my whole future?

But I kept my first feelings to myself and decided to hear her out. And I realized after a while that nothing had changed at all, and that she still wanted me to be able to dream, yet to be practical at the same time.

"You see, Corrie, most women don't spend a great deal of time thinking about what they might like to do. They just live a day at a time and life comes along, and they just do what they do without ever stopping to wonder if they might do something *else*. Or if they might *have to* do something else. I have thought about this because of losing Mr. Parrish. Women are more vulnerable. They need to be prepared in case they are suddenly on their own. But most women never think of that until it is too late. I certainly never did. Do you see what I mean?"

"I think so."

"Men don't do that, at least not most of the men I've known. Men plan and dream and work to see their dreams fulfilled. Most of the men around in these parts have dreamed of getting rich in the gold fields. Now, most of them won't, and their dreams will never come true. But at least they think and plan and *try* to do what they dream of doing. Other men want to get a spread of land they can call their own, maybe have a farm or a ranch and raise horses or cows or grow wheat. I've known other men who dream of going to sea. Some of the things they want to do happen, others don't. But most men are thinking and planning about how they want their lives to go.

"But most women, Corrie, they just take life as it comes. They're so dependent on men that they figure what happens to them will depend on what the men in their lives do—brothers, fathers, husbands. They think the men have to make the plans and do the figuring and try the new things and explore the new places and make the money and stake the claims . . . and all the while the women just have to follow along."

She stopped, this time for longer. She took a couple of deep breaths, and I could tell she was still thinking.

"I'm not saying that's wrong. In one sense, God made men to be the leaders and the doers and he made women to be the followers. God made the woman to be man's helper, that's exactly how the Bible says it, Corrie. The men are supposed to be the ones that are in charge of how the world goes, and the women are supposed to help them, not run off trying to do their own kinds of things independent of men.

"But not every woman gets married. And, married or single, a woman's still got to know how to think and how to make decisions. How else can she be a good *helpmeet,* as the Bible calls it, if she doesn't use the mind God has given her?

"And some women—and this is what I wanted to get to, Corrie—some women don't have men to depend on. Women like me, when my husband died—and like your mother, after your father left. Some women find themselves in circumstances where they *have* to be able to make their own decisions, to fend for themselves. If they take life just as it happens to come to them, well, they never know what is going to become of them.

"When my first husband died, Corrie, I had to do a lot of thinking and praying. I began to realize that a woman's got to be able to think and plan and have alternatives too. Some women more than others. When I suddenly found myself all alone, I realized that *I* had to make the decisions about what was going to become of me. I had no man to depend on. My life was *mine.* That's when I started thinking that a woman needs dreams and plans and thoughts of her own. You can never tell when *you're* going to be making the decisions that will determine what becomes of you. Do you see what I mean?"

"Alternatives?" I asked.

"Yes. Possibilities—different things you can do, choices you can make. Most women don't *have* many alternatives because they never give life or their future enough thought, and never think about the different possibilities. But some women have to. If there's no man to do it for them, they have to take hold of the reins of their own lives. And they do so because they *want* to—they *want* to make the choices that will decide what they do. Most men nowadays aren't too comfortable with women doing that. But more women than ever are getting an education and even getting jobs everyone figured were just for men."

"Like Miss Stansberry?"

"Yes. Harriet said she had wanted to be a schoolteacher ever since she was young. And though she has her brother with her, I have the feeling she probably would have come out here anyway, even if she was by herself."

"She is an adventurous lady," I said.

"But women are doing things other than just what folks figure are women-things, like teaching."

"Running a business like you do sure isn't what too many women are doing."

Mrs. Parrish laughed. "I'll say! And it was hard for many of the men around here to accept at first. But like I said, after Mr. Parrish died, I *had* to think of my options—should I go back East, take over my husband's business, try to get married again? I decided to become a businesswoman, and I've never regretted it. I love what I have done, and I am so thankful that such a possibility was available to me, even though my first husband had been the one to open the door to it for me.

"Your mother too, Corrie—it was much the same for her. She was left without a man, with a family, with decisions to make."

"Ma didn't have many things she could have done," I said. "We just stayed on the land like always. Of course, she had kin there to help us."

"What if there hadn't been kin, or what if you hadn't had the farm? Then she would have had to consider other possibilities."

"But we did decide to come west in the end."

"Exactly! You see your mother *was* a strong, thinking, deciding, trying-to-figure-what-was-best kind of woman. She did more than just take life as it happened to come. She made decisions about what she thought was best for her and her family. And, Corrie, I suspect there are a lot more women like that than some of the men realize. That's why men always seem so surprised when women like your ma or Miss Stansberry—"

"Or you!"

She laughed. "*And* me—why they seem so surprised when a women stands up and does something different than 'the weaker sex' does."

She laughed again, a humorous laugh, as though she and I were in on a secret no one else knew about. "But we have to be patient with them," she said, still chuckling. "It may take them a while, but in the end men usually come around to seeing things reasonably, as long as women aren't too pushy to begin with. Why, nearly all of my customers are men, and by now they are used to doing business with a woman, used to the fact that I have men working for me who consider me their boss. And I think most of my customers have learned to respect me as a fair and honest and intelligent businesswoman, though most of them laughed at the very notion when I first announced my plans to continue the company after my husband's death. Men just sometimes need a little time to get used to things, that's all."

A silence fell between us. I was thinking about everything she had said. I guess Mrs. Parrish was considering what to say next, because she started in from a whole new angle, talking about me this time.

"Do you see what all this has to do with you, Corrie?" she asked at length, very serious sounding again.

She stopped and waited a long time for me to answer.

"I think maybe," I replied slowly. "You figure maybe I ought to be thinking about my possibilities, too, because I'm not—"

"No, Corrie," she interrupted, "not for any reason other than because I love you very much, and I think you are an extremely gifted young woman. I want only the absolute best for you, and so I think we—your father and I *and* you—all ought to be thinking and praying about what that might be. We need to consider choices, alternatives, that are before you."

I laughed sheepishly. "I've told you what Ma said, haven't I?"

"About you not being of a marrying sort? Yes, Corrie. But if your mother could see you now—and I believe she *can*!—she would know you are the most beautiful, wonderful daughter she could ever have hoped for! That's not at all what I had in mind, Corrie."

"I'm not sure I want to get married, Mrs. Parrish," I said.

"I know. But whether you do or don't, I think a young

woman still owes it to herself to think about things *she* might want to do in life—even if she does get married."

"Is it because of you and Pa getting married," I asked, "that you figure now it's maybe time for me—you know, with me getting older and getting past school age, that I move—?"

"Oh no, Corrie!" She put her arm around me and squeezed me tight. "I love you so much! I would keep you here with us forever if I could. I never want you to go someplace away from us. Never, Corrie! And I know your pa feels the same way, too. He's real proud of you, Corrie."

You can't imagine how happy it made me to hear that! "So it isn't that you think I ought to be finding myself a man, or looking for job someplace, since I'm not a kid anymore?"

"No, Corrie. It's just that we want the best for you. We want you to be happy. And more than anything, I want to see you become the woman I think God had in his mind when he made you—a woman doing some exciting things."

"What kinds of things?" I asked.

"That's just it—I don't know, Corrie. I simply think there's a life full of opportunities out there waiting for you. And as much as I would like to always have you by my side, you're right about one thing—you aren't a child anymore. And that's why your pa and I have been talking about some of the ways you might begin preparing for whatever the future holds."

"I have wondered about teaching school," I said. "Seems that's about the only thing a young woman like me could do— like Miss Stansberry."

"Teaching is one possibility."

"I'd have to go to college."

"I thought of that," she replied. "Your father and I would have enough money to send you away to a normal school to get your certificate. Though I would hate to see you have to go away."

"There's always the newspaper writing," I added.

"That's what you *really* want to do, isn't it?"

"Oh yes!"

"But how to get you started. . . ?" Again her finger found her lips, pursed together now.

"That's another one of those areas where men don't figure a woman has much place, isn't it?"

Mrs. Parrish laughed. "Men figure that about *everything*! I'll let you in on a secret. I think they are uncomfortable because they don't like the competition. They're afraid a woman might do something just as well as they! But I fear you are right—it could be very difficult for a newspaperman to take articles by a woman seriously."

"Like Singleton," I sighed.

"There is something else I've been thinking about, Corrie," said Mrs. Parrish.

I looked at her, just waiting.

"You've had some experience teaching, helping Harriet. So that's one alternative you might explore. You've helped your pa with your brothers and sisters for two years, so we already know you could make a good wife and mother. You want to write for a newspaper, but maybe the time hasn't come quite yet for that. What would you think of learning a little about my business?"

"The Freight Company?" I asked, surprised.

"Yes. How would you like to work with me?"

"I'd never thought of that before," I said. Then I couldn't help smiling. "Did you talk to Mr. Ashton about this?" I asked.

"I think I may have mentioned it to him," she answered. "Why?"

"Well, I went in to your office last week, like you asked me to— Say, is *this* why you wanted me to do that?"

Mrs. Parrish nodded.

"I wondered what you could possibly want me to check up on. I don't know anything about the business."

"I just wanted to see what you'd think about being my family representative while I was out of town. But go on, tell me about Mr. Ashton."

"He talked to me real peculiar, all formal and stiff, calling me *Miss* Hollister! No one ever calls me that!"

Mrs. Parrish laughed loudly. "He probably thinks I'm going to make all sorts of changes now that I'm married again. He probably figures I'll turn it into a family business and he'll be out of a job."

"That's why he was being so polite."

"I'll have to talk to him and put his mind at ease," she said. "But I did speak to him about the possibility of your working in the office a little—when you're not helping Miss Stansberry, of course. What do you think, Corrie?"

"I—I don't know . . . it's such a new idea."

"I'd pay you, of course."

"You wouldn't have to do that, ma'am," I told her.

"But I *would* do it, Corrie. You're old enough now to have a money-earning job. It would be good experience. There's nothing like being in business to gain valuable knowledge. You meet people, you learn how things are run, you sometimes travel to new places. Whatever other things the Lord may in time lead you into—and we must be faithful to pray for *his* guidance—helping in the Mine and Freight Company will give you experiences you'll be able to use anywhere. And perhaps one day you'll be running the business in my place, who can tell? I've suddenly got a family to manage. I might find myself with more than I can handle."

"I'm willing to try, I reckon," I said finally, "if you think I can do it."

"I know you can, Corrie."

CHAPTER 5

ADJUSTMENTS

For the whole next year I worked with Mrs. Parrish at the Freight Company. I kept going to school every day, both to learn and to help Miss Stansberry. But most days after school I worked a couple of hours, and I even got to make some deliveries with Mrs. Parrish and Marcus Weber to some of the outlying areas in the hills.

Mrs. Parrish had been right. I learned things and met a lot of new people. I still didn't figure I was cut out to be a businesswoman like her, but it never hurt to have a few more possibilities of things I might be able to do if I needed to.

That fall after the wedding, Pa and us kids all moved into Miracle Springs to Mrs. Parrish's house so that Uncle Nick and Katie could have the cabin to themselves while they finished building their own place. Mrs. Parrish's house had seemed so huge before, but all of a sudden it was a pretty tiny place with seven of us living there!

Pa went out to the claim every morning, the kids and I went to school, and Mrs. Parrish went to the freight office. Pa and Uncle Nick would work mornings at the mine, and then afternoons on the two cabins—finishing Uncle Nick's and adding on to Pa's to make more room. Alkali Jones was there most days, and on weekends several of the other men would come out and help too. Usually Rev. Rutledge was there pounding nails or carrying lumber just about every Saturday.

Katie stayed at the claim nearly all the time, helping too,

feeding the men. The grass and trees she'd brought us from the east were all growing, and she'd started clearing a garden spot up by their new place for next year. She had plenty to keep her busy, though she started feeling poorly later in the fall and had to keep to her bed a lot. Pa said it was probably just the weather starting to turn cold.

Mr. Alkali Jones, who always seemed to know everything about everything, was now ranting every day about what a miserable winter we were fixing to have. "Them squirrels got twice the winter fur I seen on 'em in fifteen years," he'd go on. "An' they're hidin' acorns in places I ain't seen afore. I tell ya, we're in fer a heap o' snow an' cold!"

They finished the adding on to our place about the middle of October, and then with the work concentrating all at Uncle Nick's, they got his and Katie's new home closed in and the roof and the doors and windows on by about the second week of November, just before any of the big rains Mr. Jones predicted began to fall.

Two days after they moved and got Katie comfortably settled—though she was feeling better by this time—a huge storm came through. It rained for two days and the streets around Miracle turned to mud. Up in the hills to the east a lot of snow had fallen. Alkali Jones said that with a start like this—as early as it was—it was "unmistakably gonna be the dad-blamest, coldest, most ornery winter ya ever done seen!" He finished off his words with that high-pitched cackle and gave his beard a scratch with his dirty fingers. But what he said sure turned out to be right!

Once the storm had passed and the sun came back out to start drying up the mud and grass and fields, leaving big ruts in the roads with muddy water standing in brown pools in the low spots, I figured we'd all be moving back out to the cabin, especially since now it was bigger and they'd added on a couple of rooms. That's what Pa'd been thinking too.

But Mrs. Parrish was having some second thoughts about it. It was so hard not to keep calling her Mrs. Parrish! I knew someday I'd probably have to start calling her either *Mother* or

Almeda. But right then I wasn't ready for the first or old enough for the second, and I just couldn't keep from calling her Mrs. Parrish like I'd always thought of her.

Anyway, one morning I heard Pa and my new mother, Almeda Parrish Hollister—that ought to take care of just about anything I might think of calling her!—talking. The conversation was getting louder than usual. I'd never heard them argue before, and I didn't figure they ever *would* argue! But I suppose even married people who love each other have differences of opinion now and then, though never having been married I can't say for certain.

They began talking about the two houses, but pretty soon they were talking about lots of other things.

"It only seems, Drummond," Mrs. Parrish was saying, "that since we are all here now, and since the children and I all have to be in town every day, perhaps it would make more sense just to stay here in my house—at least through the winter, as long as the children are in school."

Pa was quiet for a minute. I had to admit what she said made sense, even though I hadn't thought of it before. I'd never stopped to consider what would happen to Mrs. Parrish's house when we all went back out to the claim.

Finally Pa spoke.

"I reckon you got a good point there," he said, "but I got the place all fixed up so there's more space. You and I can have a room off to ourselves, and the boys got a room, Emily and Becky can share a room, and the little one Corrie can have by herself. It's a dang sight more space than we got here, Almeda."

"But the trips back and forth into town every day, and in the cold and wet of winter . . ." She didn't finish the sentence.

"Yep, I know. But it just don't seem right somehow, livin' at a woman's house when a man's got a place of his own."

"The woman's house is not as good as the man's?"

"I didn't say that. I just said it don't seem altogether right. It's kinda like it'd be if you kept on with your Freight Company and I quit working the mine. I know we talked this out a while back. But I been doing a lot o' thinkin' on it since."

"As I told you when we discussed this before, I intend to keep my Freight Company, Drummond."

"I know, for a while. But you know as well as I do that it ain't right for a woman to support a man, and that's kinda like it'd be if we kept on living in—"

"What do you mean *for a while?*" she interrupted, her voice sounding a little agitated.

"I mean I know you can't just shut down an operation that size right away. It'll take you some time."

"Shut down? Drummond, I have no intention of shutting down my operation at all. You didn't think my marrying you meant I would give up my business? There was never any talk of that when we discussed it before the wedding."

"I guess I figured that was sort of understood." Pa's voice was quiet. I couldn't tell if he was embarrassed or was slowly getting riled. He got the same kind of quiet in both moods.

"It was not understood by me," said Mrs. Parrish. "I thought it was understood that we both had been married before, we both were involved in livelihoods of our own—your claim and my company—and I had no idea you were thinking that any of that would change. Why, I would never think of asking you to give up *your* claim or *your* cabin because of marrying me."

"That's different. I'm a man."

"What's different about it?"

"A man's work—well, it's more important than a woman's. Maybe you had to run your company so as to provide for yourself. But you got me now. You got a husband to take care of you, so you don't have to anymore."

"And if I want to?"

"Women ain't supposed to be out doin' what men do, not unless they have to, and you don't have to no more."

"Maybe I *want* to. Did you ever consider that I enjoy what I do, that maybe I'm a good businesswoman, and that I don't *want* to just be at home sweeping the floor and fixing a supper for you to eat when you're through with *your* work? Did you ever consider that?"

"I reckon I never did. Women are supposed to be at home, men are supposed to be out working. What you're saying just ain't natural. I know I never said this to you before, but it just ain't done that way."

A long pause followed. When Mrs. Parrish spoke again, her voice was calm but determined.

"Look, Drummond," she said. "I know most men, and even most women, might agree with what you say. But I'm not most women. I'm *me*! And after my first husband died, I found out some things about myself. I found out that I had a strength down inside that I could depend on. I found out that I was a good businesswoman, that I could fend for myself in this rough California world, a man's world. I found out a lot about the person I am down inside by having to stand up for myself and make it on my own when my husband was suddenly gone. I liked what I found, Drummond. The things God built into me during that time—I'm just not willing to let go of. I love you, Drummond Hollister. You are the best thing that has happened to me since my first husband died. I will love and obey and cherish you all my life. But that doesn't mean I will stop being myself—a woman, a person with my *own* dreams and goals and things I want to do in life. Please don't ask me to give up my business for you, Drummond. I would do it if you asked, because I will obey you. But I don't know what would become of me if I did. A piece of me would die. Please, don't ask me to do that."

It got quiet for a long time. The next thing I heard was the sound of Pa's boots on the wood floor, and then the back door opening and then shutting again. I guess he had to think about it all. And usually when Pa was thinking he went someplace alone, outside or in the barn or on the back of one of his favorite horses.

I never heard the two of them discussing the business or the houses again for a long time. I think they did, though, because every so often I could tell from the quiet between them that they'd been talking and had seen things differently.

But however they decided to work it out, nothing much

changed. Most of the time they were as loving and pleasant as could be to each other. Mrs. Parrish went to her office every day and the Mine and Freight Company kept doing business just as before. I went on working there after school. And Pa seemed pleased with me learning different aspects of the business. Pa kept mining with Uncle Nick and Mr. Jones, and they continued to bring gold out of the stream and out of the mountain the deeper into it they dug.

I guess Pa saw that Mrs. Parrish's idea about the houses was pretty smart. Most of the time that winter we stayed at the house in town—Mrs. Parrish's house—during the week, and then on Friday night Pa'd come in to fetch us all with the big wagon and take us out to the claim. Since there was no school, Mrs. Parrish didn't go into her office on Saturday, and so we'd stay there all weekend, and ride back in on Monday morning for the week. During the week, Pa'd come into town every evening for the night.

It was a bit of a cumbersome arrangement. But we were kind of an unusual family, and it was gonna take some time for things to get figured out.

CHAPTER 6

WINTER 1854–55

Without even thinking about it, Christmas dinner was becoming a kind of tradition. Maybe our Christmases stand out in my mind because each of the three was so different, and every time I remembered them it reminded me of how fast things had changed since we'd been in California, and how much the Lord had done for us.

This Christmas was no exception. It was the best ever!

Now we were two happy families, and Mrs. Parrish was there with us. I hadn't been happier since her and Pa's wedding day. All morning she and us three girls worked and sang away in the kitchen, baking pies and sweet potatoes and a big ham, while Pa was outside with Zack and Tad. Pa'd got Zack a new rifle for his very own, and Zack could hardly stand it, he was so excited. So as we were working, we heard the shots firing in the woods where Pa was giving him a lot of instructions about aiming, which Zack really didn't need.

We loaded the food and some extra chairs into the wagon about noon, and took it up to Nick and Katie's new place where we were going to eat. It was their first chance to show off the new cabin, and they'd invited a couple of other families, and of course the Stansberrys and the minister. Katie had been excited for days, planning and telling us she had a surprise for everyone.

We got there first, and soon the others began to gather. When Rev. Rutledge's buggy drove up, Miss Stansberry was with him, alone, with the news about her brother. Hermon Stansberry had taken sick and wasn't going to come. We all prayed for his health before sitting down to dinner, and Miss Stansberry took a nice basket of food back with her for him when the day was over.

But Katie's announcement was the highlight of the whole day!

"I have some big news to tell you all," she said, with a wider smile than I'd ever seen on her already wide mouth. "Some time along about the middle of next summer"—she looked at the five of us kids—"your Uncle Nick is going to stop being *just* an uncle and start being a pa himself!"

Mrs. Parrish was on her feet, exclaiming excitedly almost before the words had left Katie's lips. She gave Katie a great hug, which was followed by the other women doing the same, while Becky tugged at my arm asking me what all the yelling was about. I whispered to her that Katie was going to have a little baby. "And it'll be *your* cousin," I said.

The men were slapping Uncle Nick on the shoulder and shaking hands. Then Uncle Nick went to the fireplace where he picked up a small box from on top of one of the stones, and started passing out cigars that he'd bought. The minister didn't take one, but Uncle Nick shoved one into Zack's hand with a laugh.

"It's high time you tried it, Zack, my boy!" he said.

"Can I, Pa?" said Zack, expecting the usual answer.

Pa shrugged. "Maybe your Uncle Nick's right, son. I guess if he's finally old enough to be a pa, I reckon you're old enough to try one of those things."

Uncle Nick wasted no time. With a grin on his face, he struck a match and held it up to the end of the cigar that was now sticking six inches out of Zack's mouth. Zack sucked in a couple times, got a few puffs going as the tobacco caught fire, and Uncle Nick cheered him on. Pa seemed to know what was going to come of it and just stood back watching, with a half grin on his face.

It didn't take long. After only about an inch had burned

off the end, Zack's face began to turn pale. All of a sudden, amid what must have been an embarrassing roar of laughter for poor Zack, he handed the cigar back to Uncle Nick and bolted for the door and outside to get fresh air. In a minute or two Pa followed with a look on his face that seemed to say that he knew what Zack was going through, while Katie and Mrs. Parrish were talking about "these ridiculous rites of passage that men insist on putting each other through," both with disgusted looks on their faces.

But even Zack's getting sick from the cigar couldn't spoil the impact of Katie's announcement about the baby coming, and the other memories of the happy Christmas Day.

Alkali Jones was right. It was a rough winter—cold, wet, with lots of snow and frost. The stream got bigger than I'd ever seen it, and the men were saying that if the rains kept up, maybe they'd wash down lots of new gold from up in the mountains. It was so wet a time or two that we stayed at the house in town for two weeks each time. The stream was so full of water rushing by that Pa and Uncle Nick had to pull all their equipment out and couldn't do much work. They worked some inside the mine, but with the cold and wet it was a miserable job. They gave that up, too, after a while, waiting for a break in the weather. But everybody was talking about the rain being good. It had been uncommonly dry, they said, for the last couple of winters, so the crops and pastures needed the rain, and the miners were glad for it, hoping it'd shake some new gold loose. Probably the only people who weren't thankful for the rain were the children, who had to stay cooped up inside the schoolhouse all day long on the worst of the wet days.

Throughout the winter, I learned a lot about the freight and mining business and took several wagon rides with either Mr. Weber or Mrs. Parrish to deliver things that people had ordered. Mrs. Parrish always introduced me real proper-like to the people we were doing business with, saying, "Mr. So-and-So, I would like you to meet my daughter Corrie, who is helping me now in the business." She had such a way of making me feel grown-up, like she respected and appreciated me! Soon

I knew most of the roads for twenty or thirty miles around Miracle, and had been to nearly every little town or hamlet or gold camp around those parts. I'd never realized how many customers Mrs. Parrish had all over. Some of the places we went and people I met were pretty rough-looking. But she always marched right into wherever we had to go with her head high and without showing a bit of fear. That's probably why the men came to respect her, because she could be as tough as they were if she had to. And that was something I would have to learn, too—if I planned on making my way alone in California.

That winter some of the town leaders got together and decided Miracle Springs ought to have a mayor. The town had grown a lot in the last two years, and was still growing some, with new families coming in. There was no election, it was just announced one day that a retired banker, recently come from the East, had agreed to act as mayor. He'd had experience in that sort of thing before. So Jason Vaissade became the first mayor of Miracle Springs.

CHAPTER 7

LEARNING TO LET GO
AND TRUST GOD

The weather had been nice for a couple of weeks. It was warming up and folks were saying the winter had finally broken and spring was on the way. We were more than a week into March, so any other year they would probably have been right.

One morning, when we were staying at Mrs. Parrish's house in town, I woke up before dawn. I usually got up pretty early, and liked to lie in bed and read or go for walks before the rest of the family got up.

This particular morning I got up while it was still dark. I put my clothes on and sneaked out of the house as quietly as I could. The morning was beautiful. I felt as if. I were the only one alive. I took in the cold morning air in long breaths. A few stars still twinkled in the sky, with just the faintest hint of the gray dawn starting to mix in with the blackness.

I walked out into the street. It was cold and I had several layers of clothes on, but I could tell the sun was going to come up and it would be a nice bright day. Everything was completely quiet. Marcus Weber wasn't out in the stable with the horses yet, and he was usually the first person to be up and at it most mornings in Miracle Springs. The roosters weren't even about their business yet either, although they likely would be before long.

I love early mornings! After I've been up a little while, my mind gets awake and active and has its best thinking times.

Maybe it's the quiet, maybe being alone. As much as I like people, I never get tired of being alone either, and my brain always seems to take alone times to turn about some of its best thoughts. Morning is always the best for praying too.

I suppose the two go hand in hand—praying and thinking. When you're praying you *are* thinking, kind of thinking in God's direction, pointing your brain toward God and then letting your thoughts go *out* of you and *into* him. At least that's how I like to imagine what it's like when I'm praying. And the other side of praying, listening to God, works just the reverse— I try to pay attention to the thoughts that are coming *into* my brain. And if I've been talking to God about something, then I figure those thoughts coming toward me are the thoughts coming out of God toward *me*—his thoughts that he's sending in *my* direction.

Well, on that particular morning I was thinking and praying, and opening my thoughts toward God and trying to listen to his thoughts toward me. And I found myself remembering the talk Mrs. Parrish and I had about alternatives, and choices, things I might some day find myself doing, and how a young lady like me ought to be preparing herself for the future and thinking about what she wants to do. And pretty soon I was walking along not even paying attention to where I was going, talking back and forth with God—talking in my thoughts I mean, not out loud—and asking him what it was that *he* wanted me to do and prepare for.

My favorite passage in the Bible is in the third chapter of Proverbs, verses five and six: "Trust in the Lord with all thine heart; and lean not unto thine own understanding. In all thy ways acknowledge him, and he shall direct thy paths." That morning I felt as if God was directing my footsteps, because without even thinking where I was going, I found myself walking about the town praying and talking to God as I went.

I walked for five or ten minutes, and found myself standing in front of the Gold Nugget saloon, where we'd first met Pa and where we'd had our first church service in Miracle Springs. Then I walked farther on down the street past Mr. Bosely's

General store. My heart was full as I recalled everything that had happened, all that God had done since those first days here.

As I passed the bank, I thought about Mr. Royce and all the evil that had come because of him. But seeing his bank also reminded me of what Mrs. Parrish had done to save Pa's mine. Maybe that incident was the beginning of her and Pa loving each other like they did now.

God had brought me so far, would he bring me safely the rest of the way? Yet even seeing how everything had worked out in the past, it was still easy to slip into worrying about what was going to become of me.

"I'm growing up, and sometimes it's hard to know what I'm supposed to do!" I had told Mrs. Parrish in one of our talks.

"God will let you know in his time," she said. "You can trust him. If you let him, he will work in every bit of your life—you can depend on it."

Even as I was thinking these words of Mrs. Parrish's, I found myself coming back around to the Freight Company and to Mrs. Parrish's house—our house.

Oh, God, I found myself thinking, *you have been so good to me! We were so alone back then . . . and now you've given us so much! Thank you for Pa, for what a fine man he is. Thank you for Uncle Nick, for Katie, for the claim and the cabin, and for the life you've given us here, and all the new friends we have.*

I stopped and looked around me. I was standing right in front of Mrs. Parrish's office. The light was creeping up in the east, and it wasn't dark anymore, though it was still only a gray light. Inside through the window, the office was empty and black. On the glass was painted in small gold letters: *Parrish Mine and Freight Company.*

"How can I thank you enough, Lord, for . . . for my new mother?" I whispered. There was nothing else to say—that one prayer was enough. My heart was full of gratitude for her— for all she'd been to us, for the friendship she and I had, for how she had helped me love Pa better, for all she had explained to me about living with God, for how she had helped me un-

derstand myself and my own feelings more deeply, for the talks
we'd had, for our trip to San Francisco, for how I'd learned to
pray and bring God into the little things of my life because of
her. I wouldn't have been half the person I was if it hadn't been
for Mrs. Parrish—and I sure wouldn't have been standing there
praying, and thinking about verses from the Bible, if she hadn't
taught me how important it was to live my life with God as
part of it.

I didn't even realize it at first, but suddenly I was crying—
quietly, just a few tears. And a great sadness was coming up
out of my heart, although I didn't know why right at first.

I don't want to leave this place, God, I thought. *I love these
people and Pa and Almeda and Zack and Tad and Becky and
Emily . . . and Mr. Weber, and everybody, Lord! I don't want
to leave . . . I don't want to, Lord!*

All at once I knew why I was so sad. I'd been filled with
such happiness only a few moments before, in the memories
of this town and people. But retracing steps along the sidewalks
where I'd walked dozens of times in the last couple of years
was a little like saying goodbye to Miracle Springs.

"Is that why you woke me up so early, Lord," I asked, "and
drew me out of bed—to say my farewell to this place?"

My future and what was to become of me *had* been on my
heart a lot—ever since the day of Pa's and Almeda's wedding.
Even when my mind wasn't actively thinking about it, down
deeper the question was still running around inside me. Every
once in a while the doubts would surface and I'd get to thinking
again about that conversation we'd had about a girl preparing
herself for her future, or I'd remember what Ma had said about
me needing to think about growing up. I suppose I was growing
up slower than a lot of girls might—especially being a reading,
thinking person always trying to figure things out in my head.
But maybe now it was time that I *did* get on with the business
of growing up, and I couldn't help thinking about it a lot.

The town still surrounded me, still quiet just like a moment
before, but now I felt a pang of pain at the sight, as if I would
not be able to hold on to it forever.

"What are you fixing to do with me, Lord?" I asked.
"Where are you leading me? What do you want me to do?
Where do you want me to go?"

Go! Out of my own prayer the word slammed against me.
"Oh, God, you're not gonna make me go away, are you? But
I don't want to go! I've only had my pa back two years, and
now I've only had a mother again less than a year, and I don't
know if I can stand to be torn away from them! Please, God,
don't make me go away! I don't want to be *Miss Hollister,* God.
I want to be just who I've been all these years! I want to keep
being a daughter for a while longer. I'm not ready to be a
woman, a grown-up all on my own yet!"

I was crying hard now. The praying words dried up, but
not the tears.

Two or three minutes later the tears began to stop. And as
they did another set of words from the Bible crept into the back
of my mind. I hadn't thought about them for a long time—I
couldn't even remember when I'd heard or read them, but all
at once there they were, as if God had sent them to quiet down
my spirit and remind me of something I needed to remember
right then. The words were: *Delight thyself also in the Lord; and
he shall give thee the desires of thine heart.*

"Do you really mean that, God?" I asked. "Will you give
me what *I* want? You won't make me leave Miracle Springs?"

I started walking again. By now the first colors of pink were
showing in the sky to the east. Folks would be stirring before
long. The roosters were hollering their heads off all over town.

As I walked I knew God was talking to me. I didn't hear
an actual *voice* speaking out of the sky. But I had been thinking—and even crying—in God's direction. And after I'd "had
my say," maybe it was God's turn to do the talking. Walking
along I felt my mind and heart filling up with words, ideas,
feelings, verses from the Bible, reminders of things Mrs. Parrish had told me or things I'd heard Rev. Rutledge say in
church, about feeding on God's truth. When I look back on
the experience of that morning, I think God was using everything going through my mind to speak to me. *His* thoughts

were now coming in *my* direction.

I felt God speaking to me that morning. The thoughts and feelings came too fast and in such a jumble, and of course I didn't understand everything all at once. But as I wrote it down and thought about that morning after it happened, more and more of it made sense to me. It was as if God was *saying* something like this to me:

"Yes, Corrie, I *will* give you the desires of your heart. I do that with all my children who delight in me. But I cannot do it unless a man or a woman, a boy or girl . . . unless *you*, Corrie, do indeed *delight* yourself in me. That's what the psalm means. *If* you delight in me, *then* I will give you the desires of your heart."

I want to delight in you, God, I said to myself, *but I don't think I know what that means.*

Again I felt God's thoughts coming into my mind.

"Just this, Corrie—to delight in me means that you want to do what I want, not what *you* want. Your desire is to do *my* will rather than your own, because you trust me to take care of you, you trust me about everything. I created you, I created all things, and I love you so much more than you can possibly realize. You can trust me to do the very *best* for you in every way imaginable—the very best!"

I don't understand. I thought that verse said you would give me the desires of MY heart?

"When you trust me completely, as your Creator and Father and friend, when you trust me so much that you know I will do the best for you, when you trust me enough to want *my* will in your life, that becomes the desire of your heart. The desire of *your* heart is to do *my* will. And when you want *my* will for your life, and you want that more than anything else, then I will give you that—I will certainly work out my will in your life. And it will be the best possible life you could ever have! You will have the desire of your heart, and everything you could possibly hope for shall be yours—because your life is in my hands, not your own. Do you remember how that whole passage from Psalm 37 goes, Corrie?"

Suddenly I *did* remember! Rev. Rutledge had preached from Psalm 37 about two months ago and I had loved the words so much I'd memorized them:

Trust in the Lord, and do good; so shalt thou dwell in the land, and verily thou shalt be fed. Delight thyself also in the Lord; and he shall give thee the desires of thine heart. Commit thy way unto the Lord; trust also in him; and he shall bring it to pass.

"I do not always fulfill the worldly desires of my children. I do not give them everything they selfishly might *want*. But for those of my sons and daughters who want *me*, who want to know me, I will fulfill that heart's desire. And everything else in life will be given in abundance along with it. I cannot give myself without giving my blessings and my love and my abundant provision."

The flow of thoughts stopped. I was outside town now, unconsciously walking in the direction of the church and school. I looked up. There was the building off in the distance. I thought of the laughing, yelling voices of the children that'd be echoing from inside it in a few hours. I thought of Miss Stansberry and wondered if I would someday be a schoolteacher too. Then I thought of the church, about that summer when it'd been built, and about Pa and Rev. Rutledge, about the dedication of the building and the picnic and seeing Mr. Grant and the soldiers. I thought about all the many church meetings and services we'd had in that building since then, and all the growing I'd done—sometimes having to do with the church services, sometimes not.

Had the Lord directed my path here, like the proverb said, so that I could say goodbye to this church and school building like the rest of the town? Something down inside was telling me a change was coming in my life, and I was afraid. I wasn't sure I liked the idea at all.

"Trust me, Corrie . . . you *can* trust me!"

This time the words came into my mind so clearly that I *knew* exactly what God was saying.

I drew in a deep sigh from the cold morning air. Even though I was all alone, I felt suddenly embarrassed, because I knew my worrying about my future was silly. Of course I could trust God to take care of me! Even if I didn't want to leave Miracle Springs, God wouldn't lead me to leave unless it was best. I *did* want my life, my future, everything I was as a person—I wanted it to be what *God* wanted, not what I wanted. I *did* want God's will. I wanted to be able to trust him, even for my future and all its unknowns.

Then I started to realize that maybe God hadn't gotten me up early like this and had me walk around town, filling me with these thoughts about my future and what I might be doing a year, two years, three years from now, because I was going to *leave* Miracle Springs. I might leave someday, or I might not, but maybe the *goodbyes* weren't to the buildings and the things I had looked at that morning, or to the people. Maybe God was trying to get me to think about my life in a new way, wanting me to say goodbye to the old way of looking at things, goodbye to worrying about what was to become of me. Maybe the future God was wanting me to move into wasn't necessarily in a new *place,* but in a new way of trusting him, of delighting in what *he* wanted for me.

Sunrise had filled the sky with brilliant reds and oranges. I could hear the sounds of the morning in the distance—dogs barking, a few wagons moving. Marcus Weber's hammer slammed down on the anvil, ringing in the distance. He was likely fixing a wheel or shoeing one of the horses.

I walked a little way off the dirt road, behind the trunk of a huge old twisted scrub-oak tree, and knelt down. I immediately felt the cold on my knees, because the grass was still wet from last week's rain and the morning dew. But I didn't mind. I bowed my head and prayed again, this time out loud, though just barely above a whisper.

"Oh, Lord, I *do* want to delight in you! I want your will for my life, whatever you want me to do. If you want me to teach children in a school, or if you want me to keep working in the Freight Company, I'll do either of those if you want me to, God. Or whatever else. I want to trust you, and so, Lord, I want to give my life to you, like Rev. Rutledge was talking about that Sunday, to make the kind of lady you have in mind for me to be. I do give you my future and whatever you want to do with it, even if it means someday having to leave Miracle Springs, though I don't want to. Please help me to trust you more completely. I'll do what you want and go where you say, 'cause I know you know what's best for me."

That was all. No more words were there. I slowly got up and began walking back toward town, breathing in deeply of the morning air.

I felt good! In church you sometimes hear people talking about "burdens being lifted" off their shoulders, and maybe that's a little what it felt like. The worry was gone. It felt as if I had given it to God, and he had taken it, just as if I'd handed him a heavy sack and now I wasn't carrying it anymore.

I'd been crying earlier, thinking about having to say good-bye to familiar sights and faces. But now I felt like smiling. The future was going to be exciting, not fearful! Because I had given all of it to God, even though I didn't know what *it* was, and he was going to make it the very best for me—because it would be what *he* wanted for me. Maybe I felt lighter and happier because for the first time I really was trusting God to make things turn out, instead of worrying about them.

As I walked into town, more thoughts from God started coming into my mind. They were different, yet still part of that psalm which said we would be fed by truth. I hadn't thought of that part of the verse before, but now I found myself considering what it might mean. Maybe I had to get to the point of saying to God "I trust you" before he could make sense out of the rest of it to me. In my mind, God seemed to say:

"Wherever you go, and whatever you do—here in Miracle Springs or far away to wherever I might send you someday— I want you to love and follow the truth, and live by it, and let it feed you. *The truth*, Corrie Belle Hollister, my daughter that I love. I am making you into a woman, and I have plans for you—whether people call you Corrie Belle or Miss Hollister. Whatever they call you, wherever you go, whatever you do— follow the truth, Corrie . . . follow *my* truth. Find out what my truth is. Then follow it, live by it, and never let it go. For in *truth* shall you be fed, and so shall you dwell in the land, and by following the truth will I be able to give you the desires of your heart."

Like so much of what happened to me and what passed through my mind that morning, I didn't fully understand those words at the time. But now, years later, I can see how the Lord was giving me those words as a way of pointing me ahead toward a certain desire that was in my heart, getting me ready for it. That morning was the beginning of where the Lord was going to take me, the beginning of the part of my life when I began learning to trust him more completely.

At the time I realized none of this. But in going down on my knees and giving myself and my future to God in a way I never had before, I see now that when I got up and walked back into town, I had left the things of my childhood behind.

CHAPTER 8

THE BLIZZARD

The Lord shoved me right into something that was going to play a big part in my future almost immediately. But I didn't realize the significance in my life until I looked back on it years later.

That same day when I'd gotten up early to walk and pray and talk with God, about the middle of the afternoon huge clouds started to roll in from the North, coming toward the Sierras. By evening the cold, icy, blustery winds had begun to blow.

The next morning, just after dawn—which seemed later than usual on account of the dark clouds—it started to snow, very lightly to begin with. Even at noon there was no more than a fine layer of dust on things and it still wasn't collecting on the roads or where people walked.

But it kept falling, and by the middle of the afternoon the flakes were bigger and whiter, and an inch had collected. People were bundling up and starting to pack in extra firewood and oats and corn for their livestock.

Pa built a huge fire in the house that night, and it was warm and cozy. Every now and then he'd get up and go and peer out the window into the blackness. Sometimes he wouldn't say anything. Sometimes he'd come back into the room muttering. Once he just said, "I don't know, Almeda," and then he shook his head. "It looks like it could be a bad one!"

When I woke up the next morning, Pa was already downstairs in the parlor, standing still, staring out the same window into the morning gray. I walked to his side, he put his arm around me, and we both just looked and looked, neither of us saying a word. Everywhere was white—nothing but white. You could hardly tell there was supposed to be a town out there. It was just hills and mounds and bumps of white. It had to be over a foot deep, and still the sky was filled with the down-fluttering flakes.

"Ain't never seen it like this," Pa finally said. "Never this much so low down. Must be taller than a man's head up in the foothills! I hope Alkali got back to the cabin."

"Where is he, Pa?" I asked.

"He set out yesterday morning for Dolan's place, up to the high flat on Relief Hill above Missouri Canyon. He was aiming to get himself a mule. Dolan was in town last week and had several he wanted to get rid of. But Dolan's ranch'll be plumb snowed in for weeks now." He stopped and sighed deeply. "Alkali, Alkali . . . I hope you made it back in time, you old buzzard!"

The day wore on slowly. School was cancelled. Most of the places in town didn't open. If they had, nobody would have come anyway. Almeda went to her office, but only for part of the day. I could tell she was worried about Pa, he was acting real fidgety. Somehow he just had a sense that things were going wrong out there in that snow. He just kept staring out the window.

It stopped snowing about noon. A few footprints and horse tracks cut through the thick white blanket, but not too many. After lunch Pa put on his heavy winter coat and started to climb into his boots.

"You're not going out?" Almeda said.

"Can't stand sitting around here any longer, Almeda. I'm going over to Rafferty's, maybe the Gold Nugget. I gotta find out if anybody's heard anything." He made for the door.

"Can I come, Pa?" asked Tad.

"I need you to stay and protect the womenfolk, son," said Pa. The gleam in his eye said he hadn't forgotten about Marcus

Weber, who was pounding and working away out in the stable, but that he wasn't going to mention him.

"Zack, you come with me. Might be that I'll need you," he added.

Zack was in his boots and after him in a flash, leaving the rest of us sitting there wondering what Pa figured doing out in the middle of the blizzard.

Eventually we found out.

A couple of hours later Zack burst through the door.

"Pa said to get a couple of horses saddled up right away," he panted. "He'll be back in a minute."

"I'll get Marcus to help you," said Almeda, starting toward the back door. "What is it, Zack?"

"There's been an avalanche down on the west side of Washington Ridge. I guess the snow gathered so fast up on a ledge overlooking the little ravine that the powder couldn't hold together. Two or three cabins down in the wash was plumb buried. All the men are heading out there to try to dig the folks out."

"Who is it—any women or children?" asked Mrs. Parrish.

"No, ma'am. Just some old miners that camp out up there."

"What about Mr. Jones?" I asked. "Is *he* in danger too?"

"Don't know," said Zack. "Nobody's seen him."

"Let's go see to the horses," said Almeda.

"Come to think of it, we'll need three, cause Pa said to tell Mr. Weber to come too." The two of them closed the door behind them.

About ten or fifteen minutes later, Pa came in the front door almost exactly as Zack and Almeda returned from the stable.

"Horses ready, Zack?" he said.

"Yes, sir."

"I don't know when we'll be back, Almeda. Marcus coming?"

"He's in the stable."

"Good. Pray we'll find those fellas! There's a lot of snow up there—must be a good thousand feet higher'n we are here in Miracle. Come on, Zack."

They made for the back door where their horses waited.

"Oh, Almeda," Pa said, turning back at the door. "Hitch up a wagon—one with the highest axle to get through the snow—with two of whatever horses are left. The workhorses would be best in this weather. I ain't sure what we'll find, but if we need a wagon for hauling some gear up there, I want it ready."

"It will be," she replied. "Drum . . . be careful!" she added, gripping his hand.

Pa nodded seriously, then he and Zack were gone. Almost the minute they left it started snowing again.

CHAPTER 9

A RASH DECISION

About an hour and a half after Pa and Zack and Mr. Weber left—the whole time it had been still as death, hardly a sound either in the house or outside—we heard the door of the livery crash open.

Mrs. Parrish jumped up and ran out back to the stable, and I followed.

"Hey!" a man's voice was calling. "Hey . . . ain't nobody in there? Marcus, where are you, man?"

Just then Mrs. Parrish opened the stable door and looked inside. "Mr. Ward!" she exclaimed. "What are you doing here?"

"No time to explain, ma'am! Where's Weber, Hollister? I can't find any of the men around. I gotta have me some help an' I ain't got time to go tryin' to track 'em down!"

"I'm afraid all the men are gone. There was an avalanche down across the Yuba on Washington Ridge."

The man swore, slapping his hand to his forehead. But I could tell it was fear he was feeling, not anger. His face turned pale and he started to collapse.

Mrs. Parrish rushed forward and caught him in her arms before he hit the floor. "What *is* it, Mr. Ward?" she said in alarm. But the moment she felt his body and saw his face close up, she knew. "The man's nearly frozen to death!" she exclaimed back in my direction. "Corrie, come help me—we have to get him into the house!"

68

Together we half dragged the poor man, whose legs could hardly support him another step, back into the warm parlor of Mrs. Parrish's house. By the time we got him slouched in a chair he was nearly unconscious.

"The boots, Corrie!" she said. "We've got to get his boots off!" She grabbed at one as I pulled on the other. The leather was soaking wet, and when we got his boots and his stockings off, we could feel that his feet were just like ice.

"He might already have frostbite—it's a wonder he didn't die from the exposure," she said, pulling his limp legs in the direction of the fire. "We've got to get some dry cloths around his feet."

In a few minutes Mr. Ward began to come to, and almost immediately started to ramble in a panicky, exhausted voice. "My wife and three girls," he said, ". . . trapped up on Buck Mountain . . . snow caught us last night . . . blizzard up there—had to get 'em to town . . . wind blew the storm right down on top of us . . . snowing so hard I couldn't see a thing . . . too far to turn back . . . got off the trail, and the wagon went in a ditch . . . wheel broke—"

He stopped, then looked around at the two of us. His eyes were wide, as if he suddenly had become aware he was sitting in a warm room in front of a fire. His expression showed no recognition of who we were.

He struggled to rise. "Gotta get out of here," he mumbled. "Got to get back . . . gotta find help . . ."

"Mr. Ward, you can't go anywhere," Mrs. Parrish said firmly but gently. "Your feet and hands are frozen, and all your clothes are soaked."

"I've got to get back . . . they'll die if I don't . . . got to get help!"

"Where are they?" she asked.

"Snow was everywhere . . . wagon was broke down— wheel shattered . . . couldn't get us all out on the one horse . . . sheltered them best I could under the wagon . . . un- hitched the horse, took off for town. But I pushed the beast too hard in the snow . . . stumbled . . . broke a leg . . . walked rest of the way here . . . got to find some men . . . got to get back out there . . . they'll freeze to death in the blizzard!"

"Where are they—*where*, Mr. Ward?" asked Mrs. Parrish, urgency in her voice.

"Halfway down the Buck . . . off the road from our place . . . got to get back there!"

Again he struggled to rise, but fell back, unable to stand.

"There's no way this man's going out again any time soon," said Mrs. Parrish, half to me, halfway thinking aloud to herself. She paced toward the fire and back again.

Without really stopping to think, I suddenly found myself running to grab my thickest coat, putting on my gloves and hat, and then running back out to the stable and throwing the big double doors wide open. I climbed up on the seat of the wagon Marcus had hitched for Pa, and took the reins in my hands.

"Corrie, what do you think you're doing?" exclaimed Mrs. Parrish, rushing out of the house behind me.

"I gotta go after them," I said. "Mrs. Ward and the young'uns!"

"The horses can never make it! The snow's too deep, and it's still falling!"

"I can do it—I know the way."

"It'll be dark soon. Please, Corrie . . . don't. Come back inside with me." Her voice had a pleading sound in it. I could tell she was worried.

"I'm sorry, Almeda, I've *got* to. I can make it—I know I can!"

She stood there for a moment, just looking at me as if seeing me for the first time. "All right, Corrie," she said at last. "But wait a minute."

Faster than I would have thought possible, Mrs. Parrish ran into the house and came back with a package wrapped in a dish towel, with several blankets thrown over one arm.

"Some food and water," she explained. "And blankets." She threw the blankets in at my feet and stepped back. "Be careful, Corrie," she said briefly. "And God go with you."

I flipped the reins and called out to the horses, and in a few seconds I was plowing my way through the blizzard. I didn't look back. But inside I knew Mrs. Parrish was crying, and would immediately go back into the house and get on her knees to start praying. I knew God was with me, but I was glad to have two of us praying at the same time! If Pa'd been there, I might not have done what I did, but *if* I had, he'd have probably been muttering something about "that blame fool Belle blood" as he watched me disappear up the street. He probably thought the same thing when he heard about it later.

I didn't realize it then, but that was the first time I ever called Mrs. Parrish *Almeda*. I suppose I was moving toward being a grown-up faster than I realized.

I headed out of town northward, where I could still see Mr. Ward's footsteps in the snow. But I wouldn't follow them all the way. I had made a delivery up to the Wards' place last month with Mr. Weber. He had showed me a ravine along the foot of Buck Mountain where he said the snow didn't fall. He was laughing about it then, but now it just might save those peoples' lives! I'd take the wagon to the foot of the mountain, then along the length of the ravine and up the cutoff road that joined the main ridge-road about halfway to the Wards' place. Marcus had shown me where it turned off when we'd been on our way back down the mountain.

About halfway through the canyon, I heard the bray of a donkey, a strange sound through the quiet of falling snow. I stopped, and heard it again. Then I heard a familiar voice yelling and cursing. Suddenly the sounds coming from the animal made sense!

I urged my horses toward the sounds, and as I got closer I heard the voice again, this time calling out to me. "Hey! Who's there? Hold up . . . whoever ya may be!"

I called my horses to stop. Then I heard the voice again, from part way up the hillside on the slope of Buck Mountain. But it wasn't from the trapped members of the Ward family at all. I wasn't anywhere close to them yet. Instead, the voice was coming from the mouth of a small cave.

Presently a figure appeared in the black opening, looking out into the white blizzard. It was Alkali Jones!

"Mr. Jones!" I called out in astonishment. "What are you doing here? We were all worried about you!"

"I was halfway down from Dolan's when I figured I'd better git me an' my mules hurryin' a mite faster or we'd be buried by this dang blizzard. Then one o' 'em stumbled an' went lame on me an' I figured this here cave'd be 'bout the best I could do till the blame snow quit—hee, hee, hee! But am I glad to see you!"

"But you're only six or eight miles from home. Couldn't you have made it?"

"You ever tried t' pull a mule through a foot o' snow—an a lame one at that? Hee, hee! I might as well o' got on my hands an' crawled home on my knees. This blasted beast won't budge! An' I jest gave Dolan six-fifty fer the blame critter, an' I weren't about to part with my investment, ya might say, hee, hee."

"Well, come on down from there and get in! We got folks trapped up the mountain!"

Alkali left the injured mule tied at the cave and tethered the healthy one behind us. The old miner jumped into the wagon with me, and we continued on to the end of the ravine, which ended abruptly about six hundred yards farther up the canyon.

"You'll never git this pile o' lumber even halfway up the hill," said Mr. Jones. "Ain't no way a wagon like this is gonna make it up that steep path. I don't know what ya was aimin' t' do fer them folks."

"I thought there was a road from the canyon up to the ridge on top. When Mr. Weber and I were up there, he pointed down this way, and it looked like a fine road leading off down toward here."

"Fine road fer maybe two hundred yards, till it's outta sight! Then it turns into a steep trail switchin' back an' forth up the side o' the mountain. Ain't hardly wide enough fer a man, much less a beast. Jest look at it! Ain't no wagon can climb up that!"

We looked up toward Buck Mountain, one side looming against the canyon on our left. Tiny flakes of snow were falling, but above us, the mountain was lost in a dense fog of thick snow.

"'Sides that—look at it!" said Mr. Jones, still pointing upward in the direction I had been hoping to go. "Why, the snow up there's comin' down in a white blanket. There's likely a foot or two foot o' powder, maybe three, up t' the top where the other road is. That trail comin' down off the mountain t' this here ravine—why, it drops a thousand feet! Ain't no way, even if there was a road this wagon'd fit on—which there ain't! No way ya'd git it through that blizzard, not with them horses ya got."

"They're Mrs. Parrish's best," I said.

"They ain't snow animals."

"What are we going to do, Mr. Jones? Those people are trapped up there, and night's coming, and the snow's still falling!"

"That's what I was askin' you—what ya was aimin' to do."

"I thought I'd be able to get there with the wagon."

I hesitated. "What about the mule?" I exclaimed. "Could your mule make it up the steep trail?"

"'Course he could. He could make it up a mountain with no trail."

"In the snow?"

"That critter's been with me in worse snows than this! He ain't no blame tenderfoot like that beast o' Dolan's!"

"Then we'll take the mule up to the top!" I said.

"Jest how ya figure that'll help? How many of 'em ya say there was?"

"Four—Mrs. Ward and three young'uns."

"Hmm . . . lemme see, we might oughta—"

"We could bring them out one at a time, with the mule, and get them to the wagon!"

"Take too long! I tell ya, it's a three-quarter mile o' steep, rugged trail. Time ya went back an' forth, whoever was sittin' down in the wagon waitin', why they'd be plumb froze to death!

If we're gonna git 'em outta there, we gotta git 'em all at once, git back down here, an' high-tail it back to town to git them young'uns someplace warm afore nightfall brings another three foot o' snow an' they're buried till next spring!"

We were at the end of the canyon, and the trail up the mountain wound up and out of sight. I now saw the impossibility of what I had hoped to do. The wagon could go no farther. A light wet snow was falling where we were, and up higher the snow was falling in huge, thick flakes.

We stopped and I tried desperately to think.

"We'll have to try it with these horses," I said at last. "They're the best workhorses Parrish Freight has, and it's our only chance."

I jumped out of the wagon and began unhitching the straps from the two animals.

"What'n tarnation ya thinkin'?" said Mr. Jones.

"We'll both ride up there!" I answered, working my fingers as fast as I could in the biting cold. "We'll take the horses and your mule . . . leave the wagon here, then bring them all four down at once!"

"Ya got spunk, I'll say that! Let's git goin'—we still gotta find where they's broke down," said Mr. Jones, already out of the wagon and untying his mule from the back. "An' that ain't gonna be easy, neither!"

In another three or four minutes we were making our way up the narrow trail. It seemed to take forever, but we made it safely to the top. When we reached the main road that ran along the ridge, we stopped.

"Which way's the Ward place?" said Mr. Jones, half asking, half trying to remember himself.

I glanced all around. In the eerie quietness of the snowy wooded area, everything looked different.

"I . . . I'm not sure," I replied, glancing about for something I might recognize.

Suddenly Mr. Jones jumped off his mule and tromped forward in the snow several paces.

"Look . . . there's wagon tracks!" he shouted back at me

as he pointed ahead. "They been along here all right!"

He glanced hurriedly to the right and left.

"The slope's climbin' this way," he said, jumping back onto his mule. "That means they was headed down."

"Let's go!" I cried, urging the horses toward the faint wheel tracks.

Alkali Jones nodded. "I jest hope we ain't too late."

CHAPTER 10

THE ARTICLE

What happened next . . . well, I've kinda got to jump way ahead to tell you about it. You know I'd always wanted to write, and had even hoped to write newspaper articles someday—more than the one or two little things I'd done for Mr. Singleton. As it turned out, what happened to me and Mr. Jones in the blizzard was the thing that my first really big article was about. Of course, it wasn't printed in the paper till a couple months later—that's the jumping-ahead part.

But as I was writing about the blizzard, it just seemed that perhaps the best way to tell what happened would be just to let you read the article I wrote afterward. And I'm kind of proud of the article too, even after all these years, since it was the first one I got published in a big city paper. So here it is:

Sometimes danger brings with it adventures that would never have happened without it. That's how it was during the blizzard that struck the foothills northwest of Sacramento last March. Folks had already been calling the winter of '55 a bad one, and the sudden fall of snow that dropped on all the gold-mining communities of the region sure made it seem like they were right.

The blizzard brought danger, all right, because most of the citizens weren't expecting it, since it struck so suddenly and all, before anyone was prepared.

The first sign of trouble came when word got to the men gathered in Miracle Springs' Gold Nugget—one of the town's only establishments open at the time—that an avalanche had just occurred on Washington Ridge east of Nevada City, burying three cabins in the ravine below, and endangering the lives of six or eight miners trapped inside. Immediately all the town's available men set out through the snow to try to dig the men out.

No sooner had the men left Miracle Springs when another emergency came. Mr. Jeriah Ward staggered into town, nearly dead of exposure in the bitter cold and in danger of frostbite, frantically in search of help. Finding no one at the saloon or the sheriff's office, Ward made his way to the Parrish Mine and Freight Company. In a state of collapse, he desperately told Mrs. Almeda Parrish Hollister that his wife and three young girls were trapped underneath their broken-down wagon halfway up Buck Mountain.

The words had barely passed his lips when one of Parrish Freight's young employees set out through the snow with a high-axle flatbed wagon pulled by two sturdy workhorses. The Parrish Freight wagon first headed north through the snow-blanketed white countryside on the main road toward North Bloomfield and Alleghany. Following Humbug Creek, swollen full from the winter's rains, the wagon left the main road at the base of Buck Mountain, dropping down into Pan Ravine, a narrow gulch running along the south flank of the mountain. There the snow, which had been between six inches and a foot and a half deep on the main road, was only an inch or two thick. According to Mr. Marcus Weber of the Parrish Mine and Freight Company, who was interviewed afterward, this unusual phenomenon, which keeps most snowfall off the floor of Pan Ravine, is known only to the oldest natives of the region, but has been responsible for saving the lives of more than one person in winter snowstorms like this one.

Up through the ravine the young freight driver urged the two workhorses, who found the footing easier. But as the elevation steadily rose, so did the snow on the ground.

About halfway through the canyon the familiar voice of longtime Miracle Springs miner Alkali Jones was heard. Jones had left the previous day, prior to the beginning of the blizzard, for the Dolan ranch on the higher ground beyond Buck Mountain, and had been feared trapped or even lost in the snow. Like a ghost peering out from the darkness of the cave where he had been trying to wait out the worst of the storm, Jones appeared and joined the rescue effort.

The two made their way to the end of the ravine where they left their wagon. Then up the narrow trail into the blizzard they went, Jones leading on the back of his sure-footed mule, followed by his young friend on the bare back of one of the horses, pulling the other.

Steadily they climbed up the side of Buck Mountain, the snow falling heavier and heavier, but the trail under the thick foliage of the trees remaining visible. The way was slow, but all three animals proved true to their sure-footed reputations. Up the steep way they went, switching back often, always climbing, until at last they reached the main road that ran along the ridge. Snow over a foot thick covered the way.

"I hope they're still alive!" cried out the young freight driver as they began their search for the broken-down wagon.

"Ain't likely they can last long in this cold!" said Alkali Jones. "We gotta find 'em quick!"

As rapidly as they could in the thick snow, they trudged along the road, following the barely visible indentations of wagon tracks, which were growing fainter and fainter by the minute.

"I think I see it!" shouted the young driver at last. "There . . . off the road, all covered with snow!"

"Could be a wagon," replied Jones, giving his mule a hard kick in the side.

"Mrs. Ward . . . Mrs. Ward!" the two shouted as they approached, jumping down and staggering through the deep snow. "Mrs. Ward—you there?"

"Thank God!" said a faint voice from underneath the half-buried wagon. "Who is it?"

"I'm from the Parrish Mine and Freight Company. Your husband came looking for help. His horse broke a leg and he couldn't get back to you."

The two bent down. Under the wagon, protected from the snow, sat the freezing woman, the chill of death in her eyes, huddling her three children close to her under two or three blankets. The bed of the wagon, partially sloped against the wind, had kept them dry, and the blankets had preserved at least some of their body heat as the woman clutched the three children close to one another. Otherwise, all four would have been dead.

"Why, Alkali Jones!" exclaimed the woman, recognizing one of her rescuers for the first time.

"In the flesh, ma'am," replied Jones. "I haven't seen ya since last spring."

"You two can visit later! Let's wrap up the girls in these blankets. We've got to get back down to the canyon before this snow gets any deeper!"

Helping her to her feet, Jones assisted Mrs. Ward onto the back of his mule—the most sure-footed of the three animals—then handed her the smallest of the girls, tightly wrapped in a blanket. Then the other two remounted, each cradling one of the children securely.

Ten minutes later, the three animals were retracing their hoofprints toward the steep trail they had recently ascended. Downward they went this time, in tracks they had carved through the powder on the way up—still visible, though snow continued to fall. Jones, on one of the horses, with seven-year-old Julie bundled on his lap, led the way, followed by Mrs. Ward with the baby on the mule, and then the last Parrish workhorse with four-year-old Tracey in the rider's lap. In a rainstorm the footing on the steep trail would have been muddy and treacherous, but in the frozen snow the hoofs of the animals found solid footing; and though the way was slow, they made the descent into the ravine below without stumbling once.

The waiting wagon was loaded with the four Wards while the two-horse team was once again hitched to the wagon. Then the intrepid group turned for Miracle Springs.

"What about your other mule?"

"Leave it!" replied Alkali Jones, referring to the second of his two mules that he had tied back at the cave. "He couldn't make it afore ya came, an' he ain't likely t' feel none different now. I'll come back fer him when the storm breaks. You jest whip them two horses o' yers along an' git us back t' town! I'm as blamed anxious t' git outta this cold as the Missus an' her young'uns. My fingers is likely already froze clean off!"

And so the rescue of Mrs. Jeriah Ward and her three daughters off Buck Mountain took place. When her husband next saw her, Mrs. Ward was sitting trying to get warm, drinking a cup of tea, while her two older girls sipped hot milk and vanilla in front of the fireplace at Mrs. Hollister's. Waking up in a chair he could not remember being dragged to, with his family warm and safe and recovering, Ward took a cup of coffee from the hand of Alkali Jones, full of more questions than he could ask at once. Then, with many interruptions of "hee, hee, hee!" from the old miner, the relieved father and husband heard the entire story.

In conclusion, it should be mentioned that the rescue of the miners trapped on Washington Ridge was also successful, though it was after nightfall before most of the men returned to Miracle Springs.

CHAPTER 11

HOW IT GOT PUBLISHED

Well, that's the article I wrote about what happened, though you can probably tell I had a little help with it here and there. Mrs. Parrish and the man from the newspaper office added a few words and made it sound a little better, but mostly it's mine.

The Wards all turned out to be fine, and stayed in town at Mrs. Gianini's boardinghouse for five days. It snowed on and off for another two days, then it took a while before Jeriah Ward could get a wagon back up the mountain with his wife and girls. He never let the fire go out in that cabin all winter and spring, and kept his wagon in good repair. I went up to visit them several times, and they treated me like a hero, telling me that if it hadn't been for me they might have died in the cold. I hadn't really thought about the danger, but the men around had such a respect for the mountain and for the fierceness of the weather in winter that they insisted there *was* more danger to all of our lives than I realized. Although I never felt much like a hero, it was nice to have them appreciate what I did. And from that time on, the Ward place became kind of like a second home to me, and I got quite attached to Lynn—Mrs. Ward—and her three girls.

Alkali Jones went back to the cave off Pan Ravine the next day during a lull in the storm. I half think he was hoping the mule he'd left there would have frozen to death or run off so he'd have an excuse to go back to Mr. Dolan and try to get his

$6.50 back. But no such luck. The mule was still there and still lame. Mr. Jones managed to get him back to town, and got him healthy again, although he still curses at him, calling him "the blamed orneriest dang mule I ever stuck rawhide t' the rump of!" Maybe because he figured my coming along sort of saved his and his mules' lives too—or at least saved his new mule's life by keeping him from killing it himself!—he named it *Corrie's Beast*. That's what he's been calling it ever since, though most of the time he's swearing at it so loud he never has a chance to say the critter's name at all!

I wrote in my journal all about what happened during the blizzard with the Wards—even longer than I did in the article. I wasn't in the habit of showing Mrs. Parrish everything I wrote. My journal was still a private thing I did just for myself. But she asked me what I'd said about the blizzard, and if she might see it, and I agreed.

"Corrie, this is just great!" she exclaimed after she'd read only about half of it. Then she kept on reading, with a bright look in her eye. When she finally set the book down, she looked up. She was still smiling, but she tried to sound serious so I'd know she really meant what she was saying.

"Corrie," she said, "we could get this published, I'm sure of it!"

"How?" I said.

"In a newspaper. This is real news, Corrie. Papers want this kind of thing, especially personal accounts."

We talked about it some more and I asked her what I should do.

"Write it again, Corrie. Write it on separate paper, and as good as you can make it. Think of it as a newspaper story. Pretend telling folks in San Francisco or up in Oregon or back in Kansas City what it was like during that blizzard. Pretend that you're telling *real* people about what happened, and then just write it like a story."

"Should I mention my name?" I asked.

"Hmm, that is hard to know," mused Mrs. Parrish. "Why don't you see if you can write it without letting on who you are," she said after a minute. "That way it will seem more like real news reporting rather than that you're just telling something that happened to you."

Later I learned ways to do "reporting" and tell about things I was involved in without including myself. But this first time it was difficult. After I wrote everything down again as a story, Mrs. Parrish helped me make some corrections. She suggested I add a few words here and there, like *foliage* and *phenomenon*. Actually she suggested quite a few things to change, but all the time she made me think it was all my own doing.

When we were done she helped me send it to Mr. Singleton in Marysville. When he wrote back two weeks later, saying that the *California Gazette* regrettably would have to decline interest in the blizzard account, she was so upset she stormed and fumed around the house with a red face.

"That old rattlepate Singleton wouldn't know a good story if he was hit over the head with it! How he ever got into the newspaper business I can't imagine!"

All at once she had an idea. That's when she thought of her friend. "I know what we'll do, Corrie," she said. "I have a friend on the staff of the *Alta* in San Francisco. He's in advertising, but I've done quite a bit of work with him for the business. I'll send him the story, tell him it's authentic and that a friend of mine here in Miracle Springs wrote it. I'll twist his arm a bit and ask him to show it to the news editor—Kemble's his name, I believe."

"Do you really think they might print it?"

"You never know unless you try, Corrie. I've given the *Alta* a lot of my business, not just in advertising, but for various printing jobs I've needed. I think upon my recommendation, they just might consider it."

When Mrs. Parrish's friend first wrote back to us, he said, "The article's fine. Matter of fact, it's better than fine for a new reporter. But doesn't he know how important it is to identify who the hero of the story is?" He thought I was a *he* because Mrs. Parrish had suggested I send him the story as written by *C.B. Hollister*, so his editor wouldn't say no to the idea of publishing it just because I was a girl.

Mrs. Parrish answered the letter and explained why the freight driver's name shouldn't be used in the article. He responded immediately. "Kemble liked the blizzard piece. Not too well written, he said, but exciting and realistic, which is what our readers want. He complained like I did about the heroic wagon driver not being mentioned, but I told him that was a condition you'd put on publication. Anyway, he thought the piece was fine enough regardless, especially for a new reporter. Enclosed is $2.00. Whoever your friend C.B. Hollister is, Kemble says for him to get in touch. Might be that we can use something else of his in the future. Kemble likes firsthand accounts and has been looking for this kind of thing from the foothills country. We'll send you a copy of the issue when it appears."

She threw her hands in the air and let out a whoop and holler.

"Corrie, Corrie! Do you see this?" she exclaimed, shaking the check in my direction. "A check for two dollars! Corrie . . . you are going to be a published, professional newspaper writer!"

I'd been sitting beside her as we read the letter. My heart was pounding and my hands were sweating, but not because of the $2.00. In fact, I hardly even noticed that. Over and over the words from the letter spun through my brain: *Whoever C.B. Hollister is . . . get in touch . . . something else of his in the future.*

I could hardly believe it! Not just that *this* story was going to get into a newspaper—they might even want another story later, if I could write another one!

It was too good to be true!

By this time winter was over, and the story didn't appear until toward the end of April. I'll never forget what it was like sitting around the house that night after the copy of the *Alta* came, the whole family huddled near the fire, everybody looking over shoulders and around heads and through arms. Tad and Becky sat on the floor, Emily and Zack and I squatted Indian-style, Alkali Jones, Katie, Uncle Nick, Pa, and Almeda

all crowded together to read the article in the *Alta* with BLIZ-
ZARD RESCUE ON BUCK MOUNTAIN in big bold black
print across the top, and underneath the words: *by C.B. Hollister, Miracle Springs, California.*

Between the storm and the article, I'd turned eighteen. And
there couldn't have been a better birthday present than this.

When everybody was finally done reading it, Katie congratulated me, and Uncle Nick threw his arm around my shoulder and pretended to pinch my cheek. Mrs. Parrish, bubbly
and happy that it had all turned out so well, was saying things
about all the articles I was going to write in the future.

But Pa was the quietest of all. He didn't say a word until
the hubbub from everyone else had died down. Then he just
stuck out his hand toward me. I took his hand and he gave
mine a big firm shake and looked me straight in the eye.

"Corrie Belle," he said, "I reckon you're a woman now.
You done this on your own, without me or your ma, though I
guess you had your share of help from Almeda here. But no
matter—*you* went out there after them kids. And that was a
right brave thing to do—though maybe a mite foolhardy—"

Everyone laughed.

"You went after 'em. Then you thought how to write it
down. You done that too. And with whatever help you had, I
figure it's you that newspaper guy and them girls got to thank."

He paused, then added, "Anyhow, Corrie Belle, what I'm
trying to say is that you're a mighty fine young woman—and
you done your pa proud."

I held on to his hand an extra moment or two, my eyes
glistening with tears as I took in the face I loved so much. God
had been so good to me!

In that moment I was more full and more thankful and
more proud than I had ever been in my life.

CHAPTER 12

SUMMER OF '55

The snowstorm, the article, and what Pa said to me that night, all seemed to be part of the Lord pointing me toward my future. Hindsight makes it easier to see those kinds of things when your life takes new directions. And as I've looked back, I've felt that God may have brought about the events of the blizzard and then the article getting published right after the prayers I'd prayed about my future.

Even as I was still down on my knees praying in the wet grass behind that oak tree near the school, somewhere up in the clouds way up high in the sky those snowflakes were getting ready to fall. God was telling me, "You see, Corrie, even before you're through praying, I'm already sending the answers down to you. You may not realize it, but these little snowflakes are going to come down onto you, and I will use them to show you that I am answering your prayers, and will send you out into your future. I will use these snowflakes to show you that I am giving you the desire of your heart too, Corrie, which is to write."

That time of prayer and trying to give my whole self more completely to God, and then the article that came later, set me on a path I would never turn back from. I said to God, "Here is my life, my future . . . here are my worries . . . You know what I want to do . . . I am willing to do and be anything you want me to be." And then God seemed to say back to me, "I will take your life, Corrie, and I will work my will in it, and

86

at the same time I will give you more than you could ever hope for, even more than you prayed for."

Ever since, whenever I see snowflakes falling to the ground, I think of them as beautiful tiny little remembrances of God's answers to prayer. For every prayer we pray, even before we're through praying it, God is *already* sending millions of answers down to us, answers we may not see or recognize, but they are from him nevertheless. Falling snow always helps me remember that God is so completely above us that we can never escape his quietly falling blessings and answers to prayers and his love and care.

Thus, I always look back on that time as the end of my childhood and the beginning of my being an adult. Not just because I'd turned eighteen, but because I'd let go of my worries (which kind of represented my past), and God had sent me out toward my future with a glimpse (that first newspaper article) of what it was I would be doing in the years to come. Just as Pa's and Almeda's life together was just beginning, so too was mine as a grown-up.

For the rest of that school year I kept helping Miss Stansberry at the school, and then after I was done, working at the Freight Company two or three days a week. But even before school broke off for the summer in June, I think I'd decided not to be Miss Stansberry's assistant the following fall when it started back up again. Whether it was the thinking and praying about my future, I don't know. And I still considered teaching school one of my "options" that perhaps I'd think about someday. Maybe I figured it was time to take a break from school, even though I liked being part of it. It might be that God was, like the verse said, "directing my path" by getting me to think about different things. It's hard to say. I was still too new at trying to figure out about what Almeda called "God's guidance." But I felt I ought to do something else for a spell. So my plan was to work more at the Freight Company that next year, and of course Almeda thought it was a terrific idea.

The summer of '55 was one of the happiest times I can remember. The weather was nice, and everything went perfectly. The mine didn't cave in and nobody got hurt and everybody got along real fine. We all moved permanently from the house in town out to the claim. That made Pa happy, because he'd fixed up the house so nice, and it was plenty big—big enough for all seven of us.

Tad and Becky weren't just little runts anymore, but were ten and twelve. No one worried about them getting lost as we had when we'd first come, and they were all over the place. Emily was fourteen, still quiet and beautiful. Zack was well past sixteen and was a strapping tall young man with the beginnings of a beard showing on his face and muscles gradually starting to bulge out on his arms. He helped Pa at the mine on most days, although he was over at Little Wolf's most days too, riding and breaking horses. Pa'd mutter about the two of them being "plumb loco" on account of what they did with the horses. But it was plain to see that Pa was proud of Zack's being such a tough and hardworking kid. Alkali Jones was around a lot too. His hair was gradually getting more gray in it, and he seemed to do a lot more cackling and talking and directing up at the mine than working.

Uncle Nick and Katie's son Erich, named after Katie's grandfather who immigrated from Europe, was born on the next to last day of July. Uncle Nick said he had been thinking about naming the baby after his father, Grandpa Belle, if it was a boy, or if it was a girl calling her Agatha after Ma. But in the end it was Katie's name that prevailed. So we had a new cousin in the family and were mighty pleased to have him.

As you can imagine, having Katie *and* Almeda around sure did liven up the place! When I think back to that first winter when it was just us kids and Pa and Uncle Nick in that one little cabin, all I can do is laugh. The two women sure made it different, more homey, more lively. There was more laughter in the air, more flowers on the tables, better smells coming out of the pots hanging over the fires, and everything was a lot cleaner than back then!

But I think it was a good thing there were two houses separated by six hundred yards, a stream, and some woods. Those two strong women under one roof would have been like Pa putting too much dynamite in the mine! As it was, they were able to be good friends and visit and talk and invite each other over and borrow things and help each other, while they both kept track of their own houses. Just like with the naming of Erich, Katie usually got what she wanted, and anybody who knows Katie knows she was more likely to stay Katie Morgan Belle than to become *Mrs.* Anybody! She may have been Uncle Nick's wife, but she was still "Katie" to everybody around!

I suppose you could say the same of Almeda too. She had been on her own for a long time and was used to thinking independently, unlike most women with a husband and five kids. Yet she was different than Katie in how she went about things. If Katie and Uncle Nick had a dispute about something, they'd say their mind—sometimes loudly!—and somehow or another figure out what to do. They laughed and kidded and sometimes hollered at each other—you could hear them clear down across the creek at our place! They argued, and then worked out their differences, kissed, and went on. Sometimes Uncle Nick got his way, but mostly Katie got hers.

It was different with Pa and Almeda, although they laughed and had fun together too. Maybe it was because they were older, and both had been married before. Maybe it was because there were hurts in both of their past lives. They'd each had to face the death of someone they loved very much and were now married again, but with memories still lingering from before.

Both Pa and Almeda were quieter when there'd be something to decide, more thoughtful, I guess. And if they had a difference of opinion—like earlier about the houses and where to live—it would get real quiet for a spell. In some ways yelling and arguing about things like Uncle Nick and Katie did was better for the other folks around. At least you didn't have to wonder what people were thinking! When Pa and Almeda got quiet and quit talking to each other much for a day or two, it was eerie and unpleasant in the house and all us kids would tiptoe around, not knowing what to say.

But I came to realize at such times that being quiet was

their way of thinking about things. It may have been awkward for a while, but I came to see that maybe they were both quiet, not because they were angry or upset, but because they loved each other and didn't want to say something that would hurt. They needed to think and maybe pray too. And then when they did talk, you could tell they were trying hard to think of each other, not just themselves.

Both marriages were a year old that summer, and watching them develop was interesting for me. I'd never thought much about what it might be like to be married, and I wasn't thinking about it in connection with *myself*. But being older, and being Almeda's friend and getting to know Pa so much better *before* they had married made me look at them through different eyes than I could have when I was just a little kid. I did find myself wondering *if* I ever got married, way off in the future sometime, what it would be like. What kind of wife did I want to be, like Katie or like Almeda?

I didn't come to any conclusions, only that it was interesting to me, especially seeing how Almeda would try to yield to Pa as her husband. I knew that was hard for her, since she'd had to think for herself since Mr. Parrish died. And in matters like the house and how to run her business, she'd been accustomed not only to making all the decisions herself but also to thinking like a man, because she was trying to run a man's business in a man's world.

Now she was married, but she *still* had her house and business along with a husband and a family. She had to live two different lives. She'd never had children of her own before, and here she suddenly had five! Yet she still walked into her office or met with customers who looked to her as the businesswoman she was.

On most days she and I would go into town together in the morning. I was learning more about how the office itself operated and would process orders that came in through the mail or write up invoices. Mr. Ashton still called me *Miss* Hollister! With me to help in the office, Almeda had more time to go out and call on miners and see potential customers, and the incoming orders picked up as a result.

"Your being here makes a big difference, Corrie," she said. "If the business keeps growing, we'll have to change the name to *Parrish & Hollister,* or *Parrish & Daughter!*"

"How about just changing it to *Hollister* Mine and Freight Company?" suggested Pa that same evening when Almeda was recounting the conversation she'd had with me earlier. "You ain't a *Parrish* no more, you know, Almeda."

I don't think Pa meant anything by it other than just a passing comment, but afterward it was quiet for a while, and I know Almeda was thinking about how all the pieces fit. I know now that she was thinking about praying about *her* future and *her* options too, just as she was helping me do in my life. Eventually she did share with me that she went through a time of real doubt and wondering about what she and Pa ought to do. She found herself wishing Pa would give up the mine and join her in the business. Then she realized maybe she wanted it because that's the decision Mr. Parrish had come to, and that it would be hard for Pa to want to be a part of *her* business if it meant sacrificing something which was *his* own, *his* dream—like the mine was. And she had to battle within herself whether she was going to be *Mrs. Drummond Hollister,* or if she was going to keep being *Almeda Parrish* with a new last name added on. Was she going to keep everything as it had been and add Pa's family, or was she going to *become* part of the family, even if it meant sacrificing some of what she had been before?

Later, when I was quite a bit older and she told me about some of these things, she said, "Every woman doesn't have to face it the same way, Corrie. Most women just get married and their husband's home and livelihood is about all they have to consider. And they're perfectly content to just be part of their husband's world. But when I married your father, it was different. And I'm so thankful that he understood. He respected me, respected that other part of my life too that had been going on before I knew him and wanted to keep going afterward as well. I think he knew I'd never want to sell the Freight Company, or would want to change the name. As proud as I was to be Mrs. Drummond Hollister, to become a 'mother' and join your family, I couldn't help wanting, I suppose, to keep a part of myself—not 'separate' exactly, but keep it as my *own*, to keep being the *me* I have always been. As much as a man and a woman become 'one' when they are married, there is still that part of you that needs to know you are your *own* person even though you are married and have given that personhood to your husband too. I don't know if other women think about it quite like that, but I have. Anyway, I *wanted* to keep the business, and to keep calling it by the *Parrish* name . . . because of something in me that didn't go away when I married your father."

And she did keep both halves of her life going just great from what I could tell—the Almeda Parrish part and the Mrs. Drummond Hollister part. I only hoped I could do as well if there ever came a time in my life when I had to.

Some days she'd go home early, in the middle of the afternoon, and get working on supper—we were a pretty big household to feed!—and I'd ride out later by myself. On other days we'd get a big pot of beans or stew prepared in the morning to sit all day on the fire, and Emily and Becky would make corn bread or biscuits to go with it. On those kinds of days we might both come home together after the office closed. It was always different. Maybe one or the other of us would be on a delivery and would be late, and the other would tend to the supper. Almeda was gracious about making me feel like I was still needed. And I suppose I *was*, even though it took some getting used to at first, not having the others depending on me for everything. Pa was a big help. He didn't mind giving the stew a stir or adding some extra water to the pot of beans or tending lunch for the rest of the kids when neither Almeda nor I was there. We were an unusual family, but Pa didn't seem to mind that.

We had Katie to think about that summer too, and most evenings one of us would go up and help her with the washing of clothes or whatever else she had to do. Emily spent half of most days helping Katie with her new little baby cousin. Becky went over there a lot too, and tried to pitch in. But Becky always thought she was a bigger help than she really was! I could tell when Emily held little Erich that she wouldn't mind being a mother herself someday!

Even with all that was going on around home, and with the work at the Freight Company to keep me busy, I kept thinking of those words in the letter to Mrs. Parrish: *Whoever your friend C.B. Hollister is, Kemble says for him to get in touch. Might be that we could use something else of his in the future. Kemble likes firsthand accounts and has been looking for this kind of thing from the foothills country.*

All summer I kept racking my brain trying to think up some other "firsthand account" I might write about to send to the *Alta.* A little dose of success was enough to make me think I was ready to be a real-live reporter!

All of a sudden, about the middle of August, the idea hit me. Of course! I had the greatest possible story right in front of my nose! If it'd been any closer it would have bit me!

The minute it came to me I was filing the July invoices in the file drawer in the oak desk. I jumped up.

"Almeda," I said, trying to stay calm, "would it be all right if I went home early today?"

"Certainly, Corrie. Is something the matter? Don't you feel well?"

"I feel great. It's just that I think I've thought of the next story I might write and send to the *Alta.*"

"Wonderful! What is it?"

"I'd rather not say till it's done, ma'am. But I'll let you read it first."

"Go, then, Corrie!" she exclaimed, breaking into a laugh. "Go and write it. Your reading public is waiting!"

I charged out the door and onto my horse and galloped all the way back to the claim. I hardly stopped at the cabin, but ran right up to the mine where, just like I'd figured, Alkali Jones was sitting on a rock and giving out advice to Pa and Uncle Nick and Zack.

"Mr. Jones . . . Mr. Jones!" I said, all out of breath as I

ran up to him. "I gotta talk to you."

"Hee, hee, hee!" he laughed, looking me over from head to foot. "Can't be that one o' my mules has got me in a fix. I got one right there." He pointed to a tree where his trusty favorite was tied. "An' Corrie Beast's tied up where she can't git loose nohow! Hee, hee, hee!"

"No, it ain't that, Mr. Jones," I said, trying to catch my breath. "Please, would you just come down to the cabin with me for a few minutes?"

"Okay by me, Corrie Belle," he answered, "but I don't know if yer pa an' uncle can find any gold in that there stream without me. Hee, hee! I know this creek better'n I know that blame mule yonder. An' it ain't just nobody what gits the gold outta it. That's why I'm here, to show 'em where t' put their sluices an' pans an' where t' aim their shovels."

"We'll manage for five minutes, Alkali!" shouted Pa from where he stood knee-deep in the water. He threw me a quick wink as he spoke. "But don't you keep him long, Corrie! I don't want me and Nick and Zack wasting *too* much time when we don't know where the gold might be!"

"Okay, Pa," I answered him seriously. "I'll take care of my business with Mr. Jones as fast as I can."

The old prospector got up from his rock, grinning and cackling his high-pitched *hee, hee, hee* to himself, and followed me down to the cabin. I can't imagine what he thought it was all about, but once inside, as soon as I had grabbed a pencil and fresh sheet of paper, I started asking about his first days in California and about his discovery of gold in the creek, about how he first yelled "It's a Miracle," and how the stream was named, and then how the town started to grow. All it took was my first question and he was off retelling it all faster than I could write!

Well, that was my first "interview." And I never had a more willing talker! I could have written a whole book just about the adventures and exploits of Alkali Jones—founder of everything in California that was of any importance, friend of everybody, who had been everywhere and seen everything and done things nobody else in the world could hope to do! I probably would have had to call the book *Alkali Jones, the Most Important Person Ever in California's History*.

As it was, I wrote a two-page story that I called "How Gold Was Discovered on Miracle Springs Creek."

I finished it four days later. That's when I showed it to Almeda.

"It sounds just like an experienced writer, Corrie!" she said. "I am excited! Do you want me to send it?"

"If you don't mind, I'd like to send it in from myself," I answered. "I've gotta try sometime."

"You're right. And they did say to have 'my friend' get in touch with them," she laughed. "Are you going to use your whole name?"

"I don't know," I answered. "Do you really think they'd mind it being from a girl?"

"If I know men, Corrie—and I do, because I do business with them all day long!—yes, I do think they'd mind. They might not say so. No man will *admit* to looking down on those of us of 'the weaker sex.' They will always talk about 'respecting' and 'admiring' us, and they'll be more than happy to be courteous and gentlemanly if it suits them. But let a woman try to *do* something on her own, especially something they think ought to be done by a man, and they don't like it. They want to keep women what they like to call 'in their place.' And they *especially* don't like a woman doing something *well* that they think is a man's thing to be doing. Don't ask me why, Corrie— but they just don't like a woman to be successful at anything except *woman* things—you know, feeding babies and sweeping floors and washing clothes and boiling water and setting dinner on the table. Not that there's anything wrong with doing those things, but a *few* of us women, like you and me, want to do some other things besides. So to answer your question again, Corrie, I would say this—I think that if you sent in your story exactly like it is, and the editor, that Mr. Kemble, figured it was from a woman—especially just an eighteen-year-old one!—I doubt he'd even read it. But if he thought it was from a man, even though the words were just the same, I think he'd read it and like it. That's just the way the world is, Corrie, if you're a woman and you want to do something that maybe is a bit out of the ordinary for a woman to do."

"Then I reckon I ought to keep being just *C.B.* Hollister for a spell longer."

She laughed. "You boil my long-winded lecture on the frustrations of being a businesswoman right down to the basics, don't you, Corrie?"

So I sent my story to the *Alta.* I addressed it to Mr. Kemble, Editor, and included a letter. I introduced myself as the C.B. Hollister who had written the story about the blizzard, and thanked him very much for the two dollars. I had written another article, I said, which I hoped they might be able to use, and it was enclosed. The letter was in my best handwriting, and I tried not to make it look like it was written by a girl.

Two and a half weeks later, an envelope came to the freight office addressed to me, with a return address from the *Alta* in San Francisco.

The instant I saw it I started trembling with anticipation. I grabbed it out of Mr. Ashton's hands, and my sweaty fingers fumbled frantically to tear it open.

"Dear Mr. Hollister," the letter began—and I was so nervous that I didn't even notice the *Mr.* at first.

> We won't be able to use your article. Stories about gold being discovered in creeks around the foothills are what we call yesterday's news. Nobody cares about that anymore. We're looking for stories about people—*real* people. Your Alkali Jones sounds more like fiction than fact, and if he does exist, I don't believe a word of what he told you.
>
> I remain, Mr. Hollister,
> Sincerely yours,
> Edward Kemble
> Editor, California *Alta.*

I was too disappointed to think about being angry about what he'd said. As much as I wanted to be grown-up about it,

I immediately felt my eyes starting to fill up with tears. I had been so sure this story about Mr. Jones was even better than the blizzard one! At that moment, I never wanted to write another word!

I dropped the letter down on the desk and quickly went out the back door before Mr. Ashton saw me start crying and blubbering right there in the office. I was glad Almeda happened to be out on the street with Marcus Weber, checking the load for an order he was taking up to French Corral.

I went out into the back of the livery, and by then I was crying. But at least I was alone, with the smells of hay and horses and leather to calm me down instead of having to face any people.

I guess I left the door open behind me, because I never heard Almeda enter. The first I knew she was there with me was when I heard her voice close behind me and felt her hand on my shoulder.

"I guess I was wrong," she said softly. "Even from a man, he didn't like the article!"

I laughed and turned around. She was holding the letter from Kemble in her hand, and a tender smile of compassion was on her face. She knew the hurt I was feeling.

But I couldn't help it—the tears kept coming!

"No matter how old a girl—or a woman—gets, Corrie," she said, "there are times when you just have to cry. Right now, won't you just let me be—if I can say it—won't you let me be a *mother* to you?"

She opened her arms and drew me to her breast.

I laid my head against her, wrapped my arms around her waist, and melted into her tender embrace, quietly weeping. My emotions were so full, but I didn't know if it was from the letter, or from the happiness I felt at having Almeda love me as much as I knew she did in that moment. Sometimes you can't tell whether you're happy or sad, but you just keep crying anyway.

We stood there for two or three minutes, neither saying a word, holding each other tight. It was such a wonderful moment of closeness, I didn't want it to end.

Finally I felt her arms about me relax.

"You really wanted that story about Mr. Jones to be published, didn't you?" she said, looking down into my eyes, still red but at least dry now.

I nodded.

"And you thought it was . . . maybe not the best—but as good as the article you wrote about the Wards?"

Again I nodded. "I can't see that it was as much worse as Mr. Kemble said."

"But you're afraid he's right, and that you'll never amount to anything as a writer if something you liked is really as bad as he says. Is that how you feel?"

"I reckon that's about it. And he didn't say a thing about sending them anything else. I thought he said he wanted first-hand accounts. Now I'm just back to where I was before the blizzard—which is nowhere!"

"Not quite, Corrie. There's one big thing that's changed."

"What's that?"

"You *did* write that article, and it *did* appear in the *Alta,* and you *did* get paid for it. Don't you realize what that means, Corrie—you *are* a professional writer! You have done it. Maybe only once—but that's a start!"

"But what about this?" I said, pointing to the letter from Kemble.

"It's nothing! If Singleton, and now Kemble, aren't smart enough to see a future-budding reporter right under their noses, then you can send what you write to someone else. Somebody *will* be interested!"

"In my story about Alkali Jones, do you think?"

"Perhaps. But maybe not. Kemble *may* be right about it being yesterday's news. But you can't let that stop you. You'll write another article, and then another. Some of them will be published, and some won't. But that can't stop you from writing them, not if you believe in what you want to do, and believe in yourself to do it."

She paused. "*Do* you believe in yourself, Corrie—as a writer, I mean?"

"You mean, do I think I'm a *good* writer? I wouldn't say that."

"Maybe not a 'good' writer. But do you believe in yourself as someone who's *going to* be a decent writer someday—even if some day way in the future? Can you believe that about yourself? Can you believe that God can do that with you . . . and maybe even that he *wants* to?"

I thought a minute. "I reckon I can believe that," I replied.

"And you *want* it to happen, am I right? That is, if God opens the way for it to happen, then you want it?"

"Yes."

"Well, that's how I felt about this business, Corrie, after Mr. Parrish died. I desperately *wanted* to make the business work. I *wanted* to succeed, maybe because I figured most of the men around thought I'd pack right up and be on the next ship back to Boston. But no I *wanted* to stick it out, even during the hard times, and *make* it work. And it seems to me maybe that's what you might have to do too—stick it out, even through the hard times, and not give up, because you're *determined* to make it work . . . and to do it."

"That's what you mean by believing in yourself?"

"That's right. There are times, Corrie, when you've got to go after something you want, even when you think you're all alone and when nobody else believes in you or thinks you have a chance to do it. There are times when you've got to plow ahead with your own determination to succeed. That can be especially true for a woman trying to do something on her own. You can do it, Corrie. You *can* write . . . and you *will*! The day will come when you can march right into Mr. Kemble's office and lay your papers down on his desk and say, 'I'm *Corrie Belle* Hollister, if you please, and not *Mister* C.B. Hollister, and my story is as good as you're gonna get from any man-reporter!' "

"I could never do that!" I said, laughing.

She laughed too. "Maybe not in those words. But if that kind of determination is inside you, and you believe in yourself that much, then I can promise you, *Corrie Belle Hollister*, yours is a name people are going to see in print someday."

"So what do I do now," I asked, "if I'm going to try to keep believing in myself like that?"

"You keep looking for ideas, and you keep writing in your journal, and you keep thinking up stories and articles to write . . . and you keep writing them and sending them to Mr. Singleton and Mr. Kemble. And with everything you write you're going to learn a little something more, and one of these days those editors will start paying attention when they see your name on a story. Believe me, Corrie, Mr. Kemble has not seen the last of you!"

I laughed again. It was nice to hear her say it, though I couldn't be quite that confident myself.

The article about Alkali Jones never did get into a newspaper, though every once in a while I still think about writing a whole book about his life. Almeda's other words, however, about determination and believing in yourself—I never forgot them. Her encouragement came back to me more than once later, because that was not the last rejection I got for something I wrote. There were a lot more to come!

And her joking about what I might someday say to the editor of the *Alta* was something I remembered too. When that day came, it didn't happen just as she'd predicted, but I couldn't help thinking back on her words nevertheless.

CHAPTER 13

LEARNING TO BELIEVE IN MYSELF . . . AND WRITE

The following school year was very different for me. For the first time in my life I *wasn't* going to school, either as a student or a teacher's helper. It made me realize in a whole new way how much things were changing.

For everybody! Zack wasn't in school anymore either. He spent his time about equally between helping Pa and Uncle Nick at the mine and helping Little Wolf and his pa with the riding and training and selling of horses. Now that Central California had been being settled for five or six years, there were a lot more than just gold prospectors coming into the state, including farmers and ranchers. Little Wolf's pa had developed a fair business in horse selling. There seemed to be a continually increasing need for good riding and cattle horses, and they brought even more money if they were already broke and trained—which was where Zack and Little Wolf came in. The two of them loved it! Anything to do with horses made them as happy as could be.

Anyhow, with Zack and Little Wolf and I gone, and Elizabeth Darien married and moved to Oregon, Miss Stansberry chose a new helper—Emily! During that year she turned fifteen, the same age as I was when we came to Miracle Springs.

Without older boys like Zack and Little Wolf and Artie Syfer in the school anymore—and there weren't any fourteen-or-fifteen-year old boys coming up in the class—Rev. Rutledge came to check up on Miss Stansberry usually once a day, to see if she needed any help moving a desk or lifting something. She was such a capable lady it was easy to forget about her being lame, but the minister didn't forget. He was always trying to find ways to make it easier for her. Sometimes when I was on my way home from town late in the afternoon just before suppertime, I'd see Rev. Rutledge's buggy out in front of the school where he was still helping Miss Stansberry. I suppose, though, with the two of them sharing the building like that, using it both as a school and as a church, they probably had plenty to keep them both occupied.

We continued living in the cabin out at the claim. Almeda and I would take a buggy into town with Emily and Becky and Tad every morning and return in the afternoon. Sometimes only one of us might go into town. Occasionally I'd want to stay home and work on something I might be writing, and other days Almeda would want to spend part of the day with Pa. By that time, whenever she did want to stay at home, I knew most of what needed to be done at the freight office. When she wasn't there, I wasn't Mr. Ashton's or Mr. Weber's boss. They knew what to do too, and we all did our jobs together and talked about any decisions to be made before Almeda got back. Yet they would ask me questions, almost as if I *were* their boss, just because of me and Almeda being in the same family now. Although it was a mite peculiar, I got used to it—but I'm glad she was there most of the time.

I didn't forget Almeda's words about having to work for something you believed in. I figured if I had the Belle blood in me, like Pa sometimes said, then I ought to put it to work for me.

So I didn't let myself get discouraged because of that letter Mr. Kemble wrote, saying he didn't believe what I wrote about Mr. Jones was true. I just said to myself: "Well, we'll see, Mr. Editor! I'll show *you* who can write around here! You're not just talking to anybody, Mister—you're talking to a Hollister, half of whose blood is *Belle blood*! Yeah, Mr. Editor, we'll see about what's true and what's not! And what's true is that I'm gonna be a reporter for your paper someday!"

That's what I said to Mr. Kemble in my thoughts. But I was nice as could be whenever I sent a story to him. And I kept signing my name *C.B. Hollister*. Almeda had talked to me about believing in myself, but I wasn't ready to believe in myself quite enough yet to start using my real name! I figured what he didn't know about who *C.B.* was wouldn't hurt him for the time being.

So I wrote stories on anything that I thought might be interesting to the folks either in San Francisco or in Sacramento. If it seemed more to do with Sacramento, I sent it to Mr. Singleton in Marysville. If it seemed more appropriate for San Francisco, I sent it to the *Alta*. Since I didn't know exactly what kinds of things a newspaper editor would be likely to publish, I tried all kinds of different approaches. Here's one I tried.

> This fall the school in Miracle Springs begins its third year. Teacher Miss Harriet Stansberry reports an enrollment of twenty-four students, up eight from the previous year, though she says the average age of her children is younger than before.
>
> When asked about the future of the school, Miss Stansberry answered: "There are still new families coming to the area, even though the rapid growth has slowed somewhat. From the age of my students, it seems as if the enrollment will probably stay about where it is for some years to come."

I then went on to tell a little about the school and what kinds of subjects the children studied, and even had a quote or two from some of the students, including one from Emily.

I sent this to Mr. Singleton, reminding him that he had printed the very first thing I had written about the opening of the school back in December of '53. I don't know whether it was that, or whether maybe he was afraid of losing the Parrish Freight advertising, but he did print this new article about the school, though he cut most of it out, including all the quotes from Emily and the others. When it appeared it was only two paragraphs long and didn't have my name anywhere on it. And

Mr. Singleton never paid even fifty cents for anything I sent him. I began to wonder if that $2.00 was the last money I'd ever see for anything I wrote. But even if it was, I still wanted to write newspaper stories. I'd just have to keep doing other work besides.

I can't say that anything I wrote was any good compared to *real* authors like Thoreau or Hawthorne or Cooper or Irving or Walter Scott. But I wasn't trying to be a real author, only to write for a newspaper, and it didn't seem to me that you'd have to be as good to do that. Besides, I figured maybe writing was one of those things you had to learn how to do just by doing it a lot. So that's what I did—I wrote about a lot of different things, and practiced trying to make my writing more interesting. Like this one:

> Mr. Jack Lame Pony, a full-blooded Nisenan Indian, has turned his skill in training horses into a livelihood. "When white men come to California in search of gold," says Lame Pony, "many of my people went farther north, and to mountains and hills. But I had son, cabin, land. I not want to leave."
>
> After two or three years trying to scrape food out of the soil and sell furs trapped in the high Sierras, Lame Pony began to acquire a stock of riding horses. He was very bitter against the intrusion of gold-seekers into what he considered the land of his people. But when men began coming to him one by one in search of sturdy and dependable horses, he found that most were reasonable and not as different from himself as he imagined.
>
> Slowly, word about his horses spread throughout the region north of Sacramento, and he had more requests than he had horses. He also found that doing business with ranchers and farmers, and even some gold miners, was not as difficult as he had thought.
>
> "As my anger left my heart," he says, "I sold more horses. Soon had no time to trap. Had to find more horses—always more horses, then break them, train them, teach them white man's ways."
>
> Perhaps even Lame Pony's name might have helped his

reputation as the best horse trainer in the region. Wherever one goes in the foothills north and east of Sacramento, the mention of the name Lame Pony always brings a chuckle and the words, "Whatever his name says, his horses are the best." A rancher from Yuba City, who has purchased eight different horses from Lame Pony for his hands, was quoted as saying, "None of my men ever been throwed by one of his horses yet!"

Recently Lame Pony and his son Little Wolf, with the help of neighbors, enlarged their corrals and added another stable. With the continued growth of California, they foresee an even greater need for well-trained horses in the future and want to be prepared for it.

Of course I asked Little Wolf's father if I could write about him first, and Little Wolf talked him into agreeing. Mr. Singleton printed this article just as I'd written it—*after* he had signed up a small advertisement for the Lame Pony Stables to appear on the same page. The neighbors I mentioned were Pa and Uncle Nick and Zack. I didn't really talk to the man from Yuba City, but Marcus Weber knew him and heard him say those words.

I wrote a short article about Patrick Shaw, our neighbor from over the ridge, who in his spare time was getting to be a pretty well-known banjo-picker and was often invited to hoedowns from as far away as Coloma and Placerville. I drew a picture of him playing, too, to go along with the written part. But that was one of my articles that never actually made it to a paper. Mr. Shaw did ask me, though, to do a drawing of him and his banjo for him to use on a sign if he was going to be playing somewhere.

Another article I wrote was about a new church that was getting started down at Colfax. They didn't have a building yet and were meeting in a great big house. Rev. Rutledge went down there every two weeks and was more or less in charge of it, though he had people in Colfax helping a lot too, like Almeda had done when he first came to Miracle Springs.

Both the minister and Almeda were excited about the opportunity for new churches starting throughout this part of California, something I know they'd been wanting to see happen from the very first. Of course, as interested as we all were— and he would tell us what was happening in other areas on Sunday—Almeda didn't actually participate in his plans as she did at first. But at least he didn't have to make that long ride back and forth to Colfax alone every time 'cause every once in a while Miss Stansberry would go along with him to keep him company.

Religious news didn't seem to be something most folks were interested in, because that was another one of my articles that never got into a paper.

One that did, however—and I admit it surprised me, because I wrote it just for fun—was an article I called "Virginian Finds New Home After Unusual Beginning."

> When Miss Kathryn Hubbard Morgan stepped off the steamer in Sacramento in May of 1854 as a mail-order bride, she could little have foretold the strange turn of events that would make her future so different from what she had planned.
>
> Miss Morgan carried with her that day a handful of apple seeds, a seashell, a rock, a tuft of grass, some Virginia moss, and a piece of dried bark—all as remembrances of her past in Virginia and as symbols of the new life she was starting in California the moment she set foot upon the bank of the Sacramento River.
>
> As it turned out, Miss Morgan, now Mrs. Nick Belle of Miracle Springs, did not marry the man who had paid half her passage to the west, but his brother-in-law instead.
>
> "You cannot imagine the thoughts that were racing through my mind as I stood there in my wedding dress," Mrs. Belle said, "only to have the ceremony so suddenly interrupted and thrown upside-down."

I then went on to tell a little about the wedding and what Uncle Nick had done and the story leading up to that day, including quotes from Pa and Uncle Nick, and another one or two from Katie. When I was asking them questions, Uncle

Nick got to laughing and talking and said this, which people who read the article liked best of all: "When I lit outta here on the Thursday before the wedding, I figured I might never come back. I was so mad at Drum I coulda knocked his head off. But I didn't know whether to be mad at Katie and just say good riddance to the both of them, or if I oughta come back and just grab her away from him and tell her she was gonna marry me. I tell ya, I didn't know what to do. I was just all mixed up inside! And so when I rode up and saw that the wedding was going on, I don't even remember *what* I said or did!"

Then I finished the article like this:

> So now Mrs. Belle, still known to all her friends simply as "Katie," has found a new life as a full-fledged Californian. Like all Californians, she came from someplace else, but now calls this her home. Her seven-month-old son will be a Californian born and bred, one of the first in a new generation of Californians who will carry the hardy breed of pioneers— from Virginia and every other state of the union—into the future of this western region of these United States.
>
> When Katie looks out her window, if she lets her eyes go to the edge of the pine wood, she will see a thin apple tree, still too young to bear fruit, but a growing reminder of where she has come from. At its base, a different variety of grass and moss than can be seen anywhere in the surrounding woods is growing—also a reminder that this is a big land, and that its people have roots that stretch far away.
>
> One day Katie's young son will eat apples from that very tree, Virginia apples, and Katie will be able to tell him the story of how its seeds ventured to a new and strange place called California, and put down roots and began to grow, in the same way that his own mother did.

The "hardy breed of pioneers" and the "venturing to a new and strange place called California" and "roots that stretch far away" were all Mr. Kemble's words. But the ideas, even at the end were my ideas, and he just helped me to say it better.

Having this article published surprised me, especially since most of the things I'd written had been sent right back to me. But Mr. Kemble was real interested in this one. He sent me

$3.00 for it—the first time since the blizzard article that I'd gotten any money. And afterward, about a week after the story had come out in the paper (we sent for ten copies! Katie had lots of folks back east she wanted to send them to), a letter came to me from the *Alta*. I hadn't sent anything else to them and couldn't imagine what it was. But when I read the letter, the tears that came to my eyes were not tears of disappointment like the last time the editor had written to me.

> Mr. C.B. Hollister
> Miracle Springs, California
> Dear Mr. Hollister,
>
> Your recent article "Virginian Finds New Home," etc., has been very well received, both by the staff and the readership of the *Alta*. I must say, your writing has improved very much since your first story with us, "Blizzard Rescue on Buck Mountain."

As I read those words I couldn't help thinking of what he'd said when he sent back the Alkali Jones story about finding gold in the creek. I wondered if he remembered. I read on—

> I would be interested in seeing other such pieces in the future. There have already been two inquiries as to when the next piece by C.B. Hollister is going to appear. I hope to hear from you soon.
>
> > Sincerely,
> > Edward Kemble,
> > Editor, California *Alta*

I sat down and handed the letter to Almeda. She read it.

"There, you see," she said. "You never know what can happen if you believe in yourself and just keep moving in the direction you think God wants you to go."

And if you practice your writing a lot, I thought, *and don't mind getting most of your things sent back to you!*

But in an instant this one brief letter seemed to make the earlier disappointments all forgotten.

CHAPTER 14

I WRITE TO MR. KEMBLE

I took the letter from Mr. Kemble not just as an encouragement but also as an opportunity.

There was that determination in my Belle blood coming out again! But I figured I ought to make the most of the fact that he'd written and seemed interested.

So I decided to write back and ask him some questions so I'd be able to know what to do differently in the future. I had thought the story about Alkali Jones was good, and hadn't expected anybody to pay much attention to what I'd written about Katie. As it turned out, my figuring was exactly opposite from Mr. Kemble's. Not only that, two months after his letter, *another* letter came, telling me that a paper from Raleigh, Virginia, had written to ask permission from the *Alta* to reprint the Katie story! The name C.B. Hollister was going to be read clear back on the East Coast!

I wrote to Mr. Kemble and asked him just what it was about the "Virginian" article that his paper liked and wanted more of.

About three weeks later I got a reply.

"There're two kinds of stories," he told me. "First, there's straight news reporting. That's when you've got to tell your *who, what, where, when, and why*. Those are your *w's*, and no reporter better forget them for a second.

"But then you've got your human interest kind of stories. They're more personal. The *who* and the *why* are still important, but you're telling about people instead of just facts, so the other things aren't quite so important.

"Now, you take your 'Virginian' story. That was human interest if ever I saw such a thing. Once you got folks interested in your Katie Morgan, they kept reading. They weren't trying to find out news or facts; they were reading because you were telling a story about a *person*.

"I've got lots of reporters who can give me the five *w*'s. One rambunctious kid on my staff chases around this city night and day and is the first person on the scene of anything that happens. Now *he's* a newshound!

"I'm not saying that if you brought me some noteworthy news like that I wouldn't print it. Maybe I would. But from the two stories of yours we've run so far, something tells me your talent tends more toward the human interest side. You seem to see interesting things in people. And if you can keep doing that, keep finding interesting people and keep finding interesting ways to tell folks about them, then I don't doubt you might just have a future in this business. Leave the five *w's* to the newshounds like that Irish kid on my staff I was telling you about. Stick to the personal angles, Hollister, and let me see anything you come up with."

He didn't say it in that same letter, but much later when he and I were talking about similar things, he said some other things along this line.

"Women and men are different in how they read a paper," he told me. "Now we've got more men than women in California, but we still have thousands of women readers, and we've got to please them, too.

"Men want to know news and not much else. They're your five *w's* readers. Give them what happened, where, when, and why and they'll put the paper down and get on with what they got to do. Men want to know whether it's likely to rain, what kind of damage the flood caused, what price gold is fetching, whether there've been any new strikes, and how much a new pick or a fifty-pound sack of beans is going to cost.

"But a woman'll look through the paper while she's drinking her tea, and she'll want to read about Polly Pinswiggle's garden that the rain washed out. That woman reading about Polly doesn't care a hoot about how many inches it rained or about what the seed is going to cost to plant a new garden. All she's thinking about is poor Polly!

"The women are your people readers. And that's why we've got people like you writing human interest stuff. You've got to go out and find interesting people who are involved in interesting things and then write about them, mixing in a little news too, and getting three or four of the *w's* in there to please your traditional men-editors like me.

"In other words, you've got to sort of *pretend* to be a reporter, a newsperson. But really you're not. What you are is a journalist, a writer about people, not facts. And as long as you keep writing about people, you can count on having readers, whether you ever dig up any hard news or not."

All this he didn't tell me, as I said, until later. But even now, without realizing it, I think this was the way my interest in writing was heading. I'd been keeping a journal all this time, not just to record the facts of my life, like where I went and what I did and what the weather was like—what Mr. Kemble would have called the five *w's*. I kept a journal to write about a person—a person who happened to be *me*—and what she was thinking and feeling inside.

In a way, the other writing that I was starting to do now—about Mr. Jones and Katie and the Wards and Jack Lame Pony—was kind of like the writing I did in my journal, but about other people instead of me.

Having Mr. Kemble tell me about the two different kinds of writing helped me understand it a lot better. But besides the five *w's* and the human interest kind of story, there was one other ingredient that I came to see was an important part of *any* writing that anybody did. Maybe it was the most important ingredient of all.

And I have Rev. Rutledge to thank for putting this other factor in focus for me.

CHAPTER 15

A SERMON ABOUT TRUTH

One Sunday morning Rev. Rutledge preached about *truth*. Nothing he said had that much to do with writing, I suppose, but I found myself listening carefully, trying to understand everything and applying it to my own life.

"Truth means different things to different people," he was saying. "To some people truth means a set of *ideas*. Therefore, if we were talking about five statements, we might ask which of them were true:

"The sky is blue and the sun is shining today.

"California is smaller in size than New York.

"It is raining outside.

"There is no gold in Miracle Springs Creek.

"This building is used for a church and a school."

He paused a minute and let the words sink in, and then repeated the five statements.

"Now then," he went on, "which of those are *true* and which are false? We can look outside and see the sunshine and the blue above, so we know that it is *not* raining. How about New York and California—which is larger? Any of you young-sters of Miss Stansberry's school know the answer?"

Someone piped up that California was the second biggest state behind Texas.

"Right," said the minister. "So saying California is smaller than New York is a *false* statement. How about the gold? *Is* there gold in the creek?"

Some laughter spread through the room.

"Depends on who you ask, Reverend!" called out one of the miners whose claim was known not to be doing so well.

More laughter followed.

Rev. Rutledge joined in the laughter. "However, I think we would all agree that there is *some* gold still around," he said, then added, "even though it might be unevenly distributed!"

He let the chuckling gradually die away before he went on. "Then, finally, is this building used for both a church and a school?"

"Yes!" went up a chorus of young voices, enjoying being able to participate during the sermon time for a change.

"Right you are again!" said Rev. Rutledge. "Now, think back to the five statements. How many were true, and how many were false? Let me repeat them for you."

He did so. Then he waited a minute.

"All right, now—how many statements were true?"

"Two," answered someone.

"Are you all agreed? Two true, three false?" said Rev. Rutledge.

A nodding of heads and general murmur went around.

Again he waited until everyone had quieted down. When he finally started speaking again his tone was different and he was more serious.

"I must confess that I tried to trick you," he said finally. "I hope you will forgive me, but I wanted to get across a point that many people misunderstand. Now—let me answer my own question. How many *true* statements were there? My answer is . . . *none*."

He waited to let the word sink in. I don't think anyone in the whole church understood what he meant, but we were all listening for what would come next.

"Two statements were *correct*—two statements of fact; three statements were *incorrect*—three statements of *error*. But my point this morning is that *truth* is a very different thing from correct 'facts.' That's why I said in the beginning that to most people truth has to do with the factual correctness of a set of ideas. But in reality, as the word *truth* is used in the Bible, it means something very different."

He stopped, opened up his Bible, then went on. "Let me read to you what the Bible calls truth. In John, Jesus says, 'I am the truth.' He doesn't say that such-and-such an idea, or a certain set of statements or facts are the truth, he says that *he* is the truth.

"Do you remember when I said that truth means different things to different people? Let me show you two people in the Bible to whom truth meant completely different things. In the eighteenth chapter of John, after Jesus had told his disciples that *he* was the truth, Jesus stands trial before Pilate, and he again brings up the subject of truth. Jesus says to him, 'Every one that is of the truth hears my voice.' And then Pilate asks one of the most profound questions in all of the Bible. He says to Jesus, 'What is truth?'—the very question we're examining this morning.

"Can you get a picture of these two people in your minds—Pilate and Jesus—both talking about truth?

"But they mean very different things by the word. When Pilate asks 'What is truth?' he is asking for a set of ideas, facts, opinions—just like the list of statements we talked about. Pilate wants Jesus to tell him what facts and ideas comprise what he calls 'truth.' But Jesus gives him no answer. Jesus says nothing. Why doesn't Jesus answer him?"

Rev. Rutledge paused a moment.

"Jesus doesn't answer him because truth is not at all what Pilate thinks it is. There are no *ideas* that would make up what Pilate calls truth. Not even any religious ones.

"What is the truth, Pilate wants to know. Jesus *himself* is the truth, and he is standing right in front of Pilate. Pilate *has* the truth but doesn't know it!

"In other words, the truth is a *person*, but Pilate wants mere *ideas*. And even true ideas, even correct facts, are not the truth. 'The sky is blue today' is a correct statement of fact. But it is not a truth. Only a *person* can be true."

Rev. Rutledge stopped again, and took in a deep breath. I

was concentrating hard to understand what he was saying.

"I hope I've made myself clear," he said, "about the difference between truths and facts, and about the contrast between Jesus and Pilate. I know I've gone on a long time, but there's one more very important point I must make. If I don't say this one last thing, then my whole sermon may mean nothing to you. My whole sermon could amount to nothing more than just a nice set of 'ideas' that I have given you, without there being any *truth* in it.

"So, here is my final point: Jesus is not the only person who can be of the truth. So can you and I!"

Again he stopped to let his words sink in.

"Jesus said that everyone who is *of* the truth hears his voice. In other words, Jesus is *the* truth, but others—people like you and me, people who hear his voice and obey him—we can be *of* the truth. Jesus is the first truth, but we can be *of* the truth if we follow him and do as he did."

As I pondered Rev. Rutledge's words afterward, what he said next was the thing that stood out most in my mind. "Truth is people and how they live. If we want to *be* of the truth, like Jesus said, it's in how we live and what we do, not in what we think about ideas and facts. Someone sitting right here this morning—one of you in this church building—may have been mistaken in all five of those statements I gave. You might have missed every one. Yet you might be more an of-the-truth person than another one sitting here who got every answer correct— if that person with all the wrong answers went out and *lived* the truth by what kind of person he was—lived following Jesus' example.

"Was Pilate a true man?

"After asking 'What is truth?' what did he do? Knowing Jesus was innocent, knowing the charges against him were lies, and even admitting that he could find nothing wrong in him— knowing all this, Pilate still gave Jesus over to the Jews to be crucified. Pilate may have wondered what truth was, but he was not a 'true' man. He did not stand up for what he knew to be right. He was weak. He was not *of* the truth."

The minister paused again, took a breath as he closed his Bible, and went on.

"Truth is not ideas, not even religious ideas, not even Christian ideas, not even correct ideas. Truth is *life,* not thoughts. Truth is a person. That person is Jesus. And he wants us to be *of* the same truth as he is—by how we live.

"As Christians we are to be *true people*. Jesus was of the truth. Pilate was not. Jesus *is* the truth. Pilate wanted ideas, but was not a strong enough person to *live* truthfully.

"Each of us has to make the choice which of these two men we are going to be like. How are we going to live? By the truth or not? Who is going to be our example? Are we going to *live* truth, or only think and talk about it?"

CHAPTER 16

A TALK ABOUT GROWTH

It probably seems like I was forever taking walks and thinking and writing in my journal about what was going on in my mind.

But I did also try to write down things I was doing—however, the most important thing about life to me was what was going on inside me. Maybe it isn't this way for everyone, but I liked to try to figure out the meanings behind things. When I read a book, I think about what the author said, and I like to read for the ideas as much as the story. I reckon that's why I liked Mr. Thoreau so much. There was hardly *any* story in *Walden* but it was full of ideas that made me think.

Maybe that's why I wanted to be a writer, so I could think on paper, and so I could get to know other people and find out what they were thinking and write down their ideas for others to get to know too.

Ever since I began keeping my journal and started learning more about what it really meant to live as a Christian, something inside me wanted to grow, to learn, to stretch and think and explore and be more than I was. I wanted the inside part of me to get bigger so it could hold more. Thinking and talking to God and reading and writing down my thoughts and feelings in my journal were all ways to stretch and enlarge that deep-down part of me and make it grow.

Almeda and I talked once about growth. I told her this feeling I had inside about wanting to stretch that inside part of

117

me, and to be more than I was.

She thought for a long time, and then said that she felt the process of growth inside each person's heart and mind was one of the greatest gifts God has given to us.

"There is nothing in all the world," she said, "quite so wonderful as an individual soul expanding, reaching out, coming awake to itself, to its Maker, to other souls around it. The awakening of the soul, then its growth and development, then its reaching out to touch other souls that are similarly growing along the same journey—there is hardly anything in all of life so wonderful."

Her voice became quiet and her eyes misted over.

"Like you and me?" I suggested.

"I think so, Corrie," she replied in a soft tone. "I truly think so."

"What makes some people want to grow like that, and others content just to stay where they are?" I asked.

"That's a huge question, Corrie! Who could possibly know the answer to that?" she laughed.

"Is it because some people are made to be thinkers?"

"People like you, I take it you mean?"

Now it was my turn to laugh. "You know what I mean," I said. "Not everybody keeps journals and thinks about everything like I do."

"Maybe people should think more."

"But I figured God made some folks to be thinkers and others not to be. Isn't everyone different?"

"That's true. But I have the feeling God wants *everybody* to think, though maybe in different ways and to different degrees. It has nothing to do with being smart, but with using the brain you do have. The book of Proverbs, the whole of Scripture really, is full of urgings and promptings to learn and understand. One of my favorites is 'Apply your heart to understand, incline your ear to wisdom.' That sounds to me as if God meant for every person in the world to try diligently to understand things, and to get wisdom. It also says to *seek* for wisdom like silver, and to *search* for it like hidden treasures. That sounds to me like we're supposed to think!"

"It sure doesn't seem as if everybody thinks like that. Or at least they don't talk about it so you'd know."

"Most people don't think, Corrie, not like God wants them to. They aren't searching for wisdom and applying themselves to understand, and that's why not even very many people who call themselves Christians are growing as they could be."

"You mean you can't grow if you're not thinking about everything?"

"No, that's not it exactly." She paused and thought for a little bit. "Let me try to explain it another way," she said finally. "To grow, I would say—yes, you *do* have to apply yourself to understand, and you have to search and pray for wisdom, just like the Bible says. Both those things imply not only prayer but also a lot of thought. And if you're *not* doing those things, your thinking and growth and wisdom muscles, so to speak, are going to lose their power to think and grow. If you don't use a muscle, it gets weak. In the same way, if you don't think and make an effort to grow and, as Proverbs says, *apply* yourself to understand, then pretty soon you won't be able to, and you will stop growing. You become capable of thinking by thinking. You become capable of growing by growing. And thus you grow as a Christian . . . by growing. And certainly thinking and praying and searching for wisdom are all part of that process.

"But growth isn't *only* a matter of thinking—most important of all is the *doing* that goes along with the thinking. Thinking all by itself won't stretch that inside part of you. It won't make you bigger inside, won't draw you closer to God, won't make you *more* than you are now, as you said. The real growth comes *after* the thinking, when you *live* what you've been thinking about. The growth comes when we *do* what God wants us to.

"In other words, Corrie, it's a process that has two parts. First we have to try to understand, we have to search and pray for wisdom. But then after that, as the second part, we have to *live* out what our understanding has shown us. We have to *do* what Jesus says. We have to put others first, we have to be kind and do good, speak pleasantly and behave with courtesy and trust God and pray, and do all those things Jesus told us to do. That's the active part of getting understanding and wisdom.

"There's the thinking part and the doing part. And growth only happens when *both* are at work in your life together. That's how the inside part of you, the *real* you down in your heart, will stretch and grow, and will always be becoming more than it was the day before."

CHAPTER 17

A WALK IN THE WOODS

After the church service, I needed time alone to try to understand Rev. Rutledge's sermon more clearly. I had a feeling God might have more meaning for me in his words than I could know just from sitting in the church. I had to think about it some more.

So I told Pa and the others to go on ahead home without me. I'd walk back in a while. Then I went out into the woods behind the church, the same woods where Becky'd gotten lost. On the way as I walked, the conversation I'd had with Almeda about growth came back to me, and I found both her words and those of the minister mingling in my mind, trying to sort themselves out.

As all of it was tumbling through my mind—living truth instead of just thinking about it, growth, understanding, wisdom, the thinking kind of person I was, everything Almeda had said about growth and doing and Proverbs—it came to me how important all of it was if I was going to be a writer.

You couldn't even write the five *w's* without being able to think and understand things, I thought to myself, because one of them was *why*. So if you were going to write, you'd *have* to think and understand!

Then I found myself thinking, not just about the kinds of writing that Mr. Kemble had talked about, but about *why* I wanted to write in the first place. At first it had just started with journal writing. I had only needed to express myself, to think out loud.

121

But now I realized there was more to it. I still liked to think on paper—whether in my journal or in something I was trying to write. But now that I thought about it in light of Rev. Rutledge's and Almeda's words, I found myself realizing that I wanted my writing to amount to something more than *just* writing. I wanted it to *mean* something, even though I'd never really stopped to think about it before.

Then I found myself reflecting back on that early morning walk I had taken just before the blizzard began, when God had shown me so many things and when I had prayed about my future. I recalled how on that day I had thought about the *truth* too, and had felt God telling me to find the truth and to follow it and live by it and be fed by it. The scripture I had thought about that morning came vividly back to me: *In truth shall you be fed, and so shall you dwell in the land.*

Suddenly it all made so much more sense!

The truth was so much bigger than just giving a factual account of the five *w's*. Anybody could do that. That was the Pontius Pilate side, the facts, the statements, the lists of ideas that might be half correct and half wrong. That might be "reporting," but that wasn't what I wanted to spend *my* life doing.

I wanted to *grow*—in understanding, in wisdom . . . in truth.

And I wanted my writing to be true. Not just with correct facts, with the five *w's*—though that might be part of it too. But true like Rev. Rutledge talked about truth—true to the kind of person I was, true to the Bible, true to the man who *was* truth—Jesus, God's Son. I wanted my writing to point to the truth, to be *of* the truth. I wanted it to make people think and help them to grow. Even if I was writing a story about something other than Jesus, who was the truth, I wanted how I said it to make people think in a true way, not a Pontius Pilate sort of way. I wanted people like Katie, who didn't believe in spiritual things, to read my writing and think in a little more of a true way. Katie herself had said, after my article about her, that she could never think about the apple tree in quite the same way after reading what I wrote. Well, maybe if I could get her thinking about apple trees and people and roots in a true way, someday that might lead her to think about God in a more true way too.

That's what I wanted my writing to be able to do, even when I was writing about something that didn't have anything to do with God on the surface.

I remembered the verse Rev. Rutledge had quoted in church just a little while ago, the words Jesus had said: "Everyone that is of the truth hears my voice."

"Help me, God, to hear your voice," I prayed. "I want to hear your voice so that I can grow and understand. I want to hear your voice so I will know your wisdom, and so that what I write will be true."

I was deep in the woods now, the church and all the buildings of the town long out of sight.

I stopped and dropped to my knees among the decaying leaves and dead pine needles of the forest floor. I clasped my hands and closed my eyes.

"Oh, Lord," I prayed aloud, "make *me* a true person! When I hear your voice, give me strength to do what you say. Give me your wisdom and your understanding. Be the guide to my thoughts, God, and then help me to *do* what you want me to. Make my life be a true life, so that my writing will be *of* the truth."

I drew in a deep sigh, and my nostrils filled with the fragrance of the forest. It was such a lovely smell, and I couldn't help thinking right in that moment that God had made it only for me. It reminded me all over again how much he loved me.

Me—just me! The God of the universe loved little me, Corrie Belle Hollister!

Almeda had been telling me that simple truth for three years, and now I really grasped it on my own. Now maybe it was my turn to find ways to begin telling *other* people the same thing, as she had told me.

I stood and turned around and began retracing my steps out of the woods. Everywhere I looked were the signs of growth, from the fresh buds on the tips of the pine branches to the shrubs and undergrowth of the forest. Overhead the early afternoon sun poured through in tiny rays split into millions of arrows by the infinite, green needles on the trees.

I had always loved the woods, the mountains, the streams, the sky, the clouds. Yet the older I grew the more alive it all became to me. Every time I went out alone something new revealed itself to my consciousness. This was not the first time I had walked in this pine wood. But I think it was dearer to me on this day than it had ever been before. The mystery of its loveliness was somehow almost sacred. From the church building that the men of Miracle Springs had built, I had stepped into God's presence itself—into his greater, living church. All about me were signs and reflections of God himself, things he had made.

And as I left the wood that afternoon I found myself wondering about the *truth* contained in the trees and the bushes and the grass, even the truth of the blue sky and the sunshine and the smells I so enjoyed. Were all these things "true," as a man or woman might also be "true," because they came out of God, and reflected part of his nature?

That was far too big a question for my mind! I thought about it all the way home, and was no nearer to figuring it out than when I left town.

CHAPTER 18

NEW TIMES COME TO MIRACLE SPRINGS

By the time I got back to the claim, the afternoon was half gone and it was snowing again. Not real snow—it was toward the end of May, and though snow that late wouldn't have been out of the question higher up in the mountains, down in the foothills where we lived it would have been close to impossible.

A storyteller might call it snowing "figuratively." Sometimes a writer says something that has more than one meaning, like the apple tree when I was telling about Katie. So when I say it was snowing, I mean that God had already begun to answer my prayers again, my prayers about wanting to be true and to write in a true way. Like the last time, when it was *really* snowing, I didn't recognize the things that happened as God's little answering snowflakes coming down into my life.

The invisible snowflakes of answered prayer are falling down all around, millions of them. But it takes a special kind of sight to see them, and most folks never know that kind of snow's falling. You have to learn to hunt for them, learn to see them, train your eyes—your *inner* eyes, the eyes that look out of your heart and your mind. Just about everything having to do with God and the spiritual side of life is like that—they're things you have to train yourself to see.

And so I've been trying to train myself to look for buried, hidden, *invisible* things the more I grow as a Christian—the hidden meanings that are all around us, the invisible little glimpses of God that most folks don't notice.

When I got back to the house, there sat Rev. Rutledge's buggy out in front. I didn't think anything much about it until I went inside. Everyone was sitting there all quiet and talking in low tones. The reason the minister'd come was to tell us that our mayor, Mr. Vaissade, had just died, and the pastor was making the rounds to tell as many people as he knew would be interested.

Mr. Vaissade was an older man, and I don't suppose his death was all that much of a shock. But he had been in church with us just three or four hours earlier, and now suddenly was dead. He'd collapsed right on his own front porch after walking back to town from church, and was found lying there by a neighbor an hour later.

Although we all liked Mr. Vaissade, we weren't close friends, so his passing away like he did wasn't in itself an event that changed everything for me or for our family. But it turned out to have a huge effect on the future of the town, and an even bigger effect on our family.

Mr. Vaissade had been mayor of Miracle Springs for a year and a half. I don't think during all that time I heard of one thing in particular that his mayoring had done or changed. He just *was* the mayor, and everybody went on about their business as usual. Maybe he had to sign papers or something, but I never heard anything about it, and didn't really see what difference having a mayor made to Miracle Springs.

But folks had gotten kind of used to the idea of having a mayor, and almost immediately talk began to stir up about who was going to replace him. Miracle was a respectable town now. Including all the folks round about in the foothills and farms and ranches for several miles around town, there were fifteen hundred or two thousand people, and the area was growing back into the kind of size it'd boasted right after the first gold strikes. No town of the importance of Miracle Springs, they said, could be without a mayor. And in addition, political fever was in the air that summer of 1856 after Mr. Vaissade's death.

California had changed so much, even in the four years we

had been there. *We* were by now among the old-timers, the early settlers in the West. For the first several years, just about everybody coming to California from out East was coming because of the gold. Right at first it was the gold miners themselves, then later the people like the Parrishes and others— businessmen and suppliers and merchants and others who hoped to make a living *because of* the gold rush, though they may not have been directly involved themselves.

But by now, people were pouring into the West to settle it and live here, just because there was space and freedom and adventure, and because they heard the land was good. Schools and churches were being built all over the state, and thousands of families were putting down roots. Farmers were turning the valleys into land that produced food. Cities and towns were growing. Railroads joined the different parts of California, and there was even talk of a railroad someday to hook up California with the rest of the states back East.

California wasn't the only place that was growing. People were coming west—the *whole* west. California'd been made a state in 1850, and by this time there was lots of talk that Oregon would be the next new state. Settlers were coming across the Oregon Trail by the thousands.

It wasn't only because of all the new people coming west that folks were more interested in politics that year. In the only other election since California'd been in the union, statehood had been so fresh and the gold rush so much on people's minds that folks just didn't pay that much attention. After all, Washington, D.C. was thousands of miles away, and Californians didn't figure it made much difference whether they voted for Franklin Pierce from New Hampshire or General Winfield Scott.

But now in 1856, everything was different!

A new political party, the Republicans, had been formed only a couple of years earlier. The issue of slavery, though not really involving California too much, was still talked about, because the new party was more or less based on anti-slavery. I suppose Californians were interested in the Republican party too because one of the state's most well-known men, John Charles Fremont, was one of the leaders in getting it established. Fremont was rich from the gold that had been discovered on his huge estate. He had been one of the first explorers to California, had fought the Mexicans, and was one of the first new senators in 1850 right after California became a state. All in all, John Fremont was the most famous Californian there was.

And now, for the presidential election of 1856, the new Republican party had chosen John Fremont as their nominee.

That made all of California stand up and take notice of national politics. Now it made a big difference who people voted for—James Buchanan from far-away Pennsylvania, or John Fremont *from California*! We may have been the newest of the Union's thirty-one states, but all of a sudden we were one of the most important.

"Why, just think of it," everyone was saying, "a Californian in the White House!" That election of 1856 was just about the biggest thing to hit California since the discovery of gold!

John Fremont was one of those kinds of men that not everyone liked. When people talked about the election, lots of folks like Alkali Jones didn't have that much nice to say about him. But one thing was for sure—he was *our* John Fremont . . . from *our* own state! And folks figured that made him worth voting for no matter what else they thought.

So politics and John Fremont and Washington, D.C. , and slavery and Republicans and Democrats were all topics in the air and on people's minds and lips that summer.

And as part of all that, and maybe because of it, almost immediately after Mr. Vaissade's death, folks started saying Miracle Springs needed to have an election for mayor.

CHAPTER 19

THE CANDIDATE

An election for mayor in a little town like Miracle Springs may not sound like a big event, especially with an important presidential election going on at the same time. But around the Hollister-Belle claims, the minute Franklin Royce announced that he intended to run for mayor, all discussion about Buchanan and Fremont faded completely into the background. The Miracle Springs mayor's election was all at once the only election anyone cared about!

"I told ya afore, an' I ain't changed my mind none since," said Alkali Jones. "The man's a polecat!"

"A snake!" put in Uncle Nick.

They were sitting around the table in our house talking about Royce and the election. Alkali Jones' high laughter had ceased. The men didn't seem to know whether to be angry or miserable over the turn of events. So they wound up being a little of both.

"You talked t' Rafferty again, Drum?" asked Mr. Jones.

"I've talked to him half a dozen times," Pa answered, "and so has every other man in town. But he says he's got all he can do as sheriff, and he don't want to be mayor too. None of us can convince him."

"Ol' Vaissade didn't do nuthin'. What makes Rafferty think he can't jest combine the mayorin' an' the sheriffin'?"

"He says the town's growing, and needs both a mayor and a sheriff."

"Well, one thing's for sure," added Uncle Nick. "The mayor's job won't be a do-nothing job no more with Royce in it."

"Simon says he can keep him from doing any mischief," said Pa. "That's another reason he doesn't seem too worried."

"What harm *could* he do?" asked Katie, who had been listening from the other side of the room, where she and Almeda were sitting. "After all, he's still got his bank to manage."

Pa turned his head, then gave a shrug in answer. "Who knows? But if you give a man like Royce a chance, he'll find *some* way to turn it to his advantage, and I reckon that's what has the rest of us worried. Especially if we just let him have the job for the taking."

"I'll tell you what he could do," said Almeda. "Once a man like that's in power, he can do all kinds of things. I've seen it happen in other towns. There's been corruption in the governments of Sacramento and San Francisco, and any time you have money involved in political decisions it can be dangerous. As mayor *and* the town's only banker, Franklin Royce could control this town. He could bring in his own people and set up a town council. He could control decisions that were made. He could levy taxes, commission building projects, change laws. He already dictates how the money in this community flows. He could put Parrish Mine and Freight Company out of business if he wanted to. What if, as mayor, he wanted to get rid of Simon Rafferty as sheriff and appoint one of his own men? I'm sure he could find a way to manage it. Before we knew it, warrants on Drum and Nick would start to appear from the East. I tell you, the possibilities are frightening. I don't trust Royce, even though I'm forced to do business with him."

"But the mayor's never had that kind of power. Vaissade couldn't have gotten rid of Simon if he'd wanted to."

"Power has a way of sneaking up on you if you put it into the wrong hands. Once you start something, it's sometimes impossible to undo it. I for one would feel a lot more comfortable if the door were not opened in the first place."

Uncle Nick now spoke up again. "He's always wanted this land of ours," he said.

"An' every other piece he could git his slimy white hands on," Jones added.

"Then, why doesn't one of the other men in town run against him?" asked Katie.

"No one wants to," replied Pa. "Bosely, Simon, Lewis, Miller, Griffin—me and Nick and Rutledge, we talked to all of them. I even tried to get Avery to consider it, but he keeps saying religion and politics don't mix."

"Wouldn't do no good anyway," said Uncle Nick. "Royce would win, whatever anybody else tried to do. He holds mortgages and notes on eighty percent of the property in the whole area. Nobody's gonna cross him up when it could mean he'd call due what they owe him."

"But they could still vote against him," I suggested. "I can't see why everyone can't simply choose not to vote for him, or vote for nobody. "He'd never know."

"Economics, Corrie," said Almeda, looking over toward me. "Sad to say, money dictates power. If Royce doesn't win, he could call *everyone's* mortgages due. When they can't pay, he forecloses on whatever properties he wants, and winds up owning all the land for miles. Such a prospect might even be worse than calling him our mayor. Nobody *knows* whether he'd do that, but just the threat can be enough to frighten people into doing what a man like that wants. He wouldn't even have to say anything—a mere rumor circulating that foreclosures would result if he wasn't elected would probably be enough to insure his victory. That is *if* someone was running against him. As it is, he probably won't even have to go that far."

CHAPTER 20

THE TWO CAMPAIGNS

Mr. Royce continued to be unopposed in the election for Miracle Springs mayor, which was scheduled for November 4, the same day as the presidential voting between Fremont and Buchanan. He gave a couple of speeches in town in June, but nobody paid much attention since he was the only one running. And after that, he didn't do much else. About the only sign that would let a stranger know there was even an election going on was a banner in the window of the bank that said, "Royce for Mayor."

Nobody liked the idea of Franklin Royce being mayor of Miracle Springs, but gradually they got used to it and the hubbub and complaining slowly died out. Out in the open, no one really said much. I guess what Almeda said was true—they didn't want to get on Royce's bad side for fear of what would happen. Royce didn't have any "paper" against our claim (that's what Pa called it), but Parrish Mine and Freight still had business dealings with the bank, so we had to be careful like everyone else.

One other thing quieted down all the initial worries, something that was a surprise to everybody. Mr. Royce started making himself agreeable. He didn't give any more speeches, but he walked around town, smiling, shaking people's hands, visiting in the stores. He even came into the freight office a time or two for a minute, saying he was checking up on his customers, seeing how they were doing, wondering if there was any way the bank could be of service to them. He was so polite and friendly you almost couldn't help liking him!

The words "election" or "mayor" were never mentioned once. He never said a thing about asking people to vote for him. Of course, he didn't need to—there was no one else they *could* vote for!

Mr. Royce knew, I suppose, that folks were suspicious, not only of him but of bankers in general. And he probably knew that he wasn't the best liked man in Miracle Springs, and that people were nice to him only because they had to be since he was the banker.

That could hardly make a man feel too good about himself, knowing people had more fear than liking for him. I can't imagine anyone finding it pleasant inside to know that people were afraid of him. But I figured that Mr. Royce decided he'd rather have people liking him as mayor than being afraid of him, so he had vowed to himself to change his ways and be nice from now on. Rev. Rutledge talked sometimes about giving people what he called "the benefit of the doubt"—thinking the best of them. Maybe that's what I was trying to do with Mr. Royce.

When he'd come around, I'd watch his face real careful and look into his eyes to see if I could see the change. I like to watch people and try to imagine what they're thinking. But I couldn't see anything in Mr. Royce's face. His mouth had a nice smile on it when he talked, but there was just no way to tell what he was thinking. His eyes didn't seem to look exactly at you when he spoke. It was like he was looking just a little bit off to one side, and so the conversation back and forth was just a tiny bit crooked, though such a little bit that I doubt anyone else even noticed. I didn't talk to him much myself, only to answer when he'd come into the office and say "How are you today, Corrie?" before going on to talk a minute with Almeda or Mr. Ashton. So maybe that crookedness was just something I noticed that he didn't do with everyone else. But his eyes didn't sparkle, they just kind of looked past me.

I watched other people, too, as they talked to him. I was

real curious about this changed friendly Mr. Royce. Mr. Ashton seemed to be drawn into the banker's friendly smile, and their words back and forth were jovial and lighthearted. Almeda, however, always seemed to be looking into those dark gray eyes of Mr. Royce's as if she was trying to figure out the thoughts behind them too. She smiled and was very gracious, and their talk was polite. Her eyes didn't sparkle at such times either. Despite the smile on her lips, her eyes remained serious and seemed to be turning over more thoughts inside than her words let on.

Even Pa and Uncle Nick gradually started speaking more kindly about their future mayor.

"We may as well get used to him," said Pa one evening. "I never liked the man, an' I'd rather see someone else run. But we're stuck with him. He's gonna be the mayor and he's gonna be the banker, and it's for sure we don't want to be on the wrong side of *his* fence once he's *that* important."

"I reckon you're right," said Uncle Nick, "though I'll still feel a sight better once I get the $450 I owe him for lumber paid back. I don't like to be indebted to no man, least of all him. Politicians *and* bankers are both a mite too full of smiles to suit me!"

"I don't trust the varmint nohow!" put in Alkali Jones. "Jest like I don't trust ol' Fremont neither. Anyone what's been in California as long as me knows too much 'bout what Cap'n John's *really* like! I ain't gonna vote fer neither o' the skunks!"

"And a big difference *that's* gonna make, Alkali!" said Pa, laughing. "Fremont's gonna carry California so big they might as well take Buchanan off the ballot, and Royce don't need nobody's but his own vote to win."

"It's the preenciple o' the thing, I tell ya, an' I ain't gonna vote fer neither o' 'em!"

Pa chuckled to himself, but said nothing more.

"Well if *I* could vote," said Katie, who had been following the conversation with interest, "I would vote for anybody, just to have my say in what happens. You men are lucky, Alkali, to be able to vote. You shouldn't throw the chance away just because you don't like the candidates."

"Aw, but Drum's right. What blame difference is it gonna make anyhow who we votes fer, or even iffen we votes at all?"

"It's the American way, Alkali," said Pa, smiling, and giving his friend a poke in the ribs. "When you came out West it was just a wilderness. Now we're a state and our man's running for the White House, and we got our duty as citizens to do. Come on, Alkali, you got to get into the right spirit for this election!"

I couldn't tell at first how serious Pa was, but when I saw him throw Uncle Nick a quick wink, I knew. I think he meant the words but was using them to make Mr. Jones squirm a little.

When they'd get to talking about Mr. Royce, Pa was pretty kindly disposed toward him and seemed willing to forget about the past. Uncle Nick was more cautious, but not as critical as they had both once been, though he did say one time, "It's easy for you to forgive him, Drum. You don't owe him a dime. Why, you got four thousand dollars *in* his bank! But me, I gotta still worry some, till I get that house all paid for."

Pa only laughed. He'd worked hard in the mine these last two years, getting enough to add on to the house, and save money besides. Since they'd both got married, Pa and Uncle Nick had kept their earnings separate, and as much as Uncle Nick had settled down, he still wasn't half the worker Pa was. And Zack had by now begun to make a pretty big difference in the Hollister share of the output of the mine. I didn't know how Pa's and Almeda's money was being handled now that they were married—the Mine and Freight Company, that is. That's something they never talked about to me.

All through the conversation about Royce and Fremont and the elections, Almeda remained silent, although I don't think it had anything to do with the money. I could tell she was listening to every word and was *very* interested in what was being said—that much was plain from one look at her face. Just as clear was that she was thinking real hard. But what she was thinking about, she didn't let on so much as one little peep.

The weeks of summer went by. Royce kept up his pleasantness campaign. The leaves on a few of the birch trees started thinking about turning yellow. Both Mr. Singleton's *Gazette* and Mr. Kemble's *Alta* were full of the Fremont-Buchanan election, and there wasn't much room left for an aspiring girl-writer from a little foothills gold town. I hadn't seen anything of mine in either paper since May, though I kept writing. Mr. Kemble was still looking at two more articles I'd sent him—one called "Summer in the Foothills of Gold Country," and the other one of what he called his "human interest" stories about Miss Stansberry and the school, and especially about how she had learned to use her lameness as a strength instead of a weakness.

The Summer-in-the-Foothills one was mostly about the beauty of the countryside and how summer was such a special season. I had the idea out walking one day, watching Pa and Uncle Nick and Zack and Mr. Jones all working away in the stream and mine from where I was standing up on a hill behind the house. I had been thinking how much I loved the countryside God had made, and when I saw them laboring away after little pieces of gold, the realization came to me that the land itself was really the treasure, not the gold. The "real gold"—that's what I called it in the article—was the land and its people, not just the nuggets that they were digging out of the streams and rivers. Someday, I said, there might not be any gold left, but there would still be this wonderful land, and there would still be people to love and cherish the land, and that was more lasting than any riches any miner could ever dig out of even the wealthiest mine. So the article had one of those "double meanings," because I meant the word "gold" in the title to stand for the wealth of the land itself.

Anyway, I figured Mr. Kemble would be sending it back to me some time real soon. But I hoped the article on Miss Stansberry might get published. And in the meantime, the papers were full of editorials about the election and reprints from papers out East and articles about the slavery question and where the two presidential candidates stood on that and all kinds of issues. There were also other elections going on for California's senators and representatives in Washington. So much was happening so fast. Everything was growing. Sacramento had just been made the capital of all of California two years before in 1854. Now that we were so close to the center of politics, the elections for state offices had gotten everybody's attention too, and even a time or two men came through making speeches and telling everybody to vote for them, though half the time no one had ever heard of them.

CHAPTER 21

ALMEDA SURPRISES EVERYBODY!

One evening toward the latter part of July, Almeda was late coming home from town. I'd been home for some time. Supper was all ready, Pa had quit working and was cleaned up, but still she didn't come. Finally Pa said we should just go ahead and eat, though it wasn't like her to be so late. At first I think he might have been a trifle annoyed, but by eight o'clock, when she still wasn't home, he started to worry.

Finally Pa got to his feet. "I'm going into town," he said, "to find out where she is and if she's okay."

He walked out the door and toward the barn to saddle his horse. But not two or three minutes later, Almeda's little buggy came around the bend and up the road toward the house.

A moment or two passed before she and Pa came through the door together. From the look on Pa's face, she still hadn't told him what had caused her delay.

Without sitting down, she waited until everyone was quiet. We all had our eyes fixed on her, wondering what she was going to say. Her face was serious but bright, and it was obvious something was brewing inside her head that she was dying to tell us all about.

"I'm sorry to be so late," she said. "I didn't expect this, but as I got ready to come home, suddenly a great . . . a great sense . . . of God speaking to me began to come over me and I knew I had to be alone for a while. As it turns out, I've been

thinking, praying, and crying for over two hours! But now . . .
I believe I know at last what he's been trying to tell me."

She stopped and took a deep breath. Then she got a big
smile on her face, and was clearly excited about what she had
to say.

"I've reached a decision," she said. "Hopefully with God's
help—"

She paused again, then announced:

"I've decided to run against Royce . . . for mayor!"

Silence fell like a heavy cloud throughout the house. No
one said anything. Everyone was too shocked.

Becky was the first to break the silence by bolting past
Almeda and through the door.

"Where ya going?" called Pa after her.

"To tell Uncle Nick and Aunt Katie!" shouted Becky back
at him, already halfway to the bridge over the stream.

That was all Pa said for a while. He was real quiet, and
from the look of expectation on Almeda's face I could tell she
was waiting for him to say something.

"Well, if that don't beat all," he finally said. "You are a
lady full of surprises, I'll say that for you."

Almeda laughed, and finally sat down, showing some relief.
I brought a plate and set it down in front of her at the table.

Pa didn't say anything more, just sat there thinking about
this turn of events. From looking at him, I couldn't tell whether
he approved or not. I guess it was quite a thing for a man to
get used to, his wife saying she was going to run for politics.
It wasn't the kind of thing women did, or that men usually
approved of!

I decided to break the silence myself. "What makes you
think you can do it?" I asked. "If a woman can't vote, I
wouldn't think they'd let you *run* for an office."

"Well, women *ought* to be able to vote," she replied, "and
I intend to run whatever anyone thinks."

"Anyone . . . including me?" said Pa finally, looking over
at her.

"Well, I . . . ." Almeda hesitated. "I just thought, Drummond, that you'd be all for it. I've heard you say yourself you didn't like the thought of Royce as mayor."

"You're right, I don't. I reckon I just wish you'd said somethin' to me first, that's all."

"I'm sorry, Drummond," she said, genuinely surprised, as if she'd never thought about talking to Pa ahead of time. "If you'd rather—"

"No, no," interrupted Pa. "I ain't gonna stand in your way."

Then he tried to lighten the tension some by letting out a laugh. "Who knows, maybe I'll like the notion of bein' known as the mayor's husband! But what about Royce?" he asked, serious again. "He ain't gonna like this one bit!"

"Franklin Royce can think what he will. If he calls my notes due, I'll borrow the money from *you*! I don't owe him more than a couple thousand dollars."

Pa laughed again. "Well, you're determined enough," he said, sounding as if he was getting gradually used to the idea. "I reckon I'll give you my vote. But since women can't vote, and men being what they are, I can't see how you'll get many more."

"What about everything you and Nick have been saying about none of the men around caring for Royce?"

"That was before. Now that he's changed, I ain't so sure most of the men wouldn't still prefer him to voting for a woman."

"Are *you* prejudiced against the idea?" asked Almeda, still wondering what Pa thought.

"I'm just tellin' you how folks'll see it, and you know as well as I do how men are about women doing 'men's work.' "

Almeda sent a glance in my direction, as if to remind me of the conversations we had about that very same thing.

"We'll see," she said. "I'm not so sure Royce has changed as much as everyone thinks. I have a feeling he's just as conniving as ever, and if folks have a choice in the election . . . well, we'll have to wait and see. I just think they ought to have a choice."

In a few minutes Katie and Uncle Nick, led by Becky, came in. Uncle Nick was carrying fourteen-month-old Erich, but set him down as soon as they were inside. He'd been walking about three or four weeks, and now he went toddling about while Becky and Tad tried to keep up with him. Still sitting at the table, Almeda did her best to eat some supper and answer everyone's questions. Her surprise announcement caused an uproar in the house. No one knew what to think, but everybody had plenty to say in response!

"I think it's exciting!" said Katie over and over. "If I'd thought of it myself, why *I'd* have run!"

"Being the wife of this character," said Pa, tossing his head sideways toward Uncle Nick, "I wouldn't exactly have recommended you as qualified for the position."

"Why, Drummond, how dare you!" she said.

"I'm only saying," laughed Pa, "that Almeda here's got a reputation as a businesswoman that goes further back in Miracle Springs even than Royce's—when *did* he come to town, Almeda?"

"I think it was late '51 . . . maybe early '52."

"There, you see," continued Pa. "Parrish Mine and Freight has been doing business in town since '50." He stopped. "Hmm, now that I think about it, maybe you *can* put up a campaign against Royce."

"Sounds like a campaign slogan to me," said Katie. " 'Hollister for Mayor—Part of Miracle Springs from the Beginning!' "

"How about being my assistant, Katie?" said Almeda.

"No, no, no!" interjected Uncle Nick. "If a woman's gonna try to go up against a man, at least you gotta have a man runnin' it for ya."

"Are you suggesting, *Mister* Belle," said Katie, "that two women would not be able to do it?"

"*Three* women!" I added.

Katie and Almeda cheered and clapped to have me joining their debate. "Now we three outnumber you two!" said Katie. "Perhaps we should *vote* on who should be the campaign manager, right here and now!"

"Make it three against three!" chimed in Zack. "I'm sixteen. My say oughta count as much as Corrie's!"

"Now you're talking, son!" said Pa. "You just stand aside, Katie, and let us men figure out the best way to go about this thing!"

By now we were all laughing, including the kids, who had never seen a family squabble line up quite so definitely with the women against the men. It was sure good to see Pa entering into the spirit of it now, after his initial hesitation.

A lot more lively discussion followed throughout the evening. Despite all the suggestions the rest of us were free to give, the wisdom of the candidate prevailed when she said, "Perhaps the best idea is that we let this whole *committee* manage my campaign. What do you say—we six, three men, three women? That way we'll be able to give even voice to the concerns of the men *and* the women, the young *and* the old, the married *and* the unmarried, the business persons *and* the miners. We'll have our whole Miracle Springs constituency represented right on our 'Hollister for Mayor' committee—do you all agree?"

Everyone looked around at each other. What she said made sense.

"Maybe you *are* cut out to be a politician, Almeda," said Pa. "That sounds just like the kind of solution a mayor oughta be able to figure out—with a little speechmaking thrown in!"

We laughed.

"And the first thing for the committee to get busy on," she said, "is publicity. That, I think, would be your department, Corrie," she added, turning toward me.

The result could be seen the next afternoon in the window of the Parrish Mine and Freight Company, with a hand-lettered poster where the words *Vote Almeda Hollister for Mayor of Miracle Springs* suddenly declared to the whole town that the poster in the bank's window wasn't the only political message to be heard anymore.

This election had now become a two man—that is, a two-*person*—race!

It took only the rest of that day and half of the next morning for the poster to be seen and for word to begin to get around. But when it did, the news spread like a brushfire in a hot wind. Before the week was out there wasn't *anything* in the mouths of people for miles around other than what they thought of Almeda going up against Franklin Royce. Some folks thought it was ridiculous. Others said privately they would vote for her if they could, but they just couldn't afford to rile Royce. A lot of the men said women ought to stay where they belonged and keep out of politics. Of course, all the women admired Almeda and loved the idea, but none of them could vote. And most of the men, whether they liked the idea or not, said she had guts to try it, although some added it would probably ruin her business in the end. Royce wasn't the kind of man you got on the wrong side of, they said.

All of a sudden, the Fremont-Buchanan election seemed far away and uninteresting!

CHAPTER 22

THE CAMPAIGN
GETS STARTED

With the town all a buzz, there was still not much active support for Almeda against banker Franklin Royce.

People were talking *about* the election, but nobody was coming out and saying they actually supported Almeda. If anything, business around the office was quieter than usual. Almeda was right in the middle of a hurricane of talk and interest and discussion, but the Parrish Mine and Freight office was quieter than a tomb. And even the people who did come in seemed reluctant to mention the election. They just took care of their business and left without more words than were necessary.

"You know what it is," said Almeda one day in frustration to me and Mr. Ashton. "They're all afraid Franklin is standing behind his window over there watching!"

The bank and freight office, two of Miracle's busiest places and biggest buildings, sat looking right at each other across the intersection of the two main streets. There they sat, with the General Store and the sheriff's office and jail on opposite corners and lots of other little stores and buildings in between, making up the central square block of Miracle Springs.

And there stood the posters in the windows of each, saying nothing out loud, but silently saying so much about what really made Miracle Springs work and operate and "function" every day as a town. *Royce for Mayor*, said the one, promoting the

144

man who owned the bank and who as a result co-owned or part-owned three-quarters of all the farms and ranches and businesses and homes for miles around. And in the other window folks read the sign I had made that said *Vote Almeda Hollister for Mayor of Miracle Springs.* Everyone knew that it was Almeda who had gotten them their gold pans and sluice boxes and their bags, shovels, wagons, spare parts, picks, saddles, ropes, and nails. At her livery half their horses and mules were tended, and at her blacksmith's forge Marcus Weber repaired their tools, re-shod their horses, and fixed their broken wagon wheels.

I don't suppose any two people had done more to make Miracle Springs what it was in 1856 than Franklin Royce and Almeda Parrish Hollister. Yet it seemed more than likely that most folks would end up on Royce's side. Even though through the years Almeda had given credit to most of the men of Miracle Springs one time or another, she didn't hold mortgages on their property. And if she went out of business, as sorry as they might be, they could always get what they needed someplace else. If she was gone, probably Royce himself would set up a new business to replace hers!

"What we need is a flyer, a pamphlet!" Almeda exclaimed, after a few moments pause, still staring out the window, looking toward the bank. "Folks are just too nervous to be seen talking to me. But if we distributed something they could take home and read when they're alone, then they wouldn't have to worry about being seen by you know who."

She spun around and faced me. "What do you say, Corrie? A flyer—you can help me write it, and I'll take it down to Sacramento to have it printed up. We'll get five hundred, even a thousand printed up. We'll scatter so many of them around that everybody will see it eventually!"

We got started on it that very afternoon.

Almeda told me what she wanted to say. I wrote it down in the best way I could, she made some changes, and then I wrote it over again. I started to work on a couple of pictures for it, too, so that it would look interesting—a sketch of Almeda's face, and another one of the front of the Freight Company office, as a reminder of what Parrish Mine and Freight had meant to the community.

During the evening we all sat around and talked—what Almeda still called her campaign "committee"—trying to figure out what we ought to say. Katie kept talking about needing a campaign slogan, and Almeda finally settled on: Almeda Hollister—A Hard-Working Part of Miracle Springs' Past Who Will Be Faithful to Its Future. She Will Put *Your* Interests First."

That slogan would go on top of the handbill. Under it would be my sketch of Almeda. At the bottom would be words like: Integrity, Experience in Business, Familiar with Needs of Miners, Dependable, Friend of Miner and Rancher and Farmer, Working Hard for Your Prosperity.

All that would comprise the front page. Inside the fold, people would open it up and read the written part about how Almeda had come to Miracle Springs, how the business had been started, and how much she had done for the miners through the years—helping get what they needed, giving them extra time to pay if needed, delivering things at odd hours or even in rain or snow if something was needed right away, opening up her livery or blacksmith's shop in an emergency even if it meant getting Marcus up in the middle of the night—and finally saying that as mayor she would continue to do all those things for the community, always looking out for the interests and well-being of the people she represented.

During those first couple of weeks, Mr. Royce continued to be his same smiling, friendly self. In fact, three days after the poster went up in our window, we were astonished by another personal visit by the opposing candidate himself. Mr. Ashton had spotted him out the window walking in our direction from the bank.

"Here comes Royce!" he said, and he hurried back to his chair and tried to busy himself with the papers in front of him. Almeda and I braced ourselves for—well, we didn't know what, but I don't think either of us expected it to be pleasant.

But Mr. Royce walked in the door, a big smile on his face, and went straight up to Almeda.

"Well, Almeda, I must say this is a surprise! Welcome to the race!" he said.

"Thank you, Franklin," she replied, shaking his hand. "You are being most gracious about it."

"Whatever our differences in the past may have been, I congratulate your intrepid decision. California needs more women like you!"

Almeda smiled, the two wished each other well, and then the banker departed, leaving Almeda with a question on her face. "Have I completely misjudged that man?" she said after a moment, speaking more to herself than to either of us. Her eyes remained fixed on the door Mr. Royce had just left for another few seconds. Then she shook her head and went on with her work. Was she doubting whether she had done the right thing?

Thereafter, Mr. Royce kept being nice about the whole thing. Whenever anyone asked him about the election, or mentioned Almeda's running against him, his response was something nice and friendly.

"It's a free country," he might say. "Anyone is able to do as his conscience leads him, and I salute Mrs. Hollister's courage to stand up for what she believes in."

Or: "She is a strong woman, and Miracle Springs should be proud to have her as one of its leading citizens."

Or: "It is remarkable, is it not, what women are able to achieve when they persevere? She has done a great deal for this town, and I for one have the greatest respect for her as a businesswoman in what is predominantly a man's occupation."

Whether he was truly being nice, or just didn't think he had to worry about Almeda's hurting his election, I didn't know. One thing was for sure, folks were starting to change their opinion of him, and his nice comments about Almeda only made them like him all the more.

But some people didn't believe a word of it. Like Katie. When she heard that last remark he'd made to Patrick Shaw—

which his wife had told Katie—she got downright riled.

"I tell you, Almeda, he's talking out of both sides of his mouth!" she said. "All those nice words don't fool me a bit."

Almeda laughed. "Why do you say that?" she asked.

"He may be saying nice things about you, but he makes sure he always mentions that you are a woman, and that this is a man's world. He doesn't *have* to say anything—it's obvious he wants people to think for themselves that being a mayor's no job for a woman."

"He's never said a word to that effect, Katie."

"He doesn't need to. He's relying on the men around here to draw that conclusion for themselves. Patronizing, that's what it is. He's being nice to you so that folks won't take you seriously. It's almost as if he treats your running against him as a joke that doesn't *really* mean anything as far as the election's concerned."

"I don't know, Katie," Almeda replied with a thoughtful look on her face. "It just may be that Franklin Royce has changed his ways after all."

CHAPTER 23

I SURPRISE MYSELF!

Right in the middle of all the excitement of getting the handbill ready and everything else to do with the election, a letter came from San Francisco that caught me by surprise.

"Dear Mr. Hollister," it read. "I would like to run your article about Summer in the Gold Country in the *Alta* next week. Enclosed is $4 for it. I have to admit your pieces continue to surprise me. Some of the people on our staff tell me your writing is among the most favorably received of anything we print among our women readers. I don't know how you do it, but you seem to have a good feel for the kinds of things that women enjoy reading about. Keep it up! I am confident we will be able to sell this article to several eastern papers as well." It was signed, "Edward Kemble." Then underneath had been added: "It may be that we will also run your story about the lame schoolteacher. It will depend on whether we have space to spare. You're getting the picture about 'human interest.' But of course, right now we're swamped with election news."

I was elated. This was the most positive thing he'd ever written me! He actually said there were people who *liked* reading what I wrote!

Over the next two or three days, I read his letter several times. My conscious mind couldn't help feeling good at the words "favorably received," "good feel for what women enjoy reading," "keep it up" and "you're getting the picture." But down deep something was bothering me.

At first I didn't know what it was.

Then gradually thoughts began coming back to me about that Sunday when Rev. Rutledge had preached on truth. He had talked about *people* being true rather than *ideas*. I found myself wondering about it further, questioning how to make my writing "true." It seemed like I was getting to do what I had always wanted to do. Writing for a newspaper had been my dream, and now here I was actually doing it! And if I was going to keep on doing it, I wanted to write truthfully.

I thought about the two articles and about what I had written, and about what Mr. Kemble had said about them. The more I thought about them, the more I did feel like I could be proud of those articles as truthful. I honestly *did* feel there was something more special about the gold country than just the gold itself—and that was the land. And I hoped what I'd written about Miss Stansberry overcoming her lame leg would show folks something about her down inside that was a good thing for them to see, a part of her true character.

Yet something kept eating at me inside. I'd written about ideas and thoughts and feelings and people in a good and honest way, even in a way that people might like reading about. But something was still wrong.

I remembered Rev. Rutledge's words: *Truth is not ideas . . . only a person can be true.*

All at once I knew what was wrong with the two articles. It wasn't anything I said about Miss Stansberry or the gold country. It was in Mr. Kemble's letter. All the nice things he'd said were pleasant to hear. But the words that now suddenly jumped off the paper as I looked at his letter again were the very first ones: "Dear Mr. Hollister . . ."

Mister Hollister . . . Dear *Mister* Hollister . . . *Mister* . . . *Mister*. . . !

That's what was wrong! Truth wasn't the ideas, it was the person, and I was the wrong person! Mr. Kemble didn't even know who I was! He thought I was a man. How could I possibly be a writer who was trying to write about true things when I *myself* wasn't being true?

Then the words that had come out of my own mouth that same day came back to me, the words I had prayed to God in the woods after the church service: *Lord, make me a true person!*

If my writing was going to mean anything, no matter what it was I happened to be talking about, then I had to be true *myself!* And maybe this letter from Mr. Kemble was my opportunity to start. After all, being a true person isn't something you put off and figure you'll get around to some other time. You either are or you aren't. And if I had let this little lie slip in about who I really was—even though neither Almeda nor I had a thought of deceiving Mr. Kemble at first—I couldn't wait for some other time to set it right.

Setting something right is a thing you have to do now, not later. So I figured I'd better do something about this situation . . . and soon.

I'd gotten the letter at the office in the morning. All day long I thought about it. And by the middle of the afternoon I'd made a decision that surprised even me.

So that night, in as calm but determined a voice as I could, I said to Pa and Almeda:

"I'm going to San Francisco."

Almeda's eyes opened up wide as Pa exclaimed, "What in tarnation for, girl?"

"If I'm gonna keep writing for his paper," I said, "there are a few things I need to talk to Mr. Kemble about. And I just don't figure there's any way to do it but in person."

I reckon they both sensed from the resolution of my tone that there was no way I was going to let them talk me out of it.

But that didn't stop them from trying. In fact, at first Pa said if I was determined, one of them would have to go with me. But in the end, after endless instructions and warnings, they sent me off with the boys keeping me company for at least half the way.

CHAPTER 24

FACE TO FACE
WITH MR. KEMBLE

Zack and Little Wolf went with me on horseback as far as Sacramento. We camped out for one night somewhere between Auburn and Folsom. We lay around the fire and talked until after midnight before I finally drifted off to sleep.

I left my horse at a livery in Sacramento and went on to San Francisco alone. Zack and Little Wolf said they'd keep busy and see the city and would meet me back at Miss Baxter's Boarding House in three days. Miss Baxter could hardly believe it was us, and said she'd never have known Zack if he bumped into her on the sidewalk. What a feeling it was, the three of us—still kids inside, I reckon, but alone in the city and knowing we could handle ourselves. Well, Zack and Little Wolf could handle *them*selves, and I felt safe enough as long as I was with them!

Not until I was alone on the steamer floating down the Sacramento River did it begin to dawn on me what I was doing. I was on my way to the biggest city in the West—alone!

I'd climbed tall trees when I was little—terrified that I was going to fall, too frightened to look down, yet tingling with excitement as I kept climbing higher and higher . . . afraid, but glad to be afraid! And not so afraid that I didn't want to get as high up as I could.

That's how it felt as I looked out over the river and watched the shore glide past and felt the warm breeze on my face and

152

in my hair. I was nervous, and thought that anyone who saw me would have noticed my knees shaking under my calico skirt. But I wouldn't have wanted to be anyplace else.

I thought of traveling to San Francisco with Almeda exactly three years earlier. I was so dependent on her back then. It had been *her* trip about *her* business. *She'd* made the arrangements. *She* knew what to do and where to go. I had been just a little girl.

And now here I was, not only going to San Francisco alone, but going there on my *own* business, about something that concerned *my* life. It had been *my* decision to come, and I was on my own to figure out what to do. I had the name and address of a boardinghouse run by a friend of Mrs. Gianini's, but that was all.

I still felt young, but I knew I was starting to grow up. I was going to San Francisco by myself and, as fearsome as it might be, I knew I could figure out what I should do. And if I couldn't, then maybe it was time I learned. I had to grow up sometime. And maybe the best way to learn how to stand on your own two feet without your pa or ma helping you is to just go out and start walking on them without anyone's help.

I thought too about how dependent I had been on Almeda spiritually. She had been the one who had first told me how God felt about us, and about how he wanted us to think and live and behave. I hadn't known anything about God and his ways back then. When I think back to some of the questions I used to ask her, I can't help but be embarrassed at how naive I was. But on the other hand, that's how you grow and learn— by wondering, by asking, and by having someone you can look up to who can help you as you're trying to figure things out. So I'm glad I wrote in my journal about some of those lengthy conversations Almeda and I had. I still go back and reread them now and then—the talk we'd had about what sin meant when Mrs. Gianini was working on the dresses, the talk we'd had right on that same Sacramento River steamer about faith, the Easter Sunday afternoon just after I turned seventeen when I'd prayed that God would make me into the person he wanted me to be, and the long talk on the way home about obeying. Every one of those talks remains so special in my memory, and makes me love Almeda all the more as a mother.

Now those truths she had given me were part of *me*. She had taught me, helped me, encouraged me, and loved me. But the most important thing she had done for me was to help me stand on my *own* spiritual feet. She had helped me to think for myself, helped me as I learned how to pray, and encouraged me gently as I grew.

I had been grappling with the whole prospect of what growing up meant, and about my future. But the fact that I was thinking about options, about writing, about what truth was, and about growing to be a woman. The fact that I was asking God about them, showed that maybe I *was* growing up after all—or at least starting to.

And now here I was on my way to San Francisco! I would never have imagined it just a few months ago. But now . . . who could tell what the future might hold.

If being so far away from home wasn't enough to make my knees quake, the thought of facing the editor of one of California's biggest newspapers sure was! The more I thought about it, the more foolish this whole thing seemed. Yet I still knew I had to go through with it, even if it meant I never saw another word of mine in Mr. Kemble's newspaper . . . or any other newspaper! If growing as a Christian and being a "true" person had anything to do with becoming an adult, then I had to do this thing I had come to do, no matter how hard it might be. I'd never *keep* growing if I didn't do the thing that was set before me.

Another idea had been running around in my mind since just before we got to Sacramento. The closer we got to the big city, the more I found myself thinking about it—and it had to do with the election back home between Almeda and Mr. Royce. By the time I walked into Mr. Kemble's office the next day, I had figured out exactly what I wanted to say to him.

Of course, the conversation didn't quite go the way I had planned it!

The lady in the *Alta* office seemed a little surprised when I asked to see Mr. Kemble. I don't know why. I tried to look as professional as I knew how, and I had brought along my best clothes to wear. But I couldn't hide my age.

She asked if he was expecting me. I said no. Then she asked my name, and I said he didn't know me and that I wanted to wait to tell him my name in person.

That kind of annoyed her, and she told me to sit down and wait, which I did. It was a *long* wait, and I think maybe she hoped I'd get tired and go away. But I kept sitting there, and finally she got up and went somewhere out of my sight. When she came back a minute or two later, she said, "Mr. Kemble will see you now, young lady," and she led me down a hall to the editor's office.

The instant I walked in the door, a panic seized me, and I forgot everything I'd intended to say!

There sat the man I took to be Mr. Kemble behind a big desk, looking up at me with a half gruff expression that said, *I don't know who you are or why you're here, but I'm busy. So get on with your business and say what you have to say before I throw you out!* Before he had a chance to say anything, all of a sudden I was talking, hardly knowing what was coming out of my mouth.

"Mr. Kemble," I said.

"That's right," answered the man.

I walked forward and stood in front of his desk.

"My name is—"

My throat went dry suddenly and I couldn't get out the words.

"I'm not going to hurt you, Miss . . . Miss whoever-you-are. You don't need to be afraid to tell me your name."

"That's just it, sir. When I tell you my name, you may say you never want to see me again."

"I doubt that. But come on—out with it. I haven't got all day."

I tried again. "My name is—*C.B. Hollister*. Corrie Belle Hollister.

"What? You're C.B. Hollister? I don't believe it!"

"I'm sorry, Mr. Kemble. I never meant to not be truthful
. . . it was just something that happened at first, and then I
never had the courage to say anything once you started calling
me *mister* in your letters."

I was shaking from nervousness and fear and from wondering what he would do. But at least I had said it.

"You're just a kid," he said at length. "And a girl, besides!"

"But I want to be a newspaper writer," I said, though my
voice was trembling. "I *am* sorry," I apologized again, "and
that's why I came here to see you, to tell you the truth about
who I was, and so that the rest of any articles I write can have
my full name on them, so that everybody else will know too."

Mr. Kemble leaned back in his chair, thinking for a moment.

"You came all the way to San Francisco for that?" he asked.
"Just to see me and set the record straight on this *C.B.* business?"

"Yes, sir."

"Hmm," he mumbled. "That shows some spunk—I like
that." He paused again. "But as to your doing any more writing
for the *Alta* . . . most of my reporters are older, and—"

"I'm nineteen," I said. "Halfway to being twenty."

He chuckled. "That's hardly old in this business!"

"You said folks liked reading what I wrote," I ventured
cautiously. "They didn't care how old I was . . . or that I was
a young lady instead of an old man."

He leaned forward and eyed me hard for a minute. Now I
was afraid I'd said too much!

All of a sudden he threw his head back and laughed. "You
do have spunk, young Miss Hollister! And you're not afraid to
say what's on your mind," he added more seriously, "or to
come a hundred and fifty miles to make something right, even
if it's for something you shouldn't have done in the first place.
I like that. Those are good qualities for a writer—spunk and
courage. So tell me, what's on your mind to write about now—

same kind of human interest stuff our former friend C.B. Hollister's been sending me?"

He smiled at his own humor, but I had my answer ready. I'd been thinking about it all the way from Sacramento.

"I want to write about the election in Miracle Springs," I said. "I'd like to write three articles on it."

He laughed again. "The election's being covered by more experienced reporters than there are gold miners in the Mother Lode. If Fremont ever so much as sets foot in the state, there will be a hundred writers waiting. You'd never get near him!"

"I don't mean that election," I said. "I mean the Miracle Springs election—for mayor."

"What could my readers possibly care about that?"

"They'd be interested because a woman is running against the town's banker. You've heard of Parrish Mine and Freight Company."

"That's right," he said. "Run by Almeda Parrish—fine woman, from what I hear. And you say *she's* running against the town banker?"

I nodded.

"What's his name?"

"Franklin Royce."

He let out a low whistle. "I've heard of him too. A slick operator, and with plenty of dough. And you think you can write something my readers will be interested in?"

"You mentioned your women readers liking my articles—don't you think they'll want to read about a businesswoman in politics?"

"Yeah, you're probably right," he said thoughtfully, nodding his head slowly. "The thing is unheard of—though everything's new in California these days."

After a minute of silence he went on. "Now you understand, Miss Hollister, that if I agree to print something of yours about this election—well, for that matter, anything of yours in the future—"

"Three stories on the election," I reminded him.

"Whatever—whether it's the Royce-Parrish story or something else—you understand that I can't pay you near what I did before. Women only fetch a third or a half a man's wages, and a girl who isn't even twenty yet . . . let me see—I doubt I'll be able to give you over a dollar an article."

A dollar! I shouted inside. Whether it was my mother Agatha Belle Hollister or my stepmother Almeda Parrish Hollister rising up inside me—or some of both of them!—what Pa called my Belle blood started to get riled. Why should the exact words that might have been worth three or four dollars a week ago be worth only *one* dollar now? Because he had found out that I was a lady instead of a man, and a young lady besides? It didn't seem at all fair!

But before either of us said another word, the door of Mr. Kemble's office opened behind me.

CHAPTER 25

A FAMILIAR FACE

Into the editor's office walked a tall young man, carrying a stack of papers. He wore a cap tilted to the right down over his forehead, which kept me from being able to see his eyes at first, though there was immediately something familiar about the way he walked and the few blond curls coming out from beneath his cap.

The instant he spoke I remembered the voice as if I had just heard it yesterday!

"Mr. Kemble," he said, "I've got those files you asked me to dig up on—"

He stopped, apparently just as surprised to see me as I was him.

"If I didn't know better . . ." he said, pausing to look me over from head to foot. I couldn't think of a single word to utter as I stood there, probably with my mouth hanging open.

"It *is* the girl from off in the backwoods gold country!" he finally exclaimed. "Are you still trying to get into the reporting game?"

"You two know each other, O'Flaridy?" asked a bewildered Mr. Kemble.

"We ran into each other a couple years back, though I can't remember your name," he added, looking again at me.

"Robin O'Flaridy, meet Corrie Belle Hollister," said Mr. Kemble.

"Hollister, that's it!" he said. "Miracle Springs, right?"

159

I smiled and nodded. "It looks as though you've moved up a few notches from delivering papers yourself," I said. "Are you really a reporter now?"

He shifted his weight onto his other foot, as if he was embarrassed for the editor to hear me ask the question, and the pause gave me a quick chance to assess the changes that had come over the first acquaintance I had ever made in San Francisco.

In the last three years, Robin O'Flaridy had shot up, and stood a good head taller than me. But he was still lean, with a smooth face and blond hair, though a bit darker than before. And his voice, though not boyish, was still high-pitched for a man. All that made it just as hard to tell his age as the first time I had seen him as a scrappy kid delivering papers and hanging around hotels. I figured him for twenty or twenty-one, and he certainly looked as at home and comfortable in the offices of the *Alta* as he had in the lobby of the Oriental Hotel. Maybe he hadn't been exaggerating as much as I thought back then about his association with the paper. He seemed every bit the newsman now.

"Of course I'm a reporter," he answered, a little defensively I thought. "I told you that back then."

"Don't listen to a word he tells you, Miss Hollister," laughed Mr. Kemble. "To hear him talk, you'd think the *Alta* couldn't possibly put out a single edition without him. But he does occasionally bring me something I can use."

Robin's neck reddened slightly. He tried to get the conversation off himself. "So I take it you're here because you still hope to write for a newspaper someday, eh? But I can tell you from experience, just being a pretty face won't get you anywhere with this editor!" He grinned and threw Mr. Kemble a wink.

"Now don't get too cocky, O'Flaridy!" said the editor. "Miss Hollister has already written several articles for us—a couple of them have appeared back East. You may have seen the name *C.B. Hollister*."

If Robin was surprised, even halfway impressed, he wasn't about to let it show.

"What do you know about that!" he said. "So you've moved up from that other rag from the sticks! Good going, Hollister!" He gave me a slap on the back.

Now I remembered what had so irritated me about Robin O'Flaridy before. I smiled, but my heart wasn't in it. My Belle blood was flowing again!

"Careful, O'Flaridy, she may be taking your job someday! I was just about to offer her three articles on an election they're having up her way," said Mr. Kemble. "That's besides the two I've already got in the files. Can't recall *you* ever bringing me good writing quite so fast as that." He was kidding Robin O'Flaridy, that much I could tell from his tone, but whether he was being serious about my writing or making fun of me— that I *couldn't* tell.

"Three articles, huh!" he said. "That *is* something! I guess I better get my pencil busy. I can't let some girl cub reporter from out in the hills of the Mother Lode show me up!"

He set the files on Mr. Kemble's desk and then turned to leave. "See you around, Hollister!"

"Well, I think that about concludes our business too," the editor said to me before O'Flaridy was even out the door. "A dollar an article, as agreed. When will I see the first piece?"

"Uh . . . in a week or two," I said, trying to get my mind back on what I had come for and off the surprise interruption by Robin O'Flaridy.

"That sounds fine."

Mr. Kemble stood up behind his desk and offered his hand. I shook it.

"Good day, Miss Hollister," he said.

I turned and left his office, my mind half numb from all that had gone on inside, part of me thinking of the things I had intended to say to Mr. Kemble but hadn't. The whole interview now seemed awkward, even though I had accomplished what I'd wanted—he now knew who I really was, and he had agreed to let me write about the election. But somehow I still felt unsettled inside.

"Hey, Hollister, where you staying?" said the familiar voice of Robin O'Flaridy from where he was leaning against the wall of the hallway, apparently waiting for me.

I told him, then began walking toward the door where I had entered the building. He pushed himself off the wall, skipped a couple of steps to catch up with me, then continued to walk alongside me.

"That older lady with you again?" he asked.

"No."

"You came to the big city alone, eh?"

"That's right."

"And how long you planning to be around?"

I said I didn't know. To be honest, I had thought about remaining for another day or two. It was such an adventure being there on my own, I wanted to see a little of the city. However, I wasn't so sure I wanted Robin O'Flaridy escorting me around—even with his blue eyes, blond curls, and air of confidence, as if he considered the whole city and everything in it his own personal domain. I suppose most nineteen-year-old girls would have been dazzled and flattered. But something about his attentions caused me to squirm.

He started in telling me all about his latest escapades as he moved closer to my side. I felt his hand slip through my arm. Immediately I knew my cheeks were turning red.

"Say, how about I come over to Miss Sandy Loyd Bean's Boarding House tonight," he said; "and you and me, we'll go out to dinner someplace, and then I'll show you San Francisco by night?"

We were just about to the door. He opened it for me with his free hand, then continued on outside with me.

"What do you say, Corrie?"

"I . . . I don't know—I'd made plans to eat with Miss Bean. I told her I'd be back for dinner. Besides, I couldn't possibly go out with you—alone!"

"Aw, forget Miss Bean. You can eat a home-cooked meal anytime! And who needs a chaperon? Who'd ever know about it, anyway?" He laughed. "When else are you going to have an invitation to go out to a San Francisco restaurant with one of the city's well-known journalists? You're a good-looking girl and I'm not too bad-looking a fella, and it just seems right that we ought to spend some time together, you being here alone like you are. Especially with us both in the same profession now. What harm could there be in one evening of fun?"

"I really don't think I ought—"

"Listen," he said, cutting me off as I hailed a horse-drawn cab for myself from the corner of the block, "you talk to your Sandy Bean and put your mind at ease. I know she won't mind your not being there once you explain that you ran into an old friend who invited you out for the evening. I'll be by at seven o'clock."

Without giving me an opportunity to say anything further, he took my hand, helped me up onto the cab seat, gave the cab driver fifty cents and told him where to take me, then turned back toward me, smiled, tipped his cap, and as the horse's hoofs clopped off, said, "See you tonight!" He turned and pranced off down the street, obviously pleased with himself.

CHAPTER 26

WHAT TO DO?

I tried to see some of the city during the afternoon, and even took a cab out to Point Lobos where Miss Bean told me the Pacific Mail steamship was due to reach the Bay with letters and newspapers from the East. But all day I was distracted by thoughts of Robin T. O'Flaridy! There was such a battle going on inside my head that I could hardly enjoy myself.

One side of me kept thinking that I ought to throw caution to the wind and go with him. I imagined putting on my nice cream dress with the pink lace around it. He was a decent-looking young man—he'd been right about that. And we were both interested in newspapers and writing. And how many opportunities was I going to have like this? He had talked about showing me the town and it was bound to be fun.

I could hardly believe that the thought of marriage would cross my mind at a time like this! I'd never in my life thought *seriously* of getting married! But now all at once I couldn't keep the idea from entering my brain. I always figured Ma was right about me not being the kind of girl that fellas would stand in line to marry. Maybe I ought to take the few opportunities that come along and not let them pass by.

Why shouldn't I go with Robin? I might have a good time, and he probably wasn't such a bad fellow. It might be years before another young man took an interest in me. And even if he wasn't a Christian, maybe I could do him some good, or even talk to him about some of the things Mrs. Parrish and I talked about.

But the other side of me said something entirely different. I couldn't help thinking of the people who mattered to me, and what they might think. What if I did go out to dinner with him? Would I be proud to tell Almeda or would I be embarrassed? I couldn't help wondering if Robin T. O'Flaridy was the kind of person I *wanted* her to know I had been with. Was he a good person, the kind of young man she would respect and admire? And what would Jesus think to see me alone with someone I hardly knew?

The more I thought on it, the more doubts I had about what they might think. If Mrs. Parrish walked in on us together at some fancy restaurant, I *would* be embarrassed. He wasn't her kind of person—unselfish, kind, and thoughtful of others. In fact, he'd always struck me as a little egotistical and conniving. That certainly wasn't the sort of person I wanted to marry, if I ever *did* get married. If I didn't think enough of him to figure he was worth marrying, and if I would have been embarrassed to have Almeda see me with him, then what possible reason could I have for accepting his invitation? To accept would not be true to what I was thinking and feeling inside. Something about him made me very uneasy.

When Mrs. Parrish and I had first come to San Francisco, the desk clerk had said, "Nobody even knows where the boy lives. He's always on the street looking for some likely target to fleece." Robin just delivered papers, but he had told me he was a reporter. He wasn't a very honest person.

Robin T. O'Flaridy and I were different sorts of people. I couldn't believe he was a very godly young man. What would he say if I told him about how I prayed every day to obey God more and to be true?

He'd probably laugh. Or if he didn't laugh, at least he'd probably make some comment like, "Well, all that religious stuff is okay for girls and women. But I'm a man and I can make it just fine on my own without all that stuff about God."

Was that someone I wanted to spend time with, see San Francisco with? We'd be talking together and smiling and trying to have a good time, but our *real* selves would be miles apart. That didn't seem right, didn't seem honest or truthful, didn't seem any way to have a friendship between a young man and a young woman—pretending on the surface to be people we really weren't. There was really no decision to make. I couldn't even say I actually wanted to be with him. To go with him would be compromising my convictions.

By the time evening came, I had made up my mind.

He came to the door promptly at seven. I heard the knock, and my stomach lurched with a queasy feeling. I said a quick prayer as I went to answer it.

"You ready?" he asked. He stood there dressed up in a coat and tie, flowers in his hand. "These are for you," he said, holding them out toward me.

A giant knot suddenly tightened in my stomach. This was awful! A hundred doubts shot through my mind about the decision I had come to earlier. Maybe I had completely misjudged him. He probably wasn't such a bad young man after all! Yet in spite of my last-minute misgivings, I found coming out of my mouth the words I had been practicing to myself for the last hour:

"I . . . I've decided . . ." I stammered.

"Decided? Decided what?"

"I've decided that I really shouldn't go," I finally blurted out. "I'm . . . I'm very sorry."

He stood staring at me blankly, as if he hadn't heard.

"I don't believe it," he said at last. "You can't be serious?" I could see him getting angry.

"I'm really sorry. I—I—just feel I shouldn't . . . And I never really said I would go with you."

"But I had so much planned for us. I've dressed up and brought you flowers," he said, glancing at the bouquet still in his hand. "I just can't believe you'd do this to me!"

I didn't know what to say. I felt dreadful.

He just stood there staring at me, his face gradually filling with color—not the red of embarrassment, but of anger.

"Well then, enjoy your ridiculous meal in this dull boardinghouse, and your evening alone! You'll probably sit in your room reading some boring book when you could have been having the time of your life out in the city!"

With a last spiteful, glaring look, he spun around and started to leave. Then he noticed the flowers in his hand. With an angry motion, he threw them into the dirt in the street. Then he looked back at the door.

"But just don't you come crawling to me when you're a lonely old spinster!" he said vengefully. "Or when you realize you can't make it as a reporter without the help of people like me. Robin T. O'Flaridy doesn't get made a fool of twice!"

He strode off down the street with long steps, and never looked back.

I shut the door slowly and turned back into the boarding-house. Then I ran back up to my room and lay down on the bed and started to cry. All I could think was how hard it had been to refuse him when I saw his face so alive with expectation. I had almost given in and walked out the door with him. Yet even as I lay there crying, I knew that something inside me had been strengthened, and that I would look back on this moment as one more marker on the road of my spiritual life.

Robin was right. I did spend the rest of the evening alone in my room, mostly reading. I'd brought along a book of Mr. Fremont's about his exploration of Oregon and Northern California in 1843–44. Since he was running for President, I was interested in his early years in the West.

My adventure in San Francisco had lost its excitement. I had never in my life felt so lonely and far away from everybody I loved. But still I knew I'd done the right thing.

CHAPTER 27

THE CAMPAIGN HEATS UP

I tried hard to enjoy the city the next day. Miss Bean told me some things I ought to see, and I walked around a little, and took one cab. But I was afraid I'd run into Robin O'Flaridy around every corner. So it was with a great sigh of relief that I boarded the steamer the next morning back to Sacramento. And I was so glad to see Zack and Little Wolf later that afternoon that I gave them bigger hugs than I ever had before.

"What's that for?" asked an embarrassed Zack as he half returned my embrace.

"Just to remind me how much I love you," I answered. He was satisfied, in the boyish sort of way that avoids talking about such things, and I wasn't inclined to explain any further.

Little Wolf hugged me back, smiled, and pretended to give my face a little slap. Even though we were two days from Miracle Springs, I already felt like I was home! Without people to love, you can get awfully lonely in a big hurry!

Back in Miracle, the mayor's campaign had started to heat up. While I had been gone, Almeda had gotten the box of completed handbills back from the printer in Sacramento—one thousand copies printed on bright colored paper. Already Tad and Becky and Emily had been putting them around town, and Almeda had begun to call on some of the leading townsfolk, both to take them a handbill and to explain what she was doing and why. With the excitement over seeing the handbill, and then telling Pa and Almeda about my trip and the incident with

168

Robin O'Flaridy, it was late in the evening before I remembered my most important news of all.

"But guess what?" I said. "Mr. Kemble said he'd print three articles on the election if I'd write them!"

"The state election?"

"No—Miracle Springs . . . you and Mr. Royce."

"That is something—and *three*! My goodness, you *are* turning into a genuine newswoman, Corrie!"

"For pay?" asked Pa.

"More or less," I answered. "A dollar each."

"Two dollars!" exclaimed Almeda. "They paid you four times that just two weeks ago for that countryside article."

"That was before he found out I was a girl."

"Why—why, that is the most despicable, low—"

"Now hold on to your breeches, Almeda," said Pa. "Don't get all riled. You know how the world is. If Corrie's gonna try to do a man's job, she's gonna have to expect this kind—"

"A man's job! Drummond Hollister, not you too! Corrie can write just as well as any man her age, and better than some a lot older, and there's no reason she shouldn't be paid according to her ability."

"Maybe you're right, but then I figure that's Corrie's decision, not yours or mine. And if she doesn't want to write an article for a measly eight bits, she don't have to. And if she does, then it ain't nothing for you or I to stick our noses into."

Pa's practicality silenced Almeda for a minute, then she smiled broadly. "Well it's a start, Corrie." She paused. "I'm really proud of you. Proud of your courage in standing up to a powerful man like Mr. Kemble, but even more proud of your honesty, your integrity." She reached over and squeezed my hand. "Proud to have a young woman like you as my daughter."

I thanked her, inside thinking how much I would like to have known what Robin O'Flaridy made for each of *his* articles.

With the handbill circulating and Almeda making visits to people, the whole feeling of the mayor's campaign changed. People had been talking earlier, but I think it was mostly from interest's sake, almost curiosity. Just the fact that Miracle Springs was going to have an election was an event in itself. Having two of the town's most well-known people in it against each other made it all the more a topic of interest and conversation.

But now the initial novelty had worn off, and people were starting to ask more serious questions about the election. Which one of the two, Royce or Hollister, would actually make the best mayor? Who would do the most for Miracle Springs?

Almeda's visits and the handbill got people to thinking about more than they had at first, and wondering if maybe she just *might* be a better person to vote for than the banker. But she *was* a woman, and having a woman for mayor just wasn't done. And Royce was not only a man—he was the banker, and he still had financial power in one way or another over just about everybody around Miracle.

After several days Mr. Royce made another call at the freight office. This time none of us had seen him coming down the street, so when he walked in it took us by surprise.

"Almeda," he said, "I'd like to talk with you for a minute."

His voice was more serious than the last time he'd come into the office. He was trying to smile as he said the words, but you could tell he had more than just lighthearted conversation in his thoughts.

"Certainly. What is on your mind, Franklin?"

"In private?" he suggested.

Almeda nodded, then led him around the counter and into her small office. But when they went inside she made no attempt to close the door, and he did not particularly keep his voice down.

There was a pause while they both sat down. Mr. Ashton and I looked at each other sort of apprehensively and kept about our work as quietly as we could.

"Are you really sure you want to do this, Almeda?" asked Royce.

"Do what—you mean the election?"

"Yes, of course that's what I mean. What's the purpose?

You're doing nothing but getting people stirred up and confused. And what good can it possibly do in the end?"

"The last time you were in, Franklin, you welcomed me to the race and said you congratulated my intrepid decision, as I believe you so eloquently phrased it." I could almost see Almeda smiling faintly as she said the words.

"That was then," he replied, a little quickly. "I had no idea you were going to take the thing so seriously. I thought perhaps it was a ploy to help your sagging business."

"My business is not sagging. We are managing just fine."

"Nevertheless, you have taken it beyond the casual point, Almeda, and I simply suggest that it is time you paused to consider the implications. People are talking and, quite frankly, some of the talk has negative features to it that are not going to help *my* reputation and business if they persist."

"And therefore you want me to withdraw?" asked Almeda. She wasn't smiling now, that much I knew.

"Be reasonable, Almeda," Mr. Royce said. "You've had the excitement of the campaign. You've thrust yourself into the center of attention. People respect you. It cannot help but heighten your image as a businesswoman. But now it's time for you to face the realistic facts. No town is going to elect a woman mayor, and the longer you continue, the more the potential damage to *my* reputation and *my* business. And if I'm going to be the next mayor of Miracle Springs, both the bank and my image in the people's thoughts need to be solid. And all this is not to mention the lasting impression your loss will leave. Right now you are riding high in the public mind. But after the election, your image, and perhaps even the reputation of your business itself, will be tarnished and you will be seen as a loser. All I'm attempting to convey to you in the most reasonable manner I can—from one business person to another, from one *friend* to another—is that it is time you stand aside and let Miracle Springs move forward without all this dissention and strife your being part of the election is causing—for your own good, Almeda."

A long silence followed.

"So then, Franklin, you consider the outcome of the election a foregone conclusion?" said Almeda at length.

"I didn't think there was ever any doubt about that," said Mr. Royce, with the hint of a laugh.

"Maybe not as far as you're concerned," replied Almeda. "But I didn't join this race to help my business or my reputation, as you call it, or anything else. I joined it to make every effort to win."

"Surely you can't be serious?" Royce sounded genuinely surprised.

"Of course I'm serious. I wouldn't do something of this magnitude for frivolous or self-seeking motives. If you think I care about what people think of me, Franklin, then you do not know me very well."

There was another pause.

"Well, if you're determined to see it out to the bitter end," Mr. Royce finally said, "I wish you'd at least discontinue the distribution of this brochure of yours, and visiting people—a good many of them my friends, Almeda—and stirring everybody up and spreading talk about me that isn't true."

"Franklin, I have not said a single word about you to a soul! I'm surprised you would think I would stoop to such measures."

"People *are* talking, Almeda. How can it be from anything other than your stirring them up against me?"

"I tell you, I am doing no such thing. I have never even hinted anything about you. I have only been talking to people about what I feel I would be able to offer Miracle Springs as its mayor."

After the pause which followed, Mr. Royce's tone cooled. He apparently realized he was not going to dissuade Almeda from anything she had her mind made up on.

"You can't win, Almeda," he said. "The thing's simply impossible."

"We'll see," she replied.

"You're wasting time and money."

"You may be right."

"You're determined to go ahead with it?"

"I am."

"Will you stop making calls on my friends and customers?"

"They are my friends, too, Franklin. You are free to call on them yourself."

"In other words, you will not stop?"

"No."

"Will you withdraw the brochure?"

"I will not. Again, Franklin, you are free to circulate one of your own."

The next sound was that of Mr. Royce's chair scooting back on the wood floor as he rose to his feet. "At least it appears we understand each other," he said.

"So it would appear," repeated Almeda.

"Good day, Mrs. Hollister," said the banker, and the next moment he reappeared from the office and walked briskly to the street door and out, not acknowledging me or Mr. Ashton in any way as he passed. We both pretended to be busy with the papers and files in front of us.

Two or three minutes later Almeda came out of the office. Her face was red with anger.

"That pompous, egotistical man!" was all she could say before she started sputtering and pacing around the office like a caged animal. "The nerve . . . to say that I stood no chance whatsoever! To ask me to withdraw from the race, because— because of his reputation! *His* reputation—ha! Calls on his *friends*! I doubt he even has that many friends around town— everyone is too afraid of him! What harm could *I* do *his* reputation!"

She walked around the office another time or two, then burst out again:

"I've got to get out of here!" She looked at the two of us. "I'm going for a ride. I'll be back in about an hour."

With that she left the room with as much grace as she could manage. When Mr. Ashton and I heard a yell and hoofbeats galloping away down the street a couple minutes later, we looked at each other and laughed. It was plain her horse was in for a time of it!

Almeda didn't pull out of the mayor's race, which continued to get livelier and livelier as we got into the month of August.

Mr. Royce paid no more visits to the Parrish Mine and Freight Company office.

CHAPTER 28

I TRY MY HAND AT
SOMETHING NEW

I wanted to get right to work on my first article about the election. It was early August, and there were only about thirteen weeks to go.

I began by just trying to tell the five *w's* of the situation. I figured the first article needed to be a straight "news" kind of story that told folks about the election and what was unusual about it. Then for the next two I'd maybe try to write what Mr. Kemble called "human interest" things about the election and the two candidates, and maybe even about Miracle Springs itself.

I started off writing down the facts like I had for the poster about Ulysses S. Grant that Almeda had put up.

> The mining town of Miracle Springs, sixty-five miles northeast of Sacramento, will hold its first mayor's election in November of this year. The local election will be held at the same time as the general election for President and other offices. But what has the people of Miracle Springs all roused up isn't just that they're having their first election, but *who's* running in it!

Then I talked about Mr. Royce and Almeda being two of the town's leading citizens, about the bank and the Freight Company and how everyone for miles around depended on both of them for different parts of their livelihoods. But of course the fact of Almeda being a woman couldn't help but be

175

the main thing that would make folks interested in the election—and in my articles.

> The Miracle Springs mayor's election is one of the most unusual elections in all of California this year because a woman, who herself cannot even vote, is running against one of the wealthiest and most powerful men in the community. It is not known whether a woman has ever before run for such a high position as mayor in the United States, but Mrs. Hollister must certainly be considered one of the first. One might say she is a pioneer in a state full of pioneers. And if she wins, the rest of the state—if not the entire country—will be watching her, just as it is now watching the most famous Californian of all, John Charles Fremont.

I was planning to write a little bit about both of their businesses and how they both came to Miracle Springs, and then finish off the article with the last of the *w's*—a quote from both Mr. Royce and Almeda about "why" each had decided to run for mayor.

But before I got quite finished with the first article, an idea came to me that I just couldn't wait to get started on. I started putting together what I'd need for the second article, and so I got delayed a while getting the first one finished and in the mail to Mr. Kemble.

My idea was this: I'd go around to people around Miracle Springs, in private without either Mr. Royce or Almeda knowing what I was doing, and I'd ask them questions about what they thought of the election. I'd ask them their reaction to the two candidates, about what things would probably decide who they voted for, about whether they had business dealings with either candidate, and what difference that made. I would ask what they thought a mayor of Miracle Springs ought to do, what they thought was going to be the future of the community, what they themselves were most concerned about. I might even ask them who they planned to vote for.

It was such an exciting idea, I could hardly wait to get started!

If I could, I would get quotes, but if people wanted me not

to use their names, I would promise not to. I'd just tell everyone I wanted to get an idea how the whole town and its people were feeling about the election but without giving away any secrets or making it awkward for anyone.

Mostly, since they were the ones who could vote, I figured I'd talk to all the men I knew, and then to those I didn't know. And then another idea came to me! I could interview women too. Even though they couldn't vote, it would be interesting to get their opinions—especially since, according to Mr. Kemble's letter, it was the women readers of the paper who liked the kinds of things I had been writing. And I could ask the men (the married ones, at least!) if they might vote any different on account of what their wives thought.

What a great "human interest" article I could write if the women all put enough pressure on their husbands that they actually voted for Almeda! Even though the women couldn't vote, might it be possible that they could still influence the outcome? Or were there even enough women around Miracle Springs to make a difference? If the women started putting that kind of pressure on their husbands, what might the unmarried men do? There were still more unmarried men around than families. And what might Mr. Royce do?

I didn't know the answers to all my own questions. In fact, I kept thinking up new questions. And I figured the only way to find out some of these things was to get out and start talking to people and getting their ideas.

This would make a great article! It'd show Mr. Kemble I could write an article of news *and* human interest. And one worth more than $1!

The first people I talked to weren't the kind you could get a fair opinion from—they were all people who were friends of Almeda's—Pa, Uncle Nick, Katie, Mr. Ashton, Marcus Weber. But I had to begin someplace, so those were the folks I started with. I hadn't ever done anything quite like this before, so I had to learn how to ask questions and write down what people told me.

Gradually I started to talk to other people—the Shaws and

Hermon Stansberry gave me some interesting ideas, so did Mrs. DeWater, though her husband didn't say much. Rev. Rutledge was visiting Mr. and Miss Stansberry when I called on them, and so I got to talk to all three of them at once. The minister tried to be gracious toward both sides. Though obviously he had always felt fondly toward Almeda, he said some nice things about Mr. Royce too. Miss Stansberry took the woman's point of view completely, just like Katie had.

So far most of the people I'd talked to favored Almeda. But I knew to be fair I had to get the opinions of Mr. Royce's friends too. It would probably be harder than I thought to write an article that fairly represented both sides and all the people in the town!

But even as I interviewed people, I knew I had to get my first article finished up and in the mail. I went back to it, added the few parts that had been missing, rewrote it all, and then put it in the mail to Mr. Kemble. Then I got right back to visiting people, asking them questions, and writing down as much as I could about what they thought.

CHAPTER 29

I GET ANGRY

By this time there were daily stage runs from Sacramento up the valley and into the foothills. Mail usually took two or three days from Miracle Springs to San Francisco. And we'd get San Francisco newspapers most of time just two days late. They'd get the issue right off to Sacramento on the morning steamer up the river, or across the Bay and onto the train line that was now running between the two cities. Then the next day the papers would be taken by stage up the main routes to the north, which usually took a day and a half by the time it reached Miracle.

Almeda had always gotten the newspapers from Sacramento and San Francisco, besides Mr. Singleton's *Gazette*. But now that I was writing for them, I was more interested than I used to be, and the minute the stagecoach arrived in town at between two and four every afternoon, I'd be out of the office and on my way over to the depot to get whatever mail there was for Parrish Freight *and* our newspapers. On most days I spent the next ten or fifteen minutes looking over the paper, seeing what other reporters were writing about, getting ideas, reading some of the news. Then usually at night Pa and Almeda and I would pass the paper around until we all three had read every word.

The day of August 8 is a day I will always remember. At about four-thirty in the afternoon, I was sitting down in the freight office, scanning through the copy of the *Alta* that had

179

arrived about an hour before on the stage. Mostly it was full of election news. There were quotes from a speech Mr. Buchanan had made in Philadelphia, and a lot about Mr. Fremont, including two long editorials. He had been campaigning all through the East, but news of his travels and the issues surrounding the election continued to make daily news in California. The slavery situation, events in Kansas, the question of Fremont's religion had all contributed to heated debate and discussion, as well as legal battles involving title to Fremont's Mariposa estate down in the foothills east of Merced. There was a short article entitled "Fremont Estate Embroiled in Campaign Controversy," though I didn't stop to take time to read it.

A few moments later my eyes fell on a small article on the bottom of page four. When I read the caption, my pulse quickened. There was no way they could have gotten my article into print this soon, yet there were the words in bold black type: "Woman Pioneer Seeks Office in State of Pioneers."

Hastily my eyes found the small print of the article and began to read:

> The place is Miracle Springs, foothills mining town some seventy miles north of Sacramento on a tributary of the Yuba River. The occasion: an election for mayor between two of the area's most prominent citizens and members of the business community—one, the town's only banker; the other, the owner of one of the largest mining supply and freight companies in the northern foothills.
>
> What makes this an election that many observers will be watching with interest, however, is that it pits a woman—who cannot even vote in the election—against a man of great influence in the community.

I couldn't believe it! This wasn't my article, but it might as well have been—all the information was the same!

With my heart pounding, I read on:

> According to research done by this reporter, the Miracle Springs mayor's race marks one of the very few times a woman has sought higher public office in these United States, and

never has a woman held office west of the plains. It should prove a groundbreaking election insofar as the future of this great state of California is concerned.

Almeda Parrish Hollister, owner of Parrish Mine and Freight Company and recently married to one of the town's miners, has thrown her hat into the ring against Franklin Royce, Miracle Springs' only banker and financier.

There were three more paragraphs telling a little about Miracle Springs itself, and then a brief background of Mr. Royce and Almeda and their businesses and how they had come to California, with the final sentences: "Experts interviewed for the purpose of this article give Mrs. Hollister no chance to win the election. They say that besides the disadvantage of being a woman, she has taken on a man owed too many favors by too many people. But just the fact that she is in the race is of interest in its own right."

If those words weren't enough to make me downright furious, those immediately below them were:

Reported by Robin T. O'Flaridy, staff reporter for the California Alta.

I threw the paper down and jumped to my feet. How could he do this to me? The rat!

And what about Mr. Kemble? He had no right! Why, they'd stolen my ideas, my words! And if Mr. Kemble wasn't in on it, how did Robin ever get his hands on my article in the first place? They must have done it together! It wasn't so much losing the dollar. They'd taken *my* idea—and even used some of my exact words. And then, most of all, they put Robin's name under them!

I was so angry I would have clobbered Robin if he had been there! I knew why he'd done it. He wanted to get even with me for the incident over the dinner and the flowers. He was paying me back for making him feel foolish.

Well, Mr. O'Flaridy, I thought to myself, thinking up all kinds of things I could do to *him* in return to get revenge, *we'll just see who gets the last laugh!*

I fumed around the streets of town, my brain reeling back

and forth, not even stopping to think about whether my anger was right or wrong, not once thinking about God or what he might think. All I could think about was Robin O'Flaridy and how I could fix him!

And what made it even worse was that his article was *better* than mine. I couldn't stand to admit it, but he was a better writer!

I don't know how I spent the rest of the day. I think I walked around town a while longer—but for sure *this* walk wasn't one I spent in prayer! I must have gone back to the office, but whether I did any more work, I can't remember. I was just so mad!

By evening I had cooled down. In fact, I was embarrassed at myself and had to go outside for a while alone to talk to God a little about it. I told him I was sorry for getting so angry, because I knew it wasn't right. I'd been thinking so much recently on being true and everything that *truth* involved. I suppose that's what vexed me so much about what they had done—that they weren't being truthful at all, not to the people reading their paper or to me. But after a while I realized I had no business thinking about whether *other* people were truthful or not. There was only one person I had the right to criticize for not being truthful, and that was me. It was none of my affair what Robin O'Flaridy did about living honestly and doing things right. But what I did—that *was* my affair!

I walked around a while and thought and prayed. But when I went back inside I still didn't have everything figured out.

We talked about it, and Pa said something that helped me see a little more inside the situation. I had just told him and Almeda about realizing that I had to take care of myself and whether I did the right thing, rather than criticizing others for what they did.

"That's right, Corrie," Pa said. "One of the biggest things about growing up is to take responsibility for yourself without forever blaming other folks for everything that you don't like. That's something me and your Uncle Nick's had to learn—and sometimes the hard way. It still ain't easy for Nick, who gets to blaming your grandpa for things he done. And I used to blame Nick for things that I later had to face up to myself. Blame's a terrible thing, Corrie. A mind that's set to blame other folks all the time is eventually gonna destroy any chance of setting things right, 'cause all it's doing is looking at everything that's wrong."

He stopped for a minute and gave the log in the fireplace a poke with a stick.

"But on the other hand, Corrie, if you're gonna write for this man Kemble, and you're gonna work for his newspaper, then you gotta be able to trust him, and you gotta know where you stand. It's a sight different than blaming a fella when you try to get your business dealings straight so you know what's up and what's down. If I'm gonna have some kind of a deal going with your uncle or Alkali or if I walk into Royce's bank and say I want to borrow some money, then there ain't nothing wrong with saying, 'Now, Nick, here's what you gotta do, and here's what I gotta do, and since we're both men of our word, then we'll do what we say. Then we shake hands and agree on it, and that's that. Or I might say, 'Now, Mr. Royce, I don't exactly like you, but I want to borrow some money. How much'll it cost?' And then he might say, 'I don't like you either, Hollister, and I don't like your wife running for mayor against me, but if you want to borrow money, it'll cost you 6 percent.' Then if it's agreeable, we shake hands and that's the deal. We don't have to like each other, but everybody's got to know where everybody else stands, otherwise you can't do business together."

He stopped, and I waited for more. But he was finished.

"Is that all, Pa?" I asked. "What is it you think I ought to do now?"

Almeda, who had been listening to everything, laughed.

"In his wonderful roundabout way," she said, "I think your father's been trying to tell you that even though you may have to get over your anger and blaming, you still have to find out where you stand and why they did what they did. Otherwise, how can you go on writing for the *Alta*?"

"Maybe it ain't as bad as it looks, Corrie," added Pa. "Are you sure it's your article?"

"Some of the exact words, Pa. I told you about the pioneer in a state full of pioneers."

"And you and Kemble had a deal for the article."

"Well, we didn't shake hands that I can remember," I said, "but he told me he'd pay me a dollar each for three articles on the election."

Pa shrugged, and nodded his head thoughtfully.

"It sounds to me, Corrie Belle, reporter of the Mother Lode, that you need to get some things straight with your editor," said Almeda.

I gazed into her earnest face, and realized she was right. I let out a deep sigh, then got up and went into my room, where I sat down and immediately began a letter to San Francisco.

"Dear Mr. Kemble," I began. "I have to admit I was given a considerable surprise when I opened the copy of the *Alta* that arrived in Miracle Springs this afternoon. . . ."

I then went on to ask all the questions that were on my mind, as nicely as I could, though I did ask him right out if he'd let Robin put his name on my article—and if not, then how was it that I found some of my very words appearing in the paper?

It was a long letter, but I finally got everything said I wanted to say. Once I'd done it I felt a lot better. For a writer, getting your thoughts said to *somebody*—even if it's just on paper—is always a great feeling of relief. I wondered if I ought to send it at all—this might be the last I'd ever hear from Mr. Kemble. But like Pa said, I had to know how things stood if I wanted to keep having dealings with him.

The letter went south on the next morning's stage.

CHAPTER 30

MR. KEMBLE'S REPLY

The next five days were torture!

I knew I couldn't possibly hear anything back from Mr. Kemble for at least six days, yet even on the fifth day I couldn't help being there to meet the stage and frantically looking through the mail.

During that time I must have wished I had the letter back a thousand times. *What an idiot I was!* I kept saying to myself. *He's never going to print another thing I write! He's never going to even answer my letter!*

But that didn't keep me from meeting the stage every day.

I tried to do my work and to keep up with my interviews about the election just in case I got another chance with the series. But I was so distracted I finally just gave up.

On the eighth day, the seventeenth of August, there among the rest of the mail was an envelope with the return address: The California *Alta,* Montgomery Street, San Francisco, California.

I grabbed it and ran off down the street. I had to be alone. I was so afraid of what might be inside that envelope!

Finally I wound up inside the livery of the Freight Company, up in the loft. No one was around, and the silence and smells calmed me down like they always did. At home the barn was still one of my favorite places.

I took several deep breaths, then looked down at the envelope in my hands. My fingers were shaking. My whole future as a writer might be at stake. It might even be over already.

Finally I scratched off an edge of the stuck-down part, then jammed a finger through and tore the top off the envelope. Then I reached inside with two fingers and pulled out the letter, unfolded it, and began to read:

Dear Miss Hollister,

Your letter raises some interesting questions.

First, you said you thought we had a deal about you writing on the Miracle Springs election. But we had no such "deal." I said I'd pay you a buck a piece *if* you sent me something acceptable. But at the time in question I hadn't seen a word from you yet. And time was wasting! We are a *news*paper. People buy the *Alta* to read news.

In the meantime, O'Flaridy came to me with a legitimate news article. He'd researched it in our files and the limited library we have here at the *Alta* and it was a decently done bit of writing. What am I to do, turn it down? I'm an editor, he's a reporter; he brought me news, I printed the story. It's as simple as that.

Face it, Miss Hollister, he scooped you on this one. You may not like it. Maybe it doesn't seem fair. But then nobody ever accused the newspaper business of being fair in the first place. And maybe that's why you don't see too many female reporters. It's a tough business, and the reporter who gets the goods gets published. There's no place in this business for feminine emotions and for getting your feelings hurt. Talk is cheap. If you don't deliver, you get left holding the paper and reading it, while somebody else does the writing and reporting.

Now as to your chief complaint, the O'Flaridy article was set to go before I received yours in the mail. He did not take a word of yours. You can trust me on that. I would never condone such a thing. If I'm tough, you'll also find me a fair man. The title for his piece was taken from your words. That was my doing. It was a clever phrase that caught my eye and I would have written you acknowledging the fact except that your letter beat me to it. I apologize if I overstepped my bounds. I will make it up to you in the future.

As to your question about pay, I gave O'Flaridy $4 for the

article. It was solid news, and before you think of complaining, remember that he's a young man with plenty of experience that you don't have. That's why he's on our staff and why I offer him a bonus incentive like this one for bringing me something in addition to his regular assignments. If you think it's unfair, remember, this is a man's business. If you don't like the offers I make to you, then take your writing elsewhere.

Now to something more serious on my side. Given the false impression you gave initially over the whole business about the *C.B.* name, I do not feel that the payment I offered you is unfair, since you are a woman. But it does not seem you have learned your lesson about false impressions! Robin tells me this woman running for mayor is no longer Mrs. *Parrish* as you told me, but rather Mrs. *Hollister*, and none other than your own stepmother. I must tell you, Miss Hollister, I was highly annoyed when I learned that fact. You should have been clear on that point up front. It could look like you were attempting to further the campaign of your stepmother rather than to carry out objective news writing. That fact did, I must confess, contribute to my decision to run Robin's story.

We have a term in this business called "conflict of interest," and it looks to me as if you have landed yourself squarely in the middle of it. How do you possibly expect to remain objective and unbiased in writing about an election of which you are such an intrinsic part?

My first inclination was to withdraw any and all commitments and cancel all plans to publish anything else of yours, including the two prior ones I am still holding. But upon further thought I realized you may not have intentionally tried to deceive me. Thus, I have decided to keep an open mind, and if you present me with anything publishable on the election, I will run it as per our one dollar per article arrangement. Given the circumstances, I do not feel obliged to hold to our two-dollar "deal." I originally offered you one dollar, and one dollar it will be. But it will have to be well-done and objective, or I will have no choice but to send it back to you.

The two previous articles will also be run at payment of $1 each rather than the $4 stated originally. Under the circumstances, I think that is more than generous. The article received last week concerning the Royce-Hollister election, I will obviously not be able to use.

I remain, Miss Hollister, sincerely yours,

Edward Kemble

By the time I was finished reading, I was crying. Part of me couldn't help but be outraged at Robin for "scooping" me, as Mr. Kemble had called it. He'd done it on purpose, just to spite me—I knew that. And I was angry at Mr. Kemble for talking down at me about my "feminine emotions" and my "hurt feelings." No, it didn't seem fair that Robin would get $4 and I only $1! The whole thing wasn't fair!

But then my logical mind reminded me that Robin's article *was* better than mine had been. That made me mad all over again—but mad at myself, mad for being so stupid as to think I could be a writer.

I was no writer! My writing was nothing compared to everything else in the *Alta*! A dollar was too much to pay for my writing.

I thought about all the rest Mr. Kemble had said. I hadn't meant to hold back the truth about Almeda. It just never came up about our being related. I'd never even thought about what he called a "conflict of interest." That made me mad all over again. Mad at myself.

I *had* made a mistake! I hadn't told him the complete truth. Maybe it hadn't been on purpose, but what difference did that make? Why should he trust me after twice giving him the wrong impression?

I sat and cried for a long time—sad, angry, disappointed, hurt, and irritated at myself. I couldn't help but feel like a complete fool. I had wanted to be a writer, and now I realized I wasn't fooling anyone.

For years I have kept Mr. Kemble's letter. Every once in a while I get it out and read it again, because in a lot of ways—though I don't think he intended it necessarily—Mr. Kemble's words helped me in the growing-up process. Writing the letter to him had forced me to face a situation squarely. And his reply helped me to see for the first time what was involved in being part of the newspaper business. Although I didn't want to admit it, Mr. Kemble was right—it *was* a tough business.

It was time I gave it up and tried to get on to doing something else with the rest of my life.

CHAPTER 31

"HOW BAD DO YOU WANT IT?"

I moped around for a few days, keeping mostly to myself. I didn't even talk to Almeda or Pa. I was too dejected and defeated to want to talk about it.

They gave me room to wallow around in my self-pity for a while. But then eventually they both began to try to encourage me out of my despondency. When you're in one of those holes where you feel everything in your life has failed, part of you doesn't even want to get out of the hole you've dug for yourself. Strange as it seems, you almost enjoy feeling sorry for yourself.

But Pa and Almeda wouldn't let me do that.

"Ain't it about time you got back to your article writing?" Pa asked me the second evening after I'd got the letter.

I shrugged and said I didn't know if I'd do any more articles.

"What?" he exclaimed. "This from my daughter who wants to be a newspaper reporter more than anything? What're you talking about, girl?"

Finally I showed them the letter.

They both read it quietly and seriously, and neither of them said much else that night. But over the next couple of days both Pa and Almeda found a time to be alone with me.

"There's times when a body's just gotta force himself to keep going," Pa told me, "even though maybe inside everything's screaming at him to do something else. If something's the right thing to do, then you just gotta do it."

190

He looked at me carefully. "You want to keep writing, don't you?" he said.

"Of course I do, Pa. But everything Mr. Kemble said is true. And besides, my writing is terrible, and he doesn't think I was honest with him."

"But it's something you still want to do?"

"Yes."

"Then how else you figure on gettin' any better at it if you don't do it? And how you figure on gettin' Kemble to trust you if you don't keep going to him and writing for him and showing him he *can* trust you? Ain't no other way but to keep at it."

"I just don't know how I can, Pa, after that letter of his."

"I reckon it's a setback for you, all right. And I can understand how it'd hurt a mite, those things he said. But don't you want to prove him wrong, prove to him that you *can* do it, prove that a woman *can* write as well as that O'Flaridy kid?"

"Yeah."

"Then you gotta toughen up, Corrie! Get that Belle blood working for you. Toughen up, fight back, keep writing and don't let either Kemble or O'Flaridy take your dream away. Maybe they stole your idea, and even your words. But don't let them steal your dream. Fight for it, Corrie. And if Kemble doesn't like what you write, then do like he said and take it someplace else. But don't let him rob you of what God gave you just 'cause he don't have the good sense to see what a fine writer you're gonna be someday."

He gave me a hug and a kiss, and I cried a little again. It made me feel better just knowing that *he* still believed in me.

Almeda told me what it was like for her after Mr. Parrish died.

"After my husband died, Corrie, I was absolutely despondent. I felt so alone and out of place in this world. We hadn't been in California much longer than a year and our business was just getting going. I was the only woman in Miracle Springs besides the saloon girls. Mr. Parrish and I had dreamed of the life we would build in the new west, and all of a sudden it was shattered."

"But you probably didn't fall apart like me," I said.

"Oh, I did," she answered.

"I cried thousands of tears, so I think I know a little of what you are feeling right now. I wanted to just sit down and die at times. Then at other times I would decide to pack everything up and go back East. I had my reasons for not wanting to go back to Boston. Someday, when the time is right, perhaps I'll tell you about that period of my life. In light of what I've seen and been through, Corrie, God has been so wonderfully good to me. But it wasn't because of being afraid of my past that I decided not to go back. No, Corrie, it was because I finally realized I couldn't give up. That wouldn't have been fair to my husband and to the dream we'd had of a new and happy life in California. And it wouldn't have been fair to me!"

She stopped, and it was real quiet. I hadn't seen that distant look in her eyes since she and Pa had been married, but there it was again. I knew she was thinking about another time and another place, and I didn't want to disturb her.

But as usual, the silence only lasted a few moments. Then her face suddenly brightened and she spoke again.

"In every person's life, Corrie, there come times like you're going through right now. Usually everyone has several such moments, when everything you think you wanted seems suddenly gone, destroyed, unattainable. At those times a woman's got to stop and take stock of herself. Just like in business. We have to do periodic stock-checks, inventories of supplies—just like you and Marcus did out in the supply room last week. We had to know what we had on hand so we'd know what to do in the future.

"A person has to do that too—take inventory, check the supply room. Especially when you come to what you might call 'crisis' times, or times of evaluation and question, when you have to ask yourself where you're going as a person, where your life is headed. You have to take stock. You have to find out if where you've been going is still where you *want* to go, or if you need to *change* directions."

"And you think maybe that's where I'm at now?"

"Quite possibly.

"Sometimes God allows difficulties and hardships and questions and heartbreaks to come our way because he wants us to change directions. And so whenever they come we have to stop and try to listen to his voice and ask him what he's trying to get through to us. But there are other times when the disappointments come not to get us to change directions at all, but to strengthen and toughen us, so that we will be all the more dedicated to accomplishing what we felt God was leading us toward in the first place. Do you see the difference, Corrie?" she asked.

I nodded. "Like how hard it was when us kids and Pa got together," I said. "I think we all wanted to find some way out of that situation—especially Pa!"

Almeda laughed.

"But we knew we had to stick it out because it was the right thing."

"Exactly! And that's why I decided to stay here rather than go back East. After taking stock of myself, I realized that I *wanted* to make it work. I had to ask myself how willing I was to fight for what I wanted to do. And I decided I was willing to fight for it, even though I knew it would be hard and that men would probably be against me at first. But I was determined to fight for what I believed in, to fight for my dream.

"Now you're facing almost exactly the same thing. You've had a bad letdown. You're a woman up against stiff odds. The man you're up against—in my case it was the men of the community whose support and business I had to have to survive. In your case it is an editor you have to prove yourself to—such men don't necessarily make it easy for us. Now you have to take inventory of the direction you've been going and ask yourself if it's *still* the direction you want to *keep* going.

"What it boils down to, Corrie, is this—how bad do you want it?"

"I *do* want to be able to write," I said.

"I had to ask myself the same question. How bad did I want to see my business succeed? What sacrifices was I willing to make? Was I willing to fight for what I believed in? In the same way—how bad do *you* still want to be a writer? Are you willing to fight for it? What sacrifices are you willing to make? If you don't think you're a good writer now, how hard are you willing to work to improve? Are you willing to work twice as hard as a man would have to, and get only half the pay?"

She paused and looked into my eyes. "How much do you want it, Corrie?"

"I think I want it," I answered lamely.

"Well, if after taking stock of yourself, you decide you *do* still want to be a writer, then don't let Kemble or O'Flaridy or anyone else stop you. Go after it! It's your dream—so fight for it, and don't let go of it."

CHAPTER 32

MY DECISION AND WHAT CAME OF IT

Even before Almeda was through talking, I knew what my decision was!

This was one time when I didn't need to go out in the woods for a long time to think and try to figure things out. I knew what I wanted—and that was to keep writing! And if it meant working even harder than before and trying to make my writing better than it had been, I'd do it! If it meant getting only $1 an article, maybe I'd do that too. But then maybe I'd tell Mr. Kemble I wanted more. And if he said my articles weren't good enough to pay more, then I'd *make* them good enough! I'd improve my writing. I'd practice. I'd learn.

How bad did I want to do what I'd dreamed of doing? I figured I wanted it bad enough to fight for it, just like Almeda had.

Within ten or fifteen minutes I was in the saddle and on my way back toward town. It was Saturday afternoon, a good time to interview some more people about the election. If my first article wasn't good enough for Mr. Kemble, then I'd make my second one all the better—with facts and the five *w*'s and human interest all put together! I'd make it so interesting even *he* would enjoy reading it! And since I'd gotten behind during this last week, I couldn't afford to waste another minute. Most of the people in town had seen Almeda's flyer. Mr. Royce had put up a great big new banner on the side of his bank building

195

just three days ago, which said in big letters and bright paint: ROYCE FOR MAYOR. MIRACLE SPRINGS' FUTURE PROSPERITY DEPENDS ON YOUR VOTE. Folks were really interested and were talking a lot about everything. Now was the time to see everybody to get their thoughts and reactions while interest was high and they were willing to talk.

But about halfway into town a huge new idea suddenly hit me! It was such a great idea I completely forgot about Mr. Royce and Almeda and Miracle Springs in an instant. If I could write an article about someone *really* important, about news that was significant to the whole country, not just a little town like Miracle Springs, then Mr. Kemble would *have* to print it! And he'd see that I could be a reporter who could write about more than just pretty leaves and sunsets and interesting people nobody'd ever heard of.

I yanked back on the reins, swung my horse around on the trail, dug in my heels to her flanks, and galloped back to the house.

I ran straight inside and began searching through the pile of old newspapers Pa kept by the fireplace to start fires with. I hoped it was still there!

Then I remembered. I'd saved the August 8 issue with my own articles. I ran into my room. There it was, right with the others! Hurriedly I scanned through the paper until I found it. I read the brief article again, then went back into the big room where Pa and Almeda were sitting with puzzled expressions watching me scurry around.

"Look!" I exclaimed, pointing to the paper still in my hand. "It says right here that there is a controversy about Mr. Fremont's estate, but it doesn't say what it is. What if I could find out? That would sure be a story Mr. Kemble couldn't refuse!"

"There ain't no mystery there," laughed Pa. "Everyone knows they been trying to claim jump and get his gold mines away from him ever since he found gold on his land."

"Who, Pa? Who's *they*?"

"His enemies, people who want his gold—neighbors, claim jumpers, drifters, Mexicans. Anybody who's rich and powerful always has a pack of people trying to do him in, and John Fremont's both. All this time he's been back in Washington senatoring and now running for President, folks back here's trying to get their hands on his gold."

"But *who*, Pa?"

"I don't know. I suppose there's lots of 'em."

"Well, I'm gonna go find out," I said determinedly.

Pa laughed again. "What you figure on doin', girl?" he said. "The man's running for President of the United States! And *you* figure on uncovering some mystery about him that no one else knows?"

"I don't know, Pa. It's probably downright foolish—but I *know* there's a story there. I can *feel* it! A story for me . . . if I can just find it!"

"And how you figure to find this story that's waitin' just for you?" I know the smile on Pa's face wasn't meant to be making fun of me, but at the same time he just couldn't keep from chuckling. I was serious.

"I don't know. Maybe I'll just go out there and start looking around. I guess maybe that's what a reporter's got to do sometimes, and maybe it's time I learned how."

"Go where—Mariposa? That's a hundred and twenty, maybe a hundred and thirty miles."

"Through the mountains," added Almeda. "Through Sacramento and the valley roads, more like a hundred seventy-five."

"If that's what I gotta do for a story, then maybe that's just what I gotta do."

I reckon I'd been swept along in this conversation by the emotion of the moment. But the minute those words were out of my mouth, suddenly the reality of what I'd said seemed to strike us all. There was silence for a moment, and I guess somehow in the very saying of the words a determination rose up within me to *do* what I'd said, even if the words had been spoken lightly. I think Pa and Almeda realized, too, that a change had come in that instant. And maybe inside, both of them had to face how they were going to react to my growing up.

Almeda's next words were not what you'd expect from a mother who was worried about what her son or daughter was about to do, and who wanted to talk them out of it.

"I think it's a sensational idea, Corrie!" said Almeda. "If you are going to go after something and follow a dream you have, you might as well go straight to the top."

Pa had been serious for a minute, but now he chuckled again. "You're a determined one," he said. "Once you make your mind up about something, I wouldn't want to be the one standin' in your way. But how do you figure on going all that way . . . how do you figure on findin' something out that other folks don't know?"

"I don't know," I answered again with all my innocent youthful enthusiasm. "I'll find a way."

"You want me to take you down there, maybe go with you?" he asked.

I hesitated a minute before answering. "I don't know, Pa," I said finally. "Something inside me wants to do this alone, though I'm afraid at the same time. Maybe one of you should go with me . . . if you could." I was already starting to get cold feet about my idea.

A little frown passed over Almeda's forehead and I could tell she was thinking. But the reply she gave startled me.

"I don't think we ought to, Corrie," she said after a minute. "This is your idea, and you're the one who wants to go down there and uncover a story you think is waiting for you. I think it's time you figured out the best way to go about it yourself. I can give you the names of good boarding houses all the way, people I know and that we can trust. But I think perhaps it's time you saw what you were capable of. You can do it—I know you can."

"It is a fearsome thing, to go so far alone, not even knowing what I am looking for, not even knowing who to talk to, not even knowing if anybody will listen to me." My earlier resolve was fading fast.

"They will listen to you, young lady. You can be very determined . . . and very persuasive! Besides, part of the process

I was telling you about of fighting for your dream—part of it is learning to stand alone if you have to, facing the dangers and uncertainties, and learning to go where maybe no one else has gone in just the same way, or asking questions no one has voiced before. That's part of growing up—finding your own inner strength with God. Something inside tells me this might be one of those times. If there's a story there meant for you, then you have to be the one to find it."

"I don't know, Almeda," said Pa. "I ain't so sure I agree with you. There's bears and varmints and who knows what kind of hoodlums all the way up an' down that way. I don't like it. I'll go with her, just to keep an eye on things."

Neither of us said anything more. From the sound of it, Pa had made up his mind, and I knew what he said was the logical way to look at it. So I was surprised the next morning when he announced that he'd changed his mind, and that if I wanted to make the trip alone, he wouldn't forbid me. He'd still rather he or Zack went with me, but he'd trust me to make the decision.

Naturally I was fearful at first as I anticipated such a trip, such a quest for the unknown. Later I looked back at this as another one of those growing experiences. And I came to thank Pa and Almeda afterward for not doing it for me, for giving me encouragement but not actually helping me, and for forcing me not just to believe in what I wanted to do—but for forcing me to believe in myself too. Whatever I felt at the time, Pa and Almeda didn't try to make it easy for me. They pushed me out from under their wings to go after this story—whatever it was!—by myself, showed me that they really did believe in me, and were ready to treat me like an adult. There's just no other way to get your legs strong unless you stand on them without holding on to someone else. And that's what I was about to do.

I would have to finish my interviews and articles about the Miracle Springs election for mayor later. Whatever was waiting for me at the Fremont estate, I figured it had more potential for being something that Mr. Kemble would take notice of.

Two days later, my decision had been made!

With saddlebags full of a week's supply of food, and with blankets in case I couldn't put up at a boardinghouse for any reason, I set off on my faithful horse Raspberry alone, headed for Sacramento.

CHAPTER 33

TO MARIPOSA

The two-day ride to Sacramento was by now a familiar one. I had traveled the road three or four times in each direction. It was almost like coming to another one of my "homes" to stay at Miss Baxter's boardinghouse again. When I told her where I was going, she gave me several names of people she knew along the way where I could lodge.

"If you go down the valley," she said, "there are nice women who will put you up in Lodi, Modesto, Turlock, Merced. I'll write their names down for you, dearie."

I thanked her.

"But if you take the short route through the foothills, it's rougher, and mostly men. I don't know of a single reputable place from Angels Camp down through Chinese Camp and Moccasin Flat. No, you'd best stick to the valley and then cut east from Merced."

She wrote the names down for me, and having them in my pocket gave me a feeling of security. Then we talked a little about our old trail boss, Captain Dixon. She said he was just about due, and I told her to give him a hug for me.

"He'll be so proud when I tell him how you've grown and how you're a real reporter for a San Francisco newspaper!" she said.

"Not a reporter," I corrected her. "Just barely a writer, and only sometimes at that!" I laughed.

"Perhaps that will change when you find what you are seeking in Mariposa," she said.

I hoped so, too, although inside I was getting more and more fearful that I was on what Pa would call a fool's errand. But I wasn't about to turn back now, even if I did come back empty-handed.

I left the comfort and security of Miss Baxter's and Sacramento early the next morning, and went straight south on the road leading through Lodi, Stockton, and Modesto. It was hot and dry and dusty, and I was glad I had plenty of water with me. There weren't too many people on the road—now and then a rider on horseback, and two stagecoaches headed to Sacramento.

At first I rode pretty hard, but before the morning was half gone, I knew I had to slow down or poor Raspberry would drop from exhaustion in the heat. Stockton was fifty miles, and I'd thought of spending my first night south of Sacramento there. But I passed through Lodi well before noon, so I decided I'd try to make it all the way to Modesto, where I had the name of a boardinghouse. That extra thirty miles in the afternoon sun nearly wore me out, and when I got to Modesto that night I didn't think I could ever get in a saddle again in my life!

I didn't start nearly so early the next morning. I only had to go thirty miles that day, though on my sore rump it was far enough! I got to Merced in the middle of the afternoon, found Harcourt's Boarding House, took a bath, and then fell fast asleep until dinnertime.

The next morning I prepared to go to the Fremont estate, only fifteen miles from Merced. I told Mrs. Harcourt that I might be back that night, but that I couldn't be sure.

When I set off east from Merced toward the foothills, the rising sun was in my eyes. As it rose in the sky, the hills came closer and closer, with the mountains in the distance behind them. It was probably ten-thirty or eleven in the morning when I approached the Rancho de las Mariposas, estate of presidential candidate John Charles Fremont. In my heart, I must confess, I felt about as uncertain, scared, and intimidated as I had ever felt in my life. If this was "following my dream," as Almeda had put it, I began to wonder if it wasn't time to just give the whole thing up and turn around! I had no idea who I'd run into or what they'd say to me . . . or what I'd say to them!

Lord, I prayed silently, remembering my prayers before the blizzard and the article I'd written about the Wards, *I don't know what I'm supposed to do next, but please guide my steps . . . and show me what you want me to do*.

And then, taking in a deep breath of the warm dry air, I rode forward toward the gate of the estate, about half a mile outside the little village of Mariposa.

I learned later some things about the estate I didn't know at the time. In 1847, the explorer John Fremont gave a friend $3,000 to buy some land for him near San Jose, just south of San Francisco where he hoped to settle with his family. By mistake, however, the man bought a huge estate eighty miles too far inland, across the flat, dry San Joaquin Valley. At first they were disappointed, but as soon as the Fremonts saw their new land, they realized perhaps the mistake had been a blessing in disguise.

And as I entered the estate, I understood why! The Fremont ranch covered over 44,000 acres, with mountains and streams, waterfalls, trees, forest, pools, meadows, areas of rich soil, and even two small towns. I had already been through the first, for which the ranch was named, and I would later get to know the town of Bear Valley, and spend several nights in Oso House, the small hotel owned by Fremont himself. Fremont named his estate *Mariposa* after the millions of beautiful, tiny winged creatures that flew and fluttered all about it—Ranch of the Butterflies.

Even before Fremont had set foot on the land himself, farther to the north James Marshall and John Sutter discovered gold at Sutter's Mill along the American River, and the California gold rush was on. Only a year later, in 1849, huge amounts of gold were also discovered at Mariposa. Overnight John Fremont was a rich man. He had been well known already because of all the exploring he had done throughout the West for years; he became even more famous for the stories of the gold found on his land. When California became a state in

1850, John Fremont was immediately elected one of its first senators. Fremont's wife Jessie was the daughter of the well-known United States senator from Virginia, Thomas Hart Benton. Fremont was therefore a nationally known politician throughout the whole country. So when the new Republican party was formed in 1854, they nominated John Fremont to run as their candidate for President.

Fremont had not even been back to California during the whole campaign, so I didn't know what kind of story I figured to get by coming here. And as I rode up to the gate I desperately wanted to turn around and go home. But I was here, and it was too late to turn back, so I might as well see what happened.

A man was sitting in a little shed by the gate, which stood open. A painted sign on the fence read *Rancho de las Mariposas*. The man looked like a Mexican, and he stood up as I approached and glanced over me and my horse. He wasn't carrying a rifle, though he had a pistol in his holster at his waist, and he didn't seem too friendly. I suppose he was standing guard on account of the trouble Pa talked about with the Fremont mines.

"I . . . I'm a newspaper writer," I said hesitantly. "I've come to—"

But he didn't wait for me to finish and didn't seem to care what I was doing there. With a wave of his head, he motioned me to come through the gate, then pointed along the road toward some buildings in the distance, which I assumed was the ranch itself. I urged my horse along slowly, and the man sauntered back to his shed and sat down, never speaking a word.

Well, I thought to myself with relief, *at least I made it past the outside gate!*

As I approached the house, which wasn't big and fancy at all like I had expected, I could hear the sound of machinery and voices and wagons and workers in the distance. I knew that must be the gold mining going on. And as I got closer I saw more and more people about—all men, lots of Mexicans—but none of them paid any attention to me. There were several buildings, mostly adobe, a barn with corrals and stables at-

tached with both horses and cattle in the enclosed areas. Several
log buildings were scattered about, with a few men going in
and out of them, and I figured maybe that's where the mine
and ranch workers lived. The main house was made of wood
planks, but it didn't look impressive like the house of a U.S.
President. The Fremonts had never actually lived here, however. They spent most of their time back in Washington, D.C.

I stopped, got off my horse, tied her to the hitching rail in
front of the house, and took in a deep breath. I looked around
again. Still no one had taken any notice of me. I walked up
onto the porch, then knocked on the door, my knees shaking.

The door opened and another Mexican appeared. He could
not have been much older than I was.

"Hello," I said, trying to sound confident, "I am a newspaper writer and I have come to write an article—"

I paused just for a second, wondering from the fellow's
blank stare whether he understood English. But even before I
opened my mouth to continue, he spoke quickly.

"Sí, you come see Mrs. Carter!" He motioned me inside.
"Venga aquí, you seet down . . . you seet here," he said, pointing to a chair. "I get Mrs. Carter—she veesit you!" And before
I realized it, the young man had left the room and I was alone
again.

A minute or two passed. Then I heard footsteps coming
down the hall in my direction. A woman appeared and came
toward me.

"I am Ankelita Carter," she said. "Felipe says you want to
see me about something for a newspaper."

I liked Mrs. Carter immediately. From her dark brown skin
it was plain at once that she was Mexican, and her broad smile
of white teeth put me instantly at ease. Despite the color of her
skin and her overall appearance that seemed to me at first glance
that of a servant or maid, she spoke flawless English without
even the hint of an accent. There was even a cultured sound to
her tone, which made me immediately curious.

She was a stocky woman, not fat, but strongly built, and
looked well accustomed to work. She might have reminded me

of Katie, though she was taller and her broad shoulders had almost a manly quality. She was not "pretty," although her brown complexion was clear, her eyes bright, and her smile so infectious that you couldn't help but consider her attractive to gaze at and converse with. Her hair was pure black without a trace of gray, but from the rest of her appearance I would have guessed her to be somewhere in her mid-forties.

"I write sometimes for the *Alta*," I said, "and I was hoping to be able to write something about the estate or the Fremonts. My name is Corrie Belle Hollister."

"Well, Miss Hollister," replied Mrs. Carter, "I am very pleased to make your acquaintance." She held out her hand, and as I shook it I was further reassured by this woman with the friendly smile. "You must have come a long distance." She sat down in a chair opposite me.

"I have ridden four and a half days," I said.

"My, you *are* dedicated! But I must admit to some surprise. You are a woman, and a very young one at that. How do you come to be a reporter? I've never heard of such a thing."

"I don't suppose I'm *really* what you'd call an official reporter," I replied. "I try to write things I'm interested in, and then I hope the editor will want to print them."

"And he is willing to print something written by a woman?"

"Actually, the first few things he's printed appeared under the name C.B. Hollister. To tell you the truth, he hasn't printed anything of mine since he found out I was a girl not even twenty years old yet."

"How old are you, Corrie?" Mrs. Carter asked.

"Nineteen."

"Well, you are brave to try what you're doing." She paused. "Hmm . . . C.B. Hollister, you say?" She seemed to be thinking. "Did you write something about, let's see . . . it's coming to me—something about a lady from Virginia who went out to California as a mail-order bride and planted an apple tree?"

"Yes, yes!" I answered excitedly. "Did you actually read it?"

"I did indeed," she said. "It was very well done."

She smiled at me again, and gave a little nod, as if she was looking me over again for the first time.

"My, but isn't this something! For us to meet like this—a year later and all the way across the continent."

"What do you mean?" I asked. "I've only just come from north of Sacramento."

She laughed broadly. "That's not what I meant," she said. "I read your article in Virginia, when I was there with Mrs. Fremont."

"It really did get printed back there?" I said. "Mr. Kemble said it was going to be, but I never knew if it really did."

"Oh, yes, we all read it. Mrs. Fremont, the Senator."

"You were there with the Fremonts?" I asked, my surprise showing through.

"I've been with Mrs. Fremont since they were in Monterey in 1850. Her father, you know, is Senator Benton, and we were at their Virginia estate of Cherry Grove often, until the house burned down two years ago. After that and the death of Mrs. Fremont's mother, we went south less frequently. Though that is still where we encountered your article. Jessie herself is a writer, or at least she helped her husband a great deal with the memoirs of his travels. She hopes to write again one day. Just wait until I tell her I've met you! She will be thrilled. I know she will recall the article and your name because it made an impression on her at the time."

"I can hardly believe it," I said, in wonder. "To think that someone that far away actually read something I wrote out here!"

We continued to visit, and Mrs. Carter turned out to be as interesting herself as the Fremonts or the election or the estate. From a wealthy Mexican family, she had been well-educated in eastern United States, had returned to Mexico where she had married a California businessman. Her husband had been killed and most of her family's wealth lost during the Mexican war, and in Monterey, Jessie Fremont had taken her into her household, at first as a domestic. But soon realizing Ankelita's training and education, Mrs. Fremont put her in charge of most of the household, including the Fremont children. The two women fast became friends, and Ankelita had been part of the Fremont home ever since—in Washington, D.C. , during Mr. Fremont's term as senator, back in California, accompanying them to Europe. Only two months earlier had she left the Fremonts to return to California.

"But this recent trip," she concluded, "was *so* much more pleasant, now that there is a railroad across the Isthmus instead of having to walk or ride a donkey or be carried and pulled in carts by Indians." She laughed at the memory.

"Why did you return to California?" I asked.

"I felt it would be best for the campaign," Ankelita replied. She stopped as a look of sadness crossed her eyes. "I love Mr. Fremont," she went on, "and Jessie is like a sister to me. But politics is a field that attracts many enemies, where cruel things are said and done in order that men might gain their selfish ends. And many things have been said about Mr. and Mrs. Fremont that are untrue, things that others would use to defeat Mr. Fremont in the election. Some newspapers began to report that he was a Catholic. Though it is not true, the mere report has damaged him greatly. His own father-in-law, Jessie's father Mr. Benton, has spoken out harshly against Mr. Fremont, even against his own daughter."

"But why?" I asked.

"Because Senator Benton is a Democrat and his son-in-law is a Republican. The Republicans are against slavery, and most of the Democrats are in favor of slavery. And though Senator Benton himself is from the slave state of Virginia, he is personally against slavery. Yet he cannot make himself cross the party line to support his own son-in-law, though he shares his views. I find it appalling that his party has more influence than his own conscience."

"Is that why you left?" I asked.

Mrs. Carter drew in a deep sigh, and I saw a look of something like sadness on her face, even pain.

"I came to feel that my presence would ultimately do him more harm than good in the election," she said at length.

"Being raised as a Mexican, I am Catholic. It was only a matter of time before Buchanan's press writers would have discovered about my religion, and they would have used it against the Colonel. And there were those who were beginning to talk against Jessie because of me, implying that I was Mrs. Fremont's 'Mexican slave,' as they called it. Not a word of it was true. But just the darkness of my skin was enough to feed prejudices, and the hint of such a thing would have been enough to hurt the Colonel because of his strong anti-slavery position. All through the campaign people have been trying to link Mr. and Mrs. Fremont to slavery, digging up Jessie's Virginian upbringing, and asking pointed questions about their black servants, all of whom were perfectly free just like me."

"It doesn't seem fair," I said.

"Politics is never fair, Corrie. Politics is politics, and it's a matter of winning however you can and by whatever you have to say about your opponent. But *fair*—no, politics is rarely fair."

"It just doesn't seem right!"

"No, I don't suppose it's right any more than it is fair. But if you're going to be in politics, that's just the way it is."

"Did the Fremonts ask you to leave?"

"No, Jessie would never have done that. But when I told her of my decision, she knew it was best. She gave me money for passage and asked me to come back here to watch over their household affairs. Not that I could really be of much help with the business of the mine, but they want to know there is someone here they can trust completely who can tell them what is happening. So I returned, and I have been here a little over a month. After her husband is elected President, Jessie wants me to come back and live with them in the White House."

"Oh, wouldn't that be wonderful!"

"And then *you* could come visit us, Corrie, and write a story about President and Mrs. Fremont. *That* would surely make that editor of yours stand up and take notice of you—even if you are a young woman!"

I laughed. But just the thought of me ever visiting the White

House was too unbelievable to fathom.

"But you cannot have come all this way just to listen to me," Ankelita said. "You must have known the Fremonts have not been in California for five years. What did you want to write an article about, Corrie?"

I shrugged sheepishly. We'd been talking for almost an hour and the subject of my writing had hardly yet come up. If Mr. Kemble wanted "human interest," Ankelita Carter was the perfect subject. She was as "interesting" a person as I'd ever met! I could write several stories about her, without having to worry about the Fremonts or the election or the mine or anything!

"Actually, I didn't have anything to write about," I admitted. "I saw the article a few days ago in the *Alta* about the mine here having some controversy, and I just decided to come here and hope that I might find out about it. The editor of the paper has been pretty hard on me after the C.B. Hollister business, and I just have to find something to write about that'll make him see that I can be a reporter even if he doesn't like the fact that I'm a young woman."

"So you didn't knock on the door asking to see me as Felipe said?"

"No, ma'am," I said. "I just knocked on the door and was praying that somebody would be here who would take the time to talk to me and wouldn't mind that I had come."

"Well, I don't mind a bit!" she said. "And I have enjoyed talking to you."

"What is the controversy about the estate?" I asked.

"Oh, nothing new. The Colonel's mine has been in legal battles from the very beginning. Most of the miners in California believe in 'free mines'—whoever first stakes out a claim has right to the area. Colonel Fremont bought all this land before anyone knew there was an ounce of gold anywhere around here. But after 1849, miners invaded his property, and he has been having to fight them off ever since. The miners feel entitled to stake claims even though the land belongs to Mr. Fremont. And just a few months ago the Supreme Court back in Washington confirmed his title to the whole estate and Mr.

Fremont had all the independent miners driven out by force. That all happened earlier this year. But it hasn't been the end of the trouble. That's why you saw Hector out at the gate wearing a gun, and there are guards posted all around the main mining areas. Some of the anti-Fremont newspapers are stirring up the Mariposa title issue again, trying to make sure the miners of the state stay mad at Fremont until the election."

"Won't Mr. Fremont win easily here in California?" I asked. "That's what my pa says."

"I don't know, Corrie. Money and greed and power do strange things to men. Many powerful Californians are jealous of Mr. Fremont because of his fame and good fortune. They want him to fail. And they will stop at nothing. There are bad men involved, ruthless men. I have even heard Mr. Fremont say there are politicians willing to have people killed to further their own causes. It is hard to believe such people run our government. And such men are fanning the fires of contention about the title to the estate, and spreading many other false rumors about the Fremonts."

"That's terrible!" I exclaimed.

"I agree. But gold is not the only issue involved. Here in California the issue over mine ownership is big in the minds of the miners. But on a national scale, slavery is the overriding issue. And there are millions of dollars at stake over the future of slavery in the South, just as there are millions of dollars at stake over where a man is entitled to mine here in California. The pro-slavery forces of Buchanan are equally ruthless at times. They are determined to keep John Fremont out of the White House. If Fremont is elected, he will probably abolish slavery, and then their whole southern way of life will be ruined. They feel they *have* to stop him."

"Are *all* politicians like that?" I asked. "Greedy and mean?"

"No, there are many good men. Yet when otherwise seemingly good men support something intrinsically evil like slavery, it does something to them. They become different, and in a bad way. But during my years with the Fremonts, I have met many good men too. I've never forgotten the time I met a young Illinois lawyer by the name of Lincoln. The look in his eye told me that *he* was a different breed than these kinds of men I've spoken of. In fact, this Lincoln was almost Mr. Fremont's running mate for Vice-President this year, but lost out to Mr. Dayton. Lincoln is staunchly anti-slavery, just as is Mr. Fremont, and I overheard the Colonel say to his wife shortly after the nominating convention in Philadelphia last June, 'That fellow Lincoln is one to watch. I doubt the country's heard the last of him.' "

She stopped and the room grew quiet for a minute or two.

"But all this can't be that interesting," Mrs. Carter said finally.

"It's interesting to me," I replied.

"But nothing so interesting you could make an article out of. The papers have been full of this kind of thing for a year."

"But not from a woman's perspective," I said with a smile. "Maybe I could write something about Mr. Fremont in a different way that women readers would enjoy more."

"You want something women would like to read?"

"Mr. Kemble says that's one of the reasons he printed some of my articles, because women enjoyed them."

"Well, if you want a woman's story, I'll give one to you!" said Ankelita excitedly.

"What is it?" I asked eagerly.

"The best story of all in this election isn't the candidate or the election at all. It's the candidate's wife. If Mr. Fremont wins and gets to the White House, he's going to have Mrs. Jessie Benton Fremont to thank for it. *She's* the real story!"

"Should I get out my paper and pen?" I asked.

"You get them! And then you sit right here and I'll tell you all about Jessie. And when we're through, Corrie Belle Hollister, young woman reporter, we're going to have an article that editor of yours won't be able to refuse, an article that will make your name read in newspapers all over the country! Jessie's story is one that only another woman could write, and you're the first woman writer I've ever met. Oh, how I wish Jessie herself were here! She would so love to talk with you!"

I started to get my things out of my satchel, but before I got seated again, Ankelita was out of her chair.

"Let's eat some lunch together first, Corrie," she said. "Felipe!" she called down the hallway, then turned to me again. "Then afterward we'll sit down and I'll tell you everything."

Felipe appeared and she spoke a couple of hasty sentences to him that I didn't understand, then indicated for me to follow her.

CHAPTER 34

HEARING ABOUT JESSIE

An hour later we were seated in the same chairs again, each with a cup of tea in our hands.

Lunchtime had been an interesting assortment of people coming and going as we sat around a wooden table eating beans and tortillas. There were several children, an older woman, Felipe and two or three other young men about his age, and Ankelita and I. Most of the conversation among the others had been in Spanish. The ranch and mine workers must have had their midday meal someplace else, and I never did quite figure out how Ankelita was involved with everything that was going on. She could not have been in charge of the whole household, because she had only recently arrived, yet I saw no one else who seemed to be higher in authority. At least she spoke to those in this particular house in a confident manner. Maybe this wasn't the main house, even though it had been the first I had come to. There were a few other buildings about with people coming and going from them.

Once we were alone again and had seated ourselves, Ankelita began telling me about Jessie Benton Fremont, from their first days together in Monterey, right up to the present.

"It was just before I had become part of their home," she said, "that gold was found here. I've heard Jessie tell the story so many times I feel as if I'd been there: how Colonel Fremont rode up on his horse and ran into the room they were renting in Monterey and plopped down two big heavy sacks in front of her. 'Gold, Jessie!' was all he said. 'Gold! The Mariposa is full of it in every stream!' "

She told me about the Fremonts' life in Monterey before that.

"Monterey was then the capital of California, but it was a hard life for Jessie. They had no money, and Jessie had little fresh food. They had no milk, no fresh eggs. Jessie talks about eating rice and sardines and crackers during those days."

She paused and chuckled.

"A couple of months ago during the campaign, a woman started criticizing Jessie for being rich and pampered, for having tea and cake between meals.

" 'I find it a comforting break in my often wearying day,' Jessie answered her.

" 'But you allow yourself to be served by a maid?' the lady asked, thinking to make Jessie look foolish. But Jessie turned the tables on her.

" 'Yes, I confess it,' she whispered. 'But just between us, I think I make better tea myself. I had no maid in Monterey. I heated the water in a long-handled iron saucepan over a smoky fire. And instead of French cakes to eat, I lifted a sardine from his crowded can and gave him a decent burial between two soda crackers.'

"The lady and all the people around laughed, and in the next day's paper it was reported that Jessie Fremont was a good down-to-earth woman who could cook over a campfire."

We both laughed at that, and I found myself wondering if the story had made its way to the California newspapers. If not, it would be the perfect thing for me to use!

Then we talked about the Fremonts' trip to San Francisco following the discovery of gold on their estate. At San Jose, which later replaced Monterey as the capital of California, they hired some Indian women to wash their clothes by pounding them with stones in a brook. They were met there by a work-man from the Mariposa, bringing buckskin bags filled with gold dust and nuggets—wealth from their foothills mines.

After Colonel Fremont's election to the Senate to represent

the newest state in the Union, the Fremonts set sail for New York. For the next year, Jessie, who had long been a senator's daughter, now found herself a senator's *wife*.

"The years came so rapidly and were so full," Ankelita said. "Colonel Fremont was in the Senate only a year, and then we returned to San Francisco in 1851 to a beautiful big home. But within months there were two terrible fires and the house was gone. Then we spent a year in Europe before returning to the East. Jessie's mother died, her father lost his Senate seat, and the house at Cherry Grove also burned, all within a few months. And now they are running for the White House! The Fremonts' lives, especially with three young children, have been so busy and eventful."

We talked most of the afternoon. I must have asked a hundred questions. It was all so fascinating! Ankelita told me what Jessie looked like and what she felt about some of Mr. Fremont's political decisions, about the heartbreak of their decision to become Republicans, knowing that it meant driving a wedge between them and Jessie's southern relatives. She told me about the children, about what it was like for Jessie to try to be a good mother in the midst of Washington politics. She told me how Fremont would consult Jessie about political decisions, not something very many politicians did. That, too, would be perfect for an article women would really enjoy. Even though they couldn't vote, women were more interested in current events than men sometimes thought. And Jessie Fremont was the shining example of what impact a woman could have standing beside her husband in American politics.

"During the early part of the campaign, Corrie," Ankelita said, "Jessie was sometimes as popular as her husband. Crowds would call out her name after the Colonel's speeches, wanting to see her too. One campaign song went like this:

And whom shall we toast for the Queen of the
*   White House?*
We'll give them "Our Jessie" again and again.

"I only wish I could be there to see the election through,

although I know it's best that I am here."

By the end of the day, I truly felt as if I knew Jessie Benton Fremont myself. If I could just figure out how to best put it down on paper, Mr. Kemble was sure to print it! And if he didn't, I would take it to another newspaper. The Fremonts hadn't been in California since 1851 and things had been much different back then. Now Jessie Benton Fremont was only a month or two away from being the most important woman in the whole nation, and I had personal stories about her that Mr. Kemble could not possibly have heard before.

I was so excited, and hoped I'd be able to somehow write about Jessie Fremont in as interesting a way as Ankelita Carter told about her!

By the time our conversation was over, the shadows were starting to lengthen outside. The day had gone by so quickly, and had been better than my wildest dreams.

"Well, young lady," said Ankelita, "we'd best get Felipe to see about getting your horse put up for the night, and then getting you settled in your room."

From my puzzled expression she could tell I didn't understand.

"You weren't thinking of riding back down the mountain to Merced, were you?" she asked in a voice of astonishment.

"I figured I would," I answered. "To tell you the truth, I hadn't really thought about it since this morning."

"Well, you're not going anywhere, Corrie. You're staying here with us tonight. I have an extra bed in my room. Besides, you have to get started on that article of yours. And what better place than right here?"

I had supper with them around the same table, with most of the same people. Then later, at a little table with a candle, I pulled out several sheets of blank paper, got out my pen and ink, spread out my notes, and began to write the article I had come to Mariposa to find.

At the top of the page I wrote for a title: "The *Real* Jessie Benton Fremont: The Woman Behind the Candidate."

CHAPTER 35

MR. KEMBLE ONCE MORE

Five days after I'd first set foot on the Mariposa estate, I once again walked through the doors of the offices of the California *Alta* on Montgomery Street in San Francisco.

I'd arrived in the city late the evening before. I spent the night at Miss Bean's Boarding House. After a bath and a change into fresh clothes, I felt much more confident than the first time I had been there. In my hand I held eight sheets of writing, an article I was genuinely proud of as being different and publishable, and something that no other reporter could have, especially no San Francisco reporter. If Robin O'Flaridy had scooped me last time, now it was my turn!

I didn't feel like a little girl begging a powerful editor to publish my little article. For the first time I guess I felt like a real "reporter" who had uncovered a story. As I walked down the hallway—and was I ever glad there was no O'Flaridy in sight!—I felt tall and good inside.

I went straight to Mr. Kemble's office, without even asking anybody if he was in or if I could see him, and knocked on the door.

I heard a muffled sound from inside, so I opened the door and walked right up to his desk, where the editor sat just like last time. His head was down and he didn't even look up right at first.

"Mr. Kemble," I said, trying not to let my voice quiver, "I have a story for you."

At the sound of my voice he glanced up.

His eyes surveyed me up and down for a second, then it seemed to gradually come to him who was standing there in front of him in his office.

"Ah, Miss Hollister," he said, leaning back in his chair. "Come to deliver your next article in person, eh? So you can be sure no one steals any of your precious words? Long ways to come, isn't it, just to deliver a short piece?"

I think he was trying to be humorous, but I didn't smile.

"This isn't on the Miracle Springs mayor's election," I said. "It's got to do with the national election."

"Oh, national news! My, oh my!" he said, still with a little grin on his lips. "You've broken some major new story that all the other hundred newsmen in this city have never heard?"

"No, it's not a major new story," I said. It's 'human interest,' I believe you call it. However, I think you will find it of interest to your readers. And to answer your question, no, I don't think any of your other newsmen do have access to this information."

I stood straight and confident before his desk, the papers still in my hand. Gradually the smile disappeared from his face, and he eyed me carefully. I think he was starting to realize I was serious.

"All right, Hollister," he said at last. "Let me see it."

He held out his right hand. I handed him the top page.

He took the sheet, glanced over it quickly. His eyes darted up to mine again, as if looking for some clue. Then he looked down at the sheet again and read it start to finish. As he completed the last line he again held up his hand.

"I'll give you more when you agree to publish it," I said.

"Don't toy with me, Hollister!" he snapped, dropping the page. "I don't play games with my reporters, especially nineteen-year-old women!"

I reached forward and took the page from his desk, then turned around and made a step toward the door.

"Okay, okay," he said, still brusquely but apologetically. "I'm sorry. That was rude of me."

I turned back and faced him again.

"It looks good, Hollister," he went on. "I'm sure I can use it. May I please see more?"

I shuffled through the sheets and handed him page five.

He took it, and the moment he saw what I had done, he glanced up at me again, bordering on another outburst, I think. But he controlled himself, and read the page through. He set it down on his desk, leaned back in his chair, put his hands behind his head, and looked at me for a long moment.

"What is this little game you're playing with me?" he finally said.

"I just want to protect my article," I said. "What happened before was very upsetting to me. I felt we had an agreement, even if we didn't shake hands on it, and I don't think what you did was right. Now, I'm very sorry I didn't get the chance to tell you all about Mrs. Parrish being my stepmother. That was wrong of me. But it was an honest oversight. When Robin O'Flaridy walked in, I forgot a lot of what I had intended to say. But all that's past, Mr. Kemble. You explained yourself very clearly in your letter, and you were very plain about how things are if I intend to write for your paper. Therefore, it seems best to me that I make sure we come to an agreement beforehand. And after we've reached an agreement, then you can see the entire article."

While I spoke his face changed first to red then to white. I don't know if he'd ever been spoken to by any of his reporters that way, but he certainly wasn't used to it from a nineteen-year-old woman!

When I finished, I stopped and stood still. I half expected him to yell at me, or throw me out of his office and say he never wanted to see me again.

There was a long silence. I don't think he knew what to do with me either. He probably *wanted* to throw me out! But then again, I knew he wanted the article on Jessie Fremont!

Finally he spoke again.

"Where did you get this stuff?" he asked.

"My sources are confidential," I answered. I'd been prac-

ticing that line all the way from Mariposa! Ankelita told me
that's what I ought to say if asked where I'd got my information.

"Nobody could know some of the things you say unless
they knew the lady personally. *You* don't know Jessie Fremont
. . . do you, Hollister?" His voice was incredulous at the very
thought, even though he *knew* I couldn't possibly know her.

"Confidential," I repeated. "I can tell you nothing about
where any of this came from."

He squirmed in his chair. I could tell he hated not being in
control.

There was another long silence.

"All right . . . all right, Hollister, you win! I'll print it. I
don't know how you got it, but it's good, it's original, and I
want it."

"And the matter of pay?" I said, still holding the rest of the
pages.

"I told you before I would pay you a dollar an article . . .
until you've proven yourself."

"I think this is worth more than what I've sent you before."

"So now it's you who's welching on a deal, eh, Hollister?"
He chuckled.

"I never agreed to a dollar," I said.

"Okay, you're right, this is worth more. You've done some
good work here. I'll pay you two dollars for it."

"I want eight dollars."

"Eight dollars!"

I didn't say anything.

"That's highway robbery! I can't pay that kind of money
for a single article. If word got out that I'd paid a woman eight
dollars, the men would be wanting sixteen for every little thing
they brought me."

"This has nothing to do with whether a man or woman
wrote it. Somebody had to do the work to uncover this story,
and whether it was a man or a woman, it seems to me the words
would be worth the same. And I figure the words of *this* story
are worth eight dollars. She might be our next first lady, and
nobody else has some of this stuff I've written here."

"You are a huckster, Hollister, a downright rogue! All right, I'll give you four. I can't pay a penny more!"

"I'm sure the Sacramento *Union* or maybe the *Courier* would like to take a look at it."

"You can't do that. You're under contract to me—don't forget, we have a three-article deal on the other election."

"A deal you did not feel you needed to honor a couple weeks ago," I said. "I'm under no obligation to the *Alta*; I simply wanted to offer the story to you first."

I reached for the page five still lying on his desk.

"Good day, Mr. Kemble," I said, and again turned to go. This time I made it almost to the door before I again heard his voice. Even as he said it I could tell from the grating tone that it killed him to give in to the demands of a woman.

"Six" came his voice behind me.

I stopped, and slowly turned around. He was standing behind his desk, both hands resting upon it, sort of leaning toward me, his face glaring.

I stood where I was and returned his stare. Two seconds went by, then five. It seemed like an eternity that we stood there, looking deeply into each other's eyes. Whether it was a struggle of wills, or a contest of stubbornness, I don't know. But in that moment, I was thankful for Ma and her Belle blood!

Finally I spoke. My voice was very soft, but very determined. I had made up my mind even before I'd entered his office, and I wasn't about to back down now.

"Mr. Kemble, I said I wanted eight dollars. I believe the article is worth eight dollars. And if you want it for the *Alta*, you are going to have to pay eight dollars. Otherwise I am going to walk out this door and take what I have to one of your competitors."

Several more seconds went by.

Finally Mr. Kemble sat down and exhaled a long sigh.

"All right, you win. Eight dollars." His voice sounded tired. I could hardly believe it—I had beaten him.

"I'd like the money today," I said.

"Do you never stop, Hollister?" he asked in disbelief.

"Don't you trust me for payment?"

"You told me yourself, Mr. Kemble, that the newspaper business was a tough business. I'm just following your advice. You also told me that if I thought it was unfair I could take my articles elsewhere. It seems that your own advice would apply to you too. If you do not like my terms, you do not have to accept them. I'm simply saying, my terms for this article are eight dollars in advance, and then you may have my article on Jessie Benton Fremont."

He sighed again.

"Go see the cashier," he said. "Tell him I'm authorizing payment for an article. He'll check with me, and then you'll have your payment."

I turned and left his office and did as he said. An hour later I was walking back up the street to Miss Bean's. I felt like shouting at the top of my lungs.

I had done it!

CHAPTER 36

LAST NIGHT ALONE
ON THE TRAIL

Two nights later I was camping between Auburn and Colfax beside a blazing fire. I'd be home the next day.

I'd spent the previous night with Miss Baxter in Sacramento, and I could have slept this night in Auburn. But somehow I felt that I wanted to finish off this adventure alone, by myself, beside a campfire I had built, sleeping under the stars. I suppose it was a dangerous thing for a young woman to do. After all, even if Buck Krebbs was gone, there were a thousand more just like him, and California was still no tame land.

But I wanted to do it. By the time I rode back into Miracle Springs tomorrow, I would have spent eleven days alone. It was like nothing I'd ever done before. I'd gone off chasing a dream—in search of a story I didn't even know existed. I had found it, written it, and sold it for eight dollars! I'd met some interesting people. I'd taken care of myself. I'd faced some scary situations and come through them. I was eleven days older, but I felt about eleven years older! Something inside me had changed. I had learned some things about myself, about what I was capable of. And this seemed the fitting way for me to spend my last night.

I had also learned to pray in some new ways, and to depend on God more than I'd ever had to before. And now I knew a little more about what that verse in the Bible really meant about God guiding our steps. He had really guided mine!

I guess I felt I had grown up a little bit. Well . . . grown up a lot. Especially standing there staring back at Mr. Kemble and saying if he didn't pay me the eight dollars, I was leaving. I had met a lady who knew the man who might be the country's next President. The next first lady had read one of my articles, and now I'd written an article about her. Why, I practically had an invitation to the White House! I felt like I'd gone halfway around the world in those eleven days. I'd talked about and thought about some big and important things. And now here I was going back to little Miracle Springs in the foothills of the California gold country. Yet another part of me had been opened to a bigger and wider world, and I knew I'd never be the same again.

I *could* be a writer now; I already was a writer. Maybe I'd do other things. Maybe I would teach or keep working for the Freight Company. But at least I knew I *could* do it. I could go into the office of an editor of a California newspaper and put my pages down on the desk and say, "There's a story that Corrie Belle Hollister wrote, Mister. I wrote it, and folks are going to want to read it!"

So I sat there staring into my little fire, eating dried venison and hardtack and some apples Miss Baxter gave me. I felt peaceful inside. Peaceful and thoughtful and even a little melancholy. This had been an adventure, but now it was over. I knew I'd face disappointments in the future, and probably write a lot more articles that wouldn't get printed. And there would probably be times Mr. Kemble would win and would stare *me* back into a corner and make *me* give in and do it his way.

But I would always have the memory of this journey, of feeling a story calling out to me though I didn't even know what it was, of going out and uncovering it. Next time I'd have more courage to ask questions and to knock on doors and to search and try to uncover something. I was lucky this time, meeting Ankelita Carter. But I had met her because I struck out and tried something scary. Maybe next time, though it would be different, God would lead me to someone else, to a different set of circumstances that would take me in the direction of the story I was after.

There were no sounds around me but the crackling of the fire and the crickets in the woods. I hoped no wild animals came. I was especially afraid of bears and snakes, and I didn't even have a gun—only a small knife.

But God would protect me and take care of me. He had so far. Why would this night be any different?

Maybe that's one reason I wanted to spend the last night alone like this on the trail. I had been nervous and anxious plenty of times in the last ten days. Yet I hadn't been in any situation that was downright "dangerous." I wasn't really in any danger now. But I wanted to prove to myself that if I had to, if I was out tracking a story again sometime, and I did have to fend for myself—up in the mountains, or down in the valley where there was no town—I could do it. Maybe someday I'd even travel farther from home, or back East—or maybe I *would* go to the White House someday. Wherever I went, I wanted to know that even if I was all alone, I could stand on my own two feet and say to God, "Well, it's just the two of us, Lord. And that's plenty to handle just about anything that comes along!"

My eyes were fixed on the bright orange coals of the fire, and I found myself praying quietly as I sat there.

"Lord, I am grateful to you for doing like you promised, and for guiding my footsteps on this trip. I don't know whether I trusted you very well or not. I tried to, but then sometimes it's hard to remember. Yet you just kept taking care of me, anyway. And, Lord, I thank you, too, for the article, and for all the ways you have been helping my writing this last year. You showed me a while back that trusting you is the way you give us the desires of our hearts. But you've let me be a writer too! You've given me that dream, Lord, and I am so thankful to you! Help me to write just like you want me to. And teach me to trust you more! I really do want to, God. I want to do just what you want me to do, and I want to be just exactly the person you want Corrie Hollister to be."

I drew in a deep breath. I felt so peaceful. God had been good to me!

The night air was getting chilly. I lay down and pulled my blankets tight around me. And still staring into the fire, the sounds of the crickets in my ears, I gradually fell asleep.

CHAPTER 37

HOME AGAIN

I'd left Miracle on a Monday. It was now Friday afternoon, a week and a half later, the 29th of August. I wondered if Almeda would be at the office, but I was actually relieved when she wasn't. I wanted to see everyone at once.

I can hardly describe the feelings I had inside as I went around the last turn in the road and the house came into view. I felt as if I'd gone to a foreign country and was now returning after many years. Yet it had only been eleven days!

Almost immediately Becky saw me. But instead of coming to meet me, she turned around and ran inside, then out again, then up the creek, screaming at the top of her twelve-year-old lungs, "Corrie's here! Corrie's home . . . it's Corrie . . . Corrie's back!"

Within seconds people were pouring through the door of the house, and out of the corner of my eye I saw Pa and Uncle Nick and Mr. Jones running down from the mine. By then my eyes were full of tears; everybody was hugging and laughing and shouting and asking questions, and I could hardly tell who was who. I was so happy, yet I couldn't stop crying even at the same time as I was laughing and smiling and trying to talk. And I don't even remember getting off my horse, but there I was surrounded by the people I loved so much, arms and hands and voices all coming at me at once. Every once in a while I'd hear a voice I knew—Katie's one minute, then Alkali Jones's high *hee*, *hee*, *hee*, and of course all my sisters and brothers shouting at once. The only two voices I don't remember hearing were the two whose sound I loved more than all the others. But Pa and Almeda and I got a chance to visit quietly alone later. The three of us stayed up and talked around the fire way past midnight, and I told them everything.

"I've got to tell you, Corrie," said Almeda when I was through, "we were mighty concerned about you."

"I know," I said. "I'm sorry."

"You're starting to remind me of myself, girl!" said Pa with a smile. "Maybe it ain't just the Belle blood, but some of the Hollister too. Tarnation, but I'd like to see you in ten years! You're gonna be some woman, that's all I got to say."

I could tell that in spite of Almeda's concern, Pa was proud of me. I suppose he'd figured I was a mite timid—which I was!—for a daughter of his. So I think he liked what I'd done. He'd been acting a little different toward me all evening—not just treating me like I was older and wasn't a little girl anymore, but also more like a son who had done something brave. Being gone a few days wasn't all *that* courageous a thing. But because it was *me*, timid little Corrie Belle, I think it gave Pa kind of a special feeling to see his daughter do it. Zack acted different, too, as if I'd proved my right to be the oldest Hollister.

Once the article on Jessie Fremont appeared in the August 30 issue of the *Daily Alta*—on the *second* page with a big bold caption over three columns, with my name right under the title!—my life would never be the same again. Whether I liked it or not, ever after that I *was* a reporter, a writer, and much would change as a result. How many times I must have read those words over: "The Real Jessie Benton Fremont . . . *by Corrie Belle Hollister*." I was so thankful inside, so thankful to God. More and more, as I reflected back on those eleven days, I realized that none of it would have happened had he not been guiding my steps just as he promised. Even though I wasn't aware of it at the time, and even though I hadn't even been thinking of him through some of it, he had been there all the time, going along the path just in front of me.

As I read over the article and the caption and my name

underneath, I couldn't help wondering if I shouldn't have used my full given name, *Cornelia*. But when I later suggested it to Mr. Kemble, he said, "Too late, Corrie. Folks know you now. And once you're writing with one name, you can't change it any more than you can change horses in mid-river, as the saying goes. No, you stick with Corrie. It's a good name, and folks are starting to recognize it."

The excitement of my trip and the article died down, especially after church on Sunday when everybody asked me all about it, and then the following Monday I went into the office with Almeda and spent a regular day working in town.

I'd almost forgotten about the Miracle Springs election. Almeda hadn't said much about it since my return, but all of a sudden the church service on Sunday seemed to stir it up again, even more than before. People came up to me afterward, welcoming me home, asking me about the trip and what I'd done, and most everybody said something about my interviewing them earlier about the mayor's election. Sometimes it was just a little comment, like, "I been thinking about that conversation we had," or they might say, "I might like t' talk t' you again, Corrie, if yer still gonna do interviewin' about it."

Most of the folks were quiet about it, as if they didn't want anyone to hear them talking to me. And Mr. Royce acted pretty friendly at the service too, like I reckon a fellow ought to be if he's trying to make people vote for him. He was greeting the men and their wives and shaking hands. And he even came up to me and gave me a light slap on the shoulder and said "Good to have you back, Corrie!" before he went on to visit someone else.

But in the background amid all the hubbub of the after-church visiting, lots of people seemed as if they wanted to talk to me again about the election. My getting back to town seemed to stir up people's thinking in a new way.

All day Monday my mind was on the interview article, going over what I'd done and things people had told me and thinking of how to go about starting to write the article. There were only two months left before the election, so I couldn't delay too long. On Tuesday, the *Alta* came with my article in it, which set my mind running in a hundred directions at once! So it wasn't until Wednesday that I really settled myself down enough to think about the interviews and article again. That morning I gathered my papers together and put them in my satchel to take with me into town to work. I hoped to see some of the people who'd talked to me at church. There were still a few people in town I hadn't interviewed yet. As I went through my notes and quotes from what people had told me before and started to consider actually beginning to write the article in a way that Mr. Kemble'd like, I found myself getting enthusiastic about it again.

But that very evening something happened that suddenly changed my thoughts not only about the article I wanted to write but about the whole mayor's election.

CHAPTER 38

THREATS

Not long after Almeda and I got back home from town, we heard a single-horse carriage approach outside and then slow to a stop. Pa went to the window, and when he turned back inside, his face wore a look of question and significance.

"Franklin Royce" was all he said, half in statement, half in question.

We all looked at one another, but the knock on the door came before we had the chance to wonder fully what the visit could possibly be about.

Pa opened the door.

"Good evening, Mr. Hollister," I heard the familiar voice say, "might I have a word with your wife?"

Pa nodded, stepped aside, and gestured Royce into the room. Almeda stood and offered her hand. Royce shook it, though without conviction.

"Mrs. Hollister," he said rather stiffly, "I would appreciate a few moments of your time."

"Of course, Franklin," she said deliberately. It was clear from his tone this was no social call. "Please . . . sit down." She pointed to an empty chair.

"In private, if you don't mind," he added.

"Anything you have to say to me can just as well be said in front of my husband," she replied, her voice betraying a slight edge to it. I think she was perturbed by his unsmiling seriousness. She continued to look right at him, but neither said another word.

Pa had a hesitant look on his face, not seeming to know what he ought to do. But finally spoke up.

"It's no never-mind to me, Almeda," he said. "Come on, kids, let's go outside. But I'm warning you, Royce," he added to the banker. "I'm going to be right outside this door, and if you say something my wife don't like, I'll be right back in here and throw you out on your ear!"

Every one of us was curious what Mr. Royce's visit was about, but we all got up and started trooping silently toward the door that Pa held open for us. I was the next to last one, but before I reached the door, I heard Royce's voice again.

"Perhaps *Miss* Hollister could join us," he said, speaking to Almeda but gesturing his head in my direction. "What I have to say concerns her as well as you."

I glanced up at Pa. He shrugged. "If he wants to talk to you, it's okay by me." But as he said it he was staring daggers at Mr. Royce.

I turned around and went back to where I was sitting, while Pa and Zack filed outside with the others and closed the door. Once we were alone, Mr. Royce still did not take the seat Almeda offered him, but began speaking immediately.

"Almeda, when you first announced that you were going to run against me for mayor, like everyone else I was surprised, interested, even curious. And for a while I was willing to play along with your little charade of pretending to be a politician. But when matters grew more serious and when people began to talk and I began to fear for the business of my bank, then I grew concerned. You were visiting people and rousing them up against me. I came to you in your office, and I tried to be reasonable. I asked you as cooperatively as I was able to cease and desist, and to withdraw before more harm was done. But you refused. You have persisted in your efforts to undermine my reputation. Your flyers continue to circulate. And now you have set your stepdaughter to do your dirty work, talking with everyone in town, asking their opinions."

He stopped, but just long enough to take a breath of air.

"Now," he continued, "I'm here to tell you—both of you—

that I want this to stop. It's futile, it's useless. You cannot win the election, Almeda, and I will not have you stirring up the community against me any longer. I've been patient for as long as I can, but it's time I put my foot down. I want it to stop. And as for you, young lady," he said, turning and looking me straight in the face, "I do not want you talking to anyone else about the election."

"You leave Corrie out of this, Franklin," said Almeda heatedly. "This election campaign is between you and me."

"Then *you* tell her to stop with these ridiculous interviews."

"I will do no such thing. She is a newspaper reporter in her own right and I will not tell her what she can or cannot pursue."

"Newspaper reporter! That's a good one," he laughed. "That's almost as humorous as a woman mayor!"

By now we were *both* more than a little annoyed!

"My editor in San Francisco is paying me for two stories about the Miracle Springs election," I said. "I have done nothing to hurt you in any way."

"Except get people talking."

"It's hardly *our* fault if people talk," I said. "And you can't blame *us* for what they think of you."

I shouldn't have said it, but the words were out of my mouth before I realized it. Now Royce was angry too, and he made no more attempt to mask his true intentions.

"Look," he said, "Hollister may pamper the two of you in your little schemes! But he never did have much backbone. It's a rough world out there, and no two interfering women are going to spoil my plans, no matter what their fool of a husband and a father lets them get away with. Two can play this little game of yours, and you don't want to play it against me. Stop now, or I'll make life miserable for all of you!"

"How dare you talk that way of the finest man in Miracle Springs!" cried Almeda, rising from her chair.

I expected to see Pa burst through the door any minute and slam his fist into Royce's face.

"You are meddling in what is not your business, and he is a weakling if he cannot prevent you."

"You are the fool, Franklin Royce, for not knowing a real man when you see him! And as for the election, my campaign is *not* a charade. I have not roused a soul against you, and have never once even mentioned your name in a single discussion with anyone. Corrie is absolutely right—you can hardly hold *us* responsible for what people may think of you! I have done *nothing* to undermine your reputation. And I would never think of resorting to dirty work, as you call it, still less of asking Corrie or anyone else to do it for me. I resent your charges against me, Franklin, and I will *not* withdraw from this election!"

"It will not go well with you, Almeda, if you do not reconsider."

"What's more," she added, "not only will I see it through to November, after today, Franklin, you have shown me more clearly than ever that for Miracle Springs to elect you its mayor would be a grievous mistake. You have made me more determined than ever to *win* that election!"

"If you do win, Almeda," and his voice was deadly serious, "you will live to regret it! I will make life so miserable for you and your family that you will have no choice but to resign, and I will be made mayor eventually anyway."

"What can you possibly do to us?" she shot back. "You hold no mortgages on either my property or Drummond's. The little my business owes you is unsecured."

"The people of this community who *are* indebted to me will find themselves compelled to reconsider where they purchase their supplies. In fact, I have been thinking of opening a supplies outlet and freight service myself, as an adjunct to the bank."

"Dare to go into business against me, Franklin, and you will find I am a strong businesswoman, with more contacts and experience than your money alone will buy you."

I had never seen Almeda like this. She was seething.

"Perhaps that is true," replied Royce, with a sly smile. "But you will not be able to survive long without customers. And the men of this community will know they had better deal with me or else find themselves foreclosed upon. Most of the mortgages I hold have a thirty-day call."

"You are an unscrupulous man, Franklin!"

"It's called 'the fine print,' Almeda. Every standard banking contract has its share, and I simply use it to my own advantage, as does any wise businessman when it comes to matters of finances."

"When the people find out you are trying to blackmail this town into electing you its mayor, they will never stand for it!"

"They will have little choice. If they do not vote for me, I will simply call their loans due. Within a year I'll own the whole town. In the meantime, you'll be out of business for lack of customers."

"Well, you don't own *us*, Franklin! You may blackmail the rest of this town, and you may put Parrish Mine and Freight out of business. But you will never control me, or my husband, or our family! If it comes to that, I will leave the business and move out to the claim. We will manage with or without the Parrish Freight."

"Ah yes . . . the *claim*," said Royce, drawing out the words with a significant expression. "That brings up an interesting point which I have been looking into. You are correct, Almeda, in that I hold no mortgage on the property your husband and his brother-in-law claim as their own. However, according to my investigations there may be some question as to the validity of their ownership of the land."

"That is preposterous, Franklin!" Almeda nearly exploded. "You know the doctrine of *free mines* as well as anyone else in California. Whoever first stakes out a claim has exclusive right to the land. Drummond and Nick have been on that property since 1849, long before you ever got to California!"

"Granted, they have right to *use* the land, but that does not make the land itself theirs. I have been looking into the deeds to actual land ownership in and around Miracle Springs, and let us simply say the results may surprise many people."

"You wouldn't dare try to run the miners around here off their land! You wouldn't survive a month as mayor!"

"There are laws, Almeda," Royce said, trying to sound calm. "California is a state now. There are legalities to be observed. Surely you know of the recent Supreme Court decision in the Fremont case *against* free mines. I tell you, Almeda, your husband's position may be very tenuous indeed, and he may find it more pleasant to have me as his friend rather than his enemy. Especially when the authorities who might be compelled to look into the matter discover his criminal record, and learn that he is still wanted by the law in the East. I very seriously doubt that they'll uphold his claim to the property, especially given the Mariposa ruling."

"You are full of threats, Franklin," replied Almeda, and she had now grown calm as well—calm and cold. "But Sheriff Rafferty put the matter of my husband's past to rest long ago."

"Rafferty is a weakling, too!" Royce spat back. "There are others who might find his failure to uphold his duty cause for his removal as well. As mayor of Miracle Springs, I may well find that I must—"

"You will never be mayor, Franklin! Not if I can help it. You will not get away with all this!"

Suddenly the room grew silent. Royce stared back at Almeda with piercing eyes. When he next spoke, all anger, all passion, all intensity from his voice was gone. His words were icy, measured, and the look in his eyes hateful.

"I have tried to be as reasonable as a man can be, Almeda. But you have left me no choice. As a gentleman I am loathe to stoop to such measures, but you force my hand."

He paused, and his eyes squinted in a glare of evil determination.

"If the hurt to come to the rest of the town, if the loss of your business, if danger to your husband, and if the loss of all this property here on your so-called claim—if all these things do not convince you that it is in everyone's best interest for you to withdraw from the race, then perhaps what I have to tell you now *will* convince you.

"There are men in this state, even now, who will stop at nothing to see Fremont defeated in the general election, men whose interests will be more preserved under a Buchanan presidency than one led by an anti-slavery westerner."

He looked over in my direction.

"Our budding reporter here is taking a decidedly pro-Fremont stand in the *Alta*. Should these men I speak of learn that she is perhaps, as the daughter of a miner herself, planning to come out with an appeal for the miners of California to vote for Fremont, they would take such news very badly, and I would hate to see anything happen to Corrie as a result."

"I am planning no such pro-Fremont story," I said quickly. "I only wrote a story about his wife."

"Ah, but don't you see, Corrie," replied Royce, "these men do not take kindly to *any* such favorable articles. And word could begin to spread that you intended to take a more affirmative stand, and—well, you can see how a man in my position would . . . be powerless to stop such a rumor."

"Franklin, you are despicable!" said Almeda, practically shouting. "Are you now threatening Corrie with what is purely a false and—"

"Enough, Almeda!" Royce interrupted angrily. "I will do whatever I have to do! I have had people investigating you too, Almeda, as well as your husband and his daughter. If danger to your stepdaughter from the slavery people does not pound some sense into that stubborn brain of yours, then perhaps the people of Miracle Springs would like to read a little flyer that I might circulate just prior to the election concerning what I have recently discovered from my contact in Boston. You have an interesting past, Almeda!"

At the word *Boston,* Almeda's face grew white. She spoke not another word, and sank into a chair as if she had been suddenly struck a devastating blow.

"Forgive me, Almeda," said Royce. "I do not want to use the information I possess, either against you or your stepdaughter. I admit it is not the gentleman's way. But you are a stubborn woman, and I will do what I have to!"

He spun around and quickly left the house.

CHAPTER 39

MEETING OF THE COMMITTEE

The rest of that night and all the next two days Almeda was practically silent. Not a word was said about Royce's visit. Pa asked no questions. I guess he knew Almeda would tell him about it when the time was right. I didn't say anything either. I figured it was her business to share, not mine.

On the evening of the second day, Almeda got the six of us together—Zack and I, Katie and Uncle Nick, and she and Pa— for what she called a campaign committee meeting. Then she told everyone else about Mr. Royce's visit and that he'd promised to do some pretty bad things to a lot of people if she kept on with the election.

"I believe you men have an expression," she said, trying to force a smile, "when you are playing poker and realize you can't possibly win the pot. Well, I finally realize there is no way I am holding a winning hand, and it's simply time for me to throw in my cards, as you say. So I've decided to pull out of the mayor's race."

A few groans went around, but then it got quiet again.

"I am very disappointed too," she went on. "And I am convinced that Franklin Royce is more of a louse than when I began. But it just is not fair for me to continue. Too many people could be hurt. And it isn't worth it just for my pride to try to defeat him."

"But you *can* defeat him, Almeda," insisted Katie.

"The price would be too high. Many of the miners and families around Miracle Springs could be hurt."

"How?" asked Uncle Nick. "What can he do if you win?"

"He's a banker, Nick," she replied with a thin smile. "He can do whatever he wants. Specifically, he can make it very hard for folks whose mortgages he's holding. He as much as threatened to begin foreclosures if I didn't withdraw." She told them what Royce had said.

"The man is a ruthless skunk!" muttered Pa.

"But it isn't only the townspeople I'm concerned about," Almeda went on. "He threatened all of you too." She told about the questions he'd raised about ownership of the land, and about his threats to reopen Pa and Uncle Nick's problems with the law.

By now Uncle Nick was pacing about the floor angrily.

"We can fight him!" he said, waving his hands in the air. "Me and Drum ain't afraid of him. We been up against worse odds dozens of times!"

"He's a powerful man, Nick," said Almeda. "I'm not willing to run the risk of us losing our land here, or the mine. We've got a good life and I just can't take that chance. And besides all that, he threatened Corrie as well."

"He what?" Pa roared, his eyes flashing. "If he dares lay a hand on any of my—"

"Only on account of my writing, Pa," I said quickly. "He's not about to hurt me himself."

"What can your writing have to do with it? What did he say?"

"I didn't really understand it all myself, Pa," I answered, "but he said there were rich and powerful slave-state men who were determined to see Mr. Fremont lose in California, and who would do anything they could to stop him."

"His implication was that something could happen to Corrie if she got in their way," said Almeda seriously.

"What could Corrie possibly have to do with the outcome of the election?" asked Pa.

"After her article in the *Alta* about Mrs. Fremont, she could be seen as a Fremont supporter, especially if she wrote more such articles."

"Then she doesn't need to write any more."

"That's what I told him too, Pa," I said.

"Franklin implied that he knew some of these men, and that if I didn't do as he said, he would start a rumor to the effect that Corrie Hollister, a miner's daughter, was planning a major story to try to persuade California's miners to vote for Fremont. Even if it wasn't true, if he did what he said, it could endanger Corrie . . . and every one of us. The man has no scruples, and I have no doubt that he would do it just to spite me."

The room was quiet. I think any of us would have been willing to go up against Mr. Royce if the only danger was to himself. But when harm could come to so many others, no one was quite willing to take that chance.

"So you see," Almeda said at last with a sigh, "why I just cannot continue on with the election. The risk to all of you whom I love, and to others in the community, is simply too great. I'm afraid I'm just going to have to go into town and face Franklin again. And as much as it galls me to have to give in, I'm going to have to tell him he's won."

She took a deep breath, looked around at the rest of us, then got up out of her chair and slowly walked outside and away from the house. No one followed. We all understood that she needed some time alone.

During the whole discussion she had not once mentioned Royce's threats to her business, or what he said he had discovered about Boston. And after seeing the look on Almeda's face just before Royce had left, I certainly wasn't going to bring up the subject. Whatever it meant, it was clear there was a great deal of pain involved for her. Still, I couldn't help wondering how much these words of Royce's influenced her decision.

After about five or ten minutes Pa followed Almeda outside. It was an hour before the two of them came back inside. Almeda's face was red, and I knew she'd been crying. Pa was serious, but the rest of that evening whenever he'd look at her, his face was more full of love than I'd ever seen it.

Both of them were quiet, and neither said a word about their time alone together outside.

CHAPTER 40

A SURPRISE LETTER

The rest of that week things were pretty sullen and quiet around the office and at home. We were all disappointed and angry, yet there was nothing we could do. Mr. Royce had us over a barrel.

I didn't write a word or interview anyone. As much as I hated to quit on something I'd started, a dollar or two wasn't worth getting Almeda or Pa in trouble with a man like the banker of Miracle Springs. As for what he'd said about me, I have to say I didn't think of it that much. I didn't see how anything I wrote could possibly put *me* in any danger. Almeda didn't say anything to Mr. Royce, though she took the banner down from our office window.

The thought did occur to me that perhaps·I could still write an article or two about the election, even maybe with some of the quotes from talking to people, if I showed it to Mr. Royce first and he didn't see anything wrong with what I'd said. I would hate to do that! But it did seem like a possible way to be able to do the article. Maybe this was the other side of the question Almeda had put to me before I went to Mariposa: How bad did I want to write? Did I want it bad enough to crawl to Mr. Royce for approval? I didn't know if I wanted it *that* bad.

Fortunately I didn't have to decide. All of a sudden I was thrown into the middle of a new story, one that made the Miracle Springs election—or what was left of it, anyway—seem small and far away.

The following Monday a letter arrived for me in the mail. I immediately recognized the *Alta* envelope. I opened it and read:

Miss Hollister,

A major story is about to break which will doom Colonel Fremont's chance for election. We can still stop it, but time is short and I need your help. After your article on Mrs. Fremont—which I must confess turned out to be worth the $8 from all the favorable response it has received—it could well be that you have the necessary contacts to get to the bottom of this scheme to ruin the Colonel's reputation.

I must warn you, however, there could be danger. Powerful men with great resources behind them are involved. If you want to help, the *Alta* version of the story will be yours to write. I hope this reaches you in time. If interested, I will be at the offices of the *Daily and Weekly Sacramento Times* at two o'clock on the afternoon of Wednesday the 12th. Meet me there.

Edward Kemble
September 8, 1856

I could hardly believe my eyes! Mr. Kemble was asking *me* for help!

I ran across the street and burst through the door of the office. "Look at this!" I cried, waving the letter in my hand.

Almeda took it and scanned it quickly. Then she just looked up at me with raised inquiring eyebrows.

"I've got to ride home and pack my things," I said. "I've only got forty-eight hours to get there!" I reached for the letter and was ready to head back out the door.

"Are you sure you know what you're doing, Corrie?" asked Almeda.

"This could be my big chance!" I answered.

"And the danger?"

"How bad could it be? No one would try to hurt me."

"People do awful things sometimes when you try to thwart their plans. You remember what Royce said."

"This doesn't have anything to do with that."

"Just be sure, Corrie, that's all."

I paused, my hand on the knob of the half-opened door, and looked back at Almeda. Her eyes were filled with concern.

"I'm not sure," I said. "But maybe the only way I'm going to be sure is to go ahead, and see what God does. But I'll talk to Pa . . . and I'll pray. I'll try hard not to do anything foolish."

"Then God go with you, my daughter. I love you . . . and I too will pray!"

For one moment our eyes met, and in that moment worlds were spoken between us. The next instant I was out the door, onto my horse, and dashing toward home as fast as Raspberry could gallop, my hair streaming out behind me, the early autumn wind chilling my nose and ears.

I was at home in less than an hour. I threw together what food I could find, rolled up three blankets, and repacked my little tin fire box. It wasn't cold yet, but the nights would be chilly so I dressed up as warm as I could, and put extra clothes, a warm coat, an extra pair of boots, a rain slicker, and several old newspapers in a bag. Then I got together my writing satchel.

Once Pa read the letter, he figured it was too late to try to stop me. He probably wouldn't have tried, anyway. The look in his eyes said to me that he thought I was ready to face whatever the world might throw at me. And if I wasn't, then maybe it was high time I learned to be.

"You go and do your name proud, Corrie Hollister," he said. "You're a Belle *and* a Hollister. And when anyone tries to give you a hard time, you just remember that, and remember you're tougher'n any of 'em. And you're God's daughter and Drummond Hollister's little girl too—and I figure that gives you a winning hand against just about anybody. Now you go and show that fella Kemble what kind of stuff you're made of!"

"Thanks, Pa," I said.

"I love you, Corrie Belle," he added. His voice was soft and shaky.

I wheeled Raspberry around. I couldn't say anything back because of the big lump in my throat and the tears in my eyes.

I dug my heels into my mare's sides and took off down the road. Before I was out of sight, I glanced back and waved. There was Pa still standing in the same place, his hand in the air.

CHAPTER 41

SACRAMENTO

I walked into the office of the Sacramento *Times* at ten minutes after two on Wednesday.

I had ridden my mare as hard as I dared, spent both nights on the trail, and arrived in Sacramento just in time to go to Miss Baxter's to take a bath, change into presentable clothes for seeing an editor, and get directions where to go. I didn't know Sacramento very well, and it was growing so fast that it seemed to have changed every time I came.

A man sat at a desk inside an open office just inside the main door. He walked out and looked me over.

"I'm here to see Mr. Edward Kemble of the *Alta,*" I said.

"Yes, I was told to expect you," he replied. "Right this way, Miss Hollister."

He led me down a hall and opened a door for me. I walked inside. He stayed outside, closing the door behind me.

Mr. Kemble sat at a table in the center of the small office. There was no one else in the room.

"I'm sorry I'm late," I said. "I came as quick as I could. I left the minute I got your letter."

"Good . . . good, Hollister," he said. "Sit down." He pointed toward the chair opposite him.

I sat down and took off my coat. He started right in.

"I don't know how much you know about California politics," he said, "but it's a real mess this year. You would think that with Fremont's ties to the state, he'd be a shoo-in to win California."

"That's what my pa says," I added. From the look on Mr. Kemble's face, I gathered this was a time he wanted to listen to himself talk, and wasn't particularly interested in my responses. I settled back in my chair and listened.

"Well, it isn't necessarily so. Fremont's in a bunch of trouble here, and California's one of the critical states that's going to decide this election. It's all split right down the middle of the Mason-Dixon line—Fremont and the Republicans above it, Buchanan and the Democrats below it. But even with all Fremont's exploring and connections to the West, and the anti-slavery sentiment of the North, his chances are still shaky in some places—like California and Pennsylvania. The Republican party is too new. The Democrats are just plain a stronger party. They've got the South all sewed up, while at the same time there are bad fractures in the northeast and west.

"The trouble is, there's a lot of folks who don't like the idea of slavery, but they have always been Democrats. And there's some of us who are afraid that in this election we're going to find out they're more *for* being Democrats than they are *against* slavery.

"Now, you take the Germans. There's likely a hundred, maybe a hundred and fifty thousand Germans who are going to vote next month; most of them are Democrats and always have been. They don't like slavery, but they're Democrats and nobody knows how they're going to go. And so both parties are trying to win them over and are giving them money, and there are editorials aimed at the immigrant vote in the New York *Tribune* and the Cleveland *Herald* and the *Ohio State Journal* and the Detroit *Free Press* and the Cincinnati *Enquirer* and every other paper in the country. And the Democrats are stirring up fear of a Southern secession from the Union if Fremont wins. The Philadelphia *Daily News* and the *Pittsburgh Post* and the Washington *Daily Globe* are full of that stuff. The fear is worst in Pennsylvania. Listen to this."

He stopped a minute and rifled through several papers on the table in front of him. I didn't understand everything he was saying, but it was interesting, and I didn't want to interrupt again. He found the paper he was looking for.

"Listen—this is from the *Daily Pennsylvania* just a couple months ago: 'There is no disguising the fact that the great question of union or disunion has been precipitated upon us by the mad fanatics of the North, and that it is a direct and inevitable issue in the presidential contest.' "

He put the paper down and glanced across the desk at me. I think he was almost surprised to see that he'd been delivering his political speech to no one but me, who barely understood half of it.

"Do you get what I'm driving at, Hollister?" he asked.

"Some of it," I answered.

"I'm talking about this country splitting apart—that's the kind of fear the southern Democrats are putting into the people of the North. They're blackmailing the voters, threatening to pull the South out of the Union if Fremont is elected. But if Buchanan is elected, then the South wins . . . and slavery wins. The Democrats are saying, 'Give us the victory, put our man in the White House, let slavery remain, and we won't destroy this nation.' Now I ask you, can we allow this country to submit to that kind of blackmail? Of course we can't. Slavery is wrong, Hollister, and that's what John Fremont stands for, and that's why he must be elected in November. The Southern states will never secede from the Union, even over slavery. The secession issue is a bluff."

He stopped, took a breath, but then went right on.

"It's the Southerners, the Democrats, these blackmailers holding the threat of secession over the rest of the country, who are trying to ruin Fremont. They're spreading all kinds of lies and rumors about him—saying that his parents weren't married until after he was born, ridiculing him for his beard, claiming that he had once been a French actor, saying that he is secretly a Catholic, that he hates Germans because of his French blood, and hinting at improprieties, even illegalities, in how he came by his wealth. And the rumors involve his wife too—that's where you come in, Hollister. There are reports circulating that Jessie Fremont has never forsaken her Virginia upbringing, that she still keeps slaves and even watches while they are beaten at her orders, and that she herself was suckled by a slave mammy on her father's plantation.

"They're all lies. Vicious lies. But they are damaging Fremont's chances. And I don't have to tell you what that means to California. Buchanan stands for the interests of the South. His election will mean that the West will be forgotten.

"Many people feel that the future of California depends on a rail line between Chicago and Kansas City and the Pacific. Mark Hopkins, Charles Crocker, Leland Stanford, C.P. Huntington, and others like them are backing Fremont for that reason. They know that the only hope for a transcontinental railroad lies with the Republican party. And that's why our paper, the *Alta*, and the *Daily* and *Weekly Times* here in Sacramento are doing our best for him. But our competitors are working just as hard to discredit him. The Sacramento *Union*, the *Courier*, the *Democratic State Journal* are all backing Buchanan. And the worst is the *Morning Globe* in my own city, where some of my own former colleagues have defected.

"Fortunately, I have a spy at the *Globe* who keeps me informed, and only last week I learned that they are planning a major story to run just a week before the election, a story they hope will utterly ruin Fremont and insure his defeat. Their timing is intended to sway last-minute voters, and I fear they may have similar stories they will break in some of the eastern papers as well."

He paused and gave me a long, serious look.

"You understand what it's all about, don't you, Hollister?" he said after a minute. "It's slavery . . . and power . . . and greed. You've got to understand all this so you'll know the kind of men we're up against. We may be fifteen hundred miles from the nearest slave plantation, and California may be a free state. But there are men here who work for some of the most powerful and wealthy men in the South. And they're doing whatever it takes to put Buchanan in the White House and keep their power from eroding. The South controls the country right now, and they don't want to lose their hold on Washington. Men like Fremont, and that young lawyer from Illinois, Lincoln, who aren't afraid to speak up, are in danger. And *we* may be in danger too. But we've got to do what we can, and we've got to try to scoop them on their story before they print it. We've got to discredit everything they say before they say it, and print our own major new pro-Fremont piece. We may not be able to change what they do in Pennsylvania. It's too late for that. But if we can swing the vote in California, it may be enough to put your friend Jessie Fremont in the White House."

"I didn't say she was actually my friend," I corrected him.

He looked at me crooked for a second. "I thought you did," he said finally. "Well, that makes no difference. You obviously have *some* connection."

"What do you want me to do?" I asked. "I don't know anything about politics. I don't see how I can be of much help."

"One of Senator Goldwin's men is supposed to be up in the Mother Lode somewhere, digging up the last of the dirt they're planning to use against Fremont."

"Who's Senator Goldwin?"

"Herbert Goldwin—just about the most powerful man in the U.S. Senate, an entrenched slave owner, and filthy rich from his huge cotton plantations in South Carolina. Also one of the most unscrupulous men in Washington. He'd lie or cheat, steal, maybe even kill to keep his little empire secure. Fremont's spoken out against him, and Goldwin hates the Colonel. Of course he'd never soil his lily-white hands with his own dirty work. But he has plenty of people to do it for him. And one of them's up Sonora way rousing up all kinds of mischief— getting falsified documents against Fremont, getting interviews from miners Fremont supposedly ran off the Mariposa at gunpoint. Then there's the Catholic angle, and the rumors against Mrs. Fremont. My contact at the *Globe* says this guy's due back in San Francisco in a week and a half with the last pieces of the article which will, his editor claims, 'nail down the coffin on the presidential bid of John Charles Fremont.' We've got to locate that guy and find out what he's got so we can see if there's any substance to it. If they're making claims, we need to find out whether they're true or false."

"What's the man's name?" I asked. This was getting mighty interesting!

"We think Gregory, or something like that. Only heard the name once, so we can't be sure."

"And you don't know exactly where he is?"

"I had someone else on it, but they lost his trail. Sonora's the last scent we had, which makes sense—there's a lot of anti-Fremont talk among the miners that close to Mariposa. Lot of 'em think they ought to be entitled to the gold on Fremont's estate, and they don't like him getting rich while they're scratching away for tiny little nuggets. And just between you and me, I wouldn't doubt if what Goldwin *really* wants is the Mariposa for himself! Rich guys like him can't stand when a man like John Fremont comes into a lot of dough overnight. They want all the wealth and power for themselves, and it makes them crawl to have to share it."

"What do you want *me* to do?" I asked. "Why do you think *I* can help?"

"Maybe you can't, but it's worth a try. So here's what I want you to do. Find this Gregory, or whoever he is, and find out what he's got. If he has something on Fremont or his wife that's not true, then use your contact to write an article discrediting Goldwin's charges."

"How could I possibly find him? I'm just . . . a girl!"

Mr. Kemble laughed. "Here all this time you've been wanting me to overlook that fact. And now when I drop something really important in your lap, you tell me you're not old enough to do it!"

"I didn't say I wasn't old enough. I just don't know what you expect me to do when your other man couldn't do it. I don't have experience tracking someone like that."

"Don't you see—you're the perfect one, Corrie. No one will suspect you of a thing. I doubt if anyone who's involved with Goldwin will even recognize your name. I could send one of my experienced men. But they'd spot him right off. No, I think you might be able to find out things someone else couldn't. You shouldn't even have to lie."

"I couldn't do that."

"I don't think you'll have to. But you won't be able to tell them what you're after."

"I still don't see why you want *me* to follow somebody."

"I'm not just sending you to track this fellow. I'm sending you after a story. You've got to get on the trail of this thing, find out what's at the bottom of it, and then write a story that tells the truth and shows up their lies for what they are. Once their story runs, it's too late. You've got to find the guy and uncover what he's trying to do. I don't know how, but that's what you've got to try to do. I can't do it, and none of my regular guys can do it because they know them all. But you can, Corrie—at least I hope you can, 'cause the outcome of the election in California may depend on it. You get to the bottom of it, find out the truth behind the things they're planning to say, and I'll make you a reporter, Corrie Hollister. You find this guy and uncover what Goldwin's up to, and get me the story I want *before* their charges can appear in the *Globe,* and I'll give you a monthly article of your very own, as an *Alta* regular."

I was stunned. It was the very thing I'd dreamed of. Yet how could I *possibly* do all he asked? I must have said something, or asked what I should do first, though I don't remember. But I do remember his answer.

Mr. Kemble's expression changed from concern to relief. "The first thing you do is get yourself out to Sonora and start asking questions and nosing around. Real quick you'll start to find out if you're *really* a reporter, or just a kid who wants to be one. And whatever you find out, it's got to be on my desk by noon on the 22nd or else we're done for. That's ten days, Hollister. By then we'll know what kind of stuff you're made of."

CHAPTER 42

SONORA

Everyone in California had heard about Sonora. Except for the area around Sutter's Mill farther north, it was one of the heaviest populated, roughest, and richest regions of the Mother Lode. There were stories told—and we'd heard them all the way up in Miracle Springs, thanks to Alkali Jones—of single nuggets worth thousands of dollars. One was found that was supposed to have weighed twenty-eight pounds!

The whole place had been fabulously rich in the few years after the rush. There were twenty or thirty separate little towns all within ten miles of Sonora. Every one had seen thousands of hopeful miners pass through, all with a hundred stories to tell. In Shaw's Flat, only a mile away, eighty-seven million dollars had been taken from its streams. Columbia, four miles away, supposedly had a population of 30,000 with over a hundred gambling houses, thirty saloons, twenty-seven food stores, a stadium, and a theater. Farther north, Mexican Flat and Roaring Camp and Columbia and Angels Camp and Sawmill Flat—they all could have laid claim to equal riches and equal notoriety. I'd heard stories of fights and jumped claims and even murder. Most of what I'd heard, coming from the mouth of Alkali Jones, was probably considerably bigger in the tale than in the reality, but that only made it all the more fearful for me as I rode into the heart of the Mother Lode—alone, and not even knowing what exactly I was looking for. I had been praying harder than ever before in my life since leaving Sacramento! And I hadn't been about to spend the night alone in this country—at least not my first night. I'd stayed at the National Hotel in Jackson, although it wasn't much better than sleeping outside. I'd heard yelling and singing and piano playing all night, and a couple of gunshots. But at least I'd been able to lock the door to my room!

Late the next morning I rode into Sonora, still praying, still thinking every other minute of just forgetting the whole thing and galloping back to Miracle Springs as fast as I could! But I knew I couldn't. Even though Pa didn't really approve of me riding down here alone, Mr. Kemble was counting on me. And maybe Mr. Fremont too, and Jessie Fremont, and even Ankelita Carter. So I had to do what I could. Even if I failed, I had to try.

I walked my mare slowly through the main street. I hoped I could find a boardinghouse in town instead of a hotel, because most of the hotels were connected with saloons, and stayed pretty loud and raucous all night long. But I didn't see anything that looked even halfway civilized. Every other building seemed to be a saloon, and from the sounds coming from them they all seemed full of men drinking and yelling. The people on the streets were all men, and I didn't see a friendly face anywhere. The ones who noticed me looked me over as I passed, and a few yelled and whistled at me. But I just kept going and tried to keep my face from turning red. I was beginning to think I was the only female in the whole place when two or three saloon girls came out of a place called the Lucky Sluice. They started calling out worse things than the men. I didn't like their looks at all!

Finally a little ways farther on, I spotted a building with just the word "Hotel" printed across the door. I rode toward it, stopped, got down and tied my horse to the hitching rail, and walked inside.

I was glad there was hardly anyone inside, though a few tables in the lobby indicated that probably card playing went on at night. A man stood behind a counter, and I walked toward him. But before I even got across the floor, a whistle behind me let me know that the man at the counter wasn't alone after all. "If it ain't a real live female woman!" someone said.

"Hey, Fence," a voice called out, "check her into my room!"

I ignored the noises behind me and went up to the counter. Before I'd said a word the man they called Fence pushed the register in my direction.

"Excuse me," I said, putting on my bravest-sounding voice, although I probably didn't convince anyone, "do you know if there's a boardinghouse in town?"

"I got a boardinghouse, Missy!" called out a voice, followed by footsteps slowly coming across the floor.

"Shut up, Jack!" said the hotel man. "Can't you see she's just a kid?"

"So much the better!"

"Get outta here, Jack. I don't want no trouble." Then looking down at me, the man said, "There's Miz Nason's place, little lady. Down the next street to the right, 'bout a quarter mile down."

Just as I was about to turn to leave, a thought occurred to me.

"You don't have a man by the name of Gregory registered here, do you?" I asked. I glanced down at the register and tried to scan the names on the page without being too conspicuous.

"Nope. But half the fellas what come to the diggin's ain't usin' their real names anyway."

"Thank you very much," I said, turning around to go. As I did I almost bumped into the man the hotel manager had called Jack. He had been standing right behind me. I didn't know how I couldn't have known it, because he smelled terrible. He must have been working for a month without a bath! He looked even worse, and I walked on past him toward the door without even looking into his face, though he muttered a few words as I went by. Just as I was going through the door, the hotel man's voice called out after me, "If you don't find no room, Missy," he said, "I got one you can have fer four dollar a day. The lock works, an' I personally keep Jack an' his kind off the second floor."

Four dollars! When Almeda and I went to San Francisco, she'd only paid six dollars a night at the fancy Oriental, and that was for *two* of us! And he wanted four, just for me, in this ramshackle place that looked like it hadn't been cleaned since the day it was built! I kept walking back out to the street, ignoring the voices and laughter coming from behind me.

I mounted my horse again and set off again in the direction that I hoped would lead me to Nason's boardinghouse. In five minutes I found myself approaching a decent-looking two-story wood house. At least the paint wasn't peeling and some grass was growing in front. A small hand-painted sign on the fence simply said "Nason."

I stopped, got off my horse, and walked up and knocked on the door. In a minute or two a stout, broad-shouldered black-haired woman opened it. She looked me over up and down, without the slightest change in her expression, then just stared at me, waiting.

"I'm interested in a room," I said, "if you have any available."

"Rooms? 'Course I got rooms!" she said back, a little too gruffly to make me feel altogether comfortable. "How many you got with ya?"

"It's just me, ma'am."

"Just you!" she exclaimed. "You expect me to believe a young thing like you's travelin' in *this* country alone?"

"I'm sorry, ma'am, but I really am by myself."

"Well, then, guess I can't hardly send you away. Yeah, I got a room, if you got two-fifty a night."

"Two-fifty!" I said in astonishment before I could keep it from slipping out.

"Two-fifty, and a bargain at that! Only two other houses in town—one of 'em's full of dance-hall girls, and the other's full of drunken miners. An' both charge the same. If you want to stay in one of the hotels, you'll take your life in your hands—someone's gettin' shot over some gold fracas every week. An' you'll pay more besides. So it's two-fifty a day—in advance! Breakfast's included, but if you want supper, it's another two-bits."

Every other boardinghouse I'd stayed at was a dollar a night, including supper—except for Miss Bean's in San Francisco, which was a dollar-fifty. It was a good thing I'd brought money along!

Finally I nodded my head and said that would be fine. Mrs. Nason opened the door and led me inside.

I followed her through a large parlor and toward a flight of stairs. "Might you have a man by the name of Gregory lodging with you?" I asked.

"Never heard of him," she answered without turning around.

We continued up the stairs in silence, and she opened the third door we came to. "This here's the room," she said. "How many nights?"

"I—I'm not altogether sure just yet, ma'am. I guess I'll pay you for two to begin with."

"With supper?"

"Yes . . . thank you."

"That will be five dollars, four bits. And I believe I did say in advance?"

"Yes, ma'am. I'll go down and fetch my things from my horse."

"Ain't a good idea to keep nothing of value unattended in this town. They'll steal you blind. You better go down and make sure your horse is still there."

"Yes, ma'am," I said, turning back the way we'd come.

"If you want to put your horse up, there's a barn out back, with stalls an' fresh oats."

"Thank you, that will be fine."

"It's another two-bits for the horse," added Mrs. Nason. I sighed, and walked back outside to where my mare was waiting patiently.

An hour later I sat down on the edge of the bed in the bare little room. I'd fed and groomed Raspberry and put her up in the barn for a well-deserved rest. Now I had to think about what I was doing here.

I supposed if I was being a newspaper reporter investigating something, then about the only place to begin was by asking questions. No doubt Mr. Kemble might have other ideas. He'd probably have all kinds of sneaking-about-kind-of notions how to find this fellow who was working for the *Globe* and for that Senator Goldwin. But I didn't know anything but just ask around and try to find him. And if I did, then try to find out what he was up to, even if it meant just going up to him and asking him. I didn't have to blab right out that I was working for the *Alta* and that my editor told me to sabotage him.

I wasn't sure how to do what Mr. Kemble sent me to do and still be honest at the same time. This was a part of being a reporter I'd never thought about. I had always wanted to write just to express myself and tell interesting stories to people. Now all of a sudden here I was in the middle of trying to investigate a situation where wrong was being done. But even if wrong *was* being done, I couldn't do wrong myself to try to uncover it. I just hoped I'd be able to keep straight what was right myself, no matter what anyone else was doing!

I got down on my knees beside the bed.

"God," I prayed, "I'm not sure what's going to happen here. But I ask that you'd show me what to do and where to go, and guide my thoughts as well as my steps. Help me to be true, like I prayed before, and help me to find out the truth behind this article they're trying to hurt Mr. Fremont with. Help me to be a good reporter, and to be a good daughter of yours."

CHAPTER 43

THE LUCKY SLUICE

All that afternoon I walked around the town of Sonora.

After a while I got used to the rowdiness and the yelling and the horses running through the streets, and even the men talking to me and calling after me. I saw a few other women about who didn't look like they belonged in a saloon, and that helped. And luckily there hadn't been rain for a while, so the streets were dry instead of muddy.

I went into several stores, peeked over the swinging doors into a saloon or two, and got up my courage to go into two or three more of the town's hotels to ask about the fellow named Gregory. I felt rather foolish just wandering about, and it didn't seem like I was having much luck. Later on I saddled my horse and rode out of town.

I took a ride clear around through Jamestown, Rawhide, Shaw's Flat, Springfield, and Columbia. I saw signs pointing off to Brown's Flat, Squabbletown, Sawmill Flat, and Yankee Hill. I had no idea there were so many little towns and mining camps—though most of them were just a few buildings surrounded by claims up and down the streams. Once I got out of Sonora no one bothered me much. The men I passed would stare or watch to see where I was headed, but most of them were too intent on their work to mind me. All around were the sights and sounds of gold mining—men panning in the streams, mules laden down with equipment heading off the roads up toward the high country, the sounds of heavy equipment and dynamite and quartz machinery. It seemed that every square inch of this country was being dug up or mined by somebody!

Riding back to town, I decided that the only way to go about this search was to start at the beginning of Sonora and go to every hotel and boardinghouse and ask about Mr. Gregory. Then I'd go ask the sheriff. After that, I'd have to do the same things in whatever places there were in the little surrounding towns where he might be staying. I'd never find him just wandering about. There were thousands of people around here! I'd have to go to every lodging place one by one until I found where he was staying. At least by then I'd know for sure if he was in Sonora or not. If he wasn't, then I'd be able to tell Mr. Kemble I'd done everything I knew to do.

I arrived back at Mrs. Nason's just in time to unsaddle and put up my mare before supper. When I went in, Mrs. Nason introduced me to the others around the table, including her own husband who'd been out working their claim all day. Besides Mrs. Nason I was the only woman, but the men were all nice enough, although they spent most of their energy gulping down the biscuits, potatoes, roast beef, and cooked cabbage.

"She's lookin' fer a feller named Gregory," said the landlady to her husband. "You ever heard o' him, Jed?"

"Can't say as I have," the man answered. "What you want him for, Miss?"

It was the first time I'd been asked that, but I'd already planned out the answer to give.

"We're in the same line of work," I said. "And I need to ask him a few questions."

" 'Bout what? You look kinda young to be in *any* line o' work in these parts. What do you do?"

"We're in the newspaper business."

This seemed to satisfy Mr. Nason. His wife's expression didn't look like she approved, but she hadn't smiled once since I'd arrived, anyway.

Just then one of the other men at the table spoke up.

"There's a Gregory over at the saloon, least he was a couple nights back. But he weren't no newspaper man, I can tell ya. A shyster's more like it! The guy took me for my whole two days' worth of dust in an hour of five-card stud."

"Where was that?" asked one of the other men.

"The Lucky Sluice."

"The Lucky Deuce, you mean!" said the other. "They play a game of faro there with deuces countin' triple and always goin' to the player, *if* you lay down a double bet ahead of time. So if you hit it wrong, the house gets rich and you lose everything in a hurry. But they keep bringin' the suckers in! I gave it up after losin' my whole wad to 'em twice."

"When was the last time you saw this man?" I asked.

"Couple nights ago, don't remember exactly. I ain't been back since."

"Maybe I'll go over there and see if he's back," I said.

"It gets mighty wild there, Miss," said Mr. Nason. "You don't want to be mixing with drinkin' men, especially if they happen to be losin' their gold at the same time."

"Well, if it's the man I'm looking for, he's not a miner, so I won't have to worry about that. And as for the drinking, I reckon I'll just get my business done and get out before anything rough gets started."

Nobody said anything else. None of them seemed to think I was too smart to think of walking into a saloon alone. But on the other hand, they didn't seem to care that much either way. Sonora was the kind of place, I guess, where folks were in the habit of doing whatever they pleased, and where everyone else minded their own business.

After supper I went out to the barn. I was about to saddle up my horse when I remembered Mrs. Nason's words about the stealing that went on around here. Maybe it wasn't such a good idea to tie the horse on the main street of Sonora at night. I decided to walk up to the middle of town instead.

Even while I was still a block away, I heard the laughing and yelling and music coming out of the Lucky Sluice. There weren't many people out. I'm sure all the respectable people were in their homes—if there were very many of those in this town!—and the rest were already inside the brightly lit saloons.

When I got to the double swinging doors of the Lucky Sluice, I took in a deep breath, breathed a silent prayer, and, trying to hide my shaking knees, pushed through the doors and walked inside.

I was dressed in denim breeches and a man's flannel shirt, and most of the men were absorbed at the dozen or so card tables, so I didn't attract too much attention at first. If I had, I probably would have turned back around and run right out! Against the right wall a man was playing lively music on a piano, and a few women in short, bright-colored dresses were lounging about and talking with some of the men.

I walked straight to the bar, ignoring the few heads that turned and watched me. The big burly man behind it walked toward me, still finishing something he was saying to somebody else. When he looked down at me, surprise showed on his face, and I think he might have been about ready to throw me out because of how young I looked. But I didn't give him the chance.

"I'm looking for a man named Gregory," I said quickly. "I was told he might be here."

The bartender stared at me like he might *still* be thinking of throwing me out. Nobody in this town did much smiling, but they sure stared a lot! Maybe I was funnier looking or more out-of-place looking than I realized.

But finally he turned his head and shouted off toward a table near the piano, "Hey, Hap, that friend o' yers from Frisco here tonight?"

"Naw . . . who wants t' know?"

"Little lady here's askin' fer him."

The man named Hap sat up in his chair and looked in our direction. If I'd hoped to be inconspicuous, there was no chance of that now! The rest of the men he was playing cards with glanced up too, and a round of whistles and catcalls followed. But I tried not to pay any attention to them.

"I'm afraid yer luck's done run out, Miss," said Hap. "Derrick lit off fer Chinese Camp yesterday. But maybe I can help ya out, Miss," he added with a smile, and a wink at his friends. "I'm better lookin' than him by a dang sight!"

"Can you tell me where I might find him?" I asked.

"Try Shanghai Slim's at Chinese Camp, or else he might be stayin' at old lady Buford's place in Jacksonville."

"Is that a boardinghouse?"

"You can call it what ya want, Miss. Derrick's called it worse things than that! But if ya mean a place where a body can get a bed an' a meal, then that's what it is."

"Thank you kindly," I said, nodding toward him and the bartender. Then I turned and walked out as fast as I could!

I went back to Mrs. Nason's. I'd paid for the night, and it was nearly dark and much too late to think of doing anything else. I'd head south to Jacksonville in the morning. I had no way of knowing if Hap was talking about the same man as I was trying to track down. But the bartender did say Gregory was from San Francisco, and that's where the *Globe* was. So I figured I ought to follow the lead and see what came of it.

CHAPTER 44

DERRICK GREGORY

Chinese Camp was about ten or twelve miles south of Sonora. I figured I'd ride there first.

There probably wasn't much chance of finding anybody in the morning, but I could look around, ask, and then I could go on to Jacksonville three or four miles farther on and see about getting a room for the night at that boardinghouse. I didn't much relish walking into strange hotels and saloons and asking about a man I didn't know. I still couldn't figure out why Mr. Kemble had sent *me* after this Gregory when, like he said, he had other more experienced men. I couldn't believe it was only that he wouldn't recognize me. Especially when I didn't have any idea what I was supposed to be doing, or how I'd find out the information Mr. Kemble needed. But I noticed that every time I walked into a strange or uncomfortable situation, it got easier the next time.

So when I saw the sign above the door advertising "Shanghai Slim's" as I rode into Chinese Camp, I didn't feel nearly so queasy in the stomach at the thought of walking inside. I wasn't looking forward to it, but at least I knew I could do it.

I got off my horse, tied her to the rail outside, and went in.

It was obvious in a minute where the place got its name—both the town and the saloon. Inside, the decorations looked more Chinese than anything I'd seen before in California. And although there weren't very many people there, more than half of them were Chinese. A man wearing a green apron was sweep-

264

ing the floor in front of the bar. From his appearance I thought he must be the owner.

"Pardon me," I said, "are you Mr. Slim?"

He stopped his broom, glanced up at me, and answered in a thick Chinese accent, "You bet. I Shanghai Slim." The look he gave me seemed about the friendliest I'd seen in a long time, and he almost hinted at a smile. But I couldn't be sure.

"I'm looking for a man by the name of Gregory," I said.

The short little man pointed behind me, then without another word returned to his sweeping.

I turned around and saw, among the half dozen empty tables in the room, a group of men involved in a poker game at one of the tables. From the looks on their faces, I wondered if it had gone on all night, or if it was just getting started on a bad note. The only one apparently having a good time was one jovial Chinese man with a pile of money and some little bags of gold sitting in front of him. Several others who had apparently dropped out of the game stood by watching.

Slowly I approached them. No one even saw me. A pile of coins, some paper, and a couple of small nuggets of gold lay in the middle of the table, and all six of the men had their fingers curled tightly around their cards. Most of them had creases on their foreheads and were examining their hands intently. Finally a Chinese man broke the silence.

"Not me. I fold," he said throwing his cards face down in front if him. "I out this hand."

"I'll stay," said the man next to him. "That is, if you'll all take this nugget as good for the fifteen-dollar call." He held up a piece of gold between his thumb and first finger that looked to be about a half an inch thick all the way around.

"Okay by me," said a player across the table, and his words were followed by various nods and mutterings of approval.

The first man tossed the nugget into the middle of the table, where it sounded against the other coins there and rolled to a stop.

"I'm in," said a third man, laying two paper bills into the pot.

The next man eyed his cards carefully, then sent his thin Oriental eyes squinting one at a time around the table of his companions as if trying to penetrate either their thoughts or see through the backs of their cards. Finally he spoke. "I only once see man draw two cards to inside straight, and his face not look like yours. So I think you bruffing."

The look of satisfaction I had noticed on this man's face at first from his obvious winnings had now disappeared.

"I call your fifteen," he said. "And another fifty."

He reached into the pile in front of him and first tossed in two coins for the fifteen. Then with great deliberation he dropped five more ten-dollar gold pieces one at a time into the pot.

Sighs and exclamations went around the table. A couple of the men threw their cards down immediately.

To the left of the rich Chinese, a grubby looking miner laid his cards down and leaned back in his chair. "Well at least I'm glad you did that before I called with the fifteen. It's all yours, Ling. I'm out."

To his left, however, a well-dressed man, who looked somewhat out of place among both Chinese and dirty unkempt miners, cracked a tiny smile as he glanced again at his cards, then looked over into the eyes of the Chinese man who had just raised the bet to fifty. When he spoke, in spite of a deep serious look in his eyes, there was humor in his tone.

"Now, Ling," he said, "you asked for two, I took one. You figure me to be going for the inside straight. And I figure since you're so confident, then you must have three of a kind. My gut tells me you didn't pick up either the four or the full house, and that you're still standing with the same three you were dealt."

He paused, and now smiled broadly at the man called Ling.

"So if you want to see if I *did* hit on my inside straight, I'm going to make you pay for the privilege."

Still with his eyes on the other man, his hand went down in front of him and found five coins, which he tossed into the pot. It left him with only five dollars in his own pile.

One by one, all those who had previously called threw in their cards until it came again to Mr. Ling.

He laid his cards down in front of him, face up. "Three kings," he said.

"Well, Ling," said the man who had raised, "it appears at last your string of luck has come to an end. For you see, I picked up the straight . . . jack high!"

He laid down the five cards with a triumphant look of satisfaction and let out a great laugh, while various reactions and exclamations went round the table on the part of the others.

While he was scooping up the pot he had just won, I walked timidly the rest of the way to the table. He didn't see me until I was almost beside him.

"Uh . . . excuse me," I said shyly, "would you by any chance be Mr. Gregory?"

"That's me," he answered, still raking in his money. "Who wants to know?"

At last he glanced up to where I stood, and before giving me a chance to say anything more, let out an exclamation.

"Well, well! It looks like you came just in time to change my luck, honey! Derrick Gregory, at your service!" he said, flashing a grin.

He stood, took off his hat, and gave an exaggerated bow. As he rose from the table I saw that he was taller than I had realized, with curly black hair and eyes of the same color. He appeared to be in his early thirties. The smile revealed his teeth, though his voice and look didn't appear altogether genuine.

"I would like to talk with you," I said.

"Oh, I'd be right pleasured t' speak with ya, Miss," interrupted one of the other card players, a dirty man with a leering face I didn't like at all. "Now you jest come right over here t' me, an'—"

"Snap your big trap shut, Frank, or I'll stuff my fist into it!" said Mr. Gregory in my defense.

"Tarnation, Greg, I didn't mean nothin' by it."

"Well, just stay out of it!"

And though Frank didn't say another word, I still wasn't

sure what to think of Derrick Gregory either.

"Now, girl," he said, towering in front of me, "who are you, and what are you hankering to tell me?"

"I'm Cornelia Hollister," I said, "and I understand you're a newspaper writer."

The smile faded from his face. He started to lead me toward the other side of the room, saying as he did, "You fellas go on without me. I figure I owe this little lady a few minutes, the way she won that pot for me!"

As we moved away, a few whistles and jeers followed us.

"Don't pay any attention to them," he said to me. "And don't one of you think of touching my pot!" he called out over his shoulder. "I'll count every penny when I get back!"

He led me out the door and into the bright sunlight.

"You see, none of those men in there—they don't know *exactly* that I'm a reporter. They know I've been around a while asking some questions, but as long as they can keep winning some of my money at poker, they don't care too much about what I'm up to. And that's the way I'd like to keep it. So what is it *you* heard about me—what'd you say your name was?"

"Cornelia."

"So what makes you think I'm a writer?"

"I just heard about you, that's all."

"And what did you hear?"

"That you're writing about the election," I answered.

He sat down on the edge of the wood sidewalk, his long legs stretching out into the dirt street. Then he looked up and scanned me up and down as if taking stock of me for the first time.

"So you're interested in the election, eh, Cornelia?"

I nodded.

"That all?"

"I've always wanted to be a newspaper writer too," I said.

He smiled again. "A girl wanting to be a writer!" he exclaimed. "And so you figured I could give you a few pointers, eh, is that it?"

I didn't answer right off, but he didn't seem to mind.

"Cornelia what?" he asked.

"Hollister."

"Hmm . . . Hollister . . ." He rubbed his chin thought-fully, then after a few seconds went on. "Well, Miss Hollister," he said, "I'm not saying anything one way or another about what I may or may not be. But I figure I owe you one. Ol' Ling in there'd been beating me all day and all night and had just about cleaned me dry till you walked up. So just maybe this is your lucky day as well as mine."

He didn't seem to take me seriously. But on the other hand, he didn't mind talking to me either, which was all I could have hoped for.

"Where do you come from, Cornelia?"

"I rode down from Sonora."

"Well, I'll tell you what," he said, getting back to his feet. "I've been staying at a place down in Jacksonville, and I got some folks I gotta see down at Big Oak Flat. If you want to ride along with me, I'll tell you a thing or two about this elec-tion, and maybe let you watch me conduct a real live interview in person. You game?"

"Oh yes, thank you very much!" I said enthusiastically. "I would like that."

After just a few minutes with him, I wasn't worried about riding off alone with Derrick Gregory. There was nothing about him that frightened me, although I couldn't help being on my guard. He talked to me as if he were sharing his great experi-ence and wisdom with a little kid, which in this case I didn't mind.

"Let me go back in there and get my loot and tell those old coots that we're leaving. And then we'll hit the trail, *Miss* Hol-lister."

CHAPTER 45

I FIND OUT MORE
THAN I OUGHT TO

For the rest of the morning we rode south and chatted easily. Mr. Gregory seemed perfectly willing to talk to me about his work, and didn't appear to mind my questions. Gradually I learned a lot about him and what he was doing. Apparently he thought of me as nothing but a raw novice who knew absolutely nothing.

In a way I guess I *was* just a raw novice. But I knew more than he thought I knew, and I wasn't so innocent of motive as he thought. I wondered if I was doing wrong to deceive him. But I hadn't actually said anything that was untrue, he had drawn his own conclusions. I wasn't trying to hurt anyone but was just trying to get at the truth, and I thought that what I was doing was justified. If it wasn't, and if I was doing wrong, I'd have to deal with my conscience when it started to nag at me. It was a hard question, and wouldn't be the first time as a reporter when I'd wonder about the line between honesty and not saying enough. Maybe it's a problem a reporter never completely gets a handle on.

One thing was for sure, Derrick Gregory wasn't in the least concerned about truthfulness in what *he* wrote. He treated me nice enough. But he didn't care if he was fair to Mr. Fremont. Before we'd gone very far at all, he'd confided in me that his job was to get whatever he could in order to destroy John Fremont's reputation.

"But what if you write something that's not true?" I asked.

"Nobody pays you for truth, Cornelia. They pay you to watch out for their interests."

I reached into my saddlebag and pulled out a notepad and a pencil. "A *real* reporter's supposed to take notes, isn't she?" I asked innocently. "Do you mind if I write down some of what you say? I want to learn as much as possible."

Derrick looked flattered. "Atta girl, Cornelia! You wanta be a writer, you gotta *act* like a writer!" He paused, and an expression of importance crept over his face. "Now, Miss Hollister, listen close, and you might learn something about being a real newsman."

Writing notes on horseback is not an easy thing to do. My pencil went all over the page, but at least I got down the important parts. Mr. Kemble wouldn't print anything unless I was sure I had the facts straight, so I wanted to make sure I could back up what I wrote.

"If you're writing about election news," I asked Mr. Gregory, "don't you have to report the facts?"

"Facts are slippery things. One fella might look at a fact one way, and somebody else in another way. The people who hired me pay me to dig up facts that they can use against Fremont. They don't care how I get them, or even whether they're true. If they can make people *believe* they're true, then they'll have what they want, and I'll get paid handsomely for my efforts. You see how nice it works out!"

"But that's not being honest to the people who read what you write, Mr. Gregory," I said.

"What is honesty? Like I said, I don't get paid to be honest, but to do a job. And the senator who sent me out here always gets what he wants. So why shouldn't I profit from his greed?" He patted his saddlebag. "So I've got a whole lot of things here that are just what the senator wants, sworn statements, quotes from guys who saw Fremont do such and so. Why, by the time I get through writing it up, the election's as good as decided in this state. And by the way, Cornelia, no more of this Mister Gregory stuff. If you and I are going to ride together and I'm going to teach you the business of being a reporter, then you at least ought to call me by my name. Fair enough?"

I nodded. "But then why—uh, Derrick—why did you come clear out here, all the way from the South, to write stuff about Mr. Fremont?"

"That's the beauty of the senator's scheme! Right here's where Fremont kicked around before he got famous. Why, his estate runs clear up to just a few miles from here. Anything we can uncover here, people'll believe it just like it's gospel, because it's from the man's *real* past, what he was like before he got into politics."

He stopped, with a serious expression on his face, and looked around behind us.

"You hear a horse back there?" he asked, pulling his own mount to a stop. I reined in alongside him and listened. I didn't hear anything.

"Maybe I'm just too jumpy," he said, urging his horse along again. "But I've had a feeling like I'm being followed for more than a week now. Maybe I'm just nervous till I get this article written and these papers back to Frisco. But I still don't like not knowing who's watching me."

"Who would be watching you?" I asked.

"Fremont's people—maybe even Senator Goldwin's people, for all I know. Politics is a dirty business. Those guys play for keeps. To tell you the truth, it wouldn't surprise me if the senator had eyes on me, to make sure Fremont's people don't buy me off. If I will do *his* dirty work for a price, then he's got to figure I'd pull turncoat for a higher offer. You always gotta be figuring how these powerful guys think. Those slavery people are the worst. Right and wrong means nothing to them— it's strictly dollars and power."

"*Would* you turn your information over to Fremont's side— for a higher price?" I asked.

"Nah, they couldn't pay me enough to make me cross Goldwin. He'd have me killed inside a month."

"What do you have that's so valuable to him?" I asked.

"I've got the election in my saddlebag—the end of Fremont's political career forever, that's what. Once this stuff hits the press, Buchanan's election is secure. Goldwin's happy; he and his slavery boys stay in power in Washington. The anti-slavery forces go down in defeat with their champion, John Charles Fremont, caught with mud on his face and skeletons in his closet. Just think, the Union may owe its preservation to none other than an investigative reporter and man of the hour, Derrick Gregory! And you, Cornelia Hollister, had the good fortune to take it into your head to ask his advice about becoming a reporter right when he was about to finish the story that would sway the election of 1856! You are witnessing history in the making, Miss Hollister!"

"But I still don't see what you could have discovered way out here in the middle of nowhere that could be so damaging to Colonel Fremont," I said.

"All right, just for an example, take that little place where you found me, Chinese Camp," he replied. "My time there was spent doing more than playing cards. You might have seen it on your way in—little Catholic Church, St. Xavier's. I've got a quote from a Chinese man back there as an eyewitness that he saw John Fremont going into the church with a priest last time he was out here, for a private Mass."

"That can't be true," I said in disbelief. "John Fremont isn't a Catholic . . . is he?" I added, suddenly unsure of myself.

"Who knows? But haven't you been listening to anything I been telling you about this game of political reporting? Doesn't matter if it's true. Doesn't matter that I had to slip the guy ten bucks to encourage his memory along after I hinted at what I was looking for. If folks think it's true, it's good enough and you've done your job. No one's gonna come checking up on it. They couldn't check it anyway. The source's name will never be mentioned. My name won't appear on the story, won't have anything to do with it as far as the public's concerned. The story's untraceable. But the charge will persist, and even if it is only a rumor, it will do its job."

"It hardly seems right."

"Right, wrong—who cares? A reporter has a job to do, and

he gets paid by people in power with money to pay him. A writer doesn't decide right and wrong, he has to do his job. Facts are just what you make of them, no more, no less. There was another reason I was at Chinese Camp. You know about the Tong war a few months back at Crimea Flat? Well, I've got it on good authority that a bunch of Fremont's men rode up from Mariposa and instigated the whole thing because Fremont hates the Chinese and doesn't like so many of them so near his estate."

"What kind of authority—same as about the church?"

Derrick laughed. "Now you're catching on, Cornelia! No, it's a little more reliable than that. All the miners in these parts hate Fremont. They're jealous of his gold, they think some of it ought to be theirs. A few of them who got run off the Mariposa at gunpoint for poaching are willing to say just about anything to bring down Fremont. I've got sworn statements that Fremont used Chinese slave labor along with the Mexicans when he first started mining the Mariposa, that he falsified surveying reports to change his boundaries to include the richest claims. I got quotes saying they saw Negroes in chains on the Mariposa, and even that Fremont used to get away at night to take up with barmaids, leaving his wife alone at home. I got all kinds of stuff from interviewing people around here. Fremont's dead when it all gets out."

"What are you after today? Some other quote from someone who doesn't like Mr. Fremont?"

He laughed again. "In a manner of speaking. We're almost to Big Oak Flat. I'm gonna see Jim Savage, who founded the place and got rich from it. He and Fremont go back a ways. Savage led the Mariposa Battalion, the first white men into the Yosemite valley, and he has a thing or two to say about how Fremont got his clutches on all that land when he wasn't even here in person. From what I've gathered, the senator's promised Savage a big chunk of the Mariposa if he can give him enough information to contest Fremont's title. If I can get what I need, it not only makes Fremont out a crook, it might put the Mariposa right in Senator Goldwin's lap. Half of the old fat judges on the Supreme Court owe their appointments to him, and they would back him up if it came down to a law suit between Fremont and Goldwin."

"Do you think this man Savage will go against Fremont?"

"Sure. Disputes over money makes men more unforgiving than anything. Gold men and slavery men—there aren't any two groups in this country to hold a grudge longer. It would gall Savage to the core to see his old arch-rival over these gold fields be made President of the United States. I have no doubt he'll say anything and everything I want him to. And to make matters even better, Savage was involved with the Palmer & Cook Company back then at the same time Fremont was. He'll be able to confirm Fremont's role in that as well—and that one *does* happen to be in the area of true facts."

"What's that all about?"

"Just a couple months back, Palmer & Cook got into trouble for an illegal breach of faith in handling some securities belonging to the state of California. Fremont was closely involved with them when he was last here. It's the perfect smear."

We'd been talking a long time, and within another ten minutes we rode into the little village of Big Oak Flat. Derrick seemed to know where he was going. We rode straight through town, made two or three turns, and eventually arrived at the ranch called the Savage Diggings, the original name of the town in 1848. Mr. Savage must have been expecting him, because we went right in and sat down and the two men started talking. I just watched and listened, and they paid me no heed. But as I glanced around the room I noticed some old copies of the *Alta* lying around, and a momentary panic seized me.

As I sat there listening, I was astonished at what I heard. Mr. Gregory didn't just ask questions and write down Mr. Savage's answers. The two of them talked back and forth and discussed what would make it look the worst for Mr. Fremont—sometimes laughing, even making up situations and other people. By the time Mr. Gregory got to writing down some of the things they'd talked about, it might as well have been fiction. He wasn't trying to find out what *really* happened at all, but to make up what he called "facts" and quotations that he and Mr. Savage could agree on that would put Mr. Fremont in a bad light. They said things about Jessie, too, that I was sure were untrue, and I got angrier and angrier. Everything Derrick had told me on the way there was bad enough, but now I saw the deception and lies going on right in front of me, and it made me mad. How could he call himself a reporter, a newsman? He was telling lies to the whole country for that rich Senator Goldwin.

"But you say Fremont got out of the Palmer & Cook Company several years back?" asked Derrick.

"Oh yeah," answered Savage. "He's got nothing to do with this current mess of theirs. But it doesn't matter. His financial involvement in the company can be documented, and by the time he has a chance to refute it, the election will be over. Use it, Gregory. It'll bring him down in the business circles in Frisco."

Derrick was busy with his pen. He had written several pages since we'd got here, full of accusations, quotes, names, dates, places, illegalities, rumors—all slanderous against Colonel Fremont.

"But don't forget what I told you about the purchase of the Mariposa," Savage went on after Derrick's pen stopped. "It all hinges on Thomas Larkin, the guy Fremont used to buy the estate. Larkin was U.S. Consul at the time, but he had dealings back to the mid-forties with Alvarado and Michelorena, who owned the property first. I've never been able to get to the bottom of it, but if the senator could get to Larkin and, shall we say, win him over with a few hundred dollars on the side, I have the feeling Larkin might be able to provide all the ammunition the senator needs to mount a challenge to Fremont's title and get the Supreme Court to overturn their ruling."

Derrick was writing as fast as his fingers could move. Finally he glanced up.

"You are a devious one, Savage," he said. "I'm sure the senator will be deeply indebted for all your help in putting the final pieces of this article together."

"I am counting on it," smiled Savage.

"I will pass along your sentiments when I next see the senator after the election."

A pause followed. Derrick looked over his several pages of notes, then put them in a leather case along with his pen and ink. He snapped the buckle shut, patted the case with his hand, and let out a long sigh.

"Well, it's all here," he said. "I'll be writing up the article in the next few days, and within a week you should be reading the political obituary of one John Charles Fremont in the San Francisco *Morning Globe*. I'm sure future President Buchanan will be grateful for your part in effecting the demise of his opponent."

Derrick rose and extended his hand. Mr. Savage shook it, then offered me his hand also as I got up.

"Nice to see you too, Miss—"

"Hollister," I reminded him.

"Ah, yes—hmm . . . Hollister . . . seems as if I know that name. You from these parts?"

"My father's a miner," I said, evading the question. I hoped his mind didn't wander to the *Alta* right then!

"Hmm . . . well, I don't know . . . your name just seems familiar, that's all."

Derrick and I left the house, got on our horses, and started back north the way we had come.

"Looks like I've got everything I need, Cornelia!" Derrick said with a smile. "All I have to do now is write it up and take it to the city and my job's done!"

"Why do you bother with interviews," I asked, "if you're just making everything up, anyway?"

"You've got to at least give the appearance of credibility, you know! Besides, if anyone does question my sources, I want to have a credible list to give them."

We rode on a while in silence.

"Why so glum?" Derrick asked. "You've just seen political reporting at its best, firsthand. Why, you're watching how Presidents get elected!"

"It just doesn't seem right, somehow," I said.

"Still worried about honesty, Cornelia?"

"I reckon."

"Forget it. If you want to be a news reporter, this is how it works—who you know, and what kind of deal you can make with them. And watch out for your own best interests! It's the only way to get ahead in this game—just like in politics."

We were quiet again for a while.

"Are you going to Jacksonville now?" I asked.

"Nah, we still got plenty of daylight left. I think I'll get on back to Sonora and bunk there for another day or two while I'm writing this all up. I got a nice room above the Lucky Sluice where I can work."

"Maybe I could come and see what a finished article looks like," I suggested.

"Sure. Come on around, that is if your folks'll let you into a place like that." He hesitated. "But I guess if you're old enough to be tracking me down to learn how to be a reporter, you're old enough to go where you like without your pa's permission." He laughed, then sobered and asked, "Your pa's a miner, huh?"

I nodded, and immediately felt a pang of guilt for not telling him that I didn't actually live in Sonora.

All the rest of the way back that afternoon, Derrick seemed to be watching and listening, as if he still thought someone was following him. But we never saw anybody and nothing ever came of it.

CHAPTER 46

AN UNEXPECTED REUNION

We didn't get back to Sonora till pretty late in the evening. We parted at the edge of town. "See you around, Cornelia," Derrick Gregory said, then took off toward the middle of town and the Lucky Sluice. I rode back to Nason's boardinghouse, hoping I wasn't too late to get my room back—payment in advance!—for the night.

Mrs. Nason almost seemed glad to see me, in her grumpy sort of way. She even heated up some of the supper things for me to eat and said that because they had already gotten cold she wouldn't charge me for the meal.

As I lay in my room that night, I couldn't get to sleep. All I could think of was the day I'd spent and Mr. Kemble, and the election, and what I ought to do with everything I'd learned. Finally I got up, lit a lamp, and for the next couple of hours went over my notes and tried to remember everything I'd seen and heard that day. I wrote it down in as much detail as I could. Whatever came of it all, at least I had to be sure of the truth of *my* facts. I had to be accurate about Derrick's falsehoods if I was going to tell them to Mr. Kemble in a way that would help Mr. Fremont. My notes weren't very neat, but I managed to get down most of the names of people Derrick said he'd talked to and quoted from, as well as what he'd told me about making things up and bribing people to say things. And I tried to reconstruct as much of his conversation with Jim Savage as I could so that I'd be positively accurate in my *own* quotes when it came to disproving the lies that were being told against Mr. Fremont.

When I finally got to sleep, it was after midnight and I slept late the next morning. But when I woke up my thoughts were less confused and my head was gradually coming clear about what I ought to do. I didn't really stop to consider that the plan was probably foolhardy and dangerous.

First, I'd have to find out what room Derrick was in. After that I'd have to watch him and try to figure out his writing habits. If they were anything like mine, every once in a while his hand would cramp up and his brain would get dizzy and he'd have to take a break and go for a walk or something. And after that . . . well, then I'd just have to hope for the best!

A little after noon I decided to walk up to the saloon just to see if I could run into Mr. Gregory. I didn't really know what I'd do or say, but whatever happened I had to keep him in my sights. If he left town without my knowing it and got back to San Francisco ahead of me, everything was lost.

There weren't many men in the Lucky Sluice at that hour, but a couple of tables were occupied. Almost before I was fully inside I heard Derrick Gregory's voice raised in laughter and talk. He had just won a hand and was celebrating at the expense of his companions. As I walked toward him, I noticed something awfully familiar about the tall thin form sitting beside him with his back to me. Across the table facing me as I approached sat two mean-looking men—one with a beard who looked like a miner, the other clean and well dressed in an expensive suit. If they were together, they sure made an odd-looking pair!

Derrick half turned and spotted me out of the corner of his eye.

"I should have known you were somewhere close by, Cornelia!" he exclaimed. "Gentlemen," he said to the rest of the men sitting at the table, "this is my good luck companion, Cornelia Hollister. Whenever she's around, I win!" Then glancing back at me, he added, "Cornelia, these two fellas are the men I was telling you about that work for the senator and are supposed to keep me in line." He threw me a quick wink, as much as to say that in spite of their rough appearance, *he* wasn't worried about them. "And this young buck just got in from the big city," he said, indicating the young man sitting next to him.

"Meet Rob Flaridy."

It was all I could manage to keep from stumbling over my feet and gasping in amazement! I'm sure the shock must have shown on my face. I must say, if he was as surprised to see me as I was him, Robin hid his reaction better than I did mine.

"Charmed," he said, half rising from his chair and tipping his familiar cap with a smile. I knew he enjoyed my discomfort.

"Sit down . . . sit down, Cornelia!" said Derrick. "Bring me some more good luck!"

"I . . . I really can't stay," I fumbled. "I was just . . . I thought I'd find out how your article was going. I didn't mean to interrupt."

"No interruption at all!" he said boisterously. Now that I was close to him I could tell he'd been drinking, although he wasn't really drunk. "I'm half done, Hollister . . . the election's practically in the bag! I'm just having a little break with my friends here! By tomorrow at this time I'll be on my way to San Francisco, and the boys here will be on their way over-land with a copy of everything I've found for the senator's use in the East."

"You have a loose tongue," growled the man with the beard.

"Relax. Miss Hollister's on our side!"

In spite of his expensive suit, the expression on the other man's face was anything but friendly. "You just keep your mouth shut and your hand busy, and get those papers copied out for us! We're a day behind schedule as it is."

I couldn't help but notice that both the strangers had rifles leaning against their chairs. The man with the beard also wore a gun belt. The other eyed me with a questioning look.

I turned to leave.

"You come back around tonight, Cornelia," said Derrick. "I'll be right here at this table, and I'll be ready for another dose of your good luck."

I nodded sort of noncommittally.

"And maybe by then I'll be rid of these two brutes," he added, gesturing across the table, "and we can have some fun!"

I left the saloon without looking at Robin again.

I walked straight across the street into the dry goods store and pretended to look around. I kept close to the window with one eye on the swinging doors of the Lucky Sluice. In about twenty minutes the two men came out and walked up the sidewalk toward the north end of town. Five minutes later Robin emerged. He stopped, looked up and down, then started in the opposite direction, crossed the dirt street to the side I was on, and continued on toward the first hotel I had gone into when I'd got into Sonora.

I watched for another minute or two to make sure Derrick wasn't coming out. I didn't want him to see me chasing down the street after Robin. But finally I figured he'd gone back upstairs to his room. I left the store and walked southward as quickly as I could without attracting attention. I saw Robin up ahead of me, sauntering along slowly. I went out into the street so my boots wouldn't make a pounding noise on the wood walkway, and started running after him. I caught up with him just as he was passing a narrow alleyway that ran along the near side of the hotel.

Before he saw me coming, I ran alongside him and gave him a hard shove sideways into the alley and behind the building. He lost his balance and let out an exclamation, while he struggled to get back his footing. I jumped behind the edge of the wall after him, and grabbed him before he could yell.

"What are you doing here?" I exclaimed as loudly as I dared without attracting attention.

"I could ask you the same thing," he retorted. "And get your hands off me!" I hardly realized that I had hold of his coat and had pushed him up against the building.

I relaxed and took a step back.

"I am here because Mr. Kemble sent me," I said.

"As am I."

"He sent *you*?"

"How can I put this delicately, Corrie?" he said, finally cracking a meaningful grin. "He wasn't sure a girl of your tender years could—shall we say—*handle* such an important assignment. So he sent me along to make sure you didn't foul it up."

"Foul it up?" I cried, getting angry. "*You're* the one who's going to foul it up. I've practically got Gregory's whole story!"

"Ah, but I know that he's in room fourteen, and I know where those other two men are staying, and I know their whole scheme."

"How long have you been tracking him?" I asked.

"Couple weeks."

"Kemble told me he had someone on this but that it dried up and they lost Gregory's trail."

"Well, that was unfortunate. He eluded me for a while, but then Kemble told me to follow you up here and see what you turned up, and to move back in if I could. Experience, you know," he said with a superior smile. "He felt even if you did track down Gregory, I'd be better able to get what we need in the end."

"Why, that conniving rascal!" I said. "He gave me all that runaround about me being the perfect one for the story and about the election and truth all hanging in the balance, and all the time he was just using me! And you're trying to tell me that I was just a decoy so that *you* could get the story in the end?"

"The truth is sometimes painful, Corrie," said Robin, still smiling with that look of superiority.

I turned away and strode off a few steps deeper into the alley. I felt like crying and screaming all at once!

But if I was going to prove that I could compete with men like Mr. Kemble and *Mister* Robin T. O'Flaridy, I couldn't do either. I couldn't give in to all the female emotionalism flooding through me right then. I couldn't cry. I couldn't scream. I couldn't go over and punch Robin in the nose. Somehow I had to see this thing through, and prove that I was made of stronger stuff than either of them might think.

I took a deep breath, then turned back around.

"So it *has* been you following Derrick recently," I said calmly. "And you were on our trail down to Big Oak Flat yesterday."

"And you've got to admit I did a pretty good job too," said Robin. "Neither of you saw me, did you?"

I shook my head. "But Derrick knew somebody was back there."

"Nah, he knew nothing. He was guessing."

"Don't be too cocky, Robin," I said. "If you're not careful you could put your foot right in the middle of it and get us both killed."

"What could go wrong?"

"Plenty. You just watch your step. We're too close. I don't even want to think what those two men might do if they catch us or if they find out we know each other."

"They'll never find out a thing!"

"Just watch your step. Both of our names have been in print recently. It wouldn't take much and we'd be in way over our heads."

"I tell you, you worry too much, Hollister."

"And maybe it'll be my worrying that'll get you through this," I replied. "Where you staying?"

"Right here," he said, indicating the hotel.

"Well, I'm in the boardinghouse down the street. Which is where I'm going now—I've got to do some thinking. You stay out of trouble!"

In reply, he only flashed another smile of unconcerned indifference.

As I left the alley and walked off alone down the street, it hardly occurred to me how much everything had changed. I wasn't afraid of Robin anymore, as I had been in San Francisco. In fact, I'd acted as if *I* were the older and more experienced one of the team.

And for better or worse, I suppose that's what we were now, at least for a couple more days—a team. Something inside me told me it was up to me if we were going to get out of this in one piece. Robin was too cocky for his own good.

CHAPTER 47

DISCOVERY AND BETRAYAL

I didn't see either Robin O'Flaridy or Derrick Gregory for the rest of the afternoon. I spent three hours finishing writing down what I'd learned.

I didn't really know what to do next. But I had to get my hands on Derrick's batch of papers before those other two men headed east with them. If I waited too long to figure out some plan, Robin might louse it up and get us both into a heap of trouble.

Finally, late in the afternoon, I went outside. I had to do *something*. I'd been praying and thinking all afternoon, but without any ideas coming to me.

I wandered up the street toward Robin's hotel. I went inside and walked up to the counter.

"Do you know if Rob Flaridy's in?" I asked the man called Fence.

"Left an hour or two back, Miss."

"Alone?"

"Couple of men with him. They'd been lookin' fer him earlier."

"Friends of his?" I said.

"Didn't look too friendly to me," said Fence. "Looked to me they was takin' Flaridy against his will. But I don't ask no questions. You get too curious in this town, Miss, an' it's a good way t' git yerself a plot o' ground out in the cemetery."

I went back out into the street and walked back in the direction of the Lucky Sluice.

285

I approached the saloon on the wood walkway, but the instant I reached it and started to push one of the swinging doors open, I froze. Over the top of it I saw Robin seated at a table, his hands tied behind his back, with the three other men standing facing him, asking questions and talking among themselves. It was obvious in a second they'd discovered he was trying to foil their scheme. But how much they knew, I couldn't tell.

I backed up quickly so they wouldn't see me in the doorway, leaned against the wall, and strained my ears to hear through the door just to my right.

They were speaking softly to avoid attracting attention, but because they were so close to the door I could hear them clearly. It was still early. The saloon was nearly empty, and the piano player hadn't started.

"I say we take him out and put a slug through his head right now," said the man with the beard.

"No, no, Jake—too messy," said the other friend of Derrick's. "There are certain rules to be observed, even in our business. No, we'll wait till we're set to leave town, then there'll be no tracing us."

"I don't like it," I heard Derrick mutter. "I knew there was somebody trailing me!" He swore a couple of times, giving Robin a cuff on the side of the head. "But I never thought they'd send someone the likes of you after me!"

"Who's in it with ya, kid?" asked the bearded man, grabbing Robin's shirt around his neck and giving it a yank. "Tell us, an' maybe we'll go easy on ya!"

"Please . . . please! I don't know anything about what you're doing. They just told me to follow you, that's all, but I didn't find out anything. Please . . . let me go . . . I'll never say a word to anybody."

While he was whining, the nicely dressed man was apparently rummaging through his clothes.

"Well, look at this!" he said. "We shoulda searched him when we first found him snooping around your room, Gregory. It would have saved us the trouble of trying to beat the information out of him. His name's not Flaridy at all, but O'Flaridy—Robin O'Flaridy . . . and he works for the *Alta*."

"I should have known!" said Derrick. "Kemble's rag. They sent him here to kibosh the story! They've been backing Fremont from the beginning!"

"Look," pleaded Robin in a forlorn tone, "you caught me red-handed, and you know I've got nothing that can hurt you. Let me go, and you go your way and do whatever you want about the election, and I'll never say a word. You can trust me to—"

"Shut up, ya whimpering brat!" shouted the bearded man. I heard the back of his hand slap across Robin's face, and he cried out in pain.

"Wait a minute!" said the man in the suit, snapping his fingers as if he was thinking. "Wait . . . it's coming to me . . . Derrick, that girl you were so friendly with—the one you said brought you good luck."

"Yeah, what about her?"

"What'd you say her name was?"

"Hollister."

"Her first name, you idiot!"

"Cornelia . . . Cornelia Hollister. But what has she—"

"You are a bigger fool than I thought!" the man said spitefully. "I knew there was something familiar about her name the minute you said it! Blast, why didn't I think harder—don't you know who she is?"

"Yeah, she's just some miner's kid from around here who wants to be a writer."

"And you thought you'd give her a few pointers, eh?"

"I didn't see any harm in—"

"You lunkhead, she *is* a writer. And she doesn't need any pointers from you! She writes for the *Alta*, too! The name Corrie Hollister mean anything to you?"

Derrick shrugged.

"You dolt! She wrote a big pro-Fremont piece just a couple of weeks back. She's a friend of Fremont's wife! She's in it with this snivelling little creature here!"

"That's impossible—she's just a kid!" cried Derrick in disbelief.

"Impossible, huh? I saw that look in her eyes. She was watching and listening to a lot more than you thought."

"I can't believe it."

"The senator will love to hear this. What did you tell her, Gregory?"

I could hear Derrick sitting down and letting out a bitter sigh. "She was with me all day yesterday. I told her everything. She was there for the Savage interview."

"Well, you know what you got to do, Gregory," said the bearded man viciously. "The senator don't like mistakes like this. You make a mess, then you clean it up—that's what he always says."

"Yeah . . . yeah, I know," sighed Derrick. "I kinda liked the kid too, and she did seem to bring me luck at cards."

"Yeah, she brought you luck all right. *Bad* luck! She's got to be eliminated, along with this trash here!" snarled the man in the suit. "Jake'll do the boy, but *you've* got to pull the trigger on the Hollister girl, Gregory! Otherwise the senator won't know if he can trust you in the future."

"I know," sighed Derrick. "You don't have to tell me. I know the senator as well as you do. If we let these two survive, he'd be after me next."

"Where's the girl?" the suited man asked Robin.

I'll have to say this much for him, he didn't give me away immediately.

The next sound I heard was a blow to the side of the head. I was terrified! My first thought was to flee. But something held me back. I *had* to find out all I could. I looked around the corner, just in time to see Robin crashing to the floor. The terrible-looking man grabbed roughly at him and raised his fist to smack him again. "The man asked you a question!" he yelled. "Where is she?"

"You'll . . . you'll let me go if I tell you?" whimpered Robin. His mouth and forehead were bleeding. "I don't know anything . . . it's her you want, not me."

"Yeah, okay—you win, kid," said the suit-man. "Take it easy, Jake—let him loose." They set him back down in the chair.

"Okay, you got a deal, O'Flaridy. You tell us where she is, and we'll let you go."

"She's . . . she's staying at a boardinghouse—down the side street from my hotel."

I leaned back against the wall in disbelief. He had *betrayed* me!

But I didn't have time to stop to consider the implications. Immediately I heard the sounds of chairs being pushed aside and boots on the wood floor walking my way.

I turned and ran, darting into the alleyway, running alongside the edge of the saloon. I hurried into the darkened passage, and ducked quickly down behind some big oak beer kegs sitting by the back door. A few seconds later I heard the three men pass by along the sidewalk, dragging Robin along with them.

"We'll take O'Flaridy out back of the livery and tie and gag him," the suited man was saying. "You finish what you got to do, Gregory, and later you go down to that boardinghouse and sweet-talk that Hollister kid into coming out for a walk with you. We'll grab her and stash her with the kid."

"Hey, you promised to let me go!" cried Robin. "I told you what you wanted to know."

I couldn't hear what they said back to him, because by now they were too far down the street. But the man with the beard let out a huge laugh that sounded full of glee and evil intent at the same time.

I waited a few minutes after they had passed, inched out to the edge of the alley, looked both ways to be sure it was clear, then I darted across the street and made my way back to Mrs. Nason's through the back streets and alleys and over a few fences. I knew it was dangerous to go back there after what had been said. But I had to risk it.

CHAPTER 48

A RISKY PLAN

I gathered my things quickly and stuffed them into my bag.

I'd already paid for the night's lodging, but I thought it best to slip out and not tell anyone at the house. The less they knew, the less chance Derrick would have of finding me.

Dusk was just settling as I sneaked out my window and down the back stairs outside the house. I could still hear workmen's voices inside the Nasons' barn, so I crept out behind it, sat down in the grass and waited. It gave me time to collect myself, catch my breath, and rest. I was hungry, but food would have to wait! I had to spend my time thinking of a plan, not my stomach.

When time came for supper, I heard the men in the barn leave for the house. A few minutes later I heard Mrs. Nason call my name a couple of times. But eventually she gave up, and I knew everyone was at the table eating. I crept into the barn, saddled my horse as quickly as I could in the dark, then led her out and around back.

I didn't know Sonora very well, but I thought I could make a big circle around to the other side without going through any of the main streets where I might be seen. It took me twenty or so minutes to get where I was headed. I rode out past the edge of town, but stopped where most of the buildings were still visible. I got off my horse, tied her securely to a tree. I had my bag tied down behind the saddle too so I would be able to make a quick getaway when the time came.

The only thing I took back toward town with me was a handful of blank writing pages from my satchel.

Now I retraced my steps back to Nason's boardinghouse. I found a place across the street, behind some bushes, where I could see both the front door and up the street toward the hotel and the main street of town. I was sure Derrick would come that way when he came looking for me. I just hoped I wasn't too late!

I waited for a long time. I started to shiver from the cold, and I could tell the dew was beginning to creep up out of the ground. But eventually my patience was rewarded. Sure enough, in the distance down the street from the main part of town came Derrick Gregory walking toward Nason's boardinghouse.

The thought that he was coming to lure me away was incomprehensible! But I didn't have time to reflect on that now. I had to get to the Lucky Sluice and safely away before he found out I wasn't there and had time to get back to his room.

I jumped up and ran in the direction I had planned, through a couple of gardens, over a fence or two, through an alley, across a back street, into somebody's yard, through another alley, until I arrived at the main street just next to the dry goods store across from the saloon. Looking right and left I darted across, behind the saloon, and had arrived at the back stairway just about the same time, I hoped, as Derrick was knocking on the door and asking Mrs. Nason to see me.

Now came the risky part! If he got suspicious from my not being there and ran back, or if I had trouble getting in, he could catch me right in the act of breaking into his room—then I'd be a goner for sure! I only had five minutes at the most to get in, grab what I wanted, and get out!

I took the saloon's back steps two at a time as quietly as I could on the toes of my boots. I tried the door. It was open! I crept inside. The hallway had a narrow strip of carpet down the middle, which kept my footsteps quiet. I walked slowly forward.

There it was! Room 14, the second room on the right.

I tried the latch. It was locked!

The next minute I heard voices coming up the stairway from the saloon below at the other end of the hall.

I turned and bolted back for the back door, and had just closed it behind me when I saw a man and a woman come into view. I watched through the window from the landing where I stood. Luckily they didn't come much farther, but stopped and went into a room at the far end of the hall.

Now what should I do? The door to Derrick's room was locked, and he was probably already on his way back here from the boardinghouse!

I glanced around where I stood on the landing of the back stairs.

A thin ledge ran around the building at the height of the second floor, a board about six inches wide. I stuffed my batch of papers inside my pocket, then I climbed over the railing and began slowly easing myself away from the landing. If I could just keep my balance and find enough for my fingers to grasp on to!

Slipping along sideways across the ledge, my fingers barely keeping me upright by holding on to window moldings, gutters, and other projections from the building, I came even with the window of the first room. Luckily it was empty!

I continued on, my heart pounding so hard that I was afraid its beating would knock me off backward. I didn't know which would be worse—to die from a gunshot through the head, or to die of a broken neck from falling twenty feet onto hard-packed dirt!

I came to the second window. This should be Derrick's room!

As I had hoped, the window was open a crack. I got my fingers under it and jerked upward. With a great scraping sound, it gave way and opened about nine inches. I got both my hands underneath and yanked again, but only managed to open it another two or three inches.

It would have to be enough.

I leaned down, stretched one leg through, then my left arm,

then squeezed the rest of my body through.

In a few seconds I was standing alongside Derrick's bed, with visions of him already walking into the Lucky Sluice below and hurrying up the stairs three at a time to catch me red-handed!

There was enough light from the moon showing through the window for me to see his writing table. I walked toward it. There was his satchel, full of papers, as well as a stack of the papers he had just been working on. A half completed sheet lay on top of them, his dried-out pen lying across it.

Quickly I opened his satchel and grabbed out all his papers. There must have been twenty or thirty pages—interviews, quotes, names, dates, lots of notes of his own. I picked up the fresh pages off the table, apparently his completed article about Fremont and the copy he was making for Senator Goldwin. I put them all in a stack together, folded them once, and stuffed them into my coat pocket.

Then I took the blank pages I had brought with me and replaced about the same number into his satchel, and on the tabletop. I hoped that at a quick glance, seeing papers still there and still in his case, he wouldn't stop immediately to think they weren't his papers.

I hurried back to the window and started to squeeze my way back through to the outside.

Suddenly a thought struck me. One look at the table and he would instantly know his writing had been tampered with!

I reached into my pocket and grabbed the papers. I removed the half-completed top sheet. Quickly I read it over in the light of the moon. Still I heard no voices. I read it again so that it would stick in my memory.

Then I went back to the table, replaced the half-written sheet of Derrick's on the stack of blank pages I had put there, and smoothed out the fold. I laid the pen down exactly as it was before, then stuffed the rest of the pages back in my pocket, and left through the window.

It closed easier than it had opened. I crept back across the ledge, over onto the landing, and back down the stairs onto the street.

Just as I started down I heard the heated voices of Derrick and the other two men entering the hallway from the saloon. They sounded like they were in a hurry. "We'll ride out of here early tomorrow and dump the kid and the girl in a ravine up in the mountains someplace," one of the men was saying. "Then you can put a bullet into both of them. You got it, Gregory?"

I didn't want to stick around to hear any more. I leaped down the stairs three at a time, and dashed off into the night.

CHAPTER 49

ESCAPE

Taking back streets and finding my way as best I could by the light from the night sky, I hurried toward where I thought the livery stable was.

The smells and the sounds of the horses and mules inside told me I had reached the right place. I approached from out in the back of the livery. There wasn't a door into it from where I was, but I could hear two men talking on the other side of the wall. They weren't voices I recognized, probably only stable hands cleaning up and tending to the animals.

I glanced around. Where could they have stashed Robin? Inside one of the stalls? Not likely, or those two workers might have spotted him.

What had they said? I tried to remember their words. *Out back of the livery*—that's what they'd said.

He must be here someplace. There were several shacks nearby. I ran to the first and opened the door.

It was pitch black and cold inside—must have been the ice house. "Robin . . . Robin, you in here?" I said just a little above a whisper. There was no reply.

I shut the door and ran to the next little outbuilding. From the smells of leather and dirt and the shovel and pitchfork I nearly stumbled over, I figured this to be where they kept tools for repairing harnesses and wagons. "Robin . . . Robin!" I whispered. Again, I heard nothing.

I looked around yet once more. The last possible spot was

a shed for storing bales of hay and straw, made of three walls and a roof, with the one open end facing southwest, probably to protect it from the wind and rain.

I ran to the shed and inside. All I could make out in the dim light were piles of baled hay.

"Robin . . . Robin?" I called out, a little too loud, I'm afraid. But I was getting desperate. I knew those men were going to be after me any minute!

"Robin O'Flaridy, you low-down rat . . . where are you?"

I stopped and looked all around, wondering where else I could search.

Then I heard a muffled groan!

"Robin, is that you?" I cried.

The sound came again, from the back of the shed. I ran toward it, struggling to throw aside bales, and climbing over them to get to the back of the shed.

There he was, tied up in the corner—wrists and ankles bound tight, a rag stuffed in his mouth, lying on his stomach, his face buried in loose straw, and a couple of heavy bales leaning sideways on top of him. He'd probably been trying to free himself, and they'd toppled over on him, knocking him into the ridiculous position where I found him. Luckily there was no one guarding him.

As fast as I could I went to work at the ropes around his legs. But they were too tight!

I fumbled in the darkness for the knife I'd tucked at my waist, found it, and quickly slit the cords.

"Get on your feet!" I said. "Let's get out of here!"

I pulled at him to get him up. He moaned and motioned at his hands and mouth.

"After what you did to me," I said, "you want me to set your mouth free to start yapping again? You betrayed me once tonight already, Robin O'Flaridy, and I'm not likely to forget it anytime soon. And if I'm going to save your life, I don't want to have to listen to your explanations or excuses! I'll just leave your hands tied behind you and your mouth gagged until we're safe. Now come on, before those ruffians get here!"

I yanked at his arm and half-dragged him back over the bales the way I'd come. If I had seen the dried blood on his face and the welts above his eye and the bruises on his shoulders, I probably would have been a little kinder. As it was, I was both angry at him and terrified that we'd be caught any second. And by the time we got out of the shed and back out into the moonlight and I did see his condition, we were in too big a hurry. My compassion for loose-tongued and cowardly Robin O'Flaridy would just have to wait until later!

"This way!" I said, still holding on to his arm, pulling him to follow.

I ran toward the woods behind the livery, toward where I'd tied my mare earlier.

Robin was stiff and sore from being tied up, and he could barely keep to his feet. I knew I'd have to untie his hands or he'd keep stumbling along and falling every other step. I stopped and got out my knife again. But just as I was slitting through the last of the cords, I saw a figure come running out from the front of the livery to the back. He made straight for the hay shed, then stopped the instant he saw us standing about thirty yards from it toward the woods. There was no chance to hide. We were exposed in the pale glow of the moonlight.

It was Derrick Gregory!

Robin and I froze. Derrick walked slowly toward us. I hadn't noticed him wearing a gun before, but he had one now, and he pulled it from his holster.

I could feel Robin trembling and he began pulling away. I went with him and we inched backward.

"You're a clever one, Cornelia Hollister," he said, still advancing. "You had me completely fooled."

"I'm sorry, Derrick," I said, "but I had to know if you were going to write the truth about Mr. Fremont."

He gave a laugh, though this time it rang with bitterness. "I told you before, a reporter can't worry about that. You've got to do your job, that's all. And right now *my* job's to get those papers back from you."

"What papers?" I stammered nervously.

"Come on, Cornelia," he said with a sneer. "You know as well as I do you took them from my room. Now, hand them over!" He waved his pistol at us, but still we kept inching back.

"How did you know?" I asked.

He chuckled again. This time there was a little of the old humor in his tone.

"Every writer has his own little secrets, his own way of doing things. You must know what I mean, Cornelia. One of mine is that I never fold my pages. I can't stand papers with folds in them! You tried to smooth it out, but it didn't work. Very clever of you to leave the top sheet. If you hadn't folded it first, I'd never have noticed it till hours later. But then I saw all those blank papers substituted for my own, and I knew it had to be you. You're a smart girl, but I've got to have those papers back!"

"Where are the other two men?" I said.

"I sent them on a wild goose chase to the boardinghouse to look for you. I figured you'd be here, trying to save that coward who turned you in to save his own skin."

"And if I don't give you the papers?"

"Look, I don't want to hurt you, Cornelia. But I've got to have those papers! The other men'll be here any second. Now just give me the papers and get going. I'll tell them you got away. But if they get here first, they'll kill you both! Now come on, Cornelia, don't make me do something I don't want to have to do!"

He quickened his pace toward us. Robin and I began moving backward toward the woods. Derrick was still twenty or twenty-five yards from us.

"Robin," I whispered. "Make for the woods. My horse is straight up that little rise about fifty yards away. Untie her. I'll be right behind you! And you wait for me, you scoundrel!"

He hesitated.

"Get going!" I yelled, shoving him up the hill. He needed no more encouragement. He'd broken the last strand of rope on his wrists and took off for the woods as fast his spindly legs would carry him.

"Stop, Flaridy!" cried Derrick. "Stop, or I'll shoot!"

Robin kept going and in a couple of seconds was out of sight.

"Derrick," I implored, still walking backward after Robin, "you don't want to shoot anybody. I don't think you're willing to kill either of us for the sake of your rich senator."

"You'll never get away from them," he said.

"I'll just have to get back to San Francisco before you or your friends."

Behind him I heard the sounds of running footsteps and shouts.

I turned and sprinted into the woods!

My heart nearly stopped when I heard the explosive fire of Derrick's gun behind me. But he couldn't have missed! I was sure he intentionally shot wide and over my head! I heard shouts again and I knew whose voices they were. Derrick's pistol echoed in the blackness with two more deafening shots.

"They got away!" I heard Derrick yell. "After them . . . this way!"

More shots sounded, but they were not close. I reached the horse only seconds after Robin. He was fumbling with the rope.

"I'll get it!" I cried.

I loosened the rope from the tree, then jumped into the saddle and helped him up behind me. "Hang on!" I called. "If you fall off, I'm not stopping for you!"

I dug in my heels and off we galloped.

Hearing us, more gunfire rang out. It was the sound of rifles this time! Bullets smashed into trees and clipped off branches around us. But we kept on. Finally the gunshots stopped.

"Get to the horses!" I heard the man with the beard cry out. "We'll chase 'em down . . . they can't get far!"

I lashed poor Raspberry on as fast as she could go, circling the town and working our way down onto the main road west toward Chinese Camp and Modesto. Reaching the road, we pushed on as fast as we could go. But I knew the other three riders were only a minute or two behind us.

We rode hard for a couple of miles. When we came to the

junction of the southern road, I eased up on the reins, then found a place to pull off the road and hide behind several boulders and large pine trees.

A couple of minutes later, the thundering hoofs of our pursuers' three horses approached and passed us, continuing on the westward route. Once the sound had died away, I led my horse back out into the clearing, and onto the road leading south.

The stop had given Robin his first opportunity to pull the rag from his mouth.

"Hey, this isn't the road to San Francisco," he said as I urged the mare to a gallop again.

"Is that all you have to say after I just saved your skin?" I shot back at him over my shoulder.

"Of course, I'm grateful, but I only wondered where we're going."

"Well, for the moment at least, we're *not* going toward San Francisco. That is the direction they think we're going, and I don't want to make it too easy for them to find us. I happen to value my life, Robin, even if *you* don't!"

"They would never have hurt you, Corrie. I knew that. I would never have said a word if there'd been any *real* danger to you!"

"Ha!" I said. "I don't believe that for a second!"

"Where are we going?"

"Don't worry, I'll get you back to San Francisco. But first I've got a little unfinished business with regard to Mr. Gregory's article."

"Where?"

"At the Fremont estate."

The moon was practically full and I could see well enough to ride with tolerable speed. I couldn't see my map too well, but I had studied it back at Sonora. There were enough markers along the way so that I knew we were on the right road to Mariposa.

We rode pretty hard for half an hour, then eased back. The horse wouldn't be able to keep it up all night at this pace, and all I wanted to do was get far enough from Sonora so that I'd know we were safe.

We stopped about midnight. We hadn't gone very fast, but we had ridden for several hours and had covered a good distance. By my reckoning we were only eight or ten miles from Mariposa and could make it there easily in the morning. I pulled off the main road, and found a clearing two or three hundred yards away where we could spend the night.

We got down off the horse. I built a small fire, making sure to use dry wood so as not to give off any visible smoke, then got out some dried food and my canteen. I tried to wash Robin's wounds as best I could, then gave him something to eat and tried to make him comfortable with two of my blankets.

"You get to sleep, Robin," I said. "You're going to need it. I'll keep watch for a couple of hours, just till I'm sure no one's tracking us."

He was real quiet, not like his usual self. When I'd look over at him, he was just staring into the fire like he was thinking.

"How'd you learn to do all this stuff, Corrie?" he said finally.

"All what?"

"Ride a horse, escape from guys with guns, build a fire, take care of yourself out in the wilderness."

"I don't know," I said. "I never thought about it. I just did it. I guess I've been taking care of myself for a lot of years."

"Yeah," he said after another minute of staring into the fire. "I suppose it's the same for me in the city. I can take care of myself there, just like you do out here."

"The city scares me," I said, laughing. "But out here, I don't know, for me it's more like home."

"Give me buildings and lights and people and city-sounds any time!" said Robin, and for a minute I thought he might be going to laugh too.

"Not me," I said. "I love the crickets and the far-off howl of some animal and the wind in the trees and the sound of a stream."

It got quiet again.

"How's your face?" I asked. "They roughed you up pretty bad, didn't they?"

"It hurts some, but I'll be okay." He paused, but then added, and I could tell from his voice that the words were hard for him to say, "Thanks, Corrie, for what you did back there. I didn't deserve it."

"Aw, think nothing of it."

"Why did you do it? Why'd you risk everything to save me?"

"Anybody'd have done the same," I said.

"I doubt that. I'm not sure I'd have had the guts to do what you did, especially after what I did."

"Well, look at it this way," I said. "I couldn't very well go back to Kemble with the lowdown on Gregory's article and with all the papers of his, and then at the same time tell him I left his star reporter for dead. How could I tell him *that*? Don't you see, Robin, I had no choice. I *had* to save you to keep on Kemble's good side!"

Now he did let out a little chuckle, but quickly put his hand to his mouth from the pain.

"Well, whatever your reasons, thanks anyway."

"Any time," I said. "And I'm sorry I was so hard on you back there, Robin," I added. "I didn't mean to yell and call you names. I was just upset, that's all."

He nodded, then turned over and pulled the blankets around his shoulders. In two or three minutes I could tell from his breathing that he was sound asleep.

I took off my coat, wrapped my blanket around me and lay down, staring into the fire, thinking of the terrifying, unbelievable day I'd just had. At least it felt good that Robin O'Flaridy was no longer my adversary. That was one positive thing to emerge from the dangerous escapade of this night.

Still I stared into the fire, growing sleepier and sleepier, until at last I knew no more.

CHAPTER 50

MARIPOSA AGAIN

When I awoke, the gray light of dawn was just giving way to the reds and oranges of the coming sunrise.

The fire was out cold.

I glanced around. Robin wasn't where I'd left him. He must have gone down to find a stream to wash and get water.

I got up, stretched, and wandered in the direction where I figured he had probably gone. But before I had gone far, I stopped and turned back.

It was too quiet. Something wasn't right!

I ran back to the clearing where we had slept. There was no sign of Robin anywhere. And my horse was gone!

Frantically I looked around. There was the blanket I'd slept in and my coat—that was all. He'd taken both my two other blankets, my canteen of water, and all the food. I checked my coat. My notes! Every single sheet of Derrick's notes and the article he had written for the *Globe* were gone!

"Why, you underhanded rascal!" I cried.

At least he'd left me my carpetbag! There it lay on the ground right where he'd thrown it off the horse. I walked toward the bag, and then spotted a scrap of paper on the ground alongside it, torn from the bottom of one of Derrick's pages. I picked it up.

> I'm sorry, Corrie. It's an awful thing to do to a colleague.
> But I just couldn't afford to miss a shot at a really big story.
> I always wanted to write politics, and this is my chance! I'll

303

make it up to you someday.

Fond regards,
R.T. O'Flaridy

Fond regards!

I crumpled up the paper and threw it to the ground. "And *I'll* make it up to *you* someday too, Mister O'Flaridy—just you wait and see!"

I grabbed my blanket, stuffed it inside my carpetbag, put on my coat, and headed back to the road, so angry I could have walked for a week! The only trouble was, time was short and I was stuck out in the middle of nowhere!

I soon found out that even anger in the absence of food won't keep your energy up forever. After two hours, I was beat. My feet hurt, my legs ached, and I was hungry!

But still I trudged on, my carpetbag getting heavier and heavier. I don't know how far I walked. It had to be at least ten miles, although it felt like thirty! Somewhere in the middle of the morning, when the sun was getting high in the sky and the day was beginning to get uncomfortably warm, I finally reached the little village of Mariposa.

Half an hour later I was sitting with Ankelita Carter, telling her my story. Watching the various expressions on her face change from shock to grief to anger to sympathy to outrage was nearly enough to take my mind off my own trouble. As irritated as I was at Robin, Ankelita's chief concern was for her mistress and her husband.

"You must stop them, Corrie!" she exclaimed when I was through telling her everything that had happened. "You must not let them print such lies! The Colonel and Jessie are good people—these are nothing but lies!"

"I'm will do my best," I said. "But I will need your help."

"Anything!" she replied.

"First, I need to borrow a horse," I said. "A fast horse. Robin will have at least a twelve-hour lead on me. Though I doubt he will be able to ride straight through to San Francisco," I said with a smile. "He does not exactly have the adventurous pioneering spirit! Still, I have to catch up with him before he does any mischief with Gregory's parcel of papers. For all I know, he might try to sell the pack of lies back to the *Globe* rather than take it to Kemble."

"We have horses. I will have Felipe saddle for you the fastest in the stable."

"Then I need to ask you some questions, Ankelita," I said. "I need whatever proof I can get that will disprove the claims Gregory was going to make in his article. You probably know the Fremonts better than anyone in California."

"You get out your paper and pen and ask, Corrie!" she said enthusiastically. "You've got to get back to San Francisco and write the truth about Colonel Fremont! He's *got* to win that election, for the sake of the Union. We just can't let a slave man into the White House!"

"Before we start," I said with a sheepish expression, "would you mind if I had something to eat?"

She laughed, jumped out of her chair, and was on her way to the kitchen before all the words were out of my mouth.

A couple hours later, we had gone through just about everything I could remember of Derrick Gregory's charges against Colonel Fremont. I don't suppose the words of a Fremont friend and maid would constitute proof in a court of law. But perhaps they would shed sufficient doubt on the credibility of the *Globe* story to keep them from running it. I hoped so, at least.

"You can't trust anything Jim Savage might say," Ankelita said. "Why, he's been mad at the Colonel for years because he didn't get his hands on this land! And as for all that foolishness about Negroes in chains and Chinese slave labor and false surveys—why, they're just lying to make Mr. Fremont look bad. Felipe!" she called out into the other end of the house.

The young Mexican appeared after a minute. She spoke to him in Spanish, and he ran outside.

"I told him to get Bernardo. You couldn't ask for a more honest and upright man than Bernardo Garcia. He has been the Colonel's foreman here since the Colonel purchased the property. He will tell you himself that these things are not true."

"Thank you," I said. I was writing down everything as rapidly as I was able, though my fingers were already getting cramped. I would have to rely on the old newspaper gimmick of quoting "reliable sources at the Mariposa estate," and my words could be persuasive enough to convince people that what I was writing was the truth.

"As for the Colonel and barmaids in the village," Ankelita went on, incensed at the very thought. "I can tell you that Jessie never believed such things. She once told me that neither of them had ever been unfaithful to the other. She said—"

"Wait," I said, "just let me get that written down."

She paused until I caught up, then finished her sentence as I kept writing.

"What about his stirring up the Chinese in that Tong war?" I asked.

"I don't know what to say about that, except that the Colonel had nothing against the Chinese any more than he did the Negroes. But you should ask Bernardo about that. If anything like that did go on among the men here, Bernardo will know of it."

"And the rumor that Mr. Fremont is secretly a Catholic?" I asked.

"Ridiculous!" exclaimed Ankelita. "The Colonel and I had more than one discussion about matters of faith, and I know he always took the Protestant view and I the Catholic one."

"How did the rumor get started?"

"Mr. Fremont's father came from France, you know, and so I presume he was a Catholic. When he was young Mr. Fremont was educated for a time at a Catholic school, and he and Jessie were married by a priest. From all this, people merely assumed he was personally a Catholic, and his enemies stuck the label on him. He is such a private man in religious matters that he never went out of his way to refute it. His enemies knew that if it could be proven, he could never be elected President. That is undoubtedly why they are trying to dig up this old story about St. Xavier's. But don't you believe a word of it, Corrie!

John Fremont may have attended some services when he was at school as a youth, but the grown man John Fremont never attended a Catholic Mass in his life!"

"How can you be so sure?"

"Because when we were in Charleston two years ago, he showed us the church where he was baptized at the age of eight—a Protestant church!"

"Then why doesn't he make a public statement?"

"I don't know, Corrie. But just before I left the East he and Jessie had given all three of the children's baptismal records to the *Daily News* to be made public, with their admission into Protestant churches."

"Then that refutes Derrick's story completely," I said.

Just then Felipe returned, followed by a man Ankelita introduced me to as Bernardo Garcia. His English was not as flawless as hers, but I was able to understand him well enough to get along. I questioned him on all the points that were still fuzzy, especially the charges about the boundary surveys, the Chinese and Negro labor, and the treatment of local miners over squabbles about the ownership of the land. He confirmed what Ankelita had told me about Jim Savage, and was definite about everything else as well. We spoke for an hour, and when we were through I knew I had all I needed.

Bernardo went back out to the mines. Ankelita and I stood. It was already midafternoon.

"Now I must get your bed ready for you again, Corrie," she said.

"Oh no, Ankelita, I mustn't stay!"

"The article cannot get into print in less than a day," she replied. "You should stay with me again, get some rest, eat well, and sleep. Then leave early in the morning."

I stopped to think. If I took the rest of today and this evening to write my article, then I would be prepared the moment I saw Mr. Kemble. Whatever Robin might tell him, I had to have my own facts straight. And if I could have an article completed, so much the better.

I nodded. "You're right, of course. I'll stay tonight and

leave with the first light of the morning."

She led me into the room where I had slept before. I immediately began spreading my notes and previous papers over the table. I had to make sense of everything I had learned, and try to put it together into an article that was factual and true.

I worked long into the night. And when at last I laid my head down to sleep, it was with a satisfied feeling. Despite the fact that I had a journey of a hundred and fifty miles awaiting me, and even then I didn't know what might be the outcome of my efforts, at least I knew in my heart that I had uncovered the truth of what I'd been sent here to find, and I had done what I'd set out five days earlier to do.

Tomorrow was the 18th. If I gave it everything I had, just maybe I could make it to San Francisco before the offices closed on the 19th.

I might even make up the ground I'd lost and beat Robin O'Flaridy at his own game!

CHAPTER 51

SHOWDOWN

Ankelita awoke me the next morning before dawn.

She had packed food, a canteen, and an extra blanket, and Felipe already had the horse saddled and waiting for me.

"Her name Rayo Rojo," he said. "She . . . este caballo corre como el viento!"

"She's the filly of Jessie's favorite mare," added Ankelita. "She's of good stock, and Felipe's been training her to race one day."

"She run like no horse miles 'round," said Felipe excitedly. "Rapido . . . like tornado!"

"If any horse in California will get you to San Francisco ahead of that O'Flaridy scamp, Rayo Rojo will!" said Ankelita.

"What does her name mean?" I asked.

"Do you see the reddish star on her white forehead?"

I looked and did indeed see the reddish-brown star. The rest of the top of her head was white, though her predominant color was a tan or light brown.

"That red star was there from the moment of her birth. Jessie had always called the horse's mother Big Lady Red because of her color. So when the foal was born, they called her *Little* Red—until they saw how fast she could run! Then she became Rayo Rojo, or *Fast Red*. I had never seen her until I arrived back here at Mariposa recently, and Jessie has still not seen her. But we both have felt we knew her from the reports Bernardo sent. She is a favorite with all the men on the ranch."

Felipe handed me the reins, then offered his hand to help me up into the saddle.

The moment I was on her back I felt a surge of the animal's life and energy. The look in her eyes did not fully reveal the power contained within her frame and her thoroughbred legs and muscles.

"Now go!" said Ankelita, giving Rayo's rump a little swat. "Go . . . and may God be with you, our friend Corrie."

"I will get Rayo Rojo back to you as soon as I can," I shouted over my shoulder. But already I was halfway to the gate. At my slightest urging, the young filly accelerated with an ease that was astonishing. The breeze flew through my hair and I leaned forward to be sure of my seat. With my right hand I grasped the saddle horn and reins, while my left sought to make sure my hat was tied securely around my chin.

This was going to be like no ride I had ever experienced. Truly this was a faster animal than I had been on top of in all my life. I had never known such speed. Perhaps I would overtake Robin after all!

We flew through the village and eastward along the Carson Creek road, past the quarry at Negro Hill and around Cathey's Mountain, and were already in Cathey's Valley before the sun had risen over the last of the mountains in the east. I was to the central valley and Bear Creek by midmorning, and Merced by noon. I stopped and looked up Mrs. Harcourt and asked her if I could feed and water and rest my horse in her stable and refill my water canteens. The hottest and driest part of the journey still lay ahead.

It was midafternoon the following day before I reached San Jose. Poor Rayo Rojo! She was indeed fast, but I had pushed her hard, and her stamina was not equal to such a sustained effort. Now we had to walk and take many rests between gallops. She was a brave one, though, and whenever I would urge her forward, she would obey faithfully.

I rode up to the office of the San Francisco *Alta* at about half past five that afternoon. I tied Rayo outside and ran to the door. I turned the handle and it yielded. I raced down the hallway to Mr. Kemble's office.

The door was closed. I tried the handle. It was locked. I rapped on the marbled glass. There was no reply.

I turned and walked slowly back. I stuck my head in at one of the other offices where I heard someone busily at work.

"Is Mr. Kemble here?" I said.

"Gone home for the night, Miss," was the answer.

Dejectedly I left the building. Well, at least it would give me time to clean up and take a bath, I thought—and to put the finishing touches on the article I planned to present to the editor in the morning. I just hoped Miss Sandy Loyd Bean had a room left! Rayo Rojo would no doubt welcome the rest much more than I did!

Miss Bean did have a room, and I slept very soundly that night after two days of bouncing along on Rayo Rojo's back.

At seven-thirty the following morning I was standing on the walk outside the lobby of the *Alta* building, my writing satchel in my hand, awaiting the arrival of head editor, Mr. Edward Kemble.

A little while later Mr. Kemble approached along the sidewalk, with none other at his side than Robin T. O'Flaridy, walking along laughing and talking amiably together. No lady would say the things that came into my mind at that moment. Fortunately, I swallowed them and managed to keep my mouth closed. Robin wore a bandage over one corner of his mouth and chin, and one eye was pretty badly swollen and discolored, but otherwise he didn't look too much the worse for wear.

"Ah, Miss Hollister!" exclaimed Mr. Kemble the moment he saw me. "Robin told me to expect you sometime soon."

Robin gave me a nod and a smile, and I gave *him* back a look that shot daggers. I wasn't feeling much like a loving and forgiving Christian at the time!

Mr. Kemble led the way inside and down the hall to his office, and I followed in silence.

"Quite a business you and Robin got into up there, eh, Hollister?" Mr Kemble said the moment the three of us were alone. "And it looks like he scooped you again! Tough break too. I thought this was the one where you might really prove yourself."

"Scooped *me!*" I exclaimed, at last finding my tongue. "What are you talking about?"

"Right here," he replied, slapping his hand a couple times on a stack of papers that sat on his desk. "When Robin arrived yesterday afternoon—looking a mess, I have to tell you!—and put this in my hands, I knew everything had paid off in the end. Not only had he unearthed the whole of that bum Gregory's story, he had actually made off with the thing—notes, interviews, quotes and all! Can you believe it, Hollister? He scooped the whole *Globe* story—stole it out from under their noses! With this in our hands, they can't run it against Fremont!"

"What?" I stammered.

"How was I to know that he'd go back out there on his own after I pulled him off the story and sent you? Mighty determined reporter he's turning out to be! It really is too bad, Hollister, for O'Flaridy to scoop you twice in a row. Lucky for you he was there, though—to save you from those ruffians!"

The whole time Robin was standing by with a smug smile on his face, not saying a word.

"He—he told you all that, did he?" I said. I'm afraid my voice did not sound too calm.

Mr. Kemble chuckled. "He *also* told me you'd be furious and would try to tell me *you* had done it all. Look, Hollister, you're young . . . you're a bright kid. But another thing you've got to learn in this business is not to be a sore loser. When you're up against someone more experienced than yourself, like Robin, you've got to expect to be beat out for a story now and then. But you're learning."

I sat down finally, took some deep breaths, and tried to calm down. It would do no good to argue or yell or complain or call Robin a liar. That would only confirm what Mr. Kemble already thought, that I was a young and emotional female not able to think rationally. And I suppose the first two *were* true, but this was one time I had to *force* myself to think rationally!

Finally I looked up at the editor and spoke again, softly and without anger.

"And just what sort of article did Mr. O'Flaridy provide you to run in opposition to this information of Gregory's that *he* brought you?" I asked.

"We hadn't exactly settled on our response. Perhaps Robin will write a pro-Fremont piece. Perhaps you could even join that effort. Perhaps nothing need be done with regard to this aborted *Globe* information." He patted the stack of Derrick's papers again.

"I see," I said, then paused thoughtfully. "And has it occurred to you that Derrick Gregory is also an experienced writer with perhaps more at stake than either of you, and that he would be well able to reconstruct from memory much of what he was planning to divulge? Do you think that just because you have his notes and perhaps a rough draft of his article, you have stopped him entirely? I wouldn't doubt that he is already back in Sacramento or right here in San Francisco, in a hotel someplace, writing furiously to redo the very article that you think you have stopped." I pointed to Mr. Kemble's desk and the papers that I had taken from Derrick's room.

Mr. Kemble and Robin were both silent, thinking over what I had said.

"If that is true, your possessing his notes and original material will do you no good whatsoever. He'll still run his story in the *Globe,* and Colonel Fremont will suffer just as much damage as ever."

I paused and looked straight at Mr. Kemble. "What you need," I said, "is a story that refutes Gregory's charges and strengthens Mr. Fremont's position."

"And where can I get such a story?"

"I happen to have one—right here!" I patted the writing satchel on my lap. "Completed, ready to print, and refuting nearly all of Gregory's charges."

"May I see it?" asked Mr. Kemble. I think he was beginning to wonder if he'd misread the whole situation.

"Not until we have worked a few things out," I replied. "For now, I will just hold on to it myself."

"If it's what you say, Corrie, I'll pay you well. I'll give you your eight dollars without an argument this time."

"You can't buy my submission quite so easily now, Mr. Kemble. You sent me up to Sonora, as you said, to find the truth. Well, I found it. I found Mr. Gregory when Robin couldn't. I found what he was going to print. I found what I am satisfied is proof against his charges. I risked my life to steal that for you—" I pointed to the papers on his desk.

Suddenly I stopped, and the impact of what I had done hit me square in the face. I had determined not to lie to get my story, and yet I had done something just as wrong—I had broken into Derrick Gregory's room and stolen his papers, and at the same time I hadn't given it a second thought.

"Mr. Kemble," I said at last. "When I took Mr. Gregory's article, I didn't even stop to consider if it was right or wrong— I just knew I had to get my hands on that information. I had to stop his article from being published, to save the Fremonts from his deception." I paused, then went on.

"Maybe that makes me just like Derrick—willing to do anything for a story. But maybe it's different because my reasons for doing it were better. I don't really know, and I haven't had time to sort it all out yet. Maybe it doesn't matter at all to you, but it matters to *me*, and it may take me a while to get over what I've done. But your willingness to believe falsehoods about *me* is just as bad as the *Globe* being willing to print lies about John Fremont!"

I stopped, trembling with both anger and apprehension as I thought about my actions.

"I am deeply sorry, Corrie, if there has been some misunderstanding," Mr. Kemble said.

"There has been no misunderstanding. It seems simple enough to me. What Robin brought you is nothing." I turned to Robin. "That was your one mistake, Robin, leaving me my carpetbag," I said. "That's where *my* notes were. I had been with Derrick the whole previous day, and had written down everything he'd told me. He even admitted to bribing half the people he quoted! He as good as told me himself which of the charges against Mr. Fremont were false. And all *that* was in my carpetbag, which I still have. And at the Mariposa I got the rest of what I needed to destroy the credibility of Derrick's story. But you had none of that, which is why stealing Derrick's papers from me didn't do you a bit of good!"

I was angry again, and even the pale look on Robin's bruised face wasn't enough to renew the kinship I'd briefly felt with him four nights ago around the campfire.

"And you know what else you don't have?" I continued. "You don't have the last page that Derrick was in the middle of writing when everything exploded back there in Sonora. I left it behind. But I know what that page contained, and it would be dynamite if used against the Colonel. I know what that page said, and I am able to refute it. But neither of you have any idea as to either."

I looked around again at Mr. Kemble as I said these last words. I stopped and the room was silent. I had the best of the argument, and both men knew it.

"Now, Mr. Kemble," I said. "When I left, you told me to get to the bottom of the story and to find out the truth, and to have it on your desk by the 22nd. Today's the 20th. I've done everything you said with two days to spare. I reckon it's time for you to decide what you want to do about this matter, and it's time for me to decide what I want to do with what I've found and with the article I've written. I'll be staying at Miss Sandy Bean's Boarding House if you want to contact me. Otherwise, I'll be back to see you, perhaps tomorrow. That is, *if* I don't decide to take what I have to another paper!"

I got up from the chair and approached his desk, where I reached over and took hold of the stack of papers. "And if you don't mind, I think I will take these with *me*. I'm sure Robin will be glad to tell you how things *really* happened in Sonora."

I took Derrick's papers, put them under my arm with the satchel full of my own, and walked out of the office.

CHAPTER 52

COUNTDOWN TO NOVEMBER

The trip back to Miracle Springs from San Francisco was peaceful and thoughtful for me. I'd gotten my Raspberry back from Robin, and would return Rayo Rojo to Mariposa later. With both horses it was a much slower ride, and it gave me a chance to reflect on all that had happened.

After my conversation with Mr. Kemble, I went through all sorts of doubts about what I had done. Even though I was trying to stop others from doing wrong, the thought kept coming back to me that I had taken what didn't belong to me. And as I sat at Miss Bean's wondering what to do, I couldn't help finding myself confused. Finally I just had to say to myself, "Well, right or wrong, I *do* have Gregory's papers, so now I have to decide what to do with them." Maybe I'd never find any hard and fast rules that would help me know the answer to every situation I was in. I had to trust somehow that God would lead me through the dilemmas I might face as a writer.

In the end I left my entire Fremont article—explaining the charges that were being brought against him, and then showing how many of them were fabricated just so that he would not be elected—with Mr. Kemble. He said that its appearance would be a major boost to the Fremont campaign and should insure that the Colonel carried California in the election.

I took Derrick Gregory's papers to the *Globe* for them to return to him. He couldn't do much damage with them any longer, and I didn't feel right about keeping them. Without my

316

even having to dicker for it, Mr. Kemble said he'd pay me $10 for the work I had done. He called it a "major effort" in the Fremont cause. He also said the *Alta* would pay the expenses of my trip to Sonora. He would have a check sent to me for $29. We didn't get around to discussing the pledge he'd made earlier to give me a regular article in the *Alta*. But I hadn't forgotten, and I planned to remind him of it before long!

On the afternoon of September 26 I finally rode into Miracle Springs. I was so glad to be home—I'd had enough adventures for one month!

I rode up to Parrish Mine and Freight Company, stopped, dismounted, and walked inside. Almeda wasn't there, but Mr. Ashton and Marcus gave me greetings and hugs enough for all three of them.

"Miz Hollister, she left for the claim," said Mr. Weber. "She got big news for ya all, Miss Corrie! You best git on yer horse an' follow her as quick as you can."

"Can you take care of Raspberry for me, Marcus?" I asked. "As you can see, I came back with an extra horse."

"No trouble, Miss Corrie."

"Then I'll see you both again tomorrow," I said, and hurried back outside. Now I was ready to give Rayo Rojo a run, and she was ready! We flew out of Miracle Springs so fast I'm sure a few heads turned as we passed the Gold Nugget. We clattered across the first bridge over the creek and headed up the incline in less than two minutes. Never had I covered the distance so fast. *Just wait until Zack and Little Wolf see this magnificent animal!* I thought.

I galloped all the way home. As I was dismounting, all the family poured out of the house, and just like after my other trip, there were hugs and tears and shouting in plentiful measure.

I was anxious to find out the "big news" Marcus Weber was talking about. A flood of questions came out. I had all but forgotten that nobody else knew a thing of what *I'd* been through for this last two weeks. The only responses I heard were the clamoring questions of six other people shouting out and wondering what had happened to me!

Finally Pa managed to make his voice heard above all the rest. "*Everybody* inside!" he shouted. "The only way we're gonna get to the bottom of all this is to take it one question at a time!"

We trooped inside, still loud and laughing and talking. It was a happy moment. Every one of the others had big smiles on their faces and I knew they had something to tell me.

Pa got us all sat down and got my brothers and sisters to quiet down. Then he said, "Now, Corrie, tell us all about your trip."

"Oh, Pa," I groaned, "there's too much! It'll take *days* to tell you everything that happened! I want to hear *your* news! Something's up—it's written all over every one of your faces!"

The laughter erupted all over again. I had never seen Almeda so gleeful. She was laughing like a little girl.

"Come on . . . out with it!" I exclaimed, looking around at everybody. "What is going on here?"

"Well, Almeda," said Pa, looking down on her with a smile, "I reckon it's more your news than anyone else's. Go on . . . tell her!"

Almeda, who was sitting beside me on the couch, took one of my hands in hers and looked me tenderly in the eye.

"You'll never believe it, Corrie, but your father and I are going to have a baby!"

"That's . . . that's wonderful!" I exclaimed.

Without even realizing it, I discovered that I was crying. All the emotions and fears I'd had to keep to myself for the past two weeks broke loose into a well of tears that spilled over to everyone in the room. Even Pa was half laughing and crying at the same time!

When I finally dried my tears, I found that I still could not find any words to express all that was in my heart. Every word I tried to speak only started up the tears all over again.

Almeda finally came to my rescue with a long, tight hug that only a mother can give and only a daughter can receive.

At length we did manage to take some deep breaths and get

back to some normal conversation. I had so many questions, especially with the election now getting so close, and wondering what had been going on in Miracle Springs. But they were nothing compared to all *I* had to tell about my adventures!

So much had happened in two weeks, and so many stories remained to be told! In the *next* few weeks the Hollister-Parrish-Belle clan would witness a whole new series of events that would turn our lives topsy-turvy again—permanently.

All of our lives were changing. In a period of two weeks, I had found myself facing more adventure and danger, struggle and doubt, than I would have ever thought possible. I had grown so much! I'd gone out on the trail of the truth, and in finding it, I had found a little more about myself as well.

And yet in some ways the adventures were still only beginning!

———

The story that followed, and what happened in the two elections . . . you can read about in *A Place in the Sun*, The Journals of Corrie Belle Hollister, Book 4.

A PLACE
IN THE SUN

A PLACE
IN THE SUN

MICHAEL PHILLIPS
JUDITH PELLA

BETHANY HOUSE PUBLISHERS
MINNEAPOLIS, MINNESOTA 55438

Copyright © 1991
Michael Phillips/Judith Pella
All Rights Reserved

Published by Bethany House Publishers
A Ministry of Bethany Fellowship, Inc.
6820 Auto Club Road, Minneapolis, Minnesota 55438

Printed in the United States of America

Library of Congress Cataloging-in-Publication Data

Phillips, Michael R. , 1946–
    A place in the sun / Michael Phillips and Judith Pella.
        p.   cm. — (The Journals of Corrie Belle Hollister ; 4)

    I. Pella, Judith. II. Title. III. Series: Phillips, Michael R. , 1946–
Journals of Corrie Belle Hollister ; 4.
PS3566.H492P5   1991
813'.54—dc20   91–4987
ISBN 1–55661–222–2   CIP

To
Michael Oliver Cochran

CONTENTS

CHAPTER 1

ELECTION DAY

Pa walked out of the schoolhouse with a big smile on his face.

He took the stairs two at a time and ran over to where the rest of us were standing by the wagon. "Well, I reckon that's that," he said, still smiling. "Now all we gotta do is wait!"

Of course, since the rest of us were under twenty-one, we couldn't have voted, anyway—at least not Zack or Tad. But neither could Almeda, even though she was the one who got everybody for miles around interested in the political future of Miracle Springs by jumping into the mayor's race against Franklin Royce. People soon enough found out that she didn't consider being a woman to be a handicap to anything she wanted to do!

And so she stood there waiting with the rest of us while Pa went into the schoolhouse with the other men and voted. When he rejoined her, their eyes met, and they gave each other a special smile. I was well on my way past nineteen to twenty, and I'd been through a lot of growing up experiences in the last couple of years, so I was beginning to understand a little about what it felt like to be an adult. But even as the oldest of the young Hollister generation, I could have only but a bare glimpse into all that look between Pa and Almeda must have meant. If the Lord ever saw fit, maybe I would know one day what it felt to care about someone so deeply in that special way. For today, however, I was content to observe the love between

11

the two persons I called Father and Mother.

A moment later Uncle Nick emerged from the schoolhouse, and came down the steps and across the grass to join his wife Katie and fifteen-month-old son Erich, who were both with us.

"Well, Drum," he said, giving Pa a slap on the back, "we come a ways from the New York days, I'll say that!"

Pa laughed. "Who'd have thought when we headed west we'd be standing here in California one day as family men again—and *you* with a wife and a son!"

"Or doing what we was just doing in there!" Uncle Nick added. "I reckon that's just about the craziest, most unexpected thing I ever done in my life! If only my Pa, old grandpa Belle, and Aggie could see us now!"

A brief cloud passed over Pa's face. He and I had both had to fight the same inner battle over memories of Ma. We had both come to terms with her death—not without tears—and were now at peace, both with the past and the present.

As to the future—who could tell?

A lot would depend on what Rev. Rutledge and the government man from Sacramento found out when they added up all the votes later that day. For the moment, Pa and Uncle Nick had cast their ballots in the long-anticipated election for mayor of Miracle Springs, and in the Fremont-Buchanan presidential voting. I couldn't have known it yet, but my own personal future was as bound up in the latter election as the former. I had already invested a lot in the Fremont cause, and I couldn't help but feel involved in its outcome—almost as involved as in the local election for mayor.

But for the moment, the future would have to wait a spell. As Pa had said, there was nothing else to do *but* wait.

We piled in our two wagons. Pa gave the reins a snap, and off we rumbled back to our home on the claim on Miracle Springs Creek. Pa and Almeda sat up front. In the back I sat with my lanky seventeen-year-old brother Zack, who was a good five inches taller than me, thirteen-year-old Becky, and eleven-year-old Tad. Emily, now fifteen, rode with Uncle Nick and Katie, carrying her little nephew.

That was election day, November 4, 1856. A day to remember!

But there'd been so much that had happened leading up to the voting, I reckon I ought to back up a bit and tell you about it . . .

CHAPTER 2

PATRICK SHAW'S PROBLEM

After I got back from my adventure in Sonora six weeks earlier, I was certainly surprised by Almeda's unexpected news.

I had just filed my story on the Fremont-Buchanan race with Mr. Kemble at the *Alta*. After that and Derrick Gregory and the double-dealings of that ne'er-do-well Robin O'Flaridy, I sometimes wonder if *anything* could surprise me! But I'll have to say I was sure excited when I got home and Almeda said, "You'll never believe it, Corrie, but your father and I are going to have a baby!" An adventure, a baby, and two elections were almost more than I could handle!

Three or four days after I returned from Sonora, we got the first inkling that Franklin Royce, the town banker, was up to his old mischief. One afternoon Patrick Shaw rode up to the house. One look at his face, and you could tell right off that he was in some kind of trouble.

Neither Pa or Almeda had to say anything to get him talking, or ask what the trouble was. It was out of his mouth the instant he lit off his horse.

"He's gonna run us off our place, Drum!" he said. "But me and Chloe and the kids, we ain't got no place else to go. What am I gonna do, Drum? I don't know nothing but ranching, and with a family and the gold drying up everywhere, I can't pack up and try to find some new claim!"

"Hold on, Pat," said Pa. "What in tarnation are you talking about?"

14

"He's fixing to run us out, just like I told ya!"

"Who?"

"Who else—Royce! There it is—look for yerself!"

He thrust a piece of paper he'd been holding in Pa's direction. Pa took it and scanned it over quickly. He then handed it to Almeda.

"He says we got thirty days to get out!" Mr. Shaw's face went red, then white. If he hadn't been a man, he probably would have started crying.

Almeda read the paper over, taking longer than Pa, her forehead crinkling in a frown.

"It might as well be an eviction notice," she said finally, looking up at the two men. "And if I know Franklin, it's no doubt iron-clad and completely legal."

"What happened, Pat?" Pa asked. "How'd you get into this fix?"

"Well, it ain't no secret my claim's just about played out. I wasn't lucky enough to have any of your vein run across to my side of the hill. Though I suspect Royce thought it did, the way he's been after my place."

"What do you mean?" asked Almeda.

"Why, he's come out offering to buy the place three or four times the last couple of years."

"And so now he figures he'll get your place without paying a cent for it!" said Pa, the heat rising in his voice.

"A few of my cattle got that blamed infection last spring when my pond had the dead skunk in it. It spread around the herd, and I wound up losing thirty or forty head. I missed a good sale I was gonna make, and so couldn't make a few payments to the bank."

"How many?"

"Four."

"So how much you do owe him—how far behind are you now?"

"I pay him a hundred sixty-seven a month."

"So you're—let's see . . . what, about six, seven hundred behind," said Pa, scratching his head. "I'll help you with it,

Pat. I can loan you that much."

"No good, Drum! I already thought of that. I knew you'd help if you could, so when Royce delivered me that there paper, I said to him, 'I'll get you the six sixty-eight—that's how much he said I was in arrears, is what he called it. I told him I'd get it to him in a few days, because I knew you'd help me if you could. But he said it wouldn't help. He said now that I defaulted, the whole loan was due immediately, and that if I didn't come up with the whole thing in thirty days, the claim and the house and the whole two hundred-fifty acres and what cattle I got left—he said it'd all be his."

"How much is your loan, Mr. Shaw?" Almeda asked. "What do you still owe the bank?"

"Seventeen thousand something."

Pa let out a sigh and a low whistle. "Well, that's a bundle all right, Pat," he said. "I'm afraid there ain't much I can do to help with *that*. Nick and I couldn't scrape together more than three or four thousand between us."

"What about me, Drummond Hollister?" said Almeda, pretending to get in a huff. "I'm part of this family now too, you know! Or had you forgotten?"

"I ain't likely to do that anytime soon," replied Pa smiling.

"Well then, I insist on being part of this. Parrish Mine and Freight could add, perhaps, two or three thousand."

"I appreciate what you're trying to do," said Mr. Shaw, his voice forlorn. "But I could never let you loan me that kind of money, everything you got in the bank. It don't matter anyhow. Between all of us, we ain't even got half of what it'd take!"

"Yes, you're right," sighed Almeda. "And it wouldn't surprise me one bit if your loan had a thirty-day call on it even if you weren't behind in your payments. Franklin as much as told me that's how he structured all the loans around here. Of course, I couldn't say for certain without seeing the loan document, but my hunch is that your getting behind is only an excuse for the foreclosure, that legally he is perfectly justified in calling your note due at any time and giving you no more than thirty days notice."

A little more talk followed. But there wasn't much more to be said. Mr. Royce had the Shaws in a pickle, and nobody could see anything they could do about it.

CHAPTER 3

ALMEDA'S DECISION

The next surprise came a couple of days later.

Almeda had been rather quiet ever since Mr. Shaw's visit. The terrible news of what Mr. Royce had done seemed to weigh on her, and I knew she felt almost desperate to find some way to help him. Yet there just wasn't enough money to get him out from under the call on his loan.

It was getting on toward late in the evening, Pa was sitting with Tad and Becky in his lap reading them a story. I was trying to draw a picture of Zack from memory. Zack had taken Rayo Rojo for a ride that afternoon, and for one moment, just after he'd mounted, she reared up on her hind legs. Zack leaned forward, his feet tight into her flanks, one hand flying in the air, and his eyes flashing with the closest thing to pure delight I'd ever seen. The sketch wasn't turning out too well, but I didn't want to let myself forget the mental picture of that wonderful moment.

Suddenly Almeda's voice broke out loudly, as if she had been struggling all day to keep the words in and couldn't hold back the dam a second longer.

"It's just not right for a man like that to be mayor!" she exclaimed. "Drummond, I'm sorry for acting rashly, and I hope you'll forgive me, but I just don't know what else to do. We've just got to stop him, that's all there is to it! Pregnant or not, and despite his threats, and even if I am a woman—I don't know what I can do but go ahead with it! It *must* be done for

18

the good of this community—I am going to run for mayor after all!''

For a few seconds there was silence. Everyone stopped and looked at her. Pa was still holding the book steady on his lap, but his and Tad's and Becky's eyes all focused intently on Almeda where she stood over by the stove.

"If that don't beat all!" Pa said finally, shaking off the two kids from his lap, climbing to his feet, and walking over to her. "Sometimes I wonder whether I married me a wife or a hurricane! Well, if I'm gonna have me a new son or daughter, he might as well have a ma for a mayor to make up for the fact that his pa's such an old man!" He smiled and gave Almeda a big hug. I knew he was proud of her decision, even though maybe it wasn't the same one he would have made if he had to decide.

So many things immediately began to run through my heart!

What about all those threats Mr. Royce had made about what he would do to Almeda if she didn't keep out of the race? He said he'd cause trouble for Pa and Uncle Nick with the law, that he'd investigate the ownership of the land and their claim! All along we'd worried about what Royce might do to all the miners and ranchers and people around Miracle Springs who owed money to his bank if he didn't win. The incident with Patrick Shaw showed that he wasn't fooling, and I didn't see how Almeda's running would help, even if she won.

Worst of all, he had threatened *me* too! He had told me to stop interviewing and talking to people about the election, and as good as said that if I didn't, he would let it be known to powerful slavery people that I was a pro-Fremont reporter, and that I would be in danger. And after what had happened in Sonora I knew it was no empty threat! The powers behind the scenes in the national election were real . . . and *were* dangerous! For all I knew Royce might be somehow connected to senator Goldwin and his people! After my story appeared in the *Alta* exposing the falsehood of Mr. Gregory's claims against Fremont, they might try to track me down and do something to punish me. I was still so new to this whole world of politics and news reporting, I had no idea what to expect. And I certainly didn't want Mr. Royce getting me in more trouble than I was already in!

With all this worrying about Mr. Royce and his threats against *me*, I hardly even remembered at first what he'd said about opening a supplies outlet and freight service of his own, and putting Parrish Mine and Freight out of business.

But Almeda hadn't forgotten. She weighed everything, and over the next few days talked to Pa a lot. They prayed, and in the end they both concluded that her decision to run was the right one after all, and that they had to go ahead and see the election out to its conclusion on November 4.

I think Almeda felt a little like I had with the Fremont story, that there was more at stake than just the outcome of the election itself. She felt that it was her duty to fight against what Franklin Royce stood for, to fight against his underhanded and deceitful methods. She felt she was standing up for what was *right*. Even if she lost, she felt she needed to take a stand in the community for what was right and honest and true.

It was not an easy decision. Everything Royce had said was true. He *could* hurt her and her family if he chose to. He *could* put Parrish Freight out of business. He *could* challenge Pa and Uncle Nick's ownership of their land. He could hurt a lot of other people in the community, just like he was doing to Patrick Shaw, if he decided to start calling loans due. Franklin Royce was a powerful man!

But in the end Almeda and Pa decided to take the risk— because it was the right thing to do. Maybe it wouldn't help the Shaws keep their claim and their ranch and their home. But they had to do something to show that Royce couldn't just do whatever he wanted without any opposition. A man like that simply shouldn't be allowed to work his will in a town and come to power without anyone standing up to him. Sometimes you just have to do what's right, no matter what the consequences.

Realizing all the risks involved for Pa and Almeda in their

decision, within a day or two of Almeda's surprise announcement to the family, I made a decision of my own.

I decided to start up again with my article on the Miracle Springs mayor's election. And whether Franklin Royce liked it or not, I was going to pick up where I'd left off interviewing people. I *would* write at least one article, maybe two, on the election. There wasn't much time left before November, but what there was I would use. And I wouldn't settle for $1 an article either! If Mr. Kemble wasn't willing to pay me at least $3 or $4, I'd submit it to another editor—even the *Globe*, if I had to! But I was sure the *Daily and Weekly Times* in Sacramento would print it. Sacramento was closer, and both Mr. Royce and Almeda were a little bit known there.

So I dusted off my writing satchel, read over the notes from interviews I'd done earlier, and tried to figure out how I could go about telling people in the rest of the state about this election in what Mr. Kemble would call an "unbiased" way. Then I started going to visit folks again to find out their thoughts, now that the election was getting close and Almeda was back in it.

CHAPTER 4

MY FIRST INTERVIEW

One thing I was learning about being truthful was the importance of being out in the open with folks—not only being honest in what you said, but coming right out with things so that nothing was ever said or done behind another person's back. I don't think there's anything more destructive among people than thinking and saying things about someone that you're not willing to tell them to their face. And I knew that if I was going to be a writer—especially if I was going to write about people—I had to show integrity in this straightforward way.

So I figured there was only one place to begin my article about the election, especially if I was going to be fair and unbiased.

Therefore, that very afternoon, I rode into town, left Raspberry with Marcus Weber at the stable, and crossed the street to the bank. I went straight to Mr. Royce's office, knocked on the door, and walked in.

If he was surprised to see me, he certainly didn't show it. But neither did he smile.

"Mr. Royce," I said, "I would like to talk with you, if you don't mind. Either now, or some other time."

"Now will be fine, Miss Hollister," he replied, still sitting behind his desk, still not smiling or showing any sign of emotion. He motioned me to a chair with his hand.

"I imagine you know," I said, "that my stepmother has

22

decided to remain a candidate for mayor after all."

"So I understand," he replied. "It is of course her decision to make, but it is an unfortunate one that will, I fear, have most unpleasant consequences."

The squint of his eyes as he looked steadily into my face confirmed his meaning. I took a deep breath to steady myself.

"Well I have decided to go ahead with what I was doing too," I went on. "I am going to write the article or two I was planning about the mayor's election. And to do a good job I am going to have to continue talking to people around town and interviewing them."

"I am very sorry to hear that," said Mr. Royce. But his tone held a threat. "It would deeply grieve me to see a promising young writer such as you find herself on the wrong side, shall we say, of powerful interest groups and individuals who—"

"Look, Mr. Royce," I said, "I know you're trying to scare me by making it sound like I'm going to be in danger if I don't do what you say. But if Almeda can do what she's doing in spite of all the trouble you could cause her and our family, then I figure I can too. I'm going to do it whether you like it or not, and you might as well just stop trying to frighten me off by talking like that."

He stopped, his mouth half open, shocked that I would cut him off and dare to speak so brazenly.

I probably shouldn't have interrupted him, or spoken quite so boldly. But he was starting to make me angry with all his cool words and hidden threats, sitting there behind his big fancy desk as if he owned the world and could tell everyone else what to do! And I knew he was especially annoyed that Almeda and I were causing him so much trouble. He wanted us to stop interfering with his plans and the powerful grasp he used to hold on to everything around him. I'm sure he figured he could scare us into submission. Well I didn't like it! My face got red and my voice sounded a little edgy, but I couldn't help it.

For a second or two he just stared, probably wondering

whether he should threaten me further, or stand up and throw me out of his office! But before he had a chance to do either, I spoke again. And this time I went on and said everything I'd come in to say. I didn't want to give him a chance to cut *me* off.

"Now, doggone it, Mr. Royce," I went on, "I'm gonna try to be fair in this article I'm writing. It's not going to be something that's supposed to make people favor Almeda. I want to present both sides and talk to folks who are gonna vote for you *and* for her. My editor Mr. Kemble said he didn't think I could write a fair and unbiased article, being so closely involved like I am. He said I couldn't be objective—he called it a conflict of interests."

I paused to take a breath, but only for a second.

"But I'm going to prove him wrong, Mr. Royce," I said. "I'll show him that I *can* write an unbiased article about the election that will interest the people who read his newspaper. I intend to be fair, but you're not making it very easy for me to think unbiased thoughts when you're telling me and my Pa and my mother the things you're going to do to us if we don't just quit and let you run for mayor all by yourself. What would folks think if I wrote about what you said to us?"

"I would deny every word," replied the banker coolly. "It would be my word against that of a teenage girl desperately trying to sway people in favor of her father's wife. No one would believe a word you said."

"You might be right, for all I know," I said. "I don't want to write those things, and I'm not going to write them. What I came here for was to interview *you* and to ask you to give your side on some things. Whether you believe me or not, I want to write what's fair and truthful about you as well as Almeda. And it would be a lot easier to be fair to you if you'd give me a little help instead of talking mean like you're doing."

I stopped. Judging from the expression on his face, people didn't normally speak quite that plainly to Franklin Royce. And if I'd stopped to think about it, I probably wouldn't have either. But I'd done it, and it was too late to take my words back now!

He sat just staring back across his desk at me. The office was completely silent. His face didn't give away a hint of what he was thinking. I'd heard Pa and Uncle Nick talk about poker faces, and if this was one of those, then I understood what they meant!

Finally Mr. Royce's voice broke the quiet.

"What do you want to know?" he said. The red was gone from his cheeks and the meanness from his tone, although he was obviously not pleased with the whole affair.

"Why do you want to be Miracle Springs' mayor?" I asked, getting out a sheet of paper from my satchel and inking my pen. "What made you decide to run?"

He cleared his throat, but kept looking at me almost warily. The question *sounded* like what a newspaper reporter would ask, and yet he didn't quite believe it was coming from the mouth of a girl he wasn't sure he trusted.

"I, uh . . . feel that the town, growing as it is, must look to its future, and who could be better qualified to lead such a diverse community forward than one like myself, who has been such an intrinsic part of helping in its growth up till now?"

I wrote quickly to get down all his words.

"So you feel you are the most qualified person to be mayor?"

"I do."

"Because you are the town's banker?"

"That of course is a large part of it. In that role I have, as I said, helped this community grow. I have helped to finance much of the building, most of the homes. I have a stake in the community because of who I am and what I have done. As mayor I will always be looking out for the best interests of its people."

Again there was silence for a while as I wrote. Mr. Royce was getting used to the idea of an interview. He was starting to sound like he was delivering a campaign speech.

"Your opponent, Mrs. Hollister, could no doubt say the same thing about her history in the community and all the ways *she* has helped the miners," I said. "What real difference is there between you and her?"

His eyes narrowed for an instant, and I knew he thought my question meant more than I intended.

"Of course she could *say* it," he answered with just an edge of derision. "But there is a clear difference between a $13,000 loan to build a house or buy a spread of acreage, and a store where you buy a fifty-cent gold pan or a five-dollar sluice box or pay a few dollars so that a free black man can freight your supplies somewhere for you. A little supply store and a bank are hardly equal in their impact upon the community, and I am sure the voters in this area will have the good sense to acknowledge that difference on November 4."

"Do you think your position as banker might be a drawback in any way?"

"What do you mean? How could it possibly be a drawback?"

"There are some people who have said they might have trouble trusting you as mayor."

"What people?" he said, his voice rising and his eyes flashing.

"I cannot say *who*," I replied. "But I have talked with some folks who aren't sure they'd altogether like a banker in charge of their town."

"Look, Miss Hollister," he said angrily, "if you want to ask me some questions, that's one thing. But if you're going to come into my office and tell me to my face that I'm not to be trusted, and then put the lies people say about me in your article, I'll have no part of it!" He rose from his chair. "I believe it is time for this interview to come to an end. You can't say I didn't warn you what might happen if you persist in this folly. You tell that fool father and stepmother of yours that for their own good they'd better stop fighting me. I won't be denied what is rightfully mine, and I will not be responsible for people who stand in my way! Good day, Miss Hollister."

I remained seated and returned his stare. That man made it real hard to keep a Christian attitude! But I kept sitting there and didn't get up and leave like he wanted me to. Finally I spoke again, as calmly as I could.

"Please, Mr. Royce," I said, "I was only saying what some people have told me they're thinking."

"During your so-called interviews about the election!"

"That's right," I answered. "And if I'm going to write a fair article, then I ought to know how you would answer those people. Otherwise, if you just make me leave and I have to write the article with only their side of it to go on, then your perspective never gets to be told. I'm trying to give you a decent shake here, Mr. Royce, but you're making it downright hard! Do you want me to tell what *you* think or not? If you want me to leave, I will. But then I have no choice but to write just from the other interviews I get. And I am going to write this article, Mr. Royce, with or without your cooperation!"

He stood looking down at me just a second or two longer, then slowly sat down, like an eagle smoothing his ruffled feathers.

"Go on, Miss Hollister," he said calmly, "what is your next question?"

"Perhaps I should go about this differently," I said. "Why don't you tell me, Mr. Royce, how and why you first came to Miracle Springs, and how you became involved in banking in this community."

On this safe ground, Mr. Royce started up and was soon talking comfortably. I kept taking notes, and asked him more questions about himself, and the rest of my time in his office, while not "pleasant," was calmer than the beginning. When I left fifteen minutes later I had plenty of information to offer a fair look at Royce the candidate—if "fair" is the right word, considering what I knew about Royce that I couldn't say.

I never asked him about the business of calling Mr. Shaw's note due. I knew I could never mention it in the article. And for the time being I'd rather he didn't know I knew about it.

CHAPTER 5

TALK HEATS UP

I didn't need worry about trying to keep it a secret that I knew of the Shaws' problem.

Within a few days *everyone* knew. And most everyone was plenty riled. If the election had been held right then, Franklin Royce wouldn't have gotten a single vote!

Word had just begun to circulate back through the community that Almeda was going to run after all . . . *and* that she was in a family way. Those two things alone had people talking, and the "Hollister For Mayor" sign back up in the Freight Company window kept it all fresh in people's minds. But when the news got around about Mr. Shaw getting evicted by the bank, Franklin Royce wasn't exactly the most popular man in Miracle Springs that week!

Pa kept saying he couldn't figure out why Mr. Royce did it. "Gotta be the stupidest thing I can think of doing," he said, "just before the election. Why, Tad could run against him now! Anybody in the whole town could beat him hands down."

Almeda was both furious and delighted. This foolish move by the banker suddenly made it seem as if she had a good chance of winning the election. But on the other hand, what good would that do Patrick and Chloe Shaw? Even her being the town's mayor wouldn't get them their house and land back.

Finally Almeda decided to make the Shaws an issue in her campaign, to try to use it to make people think twice about voting for Mr. Royce, and at the same time to coerce the banker

28

into giving the Shaws another chance if they could get caught up and current again with their payments to the bank. "I would gladly sacrifice the election," she said one night at the supper table, "if Royce would negotiate some equitable terms with Patrick."

"Might be that you can do both, Almeda," said Pa, "win *and* make him back down."

"I'm going to do everything I can to try," she replied. "But the first order of business has to be somehow getting the Shaws out of their dilemma."

Almeda planned to give her first campaign speech the very next Sunday after church, right on the main street of town in front of Parrish Mine and Freight. Pa and Marcus Weber got busy building a three-foot-high platform for her to stand on, and the rest of us fanned out all over the community telling everybody to come, that we needed their support. She had some important things to say.

"And, Corrie, Zack, all of you," she said, "make sure the women know how important it is for them to come, even if they can't vote. If they're there on Sunday, and they hear what I say, their husbands will hear every word eventually! Women, children, dogs, horses . . . we just need a good crowd! We've got to show people that we are serious and that the opposition to Royce is real. That's the only way they'll give earnest consideration to voting for me."

By Friday, the whole community was buzzing! One of the town's most well-liked men was on the verge of getting run off his place. A pregnant woman who couldn't even vote herself was running for mayor against the town's powerful banker, and a campaign speech was scheduled in two days. Folks were talking of nothing else!

What a "human interest" item all *this* would make! I began to wonder if the article I was writing would be any good at all, leaving out all the things people were talking about. But I was almost done with it, so it was too late to start over. I thought maybe I should write a second one to come about a week after the first. I'd have to see what Mr. Kemble said.

Before I had a chance to worry about that, it began to come clear to Pa why Mr. Royce had taken the action against Mr. Shaw about his loan.

"He's a schemer all right," Pa grumbled. "He's making an example of Pat, showing folks what he'll do if things aren't to his liking."

"And demonstrating that he isn't afraid, even of what people think of him," added Almeda with a frustrated sigh. "I really don't know how to stop him, Drummond. Right now everyone's mad at him and saying they'll never accept him as mayor. But when it comes down to their decision, and their *own* homes and land that he holds the mortgages on, I'm afraid they'll worry less about how much they like Franklin Royce and more about their own security. And I can't say that I blame them. I don't want people voting for me if they're going to be hurt by it."

"He can't foreclose on everybody," said Pa. "He'd be a fool. He'd be cutting his own throat. His bank would be out of business."

"But don't you see, he doesn't have to follow through with his threats. Just the fear that he *might* will be enough. People won't run the risk. They'll give in to him. That's why he called Patrick's note due when he did. At first it looked like a foolish campaign move. But in reality it conveyed just the message to this community Franklin wanted it to—*I hold the power and the purse strings in this town, and I am not afraid to use them. I don't care if you like me. I don't even care if you all hate me. But just don't cross me or you'll end up in the same dilemma as Patrick Shaw.*"

"In other words," growled Pa angrily, "vote for me . . . or else!"

"I think that's the basic message he hopes the men of this community will glean from the Shaws' trouble. He doesn't care a bit about all this anger circulating around right now, as long as once it dies down he's succeeded in getting that message across."

Almeda sighed. She knew she had taken on a tough opponent who apparently held all the cards. Her initial enthusiasm was fading some, I could tell, and I knew from her washed-out complexion that she didn't feel well either.

"Well you just give 'em your best in that speech on Sunday," said Pa, trying to bolster up her spirits. "Maybe we can beat that rascal yet!"

Almeda smiled back at him, but it was a pale, wan smile. She rose slowly to her feet and walked to the door and outside. She needed to be alone a lot during those days. Pa knew it and let her go without any more talk between them.

CHAPTER 6

CAMPAIGN SPEECHMAKING

On Sunday morning church was packed, and folks were waiting for what was going to happen that afternoon.

A little after one o'clock, we all rode up to the front of Parrish Mine and Freight in the wagon. A few people were milling around already, and soon others began to arrive for the speech, which was scheduled for 1:30.

More people turned out than we had imagined possible! Not only were there dogs and horses and every woman for miles around and all their children, but a lot of men turned out too. Almeda was noticeably excited. By the time she was ready to stand up, the whole street was filled in front of the freight company office, all the way across to the stores on the other side, and stretching down the street almost to the Royce Miners' Bank. There must have been four or five hundred people, maybe more! The one person I *didn't* see was Franklin Royce, although I was certain he knew of the event.

At about twenty minutes before two, Pa jumped up on the platform and held up both of his hands. Gradually the crowd quieted down.

"I know it ain't necessary for me to make introductions," he said in a loud voice. "If any of you don't know who this is standing here with me by now, then I don't figure you got any business here anyway!"

Laughter rippled through the crowd.

"But this being our first campaign, well I figured we ought

to do things proper. So here I am making the speech to introduce our candidate who's gonna speak to you all today. And that's just about all I reckon I'm gonna say! So here she is, Miracle Springs' next mayor, and a mighty fine-looking woman if I do say so myself, Mrs. Almeda Parrish Hollister!"

All the women clapped as loud as they could, and most of the men joined in. Pa gave Almeda his hand and helped her up the steps to the platform. Then he jumped down onto the ground. Almeda turned to face the crowd.

"I can't tell you how much it means to me that you've all come here today," she began. "As my husband said, campaigning for public office is not something we are experienced at, and to tell the truth, I'm more than a little nervous standing up here facing so many of you. I don't really know what a political speech is suppose to be like, so I am simply going to tell you what I think of this town, why I love Miracle Springs, and why I want to be its new mayor."

She paused, looked out over the faces, and took a deep breath before continuing. As she did, some of the people sat down on the ground.

"When I came here, as a few of you know who were here at the time, the town of Miracle Springs was a far different place. My late husband and I had just arrived from Boston, and I have to tell you, all of California seemed pretty wild and rambunctious to me—Miracle Springs included. There were more saloons than stores, more gold than bread, more mules than women, and it was every man for himself. They said California was a state back then in 1850, but it wasn't like any state I'd ever seen!"

The listeners laughed and some joking comments could be heard from long-time residents who knew first-hand what she was talking about.

"That's right, Mr. Jones," Almeda called out with a smile. "I heard that. And you are absolutely correct—it was a fun place to be back then! But it was a hard life too, for those who didn't make a strike. And I don't know about the rest of you, but for myself, I will take the Miracle Springs of today to the

Miracle Springs of 1850. Yes, times have changed—here as well
as in the rest of the state—and throughout the country. It's a
new era. Our fellow Californian John Fremont is campaigning
through this great land for the abolition of slavery. And we've
all been hearing recently about some of this state's leading men,
like Leland Stanford and Mark Hopkins, who are earnestly
pursuing the railroad linkage of east and west across this great
country. California is becoming a state with a future.

"My point, ladies and gentlemen, is that as the country is
changing and growing, we citizens of Miracle Springs must
change and grow with it. Gold brought many of us here, and
it first put California and Miracle Springs on the map, but gold
will not insure our future. When the nuggets turn to dust, and
when even the dust begins to dry up, gold will no longer sustain
businesses. Gold will not feed hungry stomachs. Gold will not
educate. Gold will not keep the bonds of friendship and love
deep. Gold will not raise a church. Gold will not attract the
kind of families a community needs to put down roots and
sustain itself and grow strong that it might endure.

"You are all familiar with towns, once booming and alive
with activity, which have now become silent and empty because
the gold is gone. Ghost towns—dead today because they failed
to look to the future, they failed to establish a community fabric
where roots went down deeper than the gold they feverishly
sought."

Almeda stopped, thought for a moment or two, then took
in a deep breath and started up again.

"Now, in a few weeks you men have to decide how to vote
in Miracle Springs' first election for mayor. And I suppose I'm
telling you why I think you ought to vote for me—even though
I'm a woman!"

A little laughter went around, but mostly some cheers and
clapping could be heard from the women present.

"So I'm going to tell you why you should vote for me,"
Almeda continued. "I love this town. After my first husband
died, I was miserable for a time. I seriously considered return-

ing to the east, but in the end decided to stay here. And I cannot say it was an easy time. Some of you men made it very difficult for a woman, alone as I was, to keep a business going."

The smile she threw out as she said it showed that her words were meant in fun, not bitterness.

"Yet, on the other hand, most of you were good to me. You were considerate, you brought me your business. You treated me with courtesy and respect. And we managed to forge a pretty good partnership, you miners and Parrish Mine and Freight. This town became my home. And as the town grew, I loved it more and more. The church and school were built. A minister and schoolteacher joined our community—"

She smiled and pointed to where Rev. Rutledge and Miss Stansberry were seated together in the minister's carriage.

"Families came in growing numbers. Wives joined the miners—some from as far away as Virginia!"

She turned and threw Katie a smile behind her where she stood with Uncle Nick.

"And now I feel it is time for me to give this community back a little of what I feel it has given to me. I love Miracle Springs, and with everything that is in my heart, I desire to see it grow into a community whose strength lies in its people, and in their bonds with one another. I love it too much to see it become a ghost town, abandoned because the gold is gone from its hills and streams. My friends, even if the gold were to disappear tomorrow, you and I are what make this community vital! And that is the future to which I want to dedicate myself, as your next mayor.

"Now . . . why do I think you men ought to vote for Almeda Hollister? The chief reason is this: a Hollister vote is a vote for the future of Miracle Springs. It is a vote for the whole fabric of this community, not just one aspect of it. Money and gold may make men rich. But when they are gone, money and gold also make ghost towns.

"I am committed to the whole of Miracle Springs' future, not just its financial future." She paused, thought for a moment, and when she spoke again her voice had grown softer and more serious.

"What I say next is not easy for me," she went on. "But I suppose perhaps it is necessary in light of the purpose for which we are gathered. From the beginning, I have been instrumental in helping Miracle Springs become a real town, not just a gold camp. I helped organize the church and the school, and brought Reverend Rutledge and Miss Stansberry here. I truly believe I am qualified, both by experience and by commitment, to be your mayor. I suppose my greatest drawback as a candidate is that I am a woman, and that may be the reason many of you feel you should not vote for me. But on the other hand, perhaps that is the greatest asset I have to offer Miracle Springs, too. The fact that I am a woman makes me, I feel, sensitive to some of the deeper and longer-lasting interests of this community, important things that I fear a one-dimensional focus on gold and mining profits cannot adequately see."

I don't know whether she saw him at first, because she kept right on with the conclusion of her speech. But as I looked up I detected some movement at the back of the crowd, and then realized that a figure had emerged from somewhere near the bank and was now walking slowly forward.

"In closing then, my friends of Miracle Springs and surrounding communities," Almeda was saying, "I simply want to ask for your votes on election day. In return, I pledge to you my commitment to do all that lies in my power to insure a happy and prosperous future for all of us. Thank you very much for your attention and support."

She turned to step down off the platform, amid a lot of clapping—mostly from the women and children and *our* family, and a few enthusiastic men, like Pa and Uncle Nick and Rev. Rutledge. But suddenly the noise died down abruptly. Almeda turned around to see the cause, just as the crowd split down the middle to make way for Franklin Royce, who was striding purposefully toward the platform.

CHAPTER 7

ROYCE'S REBUTTAL

Silence fell over the street as everyone waited to see what would happen. Almeda remained where she was, watching him approach.

"Well, Mrs. Hollister," said Royce in a loud but friendly voice, "that was a very moving speech. You wouldn't deny your opponent equal time in front of the voters, would you?"

"Certainly not," replied Almeda, obviously cooled by his appearance, but trying not to show it.

The banker climbed the steps to the small platform, where he joined Almeda. He flashed her a broad grin, and then, as if he was just going on with the conversation said, "But surely you do not mean to suggest that gold and the financial interests which accompany it are of lesser importance to this community than these other things you mention?"

"I did not use such a term, Mr. Royce," said Almeda. "But now that you put it like that, I suppose I *do* believe that money is less important than people, than friendship, than churches and schools and families."

"Come now, Mrs. Hollister," said Royce with a patronizing smile. "You know as well as everyone here that gold drives this community. Without the gold Miracle Springs would not exist."

"Perhaps not. But I believe it *will* exist in the years to come, with or without gold."

"You are a businesswoman, Mrs. Hollister. You know that

money is what makes everything work. Without money, you are out of business. Without money none of these people would have homes or clothes or wagons or horses. I'm all for friendship and schools and children and churches. But a community needs a solid financial base or all the rest will wither away. Money is what makes it go, money is what it is all based on."

"Money . . . such as that represented by the Royce Miners' Bank?"

Royce smiled, although he did not answer her question directly. "And all that is why I'm not sure I can agree with your statement that a Hollister vote is a vote for the best future of Miracle Springs. In my opinion, the future must rest upon a solid financial base."

"In other words, with a vote for Royce," she said.

The banker smiled broadly. "You said it, Almeda . . . not I." Some of the men chuckled to see him getting the better of her. "Let's be practical, Almeda," he went on. "Everyone here may have done business with you at some time in the past. But I am the one who has financed their homes, their land, their businesses. Why, Almeda, I have even lent money to you to help *your* business through some difficult times! None of these people would even be here today if it weren't for my bank and what I have done for them. And the future will be no different. If Miracle Springs is to have a future, even the kind of future you so glowingly speak of, it will be because of what *I* am able to give it, both as its banker *and* its mayor."

Everyone was quiet, waiting to see what Almeda would do. Clearly, Mr. Royce meant his words as a direct challenge to everything she had said and hoped to accomplish with her speech.

When she spoke again, her voice contained a challenging tone of its own.

"Is the kind of future you have in mind for Miracle Springs the same kind as you're imposing on Patrick Shaw and his family?" she asked in a cool tone. "That is hardly the kind of future I would judge to be in the best interest of this community, no matter how much your bank may have done for it in the past."

A low murmur of agreement spread through the crowd. Her words had touched off the anger at Royce that had been circulating all week. A couple of men shouted out at him.

"The lady's right, Royce," cried one voice.

"Shaw's a good man," called out another. "You got no call to do what you done!"

Mr. Royce did not seem angered by her question. It almost seemed as though he had been expecting it, and was ready with a reply.

"Surely you must realize, Almeda," he said, "that politics and business don't necessarily mix."

"Well maybe they *should*!" she shot back. "Perhaps the incident with the Shaws tells us what kind of mayor you would be. Is this how you envision looking out for the best interests of the people of Miracle Springs—making them leave the homes they have worked so hard for?"

By now Almeda had the support of the crowd. Although not a single one of the men present would have dared go to Mr. Royce in person and tell him what he thought, in a group, and stirred by Almeda's words, all the anger that had been brewing in the community through the week spilled over into mumblings and shouts of complaint against what Royce had done.

"Listen to them, Franklin," she said. "Every man and woman here is upset by what you have done. They want to know why. They want to know if this is what you mean when you say you have *helped* the community grow! Is this the future you offer Miracle Springs—a future whose road is strewn with failed loans and eviction notices? If so, I do not think it is the kind of future the people of Miracle Springs have in mind!"

By now everyone was getting into the argument, calling out questions and comments to the banker. From the look and sound of it, it didn't seem that Royce could have any possible chance in the election! But as Pa had said earlier, Mr. Royce wasn't the kind of man who should be underestimated.

He held up his hands to restore quiet. When he could be heard again, he turned to Almeda. "What I said, Mrs. Hollister," he replied, still in a calm tone, "was that the future of

Miracle Springs must rest upon a solid financial base. Without a financial base, there can be no future."

He paused, looked into her face for a moment, then continued. "Let me ask you a question," he said. "As a businesswoman, have you ever extended credit to a bad account?"

He waited, but she did not answer.

"I'm sure you have," he said. "And what did you do when a customer did not pay you? Did you continue to let him take merchandise from you, knowing in all probability he would never pay you?"

"There are plenty of people here today who know well enough that I have given them credit during some pretty tough times," she answered at last. "When I trust someone, I do what I can to help them."

"As do I," countered Royce. "I have made loans and extended credit and helped nearly every man here. But in the face of consistent non-payment, I doubt very much if you would blithely let a man go on running up a bill at your expense. If you operated that way, you would not have survived in business so long. Well, in the case of the Shaws, I have been extremely lenient. I have done all that is in my power to keep it from coming to what has transpired this past week. You ask Patrick Shaw himself—he's standing right back there."

Royce pointed to the back of the crowd, and heads turned in that direction. "Ask him. What did I do when he missed his first payment . . . his second . . . his third? I did nothing. I continued to be patient, hoping somehow that he would be able to pull himself together and catch up and fulfill his obligations."

Royce paused a moment, seemingly to allow Mr. Shaw to say something if he wanted. But Shaw only kept looking at the ground, kicking the dirt around with his boot.

"I would say that I have been extremely patient," Mr. Royce went on. "I have done nothing that any honest businessman wouldn't have done. If you were in my position, Almeda, you would have been forced into the same action."

By now the crowd had begun to quiet down. They may not

have liked it, but most knew Royce's words were true. They didn't know he was only telling them half the truth—that he had refused to rescind the note-call even if Mr. Shaw made up the four months.

Royce turned and squarely faced the crowd. He spoke as if Almeda were not even present beside him, and gave her no opportunity to get in another word.

"Let me tell you, my friends, a little about how banking works. Banking is like any other business. When my esteemed opponent here—" he indicated Almeda with a wave of his hand, without turning to look at her, "—offers you a gold pan or a saddle for sale, she has had to buy that pan or saddle from someone else. Now as a banker, the only commodity I have to offer is money. She sells mining equipment. I sell money. Now, I have to get that money from somewhere in order to have it to lend. And do you know where I get it?" He paused, but only for a second.

"I get it from the rest of you," he went on. "The money I loaned Patrick Shaw for his house and land came from money that others of you put in my bank. I lend out *your* money to Mr. Shaw, he pays me interest, and then I pay *you* interest, keeping out a small portion as the bank's share. Mr. Shaw didn't borrow money from *me*. In a manner of speaking, he borrowed money from the rest of you! All of you who have borrowed money from the Royce Miners' Bank have really borrowed it from one another. You who receive interest from the bank are in actuality getting that interest from your friends and neighbors."

Everyone was quiet again and was listening carefully.

"If someone doesn't pay the bank what he has agreed to pay, then how can the bank pay the rest of you the interest due you? What I have done is the most painful thing a banker ever has to face. The agonizing inner turmoil it causes a man like me to have to find himself in the odious position of calling a note due, it is so painful as to be beyond words. And yet I have a responsibility to the rest of you. How can I be faithful to the whole community and its needs if I ignore such problems? My bank would soon be out of business, and then where would this community be?"

He waited just a moment to let his question sink in, then answered it himself.

"I will tell you where it would be. When a loan gets behind and goes bad, the real injury is to *you*. As much as I don't like to say it, Patrick Shaw really is indebted to the rest of you, his friends. His failure to make his payments hurts *you* as much as it hurts the bank. He has not paid *you* what he owes. And if that sort of thing is allowed to go unchecked, it puts the bank in a very serious position. Before long, I might have to call another loan due from another one of you, in order to raise the funds to make up for the note which has been defaulted upon. Do you see, my friends? Do you understand the problem? Do you see the dilemma I'm in?

"All the loans I have made are subject to a thirty-day call, just like Mr. Shaw's. In other words, the bank can legally call *any* note due at any time. Now a banker hates to call a loan due, because it is a very painful experience, as painful for a sensitive man like me as it is to a family who must pack up and leave a home where they have invested years. But if a loan is allowed to go bad, then another loan must be called from someone else, to keep the bank healthy. And so it goes. One can never tell when circumstances may force a banker to begin calling many loans due, in order to carry out his wider obligations to the entire community.

"This is why I said earlier that *if* Miracle Springs is to have a future, it must rest upon the solid financial base that I and the Royce Miners' Bank can give it. Without that solid base, I fear many loans may have to be called due, and Miracle Springs could become one of those ghost towns Mrs. Hollister spoke about. As your mayor, I hope and pray I will be able to keep that from happening."

He stepped back and began to descend from the platform, then turned back for one final statement, as if wanting to avoid any possible confusion.

"I want it to be very clear that if I am elected mayor, I will work strenuously toward a strong financial base, to make sure that what has befallen our friend Mr. Shaw, with whom I deeply sympathize, does not happen to any of the rest of you. In other words, I do not see a string of foreclosures in any way as inevitable, so long as the bank, and I personally, are able to remain in a strong position in the community. I clarify this because I did not want any of you to misunderstand my words."

No one did. Franklin Royce had made himself perfectly clear to everyone!

CHAPTER 8

POWER

The banker stepped down, passing close to Pa.

"If you know what's good for that wife of yours, Hollister," he said quietly but with a look of menace in his eye, "You'll get her out of this race before election day. If she's going to continue her attacks against me, she'll find two can play that game! And I warn you, the consequences will prove none too pleasant for either of you!"

He walked on. Pa did not say a word.

Mr. Royce strode straight back toward the bank. The crowd of people quietly began to disperse toward their homes. Hardly a man or woman anywhere liked the banker, but everyone was afraid of him. As sorry as they were for the Shaws, no one wanted to find himself in the same position. And as much as they'd have liked to help, no one had the kind of money it would take to do any good.

Almeda followed Royce down off the platform. She looked at Pa with kind of a discouraged sigh.

"Best speech I ever heard!" said Pa.

She tried to laugh, but the look on her face was anything but happy.

"I may as well have been talking into the wind for all the good it will do," she said.

"Everyone loved it," I told her. "You should have seen their faces! And they clapped about everything you said."

"Both of you are determined to cheer me up," she said,

laughing now in earnest. "But you saw what happened—Royce has let it be known that if he doesn't win, more foreclosures will follow. Nobody's going to take that chance, no matter what I say, even if they might actually prefer to vote for me."

That evening it was pretty quiet. I could tell Almeda was thinking hard on her decision to go back into the race and wondering if she had done the right thing.

"Why don't I just go to Franklin," she said at last, "and meet with him privately, and tell him that if he will reconsider the terms of the Shaws' note, I will withdraw from the race? Maybe I was wrong to think we could take him on and actually stop him. But at least maybe we could save the Shaw's place."

"Won't work, Almeda," Pa said.

"Why not? He wants to be mayor, and I'll give him the election. He will have won. He'll have beaten me."

Pa gave a little chuckle, although it wasn't really a humorous one. "As much as you like to complain about us men not understanding women, and about how your kind are the only ones who *really* know how things work, I must say, Almeda, you don't understand men near as much as you might think."

"What do you mean, Drummond?"

"This election isn't about being mayor. It might have been at first, but not anymore."

"What's it about, then?"

"It's about manhood, about strength . . . about power."

She cocked her eyebrow at him.

"Don't you see, Almeda? You challenged Royce for the whole town to see. You've had the audacity not just to run against him, but to pass out flyers, to make speeches, and to ignore two or three warnings from him to stop. You're challenging his right to be the most powerful person in these parts. And your being a woman makes it all the more galling to him. He was there this afternoon. He could see as well as everyone else that folks like you better than him. And he hates you for it. It's gone past just winning for him now. Down inside he wants to crush you, punish you for making people doubt him. Winning isn't enough. He's got to make you pay for what you've done. It wouldn't surprise me if he did what he's done to Pat to get back at us, besides telling the rest of the town not to fool with him."

"Then that's all the more reason we've got to find some way to help!"

"I don't see what we can do," said Pa.

"But why wouldn't he be satisfied with me withdrawing? How does it help him to foreclose and take the Shaws' place?"

"Well, for one thing," Pa replied, "something tells me he wants Pat's place. I don't know why, because according to Pat the gold's about played out. But if I know Royce, it's no accident that he set his sights on Pat's note. And that's just the other reason it ain't gonna do no good. He's gonna find some way to get back at you, and he's also gonna make an example of Pat that folks around here aren't likely to forget anytime soon."

"What harm would it do him to simply let it be known, 'If you elect me mayor, I'll let the Shaws keep their place. But let this be a lesson to you not to cross me, or you might find yourself in the same position'?"

"Power, Almeda—I told you already. If he did that, it would be like backing down. You would have arm-twisted him to letting Pat off, and the whole town would know it. Royce would think you made him look weak. Everyone would know that he was capable of backing down, and so they wouldn't take his threats as seriously. No, I tell you, he's not gonna back down about the Shaws, no matter what you or I or anyone else does. The memory of Pat and Chloe and them kids of theirs having to pack up and leave—that'll keep folks in line as far as Royce is concerned for a long time. Everyone'll know he means to follow through with what he says. He may hate it that folks like you better and would vote for you if they could. But he wants them to fear his power even more than he wants them to like him. And now that you've challenged that, he'll be all the more determined to run Pat off his land, *and* hurt you any way he can in the process."

Almeda sighed. "I just can hardly believe any man would

be so vindictive as you say—even Franklin Royce."

"Believe it, Almeda. I saw the look in his eye when he got down off that platform this afternoon. I've met men like him before, and I know the kind of stuff they're made of. And it ain't good."

"Do you really think he'll try to hurt me?"

"He won't go out and find a man like Buck Krebbs to send after you, if that's what you mean. He might have done that to me in the past, but he'll use different ways on you. I have the feeling we've only seen the beginning of his campaign tactics. If I know Royce, and I think I do, it's already a lot bigger in his mind than just the election. I think we may have made an enemy, Almeda, and the town might not be big enough to hold both of us."

Pa was right. It didn't take long to see that Mr. Royce did not intend to stop with mere speechmaking.

Three days later, on Wednesday morning, when Almeda and I arrived in town for the day, a man high up on a ladder was painting a sign across the front of the vacant store-building two doors down from the bank. In the window was a poster that said "Coming Soon."

By noon the words the man was painting in bright red had become plain. The sign read: *Royce Supplies and Shipping.*

CHAPTER 9

THE ARTICLE

Meanwhile, I had finished the article I'd been writing.

Going around telling folks about Sunday's speech gave me the chance to get some last interviews. Folks were really ready to talk to me now! I had a long conversation with Almeda on Friday, and then spent the rest of that day and most of Saturday writing and rewriting the final copy. By this time there was a stage running on Saturday too, and I sent off the article to Mr. Kemble by the afternoon mail, along with a letter.

Mr. Kemble had said earlier that he'd pay me $1 for an election article, but things had changed now on account of the Fremont article. I told him that since he'd paid Robin O'Flaridy $4 for his small article about Miracle Springs, I figured what I'd written here was worth at least $7. But I would be willing to settle for $4 because I knew he couldn't pay a woman more than a man. But I would not take one penny less than $4. If he didn't want to pay me that much, he could send the pages back and I would print it somewhere else.

At the end of the letter, I asked Mr. Kemble when the article about Mr. Fremont would be appearing. I thought it important that the *Alta* run my version before the *Globe* had a chance to do a story based on the false information and quotes and interviews of Derrick Gregory. Had it already run and somehow I had missed seeing it? I knew that really couldn't be possible since we got the *Alta* in Miracle Springs (though still two days late), and I had been watching for it every day. I couldn't for

48

the life of me figure out why it hadn't run yet. Nearly two weeks had passed, and the election was getting closer and closer, and I wanted the people of California to know the truth about Mr. Fremont.

Six days later, the following Friday, in the same mail pouch that brought the copies of the *Alta* to Miracle Springs, was a packet addressed to me from Mr. Kemble. In it was a check for $4, and a copy of Wednesday's edition containing my story in full. There was no letter, and no answers to any of my questions. But I hardly cared about that right then! There in the middle of the fifth page, running across two columns, were the words in bold black type: "Mayor's Race Matches Business-woman Against Town Banker."

I found a quiet place, then sat down to read over the words I had written.

> *Among the many mining towns of northern California, most of the big news in recent years always had to do with gold. But in the growing community of Miracle Springs, no one is talking about gold these days. Instead, people are talking about the town's first election for mayor, which will be held on November 4, concurrent with the national election between John Fremont and James Buchanan.*
>
> *This election is big news because of the two individuals who are running against each other. As reported in this paper last month, the election matches longtime Miracle Springs banker Franklin Royce against equally longtime businesswoman Almeda Parrish Hollister.*
>
> *That's right! Businesswoman. Mrs. Hollister, one of the first women in the west to seek office, will not even be able to vote herself. Yet she hopes to sway enough men in the community to upset rival Royce, who must be considered the favorite.*
>
> *The campaign between the two town leaders is a hot one, with emotions and reaction among the voters running high.*
>
> *Franklin Royce first arrived in Sacramento from Chicago in early 1850. He was sent west by the banking firm Jackson, Royce, Briggs, and Royce—a company begun by his father and uncle—to explore possibilities for branch offices in the new gold rush state. He opened an office in Sacramento, but later that year took out*

a $40,000 loan and moved north to the foothills community of
Miracle Springs, where he opened the doors of Royce Miners'
Bank. When asked why he chose Miracle Springs, Royce replied,
"I wanted to become involved in banking closer to the source,
where men were actually digging gold out of the streams. That
seemed to me to provide the greatest opportunity for me as a
banker, as well as open up the greatest potential for helping a
young community grow and prosper."

Within two years, Royce had made Miracle Springs his per-
manent home and had completely withdrawn from his position
with Jackson, Royce, Briggs, and Royce of Sacramento and Chicago. Since that time Mr. Royce has played an active role in
helping the young community to grow. According to Royce, his
bank has financed the building of 80% of the community's homes
and has been an active supporter of the miners and their interests.
"Who could be better qualified to lead such a diverse community
forward than one like myself, who has been such an intrinsic part
of helping in its growth up till now?" said Royce.

Mrs. Hollister came to Miracle Springs a few months before
her opponent. She was Almeda Parrish then, and she and her
husband had come to California from Boston. After a brief stint
attempting to find gold himself, Mr. Parrish started the Parrish
Mine and Freight Company. Upon his death from tuberculosis
in the early winter months of 1851, his wife decided to keep the
business going and to remain in Miracle Springs.

She has been there ever since. During those years, Parrish
Mine and Freight has been involved with the miners of the region
in nearly every phase of supply and delivery, from small gold pans
to the ordering and installation of large equipment for some of the
major quartz operations in the surrounding foothills.

Two years ago, the businesswoman and widow married Miracle Springs miner Drummond Hollister.

When asked why she felt qualified to become Miracle Springs'
mayor, Mrs. Hollister replied, "I realize the new state of California has never had a woman mayor before. However, I feel
that changing times are coming, and that women will play a vital
role in the future of this state and this great country of ours. As
mayor of Miracle Springs I would bring an integrity and forth-
rightness to the office, and the families of this town would be able
to trust that their future was being watched out for by one of their
own."

All the women, of course, although unable to vote, expressed strong support for Mrs. Hollister. "I think the idea of a woman mayor shows what a wonderful thing democracy is," commented the local schoolteacher, Miss Harriet Stansberry.

Among the men, opinions were strong on both sides. Several miners and ranchers expressed reservations about a banker as mayor. "I ain't never yet met a banker I had much a hankering to trust further'n I could throw him!" commented one old miner who said he had been in Miracle Springs longer than both candidates put together. The same prospector added, "Why, if anybody oughta be mayor of this here place, blamed if it don't seem like it oughta be me. I'm the first one in these parts to find gold anyway!"

Others, who did not want to be identified, also said from their dealings with the two candidates, they felt more trusting toward Mrs. Hollister. "She ain't one to short a feller so much as a penny," said one man. "Don't matter what kind of dealings you have with her, she always gives you the best price and a little more than you asked for. But you're never gonna get something for nothing at no bank, that's for sure!"

Many of the men said they had nothing but the highest regard for Mrs. Hollister, but some expressed concern. "She's a nice enough woman, but that don't mean she ought to be mayor. It's a man's job. I just can't see that I want no woman being leader of my town. Somehow it just ain't right. Mayoring's gotta be something a man does."

Among such men, the comment of one local saloon owner seemed to sum up what many thought, "It don't really matter what I think of Mr. Royce or Mrs. Hollister, there's only one man running. And since only men can vote, I figure they'll stick by their kind."

Whether that proves to be true, and the men of Miracle Springs elect as their mayor the only man on the ballot, Franklin Royce, or whether they go against the odds and elect California's first female mayor, Mrs. Almeda Hollister, the fact is that this election is one to watch. It is surely one of the most unusual elections in all California this year. Whether she wins or loses, Mrs. Hollister is a pioneer in a state full of pioneers. And if she should win, not only the rest of the state, but the whole country will be watching.

CHAPTER 10

THE RUMOR

We all thought Mr. Royce's decision to open Royce's Supplies and Shipping was a pretty underhanded thing to do. By the time his sign was finished, word had gotten around town about it, and a lot of people were upset that he'd try such a deceitful, lowdown tactic as attempting to run Almeda out of business.

But we didn't know the half of it yet. Within a week of Almeda's speech, we began to get wind of a rumor circulating about town. Almeda, according to the gossip, had presented herself falsely to the people of Miracle Springs. She had left Boston and come to California to escape the worst tarnish a woman's reputation could have. Some even said she had met and married Mr. Parrish on the ship north from Panama.

But the worst rumors had to do not with Almeda's past, but with her present. They said that the baby she was carrying was not a Hollister at all.

Franklin Royce, of course, never appeared as the author of the rumors surrounding Almeda. He remained too skillfully concealed behind the scenes for anyone to suspect that he was doing anything other than expressing mild curiosity at the tale as it had been told to him by others.

When the whisper first awoke it was merely the hint that the former Mrs. Parrish had not been a Parrish at all in Boston. In its later stages was added the idea that her former name—however well hidden she had kept her past—was one that all

Boston knew. Furthermore, it was said that whatever she had done, although no one could say of a certainty what exactly it was, it was enough to have barred her from the society of respected people. She had escaped the East on a steamer, leaving more than one broken heart behind her—some even said a child. On the boat she fell in with the late Mr. Parrish. The evil gossip reached its culmination with the final suggestion having to do with Pa and her present predicament—something about the chickens of her past coming back to roost. Or, more aptly, the roosters.

We went about our business as usual. Not many people came in to the freight office, and neither Almeda nor I thought much about the occasional peculiar looks on the faces of those people we saw. Whether Marcus or Mr. Ashton had heard anything, I don't know. They acted normal. It did seem activity in town was quieter than usual toward the end of that week. But still we remained in the dark about the talk that was spreading from mouth to mouth.

Sunday came, and we all went to church. The service was quiet and somber. Afterward nobody came up and greeted Pa or Almeda, but just walked off silently in the direction of their horses and wagons. It was eerie and uncomfortable, but still we suspected nothing. We all figured it was a result of the scare Mr. Royce had put into everyone the week before. But the fact that some of his best friends had seemed to avoid him and hadn't come over at least to shake his hand got Pa pretty agitated during the ride home.

All that day none of the whispers and lies and gossip reached the ears of the Hollister and Parrish and Belle clan out where we lived on the edge of Miracle Springs Creek.

Early Monday morning, a buggy drove up carrying Rev. Rutledge and Miss Stansberry. They came to the door while we were eating breakfast. Both wore serious expressions.

"We just heard," said the minister.

"Heard what?" said Pa, rising to invite them in with a smile.

"One of the children who came early to school was talking,"

he went on. "That's how Harriet heard. She put one of the older children in charge, then came right to me. We drove out here immediately. Believe me, Drummond, Almeda . . ." he glanced at them both as he spoke, still very seriously. "Believe me, I don't believe a word of it. What can we do to help?"

Pa glanced around dumbfounded, then let out a good-natured laugh. "Avery," he said. "I don't have the slightest notion what you're talking about!"

"Almeda?" said Rev. Rutledge.

"It's the truth, Avery. What is it that's got the two of you so worked up and so glum?"

"You really don't know," said Miss Stansberry, almost in amazement. "Oh, you poor dear!"

"Drummond, we have to have a serious talk," said Rev. Rutledge. "What we have to discuss has to be talked about alone."

Pa gave me and Zack a nod. "You heard the Reverend," he said. "Go on . . . git." We silently obeyed, but curious beyond belief.

We heard nothing from inside for probably ten minutes. Then the door of the house was thrown open and out exploded Pa, his face red, his eyes flaming. I'd never seen any man, much less Pa, so filled with anger!

"Drummond, please!" called out Almeda, coming through the door after him. "Please . . . wait!"

"There ain't nothing to discuss, nothing to wait for!" Pa shot back as he strode to the barn. "It's clear enough what I gotta do!"

"We don't know it was him."

" 'Course we do, woman! You told me yourself what he said. No one but him knows anything about Boston. It was him, and you know it!"

Pa was inside the barn, already throwing a saddle over his favorite and fastest horse. Almeda followed him inside.

"At least let me go talk to him first," she pleaded.

"Time for talking's over, Almeda. A man's gotta protect his own, and now I reckon it's my turn to do just that."

"Drummond, please . . . don't do something you'll regret!"

"I won't take my gun with me, if that's what you mean." He was cinching up the straps already.

"Drummond," said Almeda, more softly now, putting her hand on his arm and trying to calm him down. "I can live through this. You don't have to defend me to that evil man. The Lord has healed and restored and remade me. And I am at peace in his love, and yours. I don't care what people say, or even what they think. Drummond, don't you see? I know that God loves me just for who I am—past, present, and future. And I know that you love me in just the same way. That's all I need."

Pa seemed to flinch for just a moment in his determination. Then he said, "I understand that, Almeda. And I'm thankful for what God's done. But sometimes a man's got to stand up for truth, and stand up and defend maybe his own reputation, or maybe his wife's. And even if it don't matter to you, it matters to me what the people of this town think. That man's got no right to say dishonoring things about my wife, or about any woman! And I aim to show this town that he can't get away with it without answering to me! I'm sorry, but I just ain't gonna be talked out of this. I gotta do what's right!"

Pa pulled himself up in the saddle, then paused again and glanced around where all the rest of us were watching and listening, in fear and worry, having no idea what was happening.

"Zack, Corrie," Pa said after a couple of seconds, "you two come with me. At least having my own kids around might keep me from killing the scum!"

In an instant Zack and I were throwing saddles on our horses, and in less than two minutes we galloped out of the barn, chasing Pa down the road toward town.

CHAPTER 11

FIGHTING MAD

Zack and I never did catch up with Pa. By the time we rode into the middle of town, we were just in time to see him dismounting in front of the bank.

We galloped up, jumped off our horses, and ran inside after him. The bank had only been open a few minutes, so there were several early-morning customers inside. By the time we got through the door, Pa was already in Mr. Royce's office. His voice was loud enough that you could hear it through the whole building. Everyone else's business had ceased, and they stood stock-still with wide open eyes, listening to the argument going on in the next room.

"Look, Royce," Pa was saying, "I never had much liking for you. But I figured maybe that's just the way bankers were. So I kept my distance and held my peace. But now you've gone too far!"

"I don't have any idea what you're talking about," replied the banker, keeping his calm.

"I ain't ashamed to tell you to your face, I think you're a liar!"

"Careful, Mr. Hollister. Those are strong words."

"Not too strong for the likes of a man who's so afraid of losing an election to a woman that he'd drag her reputation through the mud and spread lies about her. Only the lowest kind of man with no sense of shame would do a thing as vile as that!"

"I tell you, Mr. Hollister, I don't know what you're referring to. I confess I have heard some rumors lately that—"

"Heard them?" exploded Pa. "You started them!"

Slowly Zack and I inched our way toward the open door of
the office. I was terrified! I think Pa forgot us after telling us
to come with him.

"Accusations, especially false ones, can cost a candidate an
election, Mr. Hollister. You would do well to guard your
tongue, or your wife will suffer even worse consequences on
election day than she has already suffered because of her past
reputation."

He still sat calmly behind his big desk, almost with a look
of humor in his expression. Pa was standing, leaning over the
desk at him. If Mr. Royce was afraid, he didn't show it. He
looked as if he had expected the confrontation, and was glad
other townspeople were hearing it.

"I ain't said a false word yet!" exclaimed Pa. "Do you deny
to my face that you've been talking about Almeda and making
up this gossip about her life before she got here?"

"I do."

"Then I tell you again, you're a blamed liar!" Pa's voice
was loud and his face was still red.

"Look, Mr. Hollister," said the banker. His eyes squinted
and his voice lost whatever humor it might have had. "I've
taken about all of your ranting accusations I'm going to take.
Now unless you want me to send for Sheriff Rafferty and have
you locked up for harassment, you had better leave."

"Simon, lock me up?" roared Pa.

"You and I both know there are worse charges that could
be brought against you. When I am mayor, I may find myself
compelled to have the sheriff look into *your* past more carefully."

"Simon knows all about my past! And you ain't gonna be
mayor of *this* town, Royce, you scoundrel. Not while I have
anything to say about it! Any low-life who'd try to hurt a
woman to make himself look good ain't the kind of man who's
good enough for anything but—"

"Your wife doesn't have a reputation worth protecting, Hollister!" interrupted the banker, finally getting angry himself. He half rose out of his chair. "You know as well as I do that everything that's being said about her is true. If you don't, and you married her thinking she's the unspoiled preacher-woman she pretends to be, then you're a bigger fool than I took you for!"

"Do you dare to tell me to my face that my wife—"

"Your wife is nothing but a harlot, Hollister! Anybody in Boston could tell you—"

But his words were unwisely spoken. Before another sound was out of his mouth, Pa had shoved the banker's desk aside. He took two steps around it, and the next instant his fist went crashing into the white face of Franklin Royce.

Stunned, Royce staggered backward. Losing his balance, he fell over his own chair and toppled backward onto the floor.

Quickly he started to scramble up. But seeing Pa standing over him, fist still clenched, trembling with righteous anger in defense of the woman he loved, apparently made Royce think better of it.

Then Royce noticed the blood flowing from his nose and around the side of his mouth.

"You'll pay for this, Hollister," he seethed through clenched teeth while his hand sought a handkerchief to stop the blood.

"Your threats don't mean nothing to me," said Pa. "You do what you think you can to me, Royce. Do it like a man, face to face—if you got guts enough! But if I hear of you speaking another word against my wife, I tell you, you'll answer to me! And next time I don't aim to be so gentle!"

He turned and strode with huge quick steps out of the office, hardly looking at us, but saying as he passed, "Come on, kids, let's get out of this scoundrel's hole!"

We followed Pa to the door, while the customers and two clerks watched in shocked silence.

Mr. Royce came running to his office door, a handkerchief to his nose and mouth, and shrieked after us, "You're through,

Hollister—you hear me? You're through! You'll regret this day as long as you live!"

But Pa didn't even slow down, only slammed the door behind us with a crash.

CHAPTER 12

REPERCUSSIONS

All Pa said on the way home was, "I'm sorry you kids had to see that . . . but maybe your being there kept me from doing worse."

About halfway back, we met Rev. Rutledge and Miss Stansberry. Pa stopped, and the minister drew in his reins.

"I'm obliged to the two of you for coming and telling us," Pa said. "I'm afraid you wouldn't approve of what I done, Reverend."

"I understand, Drummond," he replied.

"Well, I'm thankful we got you two for friends," Pa added, tipping his hat, and then moving on.

When we got home, Almeda's eyes were red. I knew she'd been crying. Pa kissed her, then put his arms around her and the two of them just stood in each other's embrace for a long time. Nothing more about the incident was said that day.

Almeda considered whether to go into town at all, now that we all understood why folks had been behaving so strangely.

"We gotta face this thing head on," said Pa. "You go into the office—I'll go with you if you like. We gotta go on with our business and show folks we ain't concerned about Royce and his rumors. We'll go around to people one at a time and tell 'em to pay no attention to what they hear, that it's all a pack of lies drummed up to make you look bad before the election."

"You know I couldn't do that," Almeda replied softly, looking Pa directly in the eyes. "But you're right—it's best we go on with our lives as usual. Corrie and I will go into the office."

"You want me to go into town with you for the day?"

"No, I'll be all right. I'll do my best to put on a brave face."

In the four years I'd known Almeda, I'd never seen her quite like this. Her voice was soft and tired, without its usual enthusiasm and confidence. It was easy to see this was really a blow to her, and that she might not get over it so quickly. All day long her eyes remained red, though I never saw her cry again. I guess the tears stayed inside.

By the time we walked into the Parrish Mine and Freight office two hours later the whole town was stirred up all over again by news of what Pa had done to Mr. Royce. Old widow Robinson had been in the bank at the time and had heard every word. And that was enough to insure that within an hour, every man, woman, and child for ten miles around knew about it! The widow's reputation for spreading information certainly proved itself true. Franklin Royce himself never appeared for two days after that, so the news had to have come through someone else who was present, and most bets were on Mrs. Robinson. In all likelihood, she was the one Royce had used to plant the rumors about Almeda. He probably told her in hushed tones, making her promise to keep it to herself, no doubt saying that he'd assured the person *he'd* heard it from that he would say nothing to anybody.

Suddenly the first rumor was old news, and began to take a back seat to steadily exaggerating tales of what Pa had done. At first it was just that he had given the banker a good sound thrashing. Then mention was made of sounds of violence, angry threats yelled back and forth, sounds of scuffling and furniture being broken, and even blood, along with vows to get even. All in all, the story as Marcus Weber said he'd heard it was a considerably wilder affair than what Zack and I actually witnessed with our own eyes.

But it did manage to lessen the impact of what had been circulating about Almeda. Even though they feared him, not too many people liked Franklin Royce much. I think the incident was talked about so much because everybody was secretly pleased to see Royce get his due for once.

Yet they were afraid too, for Pa and Almeda. If Franklin Royce promised to get even, they said with serious expressions, he was not one to make empty threats. As for the election, who could tell now? Royce was a dangerous opponent, and *they* sure wouldn't want to have crossed him! They wished someone else could be mayor, but they had to admit, with Royce as an enemy, the prospects didn't look too good for the Hollisters.

With Almeda, the distance and silence and curious looks turned into sympathy. Pa silenced the gossip once and for all, and nobody was inclined to spread the rumors any further and run the risk of Pa finding out. Whether folks believed what they'd heard—and after what Pa did, I think most figured Royce had made it all up—they didn't show it, and talk now centered around Pa.

When Mr. Royce began to be seen around town again, he kept his distance. However, he continued his subtle tactics both to make sure people voted for him, and to pressure Almeda into capitulating. By the end of the week, the sign across the street was done, and there was activity inside the place, as well as some merchandise displayed in the shop windows. Almeda muttered a time or two, "Where can he have gotten that stuff so quickly?" But there seemed to be no question about it—he *had* it, and *was* going to open a business to compete with Parrish Mine and Freight. And obviously his intent was not merely to compete, but to drive her out of business. A second paper soon appeared in the window: "Mining, ranching, farming tools, supplies, and equipment at the least expensive prices north of Sacramento. Shipping and freight services also available."

That same week, whispers of a new kind arose. If Franklin Royce did not become Miracle Springs' next mayor, it was said that he would be forced to review all outstanding loans, and would more than likely be compelled to call a good many of them due. As much as they respected Pa for standing up for his wife's honor, and as little as they cared for Royce, most of the men were agreed that they just couldn't take the chance of having what had happened to Pat Shaw happening to them. They *had* to vote for Royce. They just didn't have any other choice.

To make matters worse, Pa got an official-looking letter from some government office in Sacramento saying that the title to his land was being challenged in court by an anonymous plaintiff, and that investigators would be contacting him shortly for additional information.

"Well, if that don't just about do it!" said Pa, throwing the letter down and storming about the room. "The man's not gonna stop till he's ground us into the dirt and got our land and our business and everything!"

He walked angrily out of the house. Almeda picked up the letter and read it, then showed it to the rest of us.

"I think we'd better pray for your father," she said softly. We all sat down and took hands, while Almeda prayed out loud for Pa, for the claim, for Mr. Royce, and for God's purpose to be accomplished through all these things that were happening to us. "And show us what you want us to do, Lord," she concluded. "Make it plain, and give us the strength and courage to do it—whether we're to give in, or whether we're to stand up and fight for what we think is right. Help us not to act in our own wisdom, but to depend on you to show us what you want."

When Pa walked in a few minutes later, he was calm and quiet. He sat down, rested his chin between his hands, and let out a big sigh. Anger had obviously given way to defeat and frustration.

"We gotta quit, Almeda," he said at length. His voice was soft and discouraged. "I wish I'd never got you into this."

"You didn't get me into a thing, Drummond. I made the decision to run for mayor on my own. I brought this trouble on the rest of you."

"Well I sure didn't make it no better, flying off against Royce like I done. Though the rascal deserved it!"

"Now we've got to decide what's to be done. With Franklin threatening two claims, ours and Shaws', there's no telling where it'll end. Not to mention the business in town."

"We gotta give in," said Pa, in as depressed a voice as I'd ever heard from him. "He's got us licked. If we let him have the election, maybe he'll lay off from all this other harm he's trying to bring us."

CHAPTER 13

FIGHTING FIRE WITH FIRE

I don't know if all marriages work this way, but I'd noticed that Pa and Almeda were both quicker to defend each other than they were themselves. When Franklin Royce started spreading gossip about Almeda around town, Pa got so filled with anger that he went right into Royce's office and knocked the banker down and bloodied his nose. Pa knew it was *his* duty to defend Almeda's honor, not hers.

And in the same way, Almeda would fight for Pa. When folks were talking about her, Almeda couldn't help the discouragement it caused. But now that Mr. Royce was threatening Pa and was threatening to take away all Pa had worked for and held dear, it was *her* turn to get fighting mad, like a mother bear protecting her family. The banker could threaten her reputation and her business all he wanted, but once he dared threaten the husband she loved—look out! She wasn't about to take that lying down!

"He's not going to lay off, Drummond," she said to Pa's last statement after a few moments thought. "There are times when to lay down your arms and surrender is the best course of action. Jesus said we must deny ourselves, and do it every day. But there are also times when wrong must be fought with aggressiveness. Jesus did that too. He laid down his life without a word of self-defense, but he also drove the moneychangers out with a whip and strong words. How to know when to do which is the challenge for a Christian. And I can't help thinking

65

that this is a time for the whip and strong words."

"We've already tried it," said Pa, "you with your handbills and your speech, and me with my ranting and raving like an idiot in Royce's bank. All we've done is made him madder and made it worse for everyone around here."

"The Lord will show us what to do. The children and I were just praying while you were outside. We asked him to make it plain what we're to do and to give us the courage to—"

She stopped and her face got serious a moment, then lit up.

"You know, I just had a thought," she said. "A wild, crazy, impossible idea!" She pressed her hands against her forehead and thought hard again. "It's too unbelievable an idea ever to work, but . . . if God is behind it . . . you just never know what can happen!"

"What in tarnation is it?" exclaimed Pa. "Your face looks like you swallowed a lantern. It must be *some* notion that's rattling through that brain of yours!"

She laughed. "It is, believe me. It just might be the highest-stakes poker game you ever played, Drummond Hollister, with the mines and homes of every man in Miracle Springs in the middle of the table—winner take all. And if Franklin Royce doesn't blink first and back down, and if he decides to call our bluff, then it just might cost more people than the Shaws their places."

"Sounds like a mighty dangerous game."

"I'm afraid it is. That's why we have to pray hard for God to show us if this is *his* idea, or just something my own mind cooked up."

"Then let's pray that right now," said Pa, "before it goes any further." He got down on his knees. "Come on, kids," he said to all the rest of us. "We got some serious praying to do, and it's gonna take all seven of us. We've gotta do what the Book says and ask the Lord above for wisdom, cause if we do wrong a lot of folks are gonna be hurt. We gotta be sure we're doing what the Lord wants."

We obeyed, and Pa started to pray. We'd all heard him pray before, but somehow this time there was a new power in his voice that seemed to come from deep down in his heart. When we all got up a few minutes later, I think every one in the room had the sense that God had spoken both *to* Pa, and maybe *through* him to the rest of us. I know what *I* felt inside, and judging from the looks on Pa's and Almeda's faces I think they too thought the answer was to go ahead.

"Well, don't keep us in suspense, woman," said Pa with a smile. "What's this dangerous new plan you're thinking of?"

"Before we could even know if it had a chance to succeed," she said, "it would take a trip to Sacramento. And with the election coming up so fast, there might not be time. But here's what I'm thinking."

She paused and took a breath.

"Back when we started, and Franklin was doing everything he could to threaten us, he made a comment that I haven't forgotten. He said, 'Two can play this game as well as one.' He was, of course, referring to my flyer and Corrie's interviewing and what he considered our going on the attack against him. But the moment we started praying about what to do his words came back to me, and I suddenly found myself wondering what is to prevent us from applying the same principle. If he's going to try to undercut us by taking away business from Parrish Mine and Freight, and if he's going to start hurting our friends and neighbors by calling up their loans, then why don't we use the exact same tactic, but in the opposite way? We will take business from *him*, and will try to *help* people at exactly the point where he's trying to hurt them and pressure them into supporting him!"

"Fight fire with fire, eh?" said Pa grinning.

"Exactly! There are times to back down and admit defeat. But I don't think this is one of them. Not yet at least."

"But you shouldn't travel, not in your condition," said Pa. "Whatever's to be done in Sacramento, I can do."

"No, I have to be the one to go," insisted Almeda. "I'll need to see my friend Carl Denver and get his advice. I don't know whether there's anything his company can do, but he might know someone else in the city who can help."

"I'll at least go with you, to make sure you're all right."

"I'll be fine. Besides, you ought to stay here," said Almeda, pointing to the letter that still lay on the table where she had laid it.

The look on Pa's face said he wasn't convinced.

"I'll be fine," she repeated. "I'm a strong woman. Corrie," she said turning to me, "can you handle things at the office?"

I nodded.

"You shouldn't go alone. That I *won't* let you do," said Pa. "Zack," he said, turning his head, "you want to ride to Sacramento with your stepmother, keep her company and protect her at the same time?"

"You bet, Pa!" Zack replied brightly.

"I'm going to let you take my rifle," Pa added. "But unless there's trouble, you keep it packed in the saddle case. No foolin' around with it."

"Yes, sir."

"Do you really think that's necessary, Drummond?" asked Almeda.

"Maybe not. But I don't want to take no chances with the two of you out there alone. I don't trust Royce. It ain't been that many years ago he was hiring no-goods like Buck Krebbs to sneak around and set fire to houses. I'd feel safer if I knew Zack had the gun."

"Can I go too, Pa?" asked Tad.

"You couldn't keep up, you pipsqueak!" laughed Zack.

"I could so!" insisted Tad. "I can ride just as fast as you or Little Wolf!"

"That'll be the day! I could ride from here to Little Wolf's and back twice before you'd have your horse out of the barn."

"That ain't so! Why I could—"

"Hey, the two of you—cut it out!" interrupted Pa. "Time's a wastin', you gotta hit the road. Tad," he said, "I gotta have you here with me. If Zack's gonna be protecting your Ma, then I'll need your help here watching over the claim. You'll be my number one man, and I can't have the both of you gone."

Almeda rose, Zack ran outside to the barn, and the rest of

us did what we could to help them get ready. In less than an hour we were watching the dust settle from Almeda's buggy and Zack's horse after they'd rounded the bend in the road and disappeared from sight.

CHAPTER 14

PATRICK SHAW'S SOLUTION

Those next days waiting for Zack and Almeda to get back were dreadful, wondering all the time what was going to come of it.

How wonderful it would be if there was a railroad to Sacramento! They were laying down track for new train lines between the big cities, and the talk of a train connecting the two oceans was enough to make your head swim. I could hardly imagine it! Wagon trains took months to cross the country. Overland stagecoaches, along the southern route where there wasn't as much snow, usually took between thirty and forty days. And stories were told of madcap horsemen who rode their horses to their deaths to make it from St. Louis to San Francisco in fifteen to twenty days. I'd thought about trying to find such a man to interview for an article sometime, to find out if the stories were true about dashing across the plains at a hundred miles a day. But I could barely imagine going across the country in a comfortable train car in only eight or ten days.

Well, they didn't have a train to ride on. But they had good horses, and Zack and Almeda returned faster than Pa had expected. They left on Saturday, and about midday of the following Wednesday Zack and Almeda rode in.

It was obvious from the lather on the horses that they'd been riding hard. Their clothes and faces were covered with dust, and they both looked exhausted. But the instant Almeda saw Pa, she flashed a big smile.

"I got it!" she said excitedly, patting the saddlebags next to her on the buggy seat. "Go get Pat and we'll tell him the news!"

Pa helped her down from the buggy, then gave her a big hug and kiss. "You're a mess, woman!" he laughed, standing back to look over her dirty face.

"Don't push your luck, Drummond Hollister," she replied. "You know how a woman can get riled when she's tired!"

"Well, you heard your ma," said Pa, turning around to the rest of us. "Who wants to ride over the hill and fetch Mr. Shaw here?"

"I will, Pa," I said. "Come on, Tad. Wanna go with me?"

But he was already scampering toward the barn to start saddling his pony. One thing about Tad—he never had to be asked twice!

We took the quickest way to Shaws, the back trail around the mountain. All the way back Mr. Shaw kept quizzing us about what was up, and I said I didn't know all the details, which I didn't, but that Pa and Almeda had some exciting news for him and they'd tell him everything as soon as we got back to our place.

By the time we arrived back at the house, Almeda had gotten herself cleaned up and had changed clothes. Her eyes looked tired, but the smile still shone from her face.

"Come in . . . come in, Pat," said Pa, shaking Mr. Shaw's hand. "Sit down. Want a cup of coffee?"

"Yeah, thanks, Drum," he replied. "But what's this about anyway?"

"We'll tell you everything, Pat. Just have a seat, and I'll get you that coffee."

Bewildered, Mr. Shaw obeyed.

Pa returned in a minute, handed Mr. Shaw a steaming blue tin cup, then sat down himself. Almeda joined him.

"This has been Almeda's idea from the start," Pa said, "so I reckon I'll let her tell you about the scheme she hatched to try to foil ol' Royce." He cast her a glance, then sat back and took a sip from his own cup.

"It all began last week," Almeda began, "when we were

praying about what to do about the election. We were asking the Lord whether to quit and give in, or whether to fight on somehow, even though it seemed, as you men would say, that Franklin held all the right cards. Your note had been called due, we'd just received word that the title to our land was being questioned, and word was going around town that a vote against Franklin Royce would result in the same kinds of things happening to others. We just didn't see what could be done. But then I had an idea! And I think it was God speaking providentially to us. I certainly pray it was, but I suppose time will tell. I have no idea if it will work. And if it goes against us, it could mean doom for everybody."

"I don't understand a word of what you're talking about," said Mr. Shaw. "From where I sit, it don't appear there's nobody in any danger except you folks and us."

"Just hear her out, Pat," said Pa. "Go on, Almeda, quit beating around the bush. Pat's dying of curiosity!"

Almeda smiled. "I just returned from Sacramento," she said. "I rode down there with Zack, and on Monday morning I went to see a man I've known for several years, Carl Denver. He is one of three vice-presidents of the banking and investment firm Finchwood Ltd. I think they're connected somehow to a bank in London, but I don't know for sure. My late husband knew Carl, and when we first came west, Carl helped my husband secure a small loan to open our business in Miracle Springs. That loan was paid off long ago, but Carl and I have kept in touch through the years and I've borrowed from them a time or two, and have done some freight business with his firm as well. And now Carl's risen to a fairly prominent position.

"Well, I explained our situation to him. He said he'd read about the mayor's race in the *Alta*, and I told him the article was written by my stepdaughter."

She looked over in my direction. I couldn't help but be pleased that somebody Almeda knew had seen it!

"When I told him some of the things that have happened, he became positively livid. 'Anything I can do to help,' he said.

'Anything!' But when I mentioned the sum of eighteen thousand dollars, his enthusiasm cooled. 'That's a great deal of money, Almeda,' he said. I knew that only too well! I'd never borrowed more than five or six thousand from him before. I told him I'd secure it with my house and the business and what stock-in-trade I have, although that wouldn't amount to more than ten or twelve thousand. I knew it would be going out on a limb for him, but I assured him that the other property involved—that's yours, Mr. Shaw—was solid, and that we could add to the collateral amount later to more than cover the full amount of the loan. He said he'd have to discuss the matter with the higher-ups of Finchwood, but that he'd do everything he could on my behalf, and to come back about noon.''

"So Zack and I left and I showed him around some of Sacramento. We had a good time together, didn't we, Zack?"

Zack nodded.

"We returned to Carl's office just before twelve. From the big smile across his face, I could tell he had good news!

" 'You'll never believe this!' he exclaimed. 'I don't believe it myself. But we hit Mr. Finch on just the right day!'

" 'What do you mean?' I asked.

" 'He knows Royce,' Carl answered. 'And in plain English, Almeda—he hates him! Seems several years ago, when different companies were new to California and were trying to get firmly established, Jackson, Royce, Briggs, and Royce pulled some underhanded things against Finchwood. Nearly put them out of business, the way I understand it. And ever since, the rivalry between the two has been fierce . . . and bitter. Just last week, Mr. Finch told me, the old man of the outfit, Briggs, stole one of Finchwood's largest clients away from them. And that's why Finch is roaring mad. I told him that this Royce you're dealing with isn't with his father's firm any longer, but Finch said he didn't care. "A Royce is a Royce!" he said. "And besides, I still owe that young weasel of a Royce a thing or two from '51!" Anyway, I went on to explain your whole predicament to him, and almost before I was done, he said, "Look, Carl, you bring that lady-friend of yours in to meet me. I want to shake hands with the woman with guts enough to square off in an election against that snake. And then you tell her we'll back her up. We don't need her collateral either. I trust her from what I know of her, and your word vouching for her is good enough for me. I'd love to see her put that pretentious imposter out of business, though I don't suppose we could be *that* fortunate!" ' "

Almeda took a breath and smiled.

"I still ain't sure if I see how my property has anything to do with your banking friends," said Mr. Shaw.

"I'm just about to get to that," said Almeda. "Well, Carl took me right into Mr. Finch's office. The president of the company treated me like royalty—got a chair for me, offered me something to drink, and then shook my hand and said what an honor it was for him to meet me! Can you imagine that! An honor for *him* to meet *me*!

"We talked for quite a while. He said he'd investigated the northlands up around here a time or two, and had even thought of expanding and investing in this direction but nothing had ever come of it. The more we talked, the more interested he became, he even scratched his head once and said he thought he'd heard of the new strike at Miracle Springs. 'Had something to do with a kid getting caught in a mine and being pulled out by his brother, didn't it?' I said that indeed it did, and that those two boys were now fine young men and that I was privileged to call them my sons."

Tad was beaming as she spoke.

"He said that if worse came to worst, and he wound up holding mortgages on half a dozen pieces of property, he'd consider it a good investment, and worth every penny to put a corrupt man like Royce out of business."

Finally Almeda looked straight into Mr. Shaw's face. "The long and short of it, Patrick," she said, "is that I brought the solution to your problems with the Royce Miners' Bank home with me from Sacramento right in these saddlebags!"

She picked up the leather pouches that had been sitting beside her, stood up, and turned them upside down. Bundles of paper money poured out onto Mr. Shaw's lap.

All of us gasped. Almeda laughed at everyone's reaction as the fortune in greenbacks spilled onto the chair and floor.

"Thunderation, woman!" roared Pa. "You came all the way from the city with *that* in your bags? What if you'd been stuck up? *Tarnation*, that's a pile of money!"

"I had your son to protect me," Almeda replied. "How could I be afraid? And Zack and I prayed for the Lord's presence to go beside us. We read Psalm 91 together, and we took our Father at his word."

All this time poor Patrick Shaw just sat where he was, in speechless silence, gazing down at more money than he'd ever seen in his life.

"It's to pay off your loan, Pat," said Pa at length. "How many days you got left on the call?"

" 'Bout nine. Chloe's already started to pack up our things."

"Well you tell her to *un*pack them," said Almeda firmly, "and you ride straight into town and march into Royce's bank and put this money down on his desk, and you say to him, 'Mr. Royce, here's your money, just like your notice-of-call said. Now if you don't mind, I'd like a receipt and the clear title to my property.' "

Still dumfounded and bewildered, Mr. Shaw managed to stammer out the words, "But I can't take this . . . this ain't my money."

"Don't worry, Mr. Shaw," said Almeda. "We'll make everything legal and tidy and you don't have to be concerned about us. We're not *giving* you this money, we're *loaning* it to you. I borrowed it from Mr. Finch at four-and-a-half percent interest. We will make you the loan at the same rate. You pay off the Royce bank, and next month begin making payments to us instead. We will then pay back Finchwood Ltd. as you pay us. And since the interest rate is less, your payments every month will be less than Franklin was charging you. You'll be out from under his yoke, you'll have your land back, and as long as you keep the payments up from now on, everything will be fine."

"I—I don't know how to thank you," said Mr. Shaw.

"No thanks is needed, Pat," said Pa. "You'd have done the same thing to help us if you were in a position to."

"It's an investment for all of us," added Almeda. "For us and for Mr. Finch, for the future of Miracle Springs and its people, and against the scare tactics of Franklin Royce."

"Well, I reckon I can understand that. But I can't see how it'll help anyone else around. They're still gonna be too afraid to vote against him for mayor. And Royce is liable to be so mad he'll start calling other folks' loans due, and then we'll just be making it worse for everybody."

"You've put your finger right on the risky part of our plan," said Almeda. "Before I left for the south I told Drummond it was going to be like a giant poker game. And here's where we have to hope our bluff works."

"How's paying off my note gonna bluff him?"

"Because you're gonna tell the other men around just what you've done," said Pa. "You're gonna tell them you paid Royce off with money you borrowed, and that there's more where that came from."

"But you can't tell them where we came by it," added Almeda. "Just say that you borrowed it. And then you tell them that we'll back anybody else up whose loan gets called too."

"You mean it?" exclaimed Mr. Shaw in disbelief.

"We mean to try," answered Pa. "You just spread the word around town that nobody's got to be afraid of voting for Almeda on account of what Royce might do with their loans. You tell 'em that *you're* gonna vote for her—that is, you *are* gonna vote for Almeda, ain't you, Pat?"

"You're dang sure I am! After what you've done, how could I not? It's not every man who's got friends like you! You two are just the kind of mayoring this town needs, and I aim to tell everyone I can too!"

"Well, you tell 'em to vote for Almeda and that Royce's not likely to do a thing to 'em. If he tries and starts threatening other folks like he did you, then you tell 'em to come see us."

"I still don't see how you can do such a thing."

"What my husband has been trying to say is that we'll back

up our promise as far as we can," said Almeda, "and we're praying it's far enough. Mr. Finch said he would support us up to fifty thousand dollars. That should enable us to protect three or four others from being evicted by Royce. If he persists beyond that, then we could be in trouble. That's when we have to hope he won't call our bluff."

"Well, I'll do what you say."

"Just remember—you keep quiet about all this we talked about," said Pa. "Pay off your loan and start talking up *Hollister For Mayor*. Then we'll leave our friend Royce to stew over it."

CHAPTER 15

INTO THE HORNET'S NEST

If we thought Almeda's handbill caused a commotion, or Pa's marching in and smacking Mr. Royce in the face while the widow Robinson got an earful in the other room, that was *nothing* compared to the uproar caused when Mr. Shaw walked into the Royce Miners' Bank that same afternoon, calmly asked to see Mr. Royce, and then dumped eighteen thousand dollars in green United States bills on the desk in front of him, asking for his change, a receipt, and the cancelled mortgage note and clear deed of trust for his property.

The exclamations from the bystanders, and the look on Mr. Royce's face, according to Mr. Shaw telling us about it later, was a sight to behold.

"His greedy eyes got so big seeing all that money in front of him," he said, "for an instant I thought he was gonna dive right on top of the desk after it! But then the next second he suddenly seemed to remember this money meant he wouldn't be able to get his hands on my land *and* wouldn't be getting that six-and-a-quarter percent interest no more.

" 'What kind of a trick is this, Shaw?' he said.

" 'Ain't no trick,' I answered him. 'You called my note due, and there's the payment, just like you asked—nine days early.'

" 'Where'd you get it, Shaw?' he asked.

'Nothing in your notice of call said I had to tell you everything I do. You said I had to pay you, and I done it.'

" 'I know you don't have a dime to your name,' he growled.

And watching him when I put that money in front of him made me realize that he wasn't after the money at all, but that he wanted my place. 'What did you do, hold up a stage? Or is it counterfeit?'

"By now I was enjoying myself, and I decided to pull a little bluff of my own. 'Mr. Royce,' I said, 'that is good U.S. legal currency. I come by it perfectly legal, I'm paying you off in full with it. Now, if you don't write me a receipt and give my note back showing it's paid in full, with the extra from the eighteen thousand I got coming back, then I'll just be on my way over to the Sheriff's office!'

"Well, he blustered a while more, but finally he took the cash and put it in his safe, and got out the papers and signed everything over to me. But he didn't like it, I could tell. There he was with eighteen thousand dollars, and a look on his face like I'd gotten the best of him. And he gave me back the extra—there's $735 back from your $18,000!"

He plunked the money down on the table.

"Keep it, Pat," said Pa. "You use that to clear up your other bills, and if you still got extra, then it'll help make the first few payments."

"Then you come by the office tomorrow," added Almeda, "and we'll draw up a note and some terms. At four-and-a-half percent, it shouldn't be more than $135 or $140 a month."

"I can't tell you how obliged I am to you!"

"You just get folks over being afraid of voting for us!" said Almeda.

"Oh, I've already been doing that! Once that money fell out onto the desk in Royce's bank, it was like I'd stirred up a hornet's nest! I no more'n walked out the door of the bank and it seemed the whole town knew already. All the men came pouring out from the stores and their houses, cheering me and shaking my hand and hitting me on the back. Why, you'd have thought I struck a new vein under the mountain! And of course the question they was all asking was, 'Where'd the loot come from, Pat . . . where'd you get that kind o' cash!' But I just kinda kept to myself, smiling like I knew a big secret, and said,

'Let's just put it this way, boys. Wherever I got it from, there's more where that came from. And so you don't need to be one bit afraid of what's gonna happen if you vote for Mrs. Hollister for mayor. Matter of fact, boys,' I added, and I let my voice get real soft like I was letting them in on a big secret, 'matter of fact, it's come to my attention that our old friend Royce is charging us all close to two percent *more* interest than the going rate down in Sacramento. Unless he's a dang sight dumber than I think, he ain't gonna call your loans due. He's been making a killing on us all these years, and he ain't about to upset his money-cart now.' "

"What did they say to that?" asked Almeda. Pa was laughing so hard from listening to Mr. Shaw that he couldn't say anything!

"They were plenty riled, I can tell you that. And once I told them that I had it on the word of a man I trusted that they'd be protected in the same way if Royce called their loans due, they all walked off saying they weren't gonna vote for no cheat like him for mayor!"

"You done good, Pat," Pa said finally.

"Did you tell anyone that it was us who was behind it?" asked Almeda.

"Rolf Douglas came up to me afterward, kinda quiet. Said he was two months behind with Royce and was afraid he was gonna be next. I told him to go see you, in your office, Mrs. Hollister. I think you can likely expect a call from him real soon."

"Rolf ain't no Widow Robinson," said Pa. "But I don't doubt that word'll manage to spread around."

"Maybe I shouldn't have told him," said Mr. Shaw, worried.

"No, no, Patrick, it's just fine," said Almeda. "Word had to get around. Just so long as folks don't know *how* we were able to do what we have done—at least not for a while. We want to keep Franklin off guard and guessing."

CHAPTER 16

PA PLAYS POKER—EYEBALL TO EYEBALL

Word got around, all right—in a hurry!

Two days later we got a call from Franklin Royce that was anything but friendly. Pa must have sensed there was fire coming out of the banker's eyes while he was still a long way off. The minute he saw the familiar black buggy, he said to Almeda, "I'll handle this," and walked a little way down the road away from the house.

"I'm here to talk to you and your wife, Hollister," said Mr. Royce, hotly reining his horse up in front of Pa but remaining seated in his carriage. As he spoke he glanced over to where Almeda and I were standing near the door. His eyes threw daggers at us.

"What you got to say, Royce," replied Pa, "you can say to me. I'm not about to put up with any more of your abuse or threats to my wife or daughter. If you haven't learned your lesson from what happened in your bank last week, then maybe I'll have to knock some more sense into that head of yours."

"You dare lay a hand on me, Hollister, and I'll have you up on charges before the day's out!"

"I don't want to hurt you," said Pa. "But if you dare to threaten anyone in my family again, I won't stop with bloodying your nose. Now go on . . . say your piece."

"I'd like to know what the two of you think you're trying to do, paying off Patrick Shaw's note like that?"

"We made him a loan. I don't see anything so unusual in that."

"You're mixing in my affairs, that's what's unusual about it!"

"Ain't no law against loaning money to a friend."

"You don't have that kind of cash!"

Pa shrugged.

"I want to know where you got it!"

"There also ain't no law that gives a banker the right to meddle in someone else's private affairs," Pa shot back. "Where Pat Shaw got the money to pay you off is no more your concern than where we might have gotten it to loan him— that is *if* we had anything to do with all this you're talking about."

"You know good and well you have everything to do with it, you dirty—"

"You watch your tongue!" shouted Pa, taking two steps toward Royce's buggy. "There are ladies present. And if I hear one more filthy word from your mouth, I'll slam it shut so hard you won't speak *any* words for a week!"

Cowed but not humbled, Royce moderated his tone.

"Look, Hollister," he said, "I know well enough that you are behind that money of Shaw's. It's all over town. You know it and I know it and everybody knows it! Now I'm here to ask you—the two of you—" he added, looking over at Almeda, "businessman to businessman, having nothing to do with the election, I'm asking you what are you trying to do by meddling in *my* affairs! Banking and making loans is my business, and you have no call to step into the middle of my dealings with *my* customers! I want to know what your intentions are."

"I figure our intentions are our own business," replied Pa coolly.

"Not when they interfere with *my* business!" Royce shot back. "And word around town is that you intend to continue sticking your nose into my negotiations with people who owe my bank money. So I ask you again, Hollister, what are your intentions?"

"Our intentions are to do what's right," answered Pa.

"Paying off other mens' loans, even when they are in legal default?"

"I ain't admitted to doing any such thing."

"Cut the hog swill, Hollister!"

"You want to know my intentions," Pa said. "Then I'll tell you straight—it's my feeling that a man's duty-bound to stand by his neighbors, whatever that means. And that's what I intend to do. I'll tell you, Royce, I'm not really all that concerned about you or your banking business, because from where I stand it seems to me you're looking out for nobody but yourself. Now you can do what you want to me. You can say what you want, you can spread what lies you want. You can sic some investigator on me to try to run me off my land. You can beat my wife in this election. And maybe in the end you *will* run me out of Miracle Springs and will some day own every stitch of land from here to Sacramento. But nothing you do will make me stop standing up for what's right, and for trying to help my friends and neighbors so long as there's anything I can do for them. Now—is that plain-spoken enough for you?"

"So you intend to continue backing up the loans of others around here even if they should be called due, as people are saying?" repeated Royce.

"I said I aim to do what's right."

"What are you trying to do, Hollister, open a bank of your own?"

Pa shrugged. "I got nothing more to say to you."

"You can't do it, Hollister. You'll never pull it off. You can't possibly have enough cash to stand up to me."

Almeda began walking toward the two men.

"Franklin," she said approaching them, "do you remember just after I entered the mayor's race, you said to me, 'Two can play this game?' You were, of course, insinuating that you could be just as underhanded toward me as you thought I was being to you by the publication of my flyer. I think anyone with much sense would say that this last month demonstrates that you have few equals when it comes to underhanded tactics."

"How dare you suggest—" the banker began, but Almeda cut him off immediately.

"Let me finish, Franklin!" she said. "You have spread rumors about me throughout the community. You threatened my daughter and my husband in different ways. And now you are opening a store just down from mine intended, I presume, to drive me out of business. All we have done is help a friend. That hardly compares with your ruthless and self-serving behavior. And if it takes our going into the lending business to keep you from hurting any more of the families in this town, then so be it. Your own words condemn you, Franklin. Two *can* play this game! And if you feel compelled to enter the supplies and freight business, perhaps we will feel compelled to open a second bank in Miracle Springs, so that people can have a choice in where they go for financial help."

"That is utterly ridiculous!" laughed Royce with disdain. "The two of you—a miner and his shopkeeper of a wife—financing a bank! I've never heard of anything so absurd! It takes thousands, more capital than you'll ever have in your lives! The very notion makes me laugh!"

"You are very cocky, Franklin," she said. "It may well prove your undoing."

"Ha, ha, ha!" laughed Royce loudly.

"It isn't only capital a business needs. Besides money, it takes integrity and a reputation that people can trust. I would say that you may be in short supply of those latter assets, Franklin, however large may be the fortune behind your enterprises."

"A bank takes money, and nothing else. I don't believe a word of all this! You may have stashed away a nest egg to help that no-good Shaw, but you won't be so lucky next time."

"We were hoping there wouldn't have to be a next time, that you would see it will do you no good to call the notes you hold due."

"Don't be naive, Almeda. I'm a banker, and money is my business. And it's not *yours*! So stay out of it!"

"If you call Rolf Douglas's note, or anyone else's, Royce, you're going to find yourself straight up against us again," said

Pa, speaking once more. His voice rang with authority.

"I don't believe you, Hollister. I've checked your finances, and I know your bank account. You don't have that kind of money."

"Then go ahead and do your worst, Royce," said Pa.

"You're bluffing, Hollister. I can call any of a dozen notes due, and there's no possible way you can back them up."

Pa stared straight into Mr. Royce's face, and for a moment they stood eye to eye, as if each were daring the other to call the bluff. When Pa spoke, his words were cold and hard as steel.

"Try me, Royce," he said, still staring into the banker's eyes. "You just try me, if you want to take the chance. But you may find I'm not as easy an adversary as you think. People in these parts know I'm a man of my word, and they can trust me. I don't think you'd be wise to go up against me."

"What my husband is trying to tell you, Franklin," said Almeda, "is that you can call notes due and try to foreclose all you want. We've let it be known that if people find themselves in trouble with you, they can come see us. You may call those dozen loans due, but once they are paid off, what are you left with? A vault full of cash. Without loans, a bank cannot make a profit. You'll wind up with no loans, no land, no property, and before long the Royce Miners' Bank will be out of business, Franklin."

"That's too ridiculous to deserve a reply!"

"Do you think the people of this town will think it ridiculous when they learn that the six-and-a-quarter percent interest you have been charging them is almost two full percentage points *higher* than the current rate in San Francisco and Sacramento?"

"Rates are higher further away from financial centers."

"Your rates are two points higher than what *we* intend to charge people on *our* loans."

"You would dare undercut me?"

"No, we merely intend to charge our borrowers the fair and current rate."

"I don't believe you!"

"If you don't have better manners toward women yet, Royce," interrupted Pa angrily, "than to call them liars to their face, I suggest you go see Pat Shaw and take a look at the note we drew up for him. Four-and-a-half percent, just like my wife said! You can squawk all you want about it, but when folks find out you've been taking advantage of them, they won't take too kindly to it. They're gonna be lining up at your door begging you to call their notes due so they can borrow from us instead!"

He paused just long enough to take a breath. Then his eyes bore into Franklin Royce one final time.

"So like I said, Royce," he added, "you go ahead and do your worst. You think I'm bluffing, then you try me! You'd be doing this community a favor by calling every loan you hold due, and letting the good folks of Miracle Springs pay you off and start borrowing from somebody else at a fair rate. Then you can see what it's like trying to make a living competing with my wife in the freight and supplies business!"

Mr. Royce returned Pa's stare as long as he dared, which wasn't long, then without another word, flicked his whip, turned his horse around, and flew off down the road back toward town.

Pa and Almeda watched him go. Then she slipped her hand through his arm, and they turned and walked slowly back to the house. They seemed at peace with what they had done, because they knew it was right, but they couldn't help being anxious about the results. If Royce *did* start calling notes due, there wasn't much they could do to stop him beyond helping a handful of other men, and that would only make it worse for everybody else. If they did bail out Rolf Douglas and whoever followed him, once they reached the $50,000 limit that Mr. Finch had promised, they would have no more help to give. And then, once word got out that the Hollister-Parrish "bank" had run dry, Mr. Royce would get his chance to foreclose on everybody in sight, run Parrish Mine and Freight out of business, gobble up all the land for miles around, get elected mayor, and gain control of the whole area.

Everything Pa and Almeda had said was true, and they meant every bit of it. But there was a lot of bluff in their words too. Now there was nothing left to do but wait and see how Mr. Royce decided to play his cards.

"Well, Corrie," said Pa with a half-smile as they came toward me, "I reckon we've done it now. Your next article may be about the end of Miracle Springs and the beginning of Royceville!"

Almeda and I laughed. But all three of us knew Pa's joke was a real possibility, too real to be very funny.

CHAPTER 17

THE DOC'S VISIT AND PA'S SCARE

The election was less than two weeks away.

The moment Franklin Royce disappeared down the road in his black buggy and we went back inside the house, a last-minute let-down seemed to come over Almeda.

There was nothing more to be done. She wasn't going to give any more speeches or write any more flyers. And as far as visiting and talking with folks was concerned, she said everything had already been stirred up plenty. The people had more than enough to talk about for one year, she said, and Franklin Royce had enough fuel to keep his hatred burning for a long time. It was best just to wait for events to unfold.

Almost immediately, her whole system seemed to collapse. Even as they walked away from the conversation with Mr. Royce, her face was pale and her smile forced.

The minute they were inside, she sat down heavily and breathed out a long and weary sigh. Tiny beads of perspiration dotted her white forehead. Pa saw instantly that she wasn't feeling well at all. She didn't even argue when he took her hand, helped her back to her feet, and led her into the other room to their bed. She lay down, and Pa brought her a drink of water. He wiped her face for a minute with a cool, damp cloth, and before long she was sound asleep.

Almeda remained in bed the rest of that Friday and all day Saturday, only getting up to go to the outhouse. Pa tended her like a mother with a baby. When Katie or Emily or I would try to take Ma something or sit beside her or help her on one of her many walks outside, Pa would say, "No, she's my wife. Nobody loves her as much as me, and nobody is gonna take care of her but me. Besides," he added with a wink, "I got her into this here fix, so I oughta be the one who helps her through it!"

The rest of us fixed the meals and cleaned up the house, but Pa took care of Almeda. He even sat beside her while she was sleeping, held her hand when she got sick, and read to her now and then, either from a book or from the Bible. If the rest of the town could only have seen him, some of the men might have made fun of him for doting on her. But no woman would have thought it was anything short of wonderful to have a husband love and care for her so tenderly as Pa did Almeda.

In the midst of all the turmoil over the election and loans and money and rumors and legal questions about Pa's claim and the future of Parrish Freight, it had been easy to forget that Almeda was in the family way. Except when she'd get sick for half an hour or hour every few days, she didn't seem any different, and she wasn't showing any plumpness around her middle.

But Pa started to get concerned about her condition on Saturday afternoon when she still lay in bed, looking pale and feeling terrible. He sent Zack and Tad off on their horses to fetch Doc Shoemaker.

When the Doc came an hour or so later, he went immediately into the sick room with Pa. After examining Almeda he shook his head, puzzled.

"Everything seems fine," he said, "but she's weak, and mighty sick. I don't quite know how to account for it. Came on her sudden, you say?"

"Yep," answered Pa. "She was fine and full of pep for a day or so after she got back, and then she started to tire out pretty bad."

"Back from where?"

"Sacramento."

"Sacramento? How'd she get there?"

"In her buggy, how else?"

"She bounced around on a buggy seat for that whole trip and back?"

"I reckon so," said Pa reluctantly. By now he realized Doc Shoemaker was mighty upset.

"Drummond Hollister, you idiot! What in blazes did you let her do that for!"

"She didn't exactly ask," said Pa. "She just said she was going. I asked if she wanted me to go with her, and she said no, that I oughta stay here, and I didn't think any more about it. She just went, that's all."

"This lady's between three and four months pregnant! She can't be doing things like that. I'm surprised she hasn't already lost the child from the exertion of a journey like that. She still may."

All the color drained from Pa's face. I had never seen him so scared. "I—I didn't think of all that," he stammered. "She's the kind of woman who's used to doing what she likes, and I don't usually stand in her way."

"Well, you're her husband and the father of the baby she's carrying. So you'd just better start telling her to take it easy. If she doesn't like it, then you put your foot down, do you hear me? Otherwise you might lose both a baby *and* a wife!"

"Is she really in danger, Doc?" Pa's voice shook.

"I don't know. I hope not. But she needs rest—and you make sure she gets it!"

CHAPTER 18

A FEW MORE CARDS GET PLAYED

Almeda was up and out of bed some by Monday. Most of the color had come back into her cheeks and she was smiling again.

Pa made her stay in bed most of the day, and the minute she even had a fleeting thought about going into town or doing any last-minute campaigning, he wouldn't hear of it for a second!

"Corrie can manage the office fine without you," he said. "And whatever campaigning's to be done—which I don't figure is much—I'll do myself. There's not much we can do anyway, and the best thing for you is more rest. I don't aim to take any more chances!"

"Why, Drummond Hollister," she said, "I declare, if I didn't know better I'd take you for one of those slave-driving husbands who thinks his every word is supposed to be absolute law!" Her voice was still a little weak, but it was good to hear her joking again.

"Well, maybe it's time I started exerting my authority a mite more over an unruly wife who sometimes doesn't know what's for her own good," Pa jibed back. But joking or not, he still was determined to make her stay home and stay in bed as much as he could.

I went into town to the office, but I quickly discovered that while Almeda had been sick and we had been thinking only about her, the rest of the town had been talking about something else. And although the election was only eight days away, the elections to vote for mayor or United States President were not on people's minds.

I came back home on Raspberry about half an hour before noon. "Pa," I said, "I don't know what to do. The office has been full of people all morning."

"Don't ask me," he answered, "you and Almeda know the business, not me."

"It's not the business they're coming in about, Pa. It's about money and the worries about Royce."

"Who's been coming in?" he asked.

"Several of the men—asking to see Almeda . . . or you, when I told them she was sick. Mr. Douglas was one of the first."

"Rolf?"

"Yes, and he didn't look too happy."

A worried look crossed Pa's face. "Royce musta called his note due," he muttered. There was no anger in his voice, only a deep concern. Mr. Royce had apparently decided to play another card and call Pa's bluff.

Pa let out a deep sigh. "Reckon I'd best head into the office and see what's up," he said, "though I'm not sure I want to. What's going on now?" he added, turning to me. "What's Ashton doing?"

"I told him I was coming home to talk to you and to tell anyone who asked that I'd be back after a spell."

"Okay . . . I'll go saddle up the horse in a minute, and we'll ride back in."

He went into the bedroom to talk to Almeda a minute, then said to Emily and Becky, "You girls take care of your mother if she needs anything. And if she tries to get up and about too much, you tell her I told you to make her lie down again."

"Yes, Pa," said Emily. "Don't worry about her at all. We'll see that she keeps resting."

"Good. Corrie, we'd best be off." He went out to the barn while I went in to visit with Almeda for a few minutes. She was feeling a lot better, but she seemed quiet and thoughtful and a little sad. I suppose she was anxious about the men in town, and maybe about the election.

When Pa and I rode into town, we saw a small group of men standing around the door of Parrish Mine and Freight. A few were leaning against the building, and a couple sat on the edge of the wooden walkway, chatting aimlessly and waiting for Pa. When we rode up, they stood and turned in our direction. Worry filled all their faces. Rolf Douglas was at the head of the line right next to the door.

"He done it, Drum," said Mr. Douglas as we rode up, holding the paper he held in his hand up toward us.

"Thirty days?" said Pa, dismounting.

"Yep. I already been to see him to ask whether he would reconsider if I got back up with the two months I'm behind. But he said nope, got to have the cash or be out in thirty days."

"Well, come on in," said Pa, opening the door and leading the way into the office. "We'll see if we can't work something to help you out."

"What about the rest of us, Drum?" someone else called out. "We've got loans with Royce too."

"Any one of us could be next," called out another.

"Hold your horses, all of you," said Pa. "Right now Rolf here's the one with immediate problems with Royce. Let me get him taken care of first. Then we'll talk about what's to be done next."

He and Mr. Douglas went into Almeda's office. Ten minutes later they emerged and walked back outside. Mr. Douglas's expression was completely changed, and even Pa had the beginnings of a smile on his face. In that short time, the assembly of men outside had grown to ten or twelve.

Pa gave Mr. Douglas a slap on the back, then the two men shook hands. "You come back and see me in three weeks, Rolf," Pa said. "That'll give you eight or ten days before the money's due to Royce. We'll finish up our arrangement then."

Mr. Douglas thanked him, and by then all the other men were clamoring around, asking questions, wanting to know how things stood with them if they suddenly found themselves in the same predicament.

I don't know whether Pa was aware of it or not, but I thought I could see the outline of a familiar face in the bank window down the street. Word of the goings-on outside the Parrish Freight office would get back to Royce's ears soon enough.

"Listen to me, all the rest of you," Pa said. "We can't help you out until Royce tries to foreclose on you. Even the Hollister-Parrish bank's got limits, you know!"

He laughed, and all the men joined in.

"But we'll help you out when your time of need comes, you can depend on that. So long as we're able, whatever we got is yours. The minute Royce sends you a paper, you come see me and we'll sit down and talk. Until then, all of you just hang tight and go on with your business."

"Thanks, Drum . . . we're obliged to ya. We all owe you an' your missus, and we won't forget it!" called out several of the men as they began to disperse down the street."

"Just remember," Pa called out, "you men vote according to your consciences a week from tomorrow. I ain't gonna mention no names, but you just remember that as long as you got friends you can trust, no one is gonna be able to hurt you no matter what they may threaten to do."

He didn't have to mention any names. Every one of the men understood perfectly what Pa meant.

And as the week progressed and the days wound down toward the election, this statement of Pa's spread around town and became a final campaign pledge that stuck clearly in people's minds.

Judging from his action, it was obvious that Franklin Royce had heard Pa's statement about friends you could trust too.

CHAPTER 19

WOMAN TO WOMAN

By the middle of the week Almeda was back to a normal schedule and was going into town for at least a good part of the day. But she was unusually quiet, and it seemed as if something weighed on her mind. I didn't know if it had to do with the election or the Royce trouble or anxiety about the baby.

After all that had gone on with the build-up to the election, the last week was completely quiet—no speeches, no rumors, no new banners. No one saw Mr. Royce. Almeda kept to herself. There were no more threats of foreclosure. Business went on as usual, and Tuesday, November 4 steadily approached. The most exciting thing that happened had nothing whatever to do with the election. That was the news that Aunt Katie was expecting again. The two new cousins were both scheduled to arrive sometime in the early spring of 1857.

Time had slipped by so fast that I didn't have the opportunity to get a second article written about the election. But almost before I had a chance to think through the possibility of a post-election story, which I wasn't sure I wanted to do if Mr. Royce won, all of a sudden a realization struck me. I still hadn't seen my Fremont article in the *Alta*!

What could have happened? Did I miss it? I'd been so preoccupied with everything that was going on, I hadn't read through every single issue. Had it come and I hadn't seen it?

I couldn't believe that was the case. Mr. Kemble always sent me a copy of my articles separately. He had done so with every one he had ever printed. Then why hadn't *this* article been printed? It was the most important thing I had ever written, and it was almost too late!

I rushed home that day and frantically searched through the stack of *Alta*s from the last three weeks. It was not there. My article had still not been printed!

All that evening I stewed about it, wondering what I ought to do. By the next morning nothing had been resolved in my mind. So when we got ready to go into town, I asked Almeda if I could ride with her in the buggy instead of taking Raspberry like I usually did.

I began by telling her about the article's not appearing, and about Mr. Kemble.

"After a while," I said, "I started to get so tired of him looking down on me because I was young, and because I was a girl, that I became determined to show him that I could write as well as anyone else. But sometimes I must have sounded mighty headstrong, like I wouldn't accept anything but my own way. Do you know what I mean?" I asked.

Almeda nodded.

"I know there are times you've got to fight for something you believe in. You've taught me that. But then again, Mr. Kemble *is* the editor, and he *does* have years more experience than I do, and I *am* young. Sometimes I wonder if I'm presuming too much to think I'm so smart and such a great writer that I can just tell him what I want."

I glanced at Almeda. She was obviously thinking a lot about what I was saying, but still she let me keep talking.

"And not only am I young and inexperienced, I *am* a girl—"

"Not anymore, Corrie," Almeda interrupted. "You're a woman now."

I smiled. "What I mean," I said, "is that I'm not a man . . . I'm a girl, a lady, a woman—a female. I wish Mr. Kemble could look at something I write and *not* think of it as written by a woman. But there's a division between men and women that affects everything—it affects how people look at you and what they expect from you and how they treat you. And as much as I find myself wishing it *wasn't* that way, there's no getting around that it *is*. There *is* a difference between men and women, and maybe it *is* a man's world, especially here in the west. I don't know any other women newspaper writers. There aren't any other women in business around here but you."

I stopped, struggling to find words to express things I was feeling. "Maybe Mr. Kemble is right when he says that it's a man's world, and that a woman like me can't expect to get the same pay or have it as easy as I might like it. Maybe it *is* a man's world, and I've been wrong to think things are unfair because Robin O'Flaridy can get paid more than I do for the same article. Maybe that's just the way it is, and it's something I have to accept."

"How did your article's not being in the paper lead you to think about all that?" asked Almeda.

"I don't know. It's just hard to know how to fit being a woman into a man's world."

"Very hard!" agreed Almeda. "Believe me, Corrie, I have struggled with that exact question almost from the moment I arrived in California."

"My first reaction was anger," I continued. "I wanted to march right into Mr. Kemble's office and say, 'Why haven't you published my article?' A time or two I've been really headstrong and determined with him. Part of me still says that's the right approach. That's how a man would probably do it." I paused for a moment.

"But another side of me started thinking in this whole new way," I went on, "wondering if the way I've handled it in the past wasn't right."

"It's the Spirit of God putting these thoughts in your heart, Corrie," said Almeda. "You're maturing as a daughter of God. He's never going to let you remain just where you are. He's always going to be pulling and stretching you and encouraging you to grow into new regions of wisdom and dedication to him. And so he'll continually be putting within you new thoughts like this, so that you'll think and pray in new directions. He wants you to know both him and yourself more and more intimately."

"If it's God's Spirit speaking to me inside, then what's he trying to tell me?" I asked.

She laughed. "Ah, Corrie, *that* is always the difficult question! It's often very hard to know. Separating the voice of God's Spirit from our own thoughts is one of the Christian's greatest challenges."

The look on her face changed to one of reflection. "It's funny you should bring this up," she said after a minute. "I've been facing a real quandary myself. Different from yours, I suppose, but very similar at the same time."

"You mean about knowing if it's God saying something to you?"

"Partly. But more specifically, the issue of being a woman, and how to balance the two sides that sometimes struggle against one another inside."

"That's just it!" I said. "I feel that there's two parts of me, and I'm not sure which part I'm supposed to listen to and be like. One part wants to do things and be bold and not be looked down on for being a woman. That part of me resents hearing that it's a 'man's world' and that a woman's *place* is supposed to be somewhere different, somewhere less important, doing and thinking things that men wouldn't do. That part of me wants to think that I'm just as important as a man—not because women are *more* important, but just because I'm a human being too. Do you know what I mean?"

"Oh, I know exactly what you mean, Corrie!" answered Almeda. "Don't you think I've wrestled with that same question five hundred times since my first husband died? I've spent years trying to run a business in this 'man's world!' I always had to prove myself, to show them that I could run Parrish Mine and Freight as well as any man. Oh, yes, Corrie, I've struggled and prayed and cried over these questions you're asking!"

"Then you must feel the other half of what I've been feeling too," I went on.

"Which is?"

"Well, maybe it's not altogether right to expect to be treated the same as a man. Maybe it *is* a man's world, and I've got to accept my place in it. Even if Mr. Kemble says or does something I don't like, or even something I don't think is fair, maybe I have to learn to accept it. After all, he *is* the man, he *is* the editor, and maybe he has the right to do what he thinks best, whether I like it or not. After all, it isn't *my* newspaper. So who do I think I am to think that I have a right to expect Mr. Kemble to do what I want?"

Almeda drew up on the reins and looked at me intently. "Corrie," she said, "it seems there are two principles at work here. Maybe you're feeling the need to accept Mr. Kemble's judgment about the paper and your articles. But it's not just because he's a *man*—it's also because he's in a position of authority, and deserves your respect even when you disagree with him."

I nodded. "I guess so."

"But there's more to it than just the question of who makes the final decisions about your stories, isn't there?"

"Yes. I guess the last couple of years, since I started trying to write more seriously, I've been wanting the people I meet— first Mr. Singleton, then Mr. Kemble, and then even Robin O'Flaridy or Derrick Gregory—to treat me like an equal and not look down on me just because I'm not a man. But maybe I'm not supposed to be an equal. Maybe that isn't the way God wanted it to be. I don't like the thought that I'm not as important in the world as a man. But I've been wondering if that's the way it is."

"Corrie . . . Corrie," sighed Almeda, "you've really hit on the hardest thing of all about being a woman, especially out here in the west where we sometimes have to fend for ourselves and be tough."

"You mean accepting the fact that we're not equal to men, and that what we do and think isn't as important?"

"Oh no—not that. We *are* just as important. The question isn't about equality, Corrie, because in God's eyes, men, women, children—*all* human beings—are equal and precious. The soul of the poorest black woman is just as important to God as the soul of the richest white man. The President of the United States, in God's eyes, is no more important than a child dying of starvation somewhere in deepest India or Africa. No— men are all equal, and by *men* I mean all of mankind—men *and* women. You are just as important as Mr. Kemble or anyone else, and your thoughts are just as valid. Never think that you're not as *good* as someone else—as a man. On the other hand, never think that someone else isn't as good as you! Equality works in all directions."

"Then what's that hardest thing about being a woman?" I asked.

"I said you were wrong about us not being *equal*. But you were right when you said we were *different*! And that's what is so hard about being a woman—trying to find how we're supposed to be equal and different at the same time. That is the struggle, Corrie."

"It's a struggle, all right. Half of me wants to tell Mr. Kemble off, and the other half wonders if I've got any right to."

"That's where women make a big mistake, Corrie. We want to be treated equally, but we forget that we really *are* different. We're supposed to be. God didn't make men and women to be the same. He made us equal but different. And so we're supposed to fulfill different roles. And the minute we try to start turning our equality with men into *sameness* with men, we lose sight of what it truly means to be a *woman*. I think we become less of a woman, in the way God intended womanhood when he created it, when we try to compete with men and do everything men do."

"Do you mean maybe I *shouldn't* be trying to be a reporter, because it is something mostly men do?"

"No, it's not that at all, Corrie. I think it's all right to *do* many of the same things men do. There aren't certain limits or restrictions God places around women. But even though we may be involved in many of the same pursuits, we're still women, not men. There's still a difference. There is still a leadership role which God has given to men, and a follower's role God has given to women. That's part of the difference I spoke of. Equal but different. Man is to be the head, the spokesman, the leader. A woman is to fit into that arrangement, not try to compete with it."

"You mean, like Mr. Kemble being the editor of the paper, and so I have to realize the importance of his position?"

"Something like that."

"And even if it weren't for his being editor and me just being a raw young writer, him being a man and me being a young woman makes it that way, too."

"I suppose in a way, although I wouldn't want to assume that any man, just because he *is* a man, has the right to control your life and your decisions. I believe that God has set certain men—a husband, for example, or an employer—into positions of leadership. As women, we need to acknowledge that God-given leadership. But I have to admit that I don't always know how it works out in practice. Lately I've been struggling with it a lot myself."

"Is that how it is in a marriage too?" I asked. "Like between you and Pa?"

She didn't answer immediately, but looked down and sighed deeply. I glanced away for a moment. When I looked back toward her, to my astonishment I saw that Almeda was crying.

CHAPTER 20

ALMEDA CONFIDES

"What's the matter, Almeda?" I asked. My first thought was that something I'd said had hurt her feelings.

"I'm sorry, Corrie," she said, looking over at me. I'd never seen such an expression on her face. To me, Almeda had always been so strong, so in control, so much older and more mature than I. For three or four years she had been the one I had looked to for help and advice. I guess before that moment it had never crossed my mind that *she* had inner struggles too. But that look on her face, with tears silently running down her cheeks, was a look of confusion and uncertainty and pain—a look I had never expected to see from Almeda!

I reached over and took her hand.

The gesture made her cry even more for a minute, but I kept my hand on hers, and she held on to mine tightly. Finally she reached inside her pocket for a handkerchief, then blew her nose and tried to take a deep breath.

"I've been struggling with this for several days," she finally said, "ever since coming back from Sacramento and getting sick. I suppose I've needed someone to talk to. But I haven't even been able to bring it up to your father yet, because I haven't known how to put into words all that I was feeling."

"What is it?" I said. "Is there something wrong between you and Pa?"

"Oh, no. Nothing like that. Although it certainly has to do with your father." She paused, took another breath, then took my hand in both of hers again.

"I've always been a pretty independent sort of woman, Corrie," she said. "Just the other day, when I was sick, I heard your father saying to the doctor that I was the kind of woman who was used to doing what I liked. When the thought of going to Sacramento came to my head, just like your father said, I didn't ask him, I just said I was going and that was that—I went. Perhaps getting sick, and hearing those words of Drummond's, and realizing that my impetuousness could have cost our baby's life—all that set me to thinking about some things I hadn't ever thought of in quite the same light before. And last week, as I lay in bed recovering, I spent a lot of time in prayer. And I must tell you, I'm having to take a new look at some things in myself. It's not an altogether pleasant experience!"

She paused for a moment, dabbed at her eyes, then went on.

"Ever since I was a child I've had a determined streak. And that's not necessarily a bad thing. My past was anything but a spiritual one. I did not begin walking with God until I was in my mid-twenties, and before that I was a much different person than the one you have known. I did much that I am not proud of. And when I discovered who my heavenly Father was, and realized that he loved me and desired something more for me than what I was, I set my heart and mind to give myself to him completely. As a Christian, my inner determination has been a good thing. I have wanted to settle for nothing less than God's fullest and best for me. I have determined to give my all to him, in every aspect of my being, to let him re-make me into what *he* wants me to be, rather than just settling for what I have always been. And thus, I really am a different person than I was fifteen years ago. He *has* created in me a new heart, a new mind. And I am thankful that he gave me the determination to seek him with my whole being. Some people do not have that hunger, that earnest desire to give their all to God. But he gave me that hunger, and I am glad.

"After Mr. Parrish died, I'd have never made it in business in Miracle Springs without being what your Pa calls 'a mighty determined lady.' I had to fight for what I wanted to do, and prove myself to people, mostly to the men of this community. It's just like what we have talked about before, Corrie—fighting for what you believe in. God puts that fight, that determination into women's hearts too, not just men's. He fills women with dreams and desires and ambitions and things they want to do and achieve, and I really believe that God wants determined daughters as well as determined sons, willing to believe in things strongly enough to go after them. Like your writing. I think God is filling you not only with the desire to write, but the determination to fight for it, even when it might mean occasionally standing up to Mr. Kemble and speaking your mind.

"But on the other hand, there's a danger women face that men don't. Sometimes a single woman, who has only herself to depend on, can get too independent and lose sight of what it means to live in partnership with someone else. After I lost my first husband, I got accustomed to doing things for myself, in my own way, without asking anyone's permission or what anyone thought. I had to, I suppose.

"But when your father and I were married, I continued thinking pretty much the same way, even though I was a wife again. I didn't really stop to consider that maybe now I had to alter my outlook. I still thought of my life as *mine* to live as I saw fit. Once when we were talking about your future, I told you that I was the kind of woman who believed in exploring all the possibilities for yourself that you could. When your father suggested shutting down Parrish Freight for a while, so that I could be a more traditional wife and mother, I nearly hit the roof. I wasn't about to have any of that, and I told him so!

"The trip to Sacramento and getting sick last week suddenly made it clear to me that I have carried that independence into my marriage with your father. I haven't stopped to consider things, or to ask him about what I do, or to defer to him in any way as my husband, I've just gone on ahead and done what I wanted to do. And the instant I realized it—I have to tell you, Corrie, it was very painful. I love your father so much. Realizing that I haven't been to him what God would have me be fills me with such remorse and sadness and—"

She stopped and looked away. I could feel her hand trembling in mine. I knew she was weeping again. After two or three minutes of silence, she continued.

"Your father has been so good to me," she said. "He has never pressured me, never said a word. He has let me be myself, and even be independent. Yet now I see that I have done some things that perhaps he wouldn't have wanted me to.

"Why, this whole thing of running for mayor—I never *asked* him about it, Corrie. We prayed about it when I decided to get back in the race, but I never really sought your father's counsel as a man of wisdom. The initial decision for me to run was a decision I made. I never even sought his advice as my husband and as the leader of this family. I genuinely thought I was being led of God, and perhaps to a degree I was. But the point is, I never consulted your father in any way or allowed him to help me arrive at a decision. You were there that evening last July—I simply walked in and announced that I had decided to run against Royce."

Again she stopped, tears standing in her red eyes. "Don't you see, Corrie—I haven't been fair to your father at all! My determined nature just lost sight of the fact that we're not supposed to act independent of men, but *with* them, and following them, and allowing them to help guide us. God made women to live *with* men, not to act independently of them—especially in a marriage. And I haven't done that with your father, the man I love more than anyone else in the world!

"Probably God was trying to get my attention even before last week. From the very start of the election, all the mischief and deceit Franklin has been up to—maybe that has been the Lord's way of telling me some of my priorities haven't been as he would have them. When he started spreading those rumors about me, even then God was stirring me up, though I didn't know what he was trying to say."

"But what could all those lies about you have to do with what God wanted to say to you?" I asked.

A faraway look passed across Almeda's face. "Yes, a good portion of what people were saying was false, Corrie," she said softly. "But not everything. I lived for many years outside God's plan for me, and I had much to repent of. He had many things in my character to change. Perhaps I will have the opportunity to tell you about it one day. I would like that. Your father knows everything. I have held no secrets from him. And it is to his great credit that he married me knowing what he knew. I love him all the more for it.

"And so when Franklin began stirring up the waters of my past, God began to probe the deep recesses of my heart as well. And now I find myself wondering if this whole election came up, not so that I could become mayor of Miracle Springs, but so that I would finally face some things in my own heart that I had never let go of, so that I would put them on God's altar once and for all."

"But surely you can't want Mr. Royce to be mayor!" I said in astonishment.

"Wouldn't it be better for me to withdraw from the election, even if it means giving the mayor's post to him, than to go ahead with something that is outside of God's will for me?"

"I suppose so," I answered hesitantly. "But I just can't stand the thought of Mr. Royce getting his own way and gaining control of this town."

"I can't either," she replied. "But he is not a Christian, and I am. Therefore I am under orders to a higher power. To *two* higher powers—the Lord God our Father, and to my husband Drummond Hollister. And maybe it's time I started to ask the two of them what I am supposed to do, instead of deciding for myself."

"I just can't abide the thought of Mr. Royce being mayor."

"Look at me, Corrie," she said tenderly, placing her hand gently on her stomach. "The baby that is your father's and mine is beginning to grow. Before long I will be getting fat with your own new little brother or sister. Do I look like a politician . . . a mayor?"

"I see what you mean," I said.

"Do you remember what you said when we first started talking, about the two parts struggling inside you?"

I nodded.

"It's the same thing I've been wrestling with. It's hard. It's painful. That's why I've been praying, and crying. I *want* to be mayor. But at the same time, my first calling is to be a woman—to be your father's wife, to be a mother to his children, and this new child I am carrying. Balancing the two is very difficult! That's why I don't know what to tell you to do about your article and Mr. Kemble. Because I don't even know what I'm supposed to do in my *own* dilemma."

We both were silent for several minutes. "What will you do?" I asked finally.

"I don't know," Almeda answered. "But the one thing I *do* have to do is talk with your father—and pray with him. This is one decision I am not going to make without him!"

She looked at me and smiled, wiping off the last of the tears on her face with her handkerchief.

"Thank you for listening, Corrie," she said. "You are a dear friend, besides being the best daughter a woman could have. Pray for me, will you?"

"I always do," I replied. I leaned toward her and gave her a tight hug. We held one another for several moments.

"Oh, Lord," I prayed aloud, "help the two of us to be the women you want us to be. I pray that you'll show Almeda and Pa just what you want them to do. And help me to know what you want me to do, too."

"Amen!" Almeda whispered softly.

When we released each other, both of us had tears in our eyes. They were not tears of sadness, but of joy.

CHAPTER 21

FRANKLIN ROYCE SURPRISES EVERYBODY

All day Thursday after Almeda and I had our long talk, neither of us could concentrate on work. About three in the afternoon, Almeda suggested we go on home.

We hadn't been back more than forty or fifty minutes when Alkali Jones rode up as fast as his stubborn mule Corrie's Beast could carry him—which wasn't very fast!

Pa was just walking down from the mine to wash up and have a cup of coffee. We'd been inside the house, but hadn't yet seen Pa since getting home. Mr. Jones spoke to all of us at once as he climbed down off the Beast.

"Ye left Miracle too blamed early!" he said to me and Almeda. "Weren't five minutes after ye was gone, ol' Royce come out o' his bank, an' starts talkin' to a few men who was hangin' around the Gold Nugget. Told 'em he was gonna be givin' kinda like a speech tomorrow mornin', though not exactly campaignin'. But he said whatever men owed his bank money oughta be sure an' be there. He said he'd like to notify 'em all by letter, but there weren't enough time, so would the men spread the word around town."

"And what else?" asked Pa.

"That's it," said Mr. Jones. "He's gonna be sayin' something he says is mighty important an' folks oughta be there."

Pa looked at Almeda. "Well, I reckon this could be it," he

said. "Looks like he's gonna call our bluff and foreclose on the whole town at once."

"He wouldn't dare," said Almeda.

"As long as you've known Franklin Royce," said Pa, "you still think he'd be afraid to do anything? Nope, that's what he's gonna to do all right. One last threat to finalize his election on Tuesday."

"I just can't believe he'd have the gall."

"He'll do anything to win."

Everybody was silent a minute.

"Well, I can't be there," said Almeda finally. "I wouldn't be able to tolerate that conniving voice of his addressing the men of this town. I'm afraid I would scream!"

"I'm not gonna be there, that's for sure!" added Pa. "I'd be afraid I'd clobber him, and then Simon'd have to throw me in the pokey. Alkali, you want to go and hear what the snake has to say? You'd be doing us a favor."

"You bet. Maybe I'll clobber the varmint fer ye! Hee, hee, hee! I don't owe him nuthin'. He cain't do a thing to me!"

"No, you just stand there and listen. Won't be doing our cause no good for *anybody* to clobber him, as much as I'd like to!"

They went into the house and had some coffee and talked a while longer, and then went back to the mine where Pa worked for another couple of hours.

That evening was pretty quiet. It felt as if a cloud had blown over the house and stopped, a big black thundercloud. I think Pa and Almeda were afraid that whatever Royce did in the morning would send a dozen or more men running to them for help with their loans, and then the cat would be out of the bag that they didn't have enough money to help them all. They didn't actually have any money at all! Once they were forced to admit that fact, like Pa said, the jig was up. Royce would then have everyone over a barrel and could do whatever he liked.

The next morning we all tried to keep busy around the house, but it was no use. We were on pins and needles waiting for some news from town. I think Pa was halfway afraid that he'd suddenly see ten or twenty men riding up, all clamoring for help with their loans, and when he had to level with them and say there was no way they could back them all up, that they'd turn on him and lynch him from the nearest tree!

The morning dragged on. Two or three times I could tell from Pa's fidgeting that he was thinking of riding into town himself to see what was up. But he stuck with his resolve, and attempted to busy himself in the barn or around the outside of the house.

The first indication we had that word was on the way wasn't the sight of dust approaching or the sound of galloping hoofbeats rounding the bend. Instead it was the high-pitched voice of Mr. Jones shouting at his mule as he whipped it along. Long before he came into view, his voice echoed his coming.

"Git up, ye dad-blamed ornery varmint!" he yelled. "Ye're nuthin' but a good-fer-nuthin' heap o' worn-out bones! If ye don't git movin' any faster, I'm gonna drive ye up the peak o' Bald Mountain an' leave ye there fer the bears an' wolves—ye dad-burned cuss! Why, I shoulda left ye in that drift o' snow last winter! Ye're slower than a rattlesnake in a freeze!"

By the time he rounded the bend and came in sight, Pa was already running toward him, and the rest of us were waiting outside the house for news.

Seeing Pa and the rest of us, Alkali's jabbering changed and his face brightened immediately.

"Ya done it!" he shouted out. "Ya done it, ye wily rogue!"

"Done what?" said Pa. "Who's done what?"

"*You* done it!" repeated Mr. Jones. "Ya made the rascal blink, that's what! Hee, hee, hee!"

"Alkali, I don't have a notion what you're babbling on about!"

"He backed down, I tell ye! Your bluff worked!"

"What did he say, Mr. Jones?" said Almeda, "Are you telling us he *didn't* call all the mens' notes due like we feared?"

"He didn't do nuthin' o' the sort, ma'am. Why, he plumb was trippin' over his own tongue tryin' to be nice, 'cause he ain't used enough to it."

"What did he say, Alkali? Come on—out with it!" said Pa.

"Well, the varmint got up on top of a table so everybody could hear him. There was likely thirty, forty men gathered around, all of 'em that owes the rascal money. An' they was all worried an' frettin', and your name came up amongst 'em afore Royce even got started, and they was sayin' as how they'd have to be over t' see you next.

"But then Royce climbed up there, all full of smiles, and said he'd been thinkin' a heap 'bout the town an' its people and about his obligation as the banker an' the future mayor. An' he said he had come t' the realization that ye gotta have friends ye can trust when times get rough—"

"He stole that from you, Pa," I interrupted.

Pa just nodded, and Mr. Jones kept going.

"An' he said that as Miracle Springs' banker, he was proud of bein' a man folks could trust. An' then came the part that jist surprised the socks clean off everybody listenin'. He said that he'd been thinkin' an' was realizin' maybe he'd been a mite too hard on folks hearabouts. An' so he said he was gonna do some re-figurin' of his bank's finances and had decided fer the time bein' t' call no more loans due. An' he wanted t' git folks together 'cause he knew there'd been some worry around town and he wanted t' put folks' minds at ease.

"An' then blamed if he didn't hold up a piece a paper, an' he said that it was the call notice on Rolf Douglas's note. An' he said he'd reconsidered it too, an' then all of a sudden he ripped that paper in half right afore our eyes! An' then he said he wanted them all to remember that he was their friend, an' a man they could trust."

"That was all?" asked Pa, stunned by the incredible news.

"The men was jist standin' there with their mouths hangin' open, an' no one knew whether t' clap fer him or what t' do, they was all so shocked. An' then he said he hoped they'd remember him on election day. But if ye ask me, gatherin' from the gist of what I heard as the men was leavin', I figure the only person they's gonna be rememberin' next Tuesday is this here missus of yours, Drum, now that they don't figure they need to be afeared of Royce!"

He stopped and looked around at all our silent amazed faces.

"Hee, hee, hee!" he cackled. "Ye all look like a parcel of blamed ghosts! Don't ye hear what I'm tellin' ye? Mrs. Hollister, ma'am, I think you jist about got this here election in the dad-burned bag!"

Pa finally broke out in a big grin, then shook Alkali Jones' hand, and threw his arm around Almeda.

"Well, maybe we have done it after all, Mrs. Hollister!" he exclaimed. "I just don't believe it."

But Almeda wasn't smiling. One glance over in my direction told me this latest news was like a knife piercing her heart. Knowing that suddenly she had a chance after all was going to make what she had to do all the more difficult.

CHAPTER 22

TWO OPPOSITE MOODS

All the rest of that Friday Almeda was quiet and kept to herself, while everyone else was happy. Around the house Pa was all smiles, laughing and joking. I'd hardly ever seen him like that! To know they had gone up against a skunk like Royce and won was more than he'd expected. We still didn't know what effect it would have on the trouble he was trying to cause about *our* claim. But at least the men with overdue loan payments appeared out of danger.

Uncle Nick and Katie came down to the house, and the minute they walked in, Pa took Katie's hand, even in her condition, and did a little jig, and then said to her and Uncle Nick, "The two of you watch how you talk around here from now on—this is the home of the soon-to-be mayor of Miracle Springs!" And that set off the celebrating all over again!

Even more than being glad about Royce's backing down about the loans, Pa was jovial because he figured Almeda was a cinch to win the election on Tuesday! Pa was so excited he could hardly stand it. They were going to beat Royce in two ways!

Despite Royce's last-minute ploy with his speech, tearing up Mr. Douglas's call notice and trying to convince folks he was their friend, the word around town was that most of the men were going to go with the person their gut had told them all along they could trust. The words *Mayor Hollister* went down a lot smoother than *Mayor Royce*.

Uncle Nick was in town a couple of hours after the banker's speech, and when he came back he confirmed exactly what Mr. Jones had said. People were relieved at what Royce had done. But a lot of them said they hadn't been that worried anyway because they knew Drum would help them out. And now more than ever they knew who they were going to vote for, and it wasn't the man with all the money in the fine suit of clothes from New York.

"Everybody's sayin' the same thing, Drum," said Uncle Nick, "and what Alkali said is right—she's just about got the election in the bag!"

When Almeda and I went into the office for a couple of hours, people on the street shouted out greetings. Mr. Ashton was all smiles, and when we saw Marcus Weber a bit later, his white teeth just about filled his dark face in the hugest grin I'd ever seen him wear. The two men did everything but address her as Mrs. Mayor.

Poor Mr. Royce! He had tried being mean, and now he was trying to be nice. But neither tactic made people like him nor trust him.

Almeda was silent, unsmiling, even moody. Pa, and I think most other folks, just figured she wasn't feeling well on account of the baby.

But I knew that wasn't it. I knew what she was thinking— she was going to withdraw from the election! After all that had gone on, she had victory in her grasp . . . and now she was going to have to let go of it and hand the election to a man she despised.

It took her the rest of the day to get up the nerve to talk to Pa, because she knew how disappointed he would be. Finally, after supper, she asked him if he'd go outside with her for a walk. He was still smiling when they left. But when they came back an hour or so later, his face was as downcast as hers had been all day, and Almeda's eyes were red from crying. I knew I'd been right. She'd told him, and the election was off.

The instant they walked in the door, a gloomy silence came over the five of us kids. All the rest of them knew something was up, just from Pa's face, although neither Pa nor Almeda said anything about what they were thinking.

Before long we got ourselves ready and off to bed, leaving Pa and Almeda sitting in front of the fire. The last thing I remembered before falling asleep was the soft sounds of their voices in the other room. I couldn't tell if they were talking to each other or praying.

Probably both.

CHAPTER 23

THE COMMITTEE GETS
TOGETHER AGAIN

On Saturday, three days before the election, when I got up
Pa was already gone. Almeda was still in bed. Pa finally returned a little before noon. His first words were to Almeda,
who was up and about but who hadn't said much to any of the
rest of us yet that morning.

"You still want to tell everyone all at once?" he asked her.

"I think it's the best way, don't you?"

"Yeah, I reckon. They gotta know sometime, and it's probably easiest that way."

Then Pa turned to the rest of us. "Listen, kids—we're
going to have another meeting of our election committee. So
you all be here right after lunch. Don't go running off if you
want to hear what your mother and I have been discussing, you
hear? Plans have changed some, and we're gonna tell you all
about it."

He spoke again to Almeda. "I already told Nick and Katie
to come down. What do you think—anyone else we ought to
tell personally, so they don't just hear from Widow Robinson
and the rest of the town gossips?"

"Maybe it would be good to tell some of our friends," suggested Almeda, "now that you mention it. I'd like Elmer and
Marcus to hear it from us."

"And Pat," said Pa. "And maybe the minister—"

"And Harriet," added Almeda.

116

They both thought another minute.

"Guess that's about it, huh?" said Pa. Almeda nodded.

"Zack, son," said Pa, "You want to ride over to the Shaws' and ask Pat if he could come over around half past one?"

"Sure, Pa."

"Come to think of it," Pa added, "ask him if he's seen Alkali today. Alkali's gotta be here too."

"He was by Uncle Nick's earlier," said Zack. "I heard him say he was going into town."

"Well, we'll round him up somewhere. Between him and his mule, it shouldn't be too hard to find him."

"Corrie, would you ride into town and deliver the same message to Mr. Ashton and Mr. Weber?" said Almeda.

"Can I go see Miss Stansberry?" asked Emily. "I'll tell her."

"Sure, said Pa. "What about Rev. Rutledge? Who wants to ride over—"

"I'll ask him to come too," said Emily. "He'll be at Miss Stansberry's—he's always with her."

"You noticed, eh?" said Pa with a smile.

"Everyone knows about them, Pa," said Becky. "They're *always* together!"

"Okay, all of you get going with your messages. Tell everyone we'll meet here at half past one."

Two hours later, we were all back, and the house was full of the election committee and our closest friends—sixteen in all, probably the most people we'd ever had in the house at one time.

"We're obliged to you all for coming," Pa began. "What we've got to tell you isn't exactly the best news we could have. But we talked and prayed the whole thing through and this is the way we figure things have to be. You all are family, and the best friends we've got, and we want you to hear how things stand from our own lips instead of just hearing it around town.

"Now in a minute Almeda's got some things she wants you to know about how she's been thinking. When she first unburdened all this to me, I didn't see what the problem was with her being mayor. But I gotta tell you, we done some praying on this dilemma last night, and I went out myself for a couple hours this morning and was asking the Lord some mighty hard questions. And I'm coming to see that maybe what she's doing is the right thing after all.

"You see, we've been thinking mighty hard about this here marriage of ours, and we've been asking God to show us how things are supposed to work between a man and a woman who say they want to live together and try to be one like the Book says they're supposed to be. Almeda figures maybe she hasn't been deferring to me like she ought to have been. At first when she said it, I didn't see how that should prevent her from running for mayor. But I have to respect what she thinks is the right thing to do. And then something began to speak inside me too. I have to hope it was God's voice, just the same as I have to think it's him that's speaking to Almeda's heart.

"I began to see that maybe I had some changing to do too. Maybe I haven't been quite the leader of this marriage that I'm supposed to be. I mean, I don't have any complaint with what Almeda does or wants to do. And I don't want her asking my permission to do things. She's a grown woman, and she's a heap sight more experienced than I am about trying to live the way a Christian should and listening for how to obey what God wants us to do. When it comes to that sort of thing, why she's the one who ought to be leading me! If she comes and says, 'I don't know what to do about such-and-such, and you're my husband and I want to do what you think is best,' I'm more'n likely to answer her, 'You're a grown woman, and I trust you, so do what you think's best.' In other words, I don't figure she needs me telling her what do all the time.

"Yet I can see that maybe I need to take more responsibility in the way of thinking of myself as head of this family and this marriage. I'm not really sure what that will mean because all this is mighty new to both of us. But I reckon that if you don't start someplace, you're likely never to get the thing done. So we're aiming to start here and now, even though it means having to turn back from something we worked so hard get. If we got started with this election on the wrong foot, then it's not gonna do nobody any good to keep pushing forward. The only way to make things come out right in the end is go back and start over, even if it means having to let go of something in the process."

He stopped and let out a big sigh. The whole house was silent as Pa looked around the room. His eyes fell on Almeda last of all. "Well," he said, "I reckon I had *my* say . . . now it's your turn."

"Drummond has really put his finger on what has been bothering me for the last week," Almeda began. "This whole election thing, as he said, got off on the wrong foot. I am coming to see that perhaps I'm a more independent woman than I realized—more independent than I should be. I have been in the habit of doing and thinking for myself, of making up my *own* mind about things, of running my *own* life and never really asking how what I do affects anybody else. And I see that in certain ways I have been headstrong when things stand in my way.

"I suppose it all boils down to the simple question: Is this the way for a woman, a wife, to behave in a marriage? I can't say as I even have the answer. As Drummond told you, neither does he. I don't intend to suddenly start asking him about everything I do. And I know the last thing he would ever do is to start lording it over me like a king. He is the most tender, most thoughtful man I have ever known.

"Yet somehow, we need to make some changes about my being less independent, and maybe him being a little more forceful. Neither of us understands very much about what we're trying to explain, because it's new to both of us."

Almeda then went on to tell how she had made the decision to run for mayor on her own. She shared some of what she and I had talked about, how she realized she had brought her independent streak into the marriage with Pa. And now, she said, she felt that the only way to make right what she had done was to go back and undo it, and then start anew.

"Drummond explained how I feel," she said. "I should have paid more attention to his initial hesitations, but I was determined it was the right thing. You can't make something come out right in the end if you got started with it in the wrong way. You have to go back and start over. The foundation has to be built right, or else everything that comes along and gets put on top of it will be shaky. It's like the old parable of building a house on either rock or sand. And I fear my running for mayor of Miracle Springs was a decision built on sand. Nothing I can do now will change that, or change the sand into rock. I don't know anything to do but go back and rethink the original decision in a new light."

She stopped, drew in a deep breath, and then went on with the hardest part of what she had to say.

"This new light cast on my decision to run for mayor, shows me that it was an ill-advised decision—one made independently, maybe even with some pride mixed in, a determination not necessarily to do what was right or what God wanted, but rather to do something that pleased my ego—that is, prevent Franklin Royce from becoming mayor. I never stopped to ask whether running for mayor was right for my husband, for this wonderful family of mine—"

Her hand swept around the room as she spoke, and she glanced around at all of us.

"I just said to myself, 'I can do this. I *will* do it!' And so I did. I made the decision without consulting a soul. Of course I prayed about it. But even my prayers were so full of self that God's voice could only speak to me through a heart that was still thinking independently.

"Well, the long and the short of it, as I'm sure all of you have guessed, is that we feel we must go back and undo that original decision I made.

"Now, no doubt you will all find yourselves full of reasons to try to convince us to reconsider. I know Franklin Royce is a dangerous man to let become mayor. I know every possible thing you could say to try to convince me to remain in the race. I've said them to myself. At first Drummond would not hear of my withdrawing, and he gave me every reason he could think of too. But as we talked and prayed, and as time settled our thoughts, we both became convinced that this is the right and proper course of action. Neither of us can give you every reason why—but we feel it is the right thing to do. So please, don't try to change our minds, unless you truly feel we've missed something God might have wanted to say to us.

"So," she concluded, in a quiet tone full of resolve, "I have decided—that is, *we* have decided . . . together, both of us— that it is best for the name Almeda Hollister to be withdrawn from consideration in the election for mayor of Miracle Springs. Since it is obviously too late for my name to be taken off the ballot, I would like to make a public announcement tomorrow at church, if that would meet with your approval, Avery, and simply tell people that I am no longer a candidate. If despite this, people still check my name on the ballot on Tuesday, I will not accept the position. In any case, Franklin Royce will become the next mayor of Miracle Springs."

CHAPTER 24

WHAT AN IDEA!

The room was silent.

Pa and Almeda both felt relieved, I think. I could tell a burden had been lifted from Almeda's shoulders. The peace on her face was visible. And since I had been expecting it, the shock wasn't as great for me.

But for everybody else, the news was awful!

I knew every single person wanted to start shouting out reasons to make them reconsider. But because Almeda had said not to, no one spoke.

The silence went on and on for a minute or two. Finally Rev. Rutledge broke it.

"Does this represent your decision too, Drummond?" he asked. "Is this what you want?"

"I reckon," Pa answered. "At first I didn't like it any better than the rest of you. And she's right—I spent an hour trying to convince her that I *did* want her to be mayor. But then after a while I saw what she'd been driving at. And so I reckon I do agree that maybe a woman—at least a wife, who's carrying my baby!—ought not be mayor. I'm not saying that *no* woman should do something like that. But we got ourselves a family here, and it's gonna be an even bigger family in a few months. We got our hands full without her trying to manage a town's business besides. So yeah, Reverend, I'm in agreement with this decision, even though I can't abide the thought of Royce being mayor any more than the rest of you can."

The silence fell again, and Rev. Rutledge seemed satisfied. A long time passed before anyone said anything.

"Well, I reckon there ain't but one solution t' this here fix," cackled Mr. Jones at length.

Pa looked over at him with a blank expression. I know he was expecting one of his old friend's wisecracks.

"And what's that, Alkali?" he asked.

"Fer you t' take the lady's place. Hee, hee, hee!"

As his high-pitched laughter died down, silence again filled the house. We could all *feel* an unexpected energy of hope rising out of the disappointment of only seconds earlier.

Faces gradually started glancing around the room at each other. Eyes grew wider and wider.

Mr. Jones' words were like a stick of dynamite exploding right in the middle of the room! For the first few seconds everyone wondered if they'd heard him right.

Then light began to dawn on face after face!

Uncle Nick was the first to say what everyone else had felt instantly. "If that ain't the dad-blamedest best idea I've ever heard!" he exclaimed, jumping out of his seat. He walked over to Pa and stuck out his hand.

Dazed, Pa shook it, still hardly believing what he'd heard. The moment he took Uncle Nick's hand, everyone in the room began letting out cheers and shouts of approval. The next instant we were all out of our seats and crowding around Pa, who still sat bewildered.

"Drummond," said Rev. Rutledge somberly, "I think Mr. Jones has hit upon an absolutely wonderful idea."

"The perfect answer!" chimed in Katie and Miss Stansberry almost in unison.

"Will you do it, Drummond?" asked the minister. "We're all behind you one hundred percent."

Almost in a stupor in the midst of the sudden excitement, Pa still didn't seem to grasp what all the fuss was about.

"Do what?" he said.

"Take Almeda's place, you old goat!" said Uncle Nick. "Just like Alkali said."

Still Pa's face looked confounded. The idea was just too unbelievable for him to fathom.

Finally Almeda turned from where she was sitting beside him. She took one of his hands in hers and looked him full in the face with a broad smile. "Drummond, what these friends of yours are saying is that they want *you* to run for mayor . . . *yourself!*"

"*Me* . . . run for mayor?" he exclaimed in disbelief. "The notion's crazier than Alkali shaving his beard and taking a bath!"

"No crazier than me being hitched and having a family, Drum," rejoined Uncle Nick.

"This here's Californeee, don't ya know! Things is done a mite looney out here. Hee, hee, hee!"

"Times are changing. You might as well change with them," added Mr. Shaw.

"But I'm no politician," objected Pa. "I don't know anything about that kind of stuff."

"Nobody else does either, Drummond," said Almeda, growing in enthusiasm over the idea herself. "I'm no politician either, and Franklin is only running so that he can gain more power for himself and his bank. Surely you don't want *him* to be elected?"

Her words sobered Pa and quieted everybody down.

For the first time the look on Pa's face indicated that he was giving serious thought to the reality of the possibility—as outlandish as the whole thing still seemed to him.

"My name's not even on the ballot," he said at length.

"If enough people voted for me and I should happen to win," suggested Almeda, "I could then step down and appoint you mayor."

"Is that legal?" asked Miss Stansberry.

"Royce would probably challenge it and call for a new election," said Katie. "Something similar happened in Virginia a few years back."

"And then once that happened, he'd think we'd deceived him and would no doubt start in again with his shenanigans and financial pressure on everyone," said Almeda, thinking aloud.

"There's got to be some way to get Drum elected mayor," said Mr. Shaw, "even if the election's only three days off."

The room got quiet for a minute. When Almeda spoke next, her voice was soft and earnest. It was almost as if the two of them were alone, continuing a conversation they'd been having in private.

"Drummond," she said, "it seems to me that this could be exactly what the Lord has had in mind all along. Perhaps this is the reason things have worked out as they have, and why he unsettled my heart about my being out in public view trying to make something of myself. Maybe all along God wanted me, and perhaps the whole community, to be looking to my husband for leadership. I see God's hand in the way events have unfolded. And I can't think of a better way for me to defer to you, and for you to move up a step in taking hold of the firm hand God might want you to exert, than for me to step aside so that you can take the lead in this election."

She paused, and her eyes were filling with tears of love as she went on. "I can't tell you how pleased it would make me," she said softly. "It would make me feel as though these past two months had not been in vain, that maybe God was even able to use my independence to accomplish his purposes. But of course," she added, "it has to be your decision, and I will understand and stand by you whatever you think is best."

She stopped, and now all eyes rested on Pa as he considered everything that had been said. A long time—probably two or three minutes—passed before he said a word.

"Well, you're all mighty convincing," he said finally. "And I have to say it's flattering that you'd think I could even do the thing—that is, if I had a chance in the first place."

He paused and took a breath.

"But it occurs to me," he went on, "that one of the first things a mayor probably has to do is make decisions of one kind or another. And it occurs to me, too, that if I'm gonna start taking more of a lead in this marriage partnership Almeda

and I are trying to figure out, then I have to get more practiced
in finding out what the Almighty wants me do, instead of just
taking things as they come, or figuring that Almeda's supposed
to handle most of the spiritual side of things, while I just go
on without paying much attention.

"All that is my way of saying that I guess I *do* have to make
the decision myself. I appreciate all your thoughts and advice.
And I'd appreciate all of you praying for me, because I'm gonna
need it. But first I have to get alone and ask God what decision
he wants me to make, and then hope that he'll put the thoughts
into my heart and head plain enough that I can figure out what
he's saying."

He let out a deep sigh, then hitched himself to his feet.

"So that's what I'm going to do before I say anything else,
and before you all try to do any more convincing."

He went to the door, opened it, and walked outside.

Gradually those of us left in the house started talking a little.
Katie had to entertain little Erich, and Becky and Tad had had
enough sitting for one stretch and had to get themselves moving
again. Almeda went into her and Pa's bedroom and closed the
door, to pray for Pa and the decision he was wrestling with.

About twenty minutes later Mr. Shaw was about to leave,
and Rev. Rutledge was helping Miss Stansberry with her coat,
when the door opened and Pa walked in.

From the look on his face, every one of us knew instantly
that he'd made his decision.

Almeda had heard him return and emerged from the bedroom just as he spoke. "It'd be a shame to waste all those good
'Hollister For Mayor' signs and flyers," he said with a big grin.
"So if it's not gonna be one Hollister, it might as well be the
other! Move over, Royce—I'm in it now too!"

"Now the varmint'll find himself in a *real* scrape!" cackled
Alkali Jones. "Hee, hee, hee!"

More hollering and hand-shaking went around the room,
while Mr. Shaw and the others took off their coats again. Over
to one side of the room I could see the person more involved
in this turn of events than anyone but Pa, and she wasn't yelling
or whooping it up.

Almeda closed her eyes briefly and softly whispered the words, "Thank you!" Then she opened them, and walked forward with a smile to join her husband in the midst of the commotion.

CHAPTER 25

DEVISING A STRATEGY

"Well, I suppose you'll still be wanting to make an announcement at church tomorrow," said Rev. Rutledge at length. "Although it looks like it will be quite different than what you first had in mind, Almeda!" he added with a big smile.

"I don't know, Reverend," replied Pa hesitantly. "I don't know if it strikes me as quite right to use your pulpit to further my own plans. Seems like it might have been okay to make a public announcement like Almeda was fixing to do. But without Royce having the same advantage, it hardly seems like it'd be fair for me to do it."

All this time Pa had been so angry at Mr. Royce for everything he'd done, and now all of a sudden he was worrying about being fair—even to him. It didn't take long for him to start thinking like a politician—and a good one at that, not like the kind who are always trying to twist things for their own advantage. Maybe Pa was gonna be cut out for this kind of thing after all!

"Aw, come on, Drum," said Alkali Jones. "How considerate has that snake been t' you an' yer missus here?"

"All's fair in love and war—and politics—that's what they say, Drum," added Mr. Shaw.

"Now let's have no more of this, the rest of you," said Almeda. "My husband has made his first decision as a candidate for mayor, and I think we should support him to the fullest in it. And besides that, I think he's absolutely right. Ethically speaking, it would give him an unfair advantage to speak in church.''

"Not to mention mixing religion and politics," added Miss Stansberry.

"Even if there weren't anything wrong with it," Pa said, "Royce'd squawk and complain of an unfair advantage and might get so angry he'd start causing who knows what kind of mischief all over again. Just because I have to be fair to the man doesn't mean I trust him any more than I ever did—which isn't much. No, there's not gonna be no speaking out about this change of plans in church. If I'm going to win this election, I'll do it fair and square, so that Royce hasn't got a straw of complaint to stand on.''

The room got quiet and people sat back down again. Only Pa remained on his feet, slowly pacing about, as if he had to keep moving while he was trying to think. But when he spoke, since he was standing and all the rest of us were sitting, it was almost like a speech, although I knew speechmaking never crossed Pa's mind. I couldn't help being intrigued by the changes I saw coming over him already! He was taking command of the situation, just as Almeda had said she had hoped he would.

"And that brings us straight back to the question I asked a little while ago," Pa went on, "which seems to be the crux of the whole matter. My name isn't even on the ballot. I don't see how I *can* run against Royce for mayor, even if I want to. There just isn't enough time.''

Silence fell again. He was right. Time was short. What could be done? The ballot obviously couldn't be changed.

"What about a write-in vote?" suggested Katie after a long pause.

"What's that?" asked Pa.

"A write-in vote. People write in someone's name who isn't officially running. You hear about it all the time in the east—although nobody ever wins that way because they just get a few votes.''

"That's it! That's the perfect way!" exclaimed Almeda excitedly. "What do you think, Drummond?" she asked, turning toward Pa. "We'll get word out that everyone who was going to vote for me should write in your name on the ballot instead."

"That's a lot of folks to get word to," replied Pa, "because I still don't want an announcement made in church."

"We could do it, Pa," said Zack, getting into the spirit of it. "Look how many of us there are right here. We'll just go out and tell everybody!"

"He's right—we could!" said Almeda. "With eight or ten of us, each calling on five or six families, telling them to let it be known—why, the whole community would know in no time."

"What are we waitin' for?" cried Uncle Nick. "Let's get the horses saddled and the buggies hitched and be off!"

"Hold your horses!" said Pa loudly. "I figure if all this is going on because of me, I ought have some say in it too!"

Everybody quieted down and waited. Pa thought for a moment. He was still standing up and slowly walking back and forth.

"All right," he said finally, "like I said a bit ago, I'm in this thing, so maybe Zack's got himself a good idea. If you're all of a mind to help, then you've got my permission to tell anybody you want—"

A fresh round of whooping and cheering went around the room. Even Rev. Rutledge dropped his normal reserve and got into the act with some noise.

"Wait a second . . . hold on!" shouted Pa. "Don't you go chasing off before the wagon's hitched! I was about to say you could tell anybody you want . . . *but* ye gotta keep word of this quiet—just one person to the next. I don't want this being talked about on the streets of Miracle Springs. I don't want Royce getting wind of it. You just tell people to spread the word around quietly and not to make a big ruckus about it, but just to walk into that schoolhouse on Tuesday and do what they feel they oughta do. The less Royce knows the better. I don't want to give him any more fuel to try anything else that's gonna hurt somebody. After the election's done, he can come and see me if he's got a complaint."

"That sounds easy enough," said Uncle Nick. "Now can we git going, Drum?"

"Nobody goes anywhere till after church tomorrow," answered Pa. "I don't want it talked about, you hear? Tomorrow afternoon, once folks are back home, then we'll see what can be done. But we're all going to go to church as usual, and we're not going to say anything. You all promise?"

Everyone nodded, although Uncle Nick and Alkali Jones didn't like the idea much. I think they would have liked to go and shout the news in the middle of the Gold Nugget so the whole town would know everything in five minutes!

Rev. Rutledge rose from his chair and walked over to Pa. "May I be the first to offer you my congratulations, Drummond?" he said, extending his hand. "I think you have chosen a reasonable and a wise course of action, and I want to wish you the best."

"Well, I reckon we'll see what'll come of it in a few days!" replied Pa, shaking his hand. The two men looked at each other for a couple seconds as their eyes met. I can't say it was a look of love so much as a look of mutual respect, and even friendship. They had sure come a long way together.

We went to church the next day, like Pa had said, but we all sat there with half-smiles on our faces, as if we all knew a secret we were keeping from the rest of the town.

Which, of course, we did!

But we didn't keep it from them for long. That afternoon, everyone who had been at our place the day before—everyone except Pa, that is. He didn't feel he ought to go to people and ask them to vote for him—rode on horseback or by buggy all throughout the community to pay short visits to everyone we could. Almeda and Miss Stansberry and Rev. Rutledge had planned out where we would all go. Even Tad and Becky had their calls to make.

The visits continued on Monday, although Almeda and I went into the office and tried to conduct a normal day's work in spite of the distraction of knowing the election was the next day. Smiles and nods and whispered words of hope and encouragement as the day progressed told that the word of Pa's write-in candidacy had spread through the town as quickly and successfully as anyone could have imagined.

Late in the day, Franklin Royce paid another call. He came into the office, asked for Almeda, then extended his hand and shook hers in one last election formality.

"Well, Almeda," he said, "by tomorrow evening this will all be over. So may the best man win, as it were."

Almeda smiled, thinking to herself—as was I—that he could not possibly have realized the significance of his own words. He obviously knew nothing about Pa, or Almeda's decision to remove herself from the race.

We all went to bed tingling with anticipation and excitement . . . and a little fear besides!

The next morning, the fateful day of November 4, 1856, we all got up and rode into town in the wagon with Pa, so he could cast his vote.

CHAPTER 26

ELECTION RESULTS

The voting stopped at six o'clock that night.

The government man from Sacramento, Rev. Rutledge, and a few people they'd gotten to help locked the door right then and started to count the ballots. They figured to be done and announce the results by eight-thirty or nine o'clock.

By eight a pretty big crowd was beginning to gather around the schoolhouse. Lots of people had come back to town, whole families in wagons, carrying lanterns and torches. At eight-fifteen, Mr. Royce drove up in his fancy black buggy. We were all bundled up warm in the back of our wagon. People came over now and then to speak briefly to Pa and Almeda, but mostly we just waited nervously. We tried to figure out how many voters there were. Pa and Almeda thought there would be somewhere between three and five hundred men who lived in and close enough to Miracle to vote for its mayor. There were probably another hundred or two hundred men who lived farther away who would have come to town to vote in the presidential election.

At about eight-forty the door to the schoolhouse opened. Some men came out, and everybody who was waiting came and clustered around the stairs to hear the news. The government man held a paper in one hand and a lantern in the other.

"I have some results to report to you," he said, and silence fell immediately over the crowd. "First of all, in the election you're most interested in, that for mayor of Miracle Springs, we have tallied the unofficial vote as follows. These will have to be re-confirmed, but this is the first count. For Mrs. Almeda Parrish Hollister, the first name on the ballot, there were 67 votes cast."

A small ripple of applause scattered about. Already I could see a smile starting to spread across Mr. Royce's face where he stood not too far away.

"For the final name to appear on the ballot, Mr. Franklin Royce, we have a total of 149 votes."

Again there was some applause, though it was not as loud as Royce had expected. His smile grew wide. The turnout was not very high, but he was willing to take the victory any way it came. He began making his way through the crowd and toward the steps where he was apparently planning to address the people of Miracle Springs with a short victory speech. He had just taken the first two steps when he was stopped by the sound of the man at the top of the landing again.

"And in what is a most unusual and unexpected occurrence, we have a third unregistered candidate. . . ."

Everybody could almost feel the chill sweep through Mr. Royce's body. The smile began to fade from his lips.

"This candidate has received a sizeable number of write-in votes. In fact, by our unofficial tabulation, a certain Mr. Drummond Hollister, with 243 write-in votes, would appear to be the winner. . . ."

Before these last words were out of his mouth, a huge cheer went up from the crowd gathered there in the darkness. Instantly scores of people clamored around Pa and Almeda, shouting and shaking hands and clapping and whooping and hollering. In the middle of it, suddenly Mr. Royce appeared. His smile was gone, and even in the darkness I could see the rage in his eyes.

"I don't know what kind of trick this is, Hollister," he said. "But believe me, you won't get away with it!"

Without waiting for a reply, he spun around and walked back to his buggy. No one took any notice as he turned his horse and cracked his whip and flew back toward town. Nothing ever came of this last threat. There was not a thing he could do. Pa had won the election fair and square!

CHAPTER 27

LOOKING PAST THE ELECTION

After the headlong rush of events for the four or five months leading up to the election, the months of November and December of that year seemed like a sudden calm. Like a river tumbling over rocks and through white, foamy rapids, our lives suddenly opened out into a calm pool.

Everyone, myself included, felt like just sitting back and breathing out a sigh of relief. It was good to know there were no more stories I had to write immediately, no more dangers facing anyone, no more elections, no more trips, no more handbills to pass out. The next morning I lay in bed for a long time, just enjoying the quiet. I didn't want to get up, I didn't want to write, I didn't want to think about anything!

The whole town seemed to feel that way. People seemed relaxed, but they were talking plenty about the election results! The men spent a lot of time hanging around the street in front of the Mine and Freight, although we hardly had a customer for three days. They weren't interested in seeing any of *us*, or in doing business. They were waiting to catch sight of their new mayor!

When Pa rode into town that Wednesday afternoon, I knew by the look on his face that he had no idea what was waiting for him. He was such a down-to-earth and humble man that he still didn't realize that he was suddenly a local hero. He had hardly gotten past the first buildings of Miracle Springs when word began to spread, faster than the time it took him to ride the rest of the way in. By the time he got off his horse and was tying the reins to the rail in front of the store, fifty men and women had gathered around him—shouting, cheering, throwing out questions—with kids running through the streets like miniature town-criers, telling everybody that the new mayor was in town!

Pa just looked sheepishly at everybody, confused and not sure what all the fuss was about. After a minute or so they all quieted down, as if they were waiting for Pa to make a speech or something. But when he finally spoke, all he said was, "Tarnation, what are you all raising a ruckus about? I just came to fetch my wife, and I can't even get through the door!"

———————

Almeda wasn't due until April or May, but Katie, who was due earlier, was starting to show a lot. And once the election was over, the anticipation of two new babies on their way into the Hollister-Belle-Parrish clan started to take more of everybody's attention. I could see both Pa and Uncle Nick treating Katie and Almeda with more tenderness, pampering them more than usual. Katie still could be reserved and distant, and every once in a while she would say or do something that made me wonder whether she liked Almeda at all. Sometimes I saw a look on Uncle Nick's face as if he might be thinking, "What's going on inside this lady I married?" Nick tried to be gentle with her, helping her across the bridge with his hand, or fixing her some soup when she didn't feel well. Sometimes she'd be appreciative and smiling, but at other times she seemed to resent it, and would snap, "Let me alone. I can take care of myself!" Uncle Nick would stomp around muttering, or go off for a ride or a walk alone in the woods if Katie got after him. It was obvious he didn't know what to do. Being a husband was still pretty new to him. But Almeda never seemed to take it personally or be hurt by it. Once she said to me quietly after Katie and Uncle Nick had left and we were alone for a minute, "I know what she's going through, Corrie, and I know how hard it is."

"What is it?" I asked. "You mean with the baby and feeling sick and all?"

She smiled. "Oh, that upsets our system a bit," she answered, "but there's more to it than that. The Lord is at work in your Aunt Katie's heart, Corrie, and she doesn't like it. We must continue to pray. Her time is coming."

That was all she ever said. But ever after that, when I'd look into Almeda's face when Uncle Nick and Katie were around, or when we'd go up to visit them or to help Katie, I saw an even more tender look in Almeda's eyes. Maybe she was praying at those times too. After what she'd said to me, I noticed Almeda paying all the more attention to Katie, looking for every opportunity possible to help her or do something for her. I wondered if she would say something to Katie about God as she had with me several years before. But as far as I know, nothing was ever said.

In the meantime, more visitors began to show up around our place, men coming to ask Pa's advice about things. They came both to the claim and to the office in town. Sometimes it was about a little thing that didn't have anything to do with Pa, but maybe they figured that since he was mayor and was a man they could trust, he was the one to ask. And once he realized this was going on, something in Pa's bearing began to change. There seemed to be a confidence growing inside him. Around town, people would greet him with, "Hey, Drum!" and he'd wave and answer back. Gradually he seemed to get used to the attention folks paid him and quit minding it so much, as if he realized it was his duty now to be something more to them than he had been before.

CHAPTER 28

DIRTY POLITICS

It took some time before we found out the results of the national election. We knew the following week that Mr. Fremont had lost his home state of California, but it was weeks before we found out that he had lost the rest of the country too. James Buchanan had been elected the 15th President of the United States.

By that time I was sure my story had never run in the *Alta*. I was disappointed for the Fremonts, and I didn't know what to think about my story. I was sure it would have helped counteract all the rumors and lies being told about Mr. Fremont during the campaign. And Mr. Kemble had seemed to want the information so badly. I couldn't imagine what had happened. I wrote to Mr. Kemble to find out, but it was well toward the end of November before I got a reply from him.

Dear Miss Hollister,

I understand your concern over your Fremont article, especially after the hard work and dangers you undertook on the Alta's *behalf. It was a fine bit of legwork you did, and now that I have been able to extract more of the full scope of what happened from your colleague, Mr. O'Flaridy, I realize just what a powerful article it was and how fortunate I am indeed to count you as one of my reporters. I commend you once again for a fine piece of journalism!*

Unfortunately, as it turned out, I was unable to run the story in the Alta *prior to the election. Apparently your man Gregory got back to the* Globe *and immediately began trying to cover his* tracks with accusations against you and our paper. I received a not-so-friendly visit from the editor of the Globe, and he told me that if we tried to run a pro-Fremont piece there was sure to be trouble, for the paper as well as for you. I told him I didn't believe a word of it and that I fully intended to stand by my reporter and run the story. The world needed to hear, I said, that what was being said about John Fremont was nothing but a pack of lies. He left in a huff and I made plans to print your story just as you gave it to me.

However, the next day my publisher ordered me to kill the story. "What?" I said. "They didn't get to you, did they?" He didn't say anything except to repeat his order. "Listen," I told him, "the country's got to know the rumors and charges against Fremont are unfounded. It could turn the election!"

"It doesn't matter now," he said. "You just kill that story. John Fremont will have to take care of himself without any help from us. If we run that story they could ruin us—both you and me and the paper, do you understand, Kemble? And they could hurt your young reporter friend too. We have no choice. They've made that clear, and I don't intend to see how far they're prepared to back it up."

"Goldwin?" I asked.

"Goldwin . . . and others," he answered. Then he left the room.

So I'm sorry, Miss Hollister, but he left me no choice. My publisher's a strong man, and a major influence in this city. I don't know how they got to him, but whatever they were holding over his head, it must have been powerful. I've never seen him so beaten down and defeated. But it was for your good as well as the paper's that we didn't run it, as much as it galled me to see the Globe get away with printing Derrick Gregory's phony interviews. I truly believe your story could have influenced the election, if it had run in time to be picked up by the Ohio and Pennsylvania papers. But sadly, we will never know.

Perhaps John Fremont will be able to make another run at the White House in 1860, and we can try to help his cause again. In the meantime, I hope you will be working on some articles for me. You have shown a flair for politics as well as human interest. I would be happy to see you pursue more along that line in the future.

O' Flaridy sends his regards. I remain
Yours Sincerely,
Edward Kemble, Editor
San Francisco Alta

I almost expected my reaction to be one of anger. Most of Mr. Kemble's letters aroused all kinds of hidden emotions in me and put me through all kinds of ups and downs and doubts and questions. But this time I just put down the letter with a deep sense of sadness and regret. It almost confirmed everything Derrick Gregory had told me about politics being a dirty business where everything depended on money and what people wanted out of you rather than truth. Was that really what political reporting boiled down to? If so, then I for one didn't want to have any more to do with it. However flattering Mr. Kemble's words might have been, I would stick to human interest from now on. And as for Robin O'Flaridy's regards—those I could do without!

During the next several days I alternated between being upset, then depressed and disillusioned all over again. I had spent so much time and had invested such effort in that story, not to mention risking my life! And for what? The bad guys had won anyway. The powerful senator had used his influence to get his way and to keep the truth from being printed. A slave supporter would be in the White House for another four years. And all I *thought* I had accomplished seemed wasted. It really made me stop and question why I wanted to be a newspaper writer in the first place.

But then I got to thinking about the *other* election I had been part of. Who could deny that good *had* come through in the Miracle Springs mayor's race? It wasn't that I had much to do with the outcome—I probably hadn't at all. But the truth did come out in the end. The most truthful person, Pa, had won the election. And so in this case at least, politics wasn't a dirty business at all. The good guy had defeated the underhanded banker!

I never did come to much of a conclusion about myself and whether I would do any more writing about politics. But I finally realized that politics itself wasn't necessarily a bad thing. If you're going to run a country or a state or a town you've got to have elections and officials and Presidents. And I was glad that Pa was mayor now rather than Franklin Royce. Maybe what was needed was for good men like him to be in politics, not men like Mr. Royce and Senator Goldwin. I just hoped Mr. Buchanan would be a good man too, and a good President, and that some day someone would get elected who would free the slaves like Mr. Fremont had wanted to do.

I wrote to Ankelita Carter about returning Rayo Rojo to Mariposa. I had wanted to do so before the election but there hadn't been time. I told her about the article being scuttled and how sorry I was for the way the election had turned out. When I heard back from her, shortly before Christmas, she was furious. She said she was sure the election would have turned out different, especially in California, if people had known what she told me. She'd written to the Fremonts before the election and told them about what I was trying to do. She hadn't heard back from them since news of the loss, but she knew what Jessie and Mr. Fremont must be going through, and she said she intended to write them that very day with news of what had happened with the *Alta* story. There was nothing Mr. Fremont could do about it now, but he ought to know what Senator Goldwin had been able to do, even in far off California. She wanted to see me again, whenever it might be possible, and if I wanted to do *another* article on the Fremonts, she would be more than happy to oblige. There was no hurry about getting Rayo Rojo back, but when I was able to come, I should plan to spend at least two or three days with her.

She wrote as if I were her friend, and it set the wheels of my mind in motion again. Why couldn't I do an article on Mr. Fremont about the lies that had been told? It might not win him the election now, but at least it would vindicate his reputation and might help him in the future.

Time would tell. In the meantime, I wanted to think of some less controversial subjects to write about.

CHAPTER 29

PREPARATIONS FOR THE HOLIDAYS

Our Christmases always seemed to be times of exciting announcements, high-running emotions, family, friends, guests, food, and the unexpected. The Christmas of 1856 was no exception.

We had been looking forward to Christmas all the month of December. Almeda had such a way of making the holiday a happy time, and of course my sisters and I couldn't have enjoyed anything better than being part of all the preparations. We made decorations out of ribbons and popped corn, colored paper, and greenery cut from the woods, bells and dried berries.

And what Christmas celebration would be complete without a feast, and people to share that feast with? So along with everything else, we were thinking of who to invite to our place for the day. Pa and Almeda always included all five of us kids in most of the talking and discussion that had to do with our family. Sometimes they'd talk alone, walking together, or whispering in low tones in their room late at night, but they included us in everything they could. It really made us all feel that we were a *whole* family. And both of them would include *me* in even a more personal way in their decisions too. To say I had a *friendship* with my own Pa sounds a little funny, but in a way, that's what it was. He *was* my friend! And so was Almeda—friend and mother and an older sister all rolled up into one.

142

And so we talked and planned the Christmas as a family. Of course we intended to invite our friends like Alkali Jones and Rev. Rutledge and the Stansberrys, and of course Uncle Nick and Katie and little Erich. Zack said he'd like to invite Little Wolf and his father, and after a brief glance at Almeda, Pa looked back at Zack and replied, "I think that's a mighty good idea, son. You go right ahead and ask them if they'd join us for the day!"

Pa fell silent for a few moments. I hadn't noticed the look that had come over his face, but when he next spoke I could see in his eyes that he'd gone through an intense struggle just in those brief moments. The tone in his voice spoke much more than the words that came out of his mouth.

"You know, Almeda," he said quietly, "there is someone else we might pray about asking to join us."

"Who's that, Drummond?"

Pa paused again, and when he answered her, though his voice was soft, the words went like an explosion through the room.

"Franklin Royce," he said.

Becky and Zack immediately let out groans, but Almeda's eyes were fixed on Pa with a look of disbelief and happiness at the same time.

"You're right," she said after a moment. "He is a lonely man, with probably no place to go on Christmas."

"It just seems like the right thing to do," Pa added. "I'm not all that anxious to strike up a friendship with him after what he's done. But we have to put the past behind us, and I believe it's got to start with us. One thing's for sure—he's not going to be inviting us to his place anytime soon!"

Almeda laughed. "I think it's a wonderful idea, Drummond!"

The rest of that week before Christmas we did lots of baking—wild huckleberry pies, an *olia podrida* (a stew with a lot of meats and vegetables mixed together), and honeyed ham. Then Christmas morning we baked biscuits, potatoes, carrots, yams, and two pumpkin pies.

There was also a lot of sewing and stitching and trying-on to be done too, everyone pretending they didn't know what it was all for. Almeda made Pa close his eyes to try on the new vest she was making him, telling him to pay no attention to anything that was going on. I did the same for a shirt I was making for Zack. We kept poor Mr. Bosely so busy that week—buying extra bits of linen or cotton fabric, lace, buttons, and thread.

It was so funny to watch Pa going about Christmas business of his own, and with Zack and Tad. Men have such a hard time knowing how to do and make things, especially for wives and sisters and daughters. Most of the preparations at holiday time came from the women. But Pa entered into the spirit of it, and kept his little secrets too, and would sometimes shoot a wink at one of the boys about the things that *they* were planning that none of us knew about. I could tell it made Almeda love him all the more to watch him try to do his part to make it special.

CHAPTER 30

A CHRISTMAS DAY TO REMEMBER!

Christmas morning everyone was up at the crack of dawn.

It was one of those crisp, sunny winter days that made me love California so much. And as the day wore on, though it would never get hot, I knew it would warm up enough to draw the fragrances up out of the earth and from the trees and out of the grasses and pinecones and dew. Days like that always made me want to go find a quiet place in the sun where I could just sit down and lean my back up against a tree trunk and read a book or draw or just think.

While Pa stoked up the fire with a new supply of wood and Almeda put the ham in the oven to bake, Tad scurried around making sure the rest of us were up and ready. Then he was off across the creek to fetch Uncle Nick and Aunt Katie to make sure they got down to our place the minute they were dressed. He didn't want to have to wait one second longer than he had to before Pa turned him loose in the pile of packages and presents next to our Christmas tree.

If the giving of gifts at Christmas is an expression of a family's love, then there couldn't have been a greater outpouring than there was that year. Pa gave Zack a beautiful new hand-tooled saddle with a matching whip. If Zack could have carried the saddle around with him all day, he would have. He *did* carry the whip, feeling its tightly wound leather handle, smelling it, examining every inch with his fingers and fine eye. He was truly a horseman, and nothing could have pleased him more.

Almeda gave me a beautifully-bound copy of *The Pilgrim's Progress*, and a new journal. Like Zack, I carried around my two new books most of the day, just looking at them and feeling them.

She and I had made dresses for Emily and Becky. We three girls, with Katie's help, had nearly completed a new quilt for Pa and Almeda's bed, with a big "H" in the middle of it. But we had to give it to them not quite finished, saying we'd get the stitching done later.

There was a new doll for Becky, scarves for all three of us girls, a harmonica for Tad, Pa's new leather vest, and other smaller things—candies, fruits, nuts—as well as what we gave Uncle Nick and Aunt Katie.

Two of the most memorable gifts of the day were given to the two mothers. Almeda had bought a small New Testament. She had been praying a lot for Katie, and trying to find ways to talk to her about her life with the Lord. And so I knew how deeply from the heart the gift of the small book was. But when Katie opened it and saw what was inside the package, she was very quiet for a moment. "Thank you," she finally said, her words stiff and forced. When I glanced over at Almeda, I saw clearly the disappointment on her face from Katie's lack of enthusiasm.

Pa had made Almeda a nice wood shelf for the wall in her kitchen. It had three levels, with a decorative top-piece he'd carved out with a design. Almeda raved excitedly about what fine workmanship it was and all the things she would put in it. But then Pa pulled out one last wrapped package, one he'd kept hidden somewhere.

"Well, you've gotta keep a place on one of the shelves for this," he said as he handed it to her. "This is what gave me the idea of making the shelf in the first place, so you'd have somewhere to put it so you could see it."

She took it from him and opened it. Out came a beautifully painted little china replica of a two-story house, like I'd seen drawn in books and magazines of city buildings in the east.

"I ordered it from one of Bosely's catalogs," Pa said, and I could tell he was excited. "It's called 'Boston Home.' The minute I saw it, I wanted you to have it."

Almeda fought back tears. "Thank you, Drummond," she said finally in a soft voice. "It is beautiful."

"And look there behind," said Pa, taking it from her hand and turning it around, "here's a place for a candle, so it lights up and looks like there's lights in the windows. I hope you like it," he added. "I thought it would remind you of your home back East."

She looked up at Pa, then reached forward and kissed him.

"Whenever I look at it," she said, "it will remind me of how grateful I am to be here with *you* in California!"

Then she stood up and left the house for a few minutes. There *were* tears in her eyes by now. The room was silent for a short spell, then Pa tried to liven things up again.

"Play us a tune on your new mouth organ, Tad, my boy!" he said.

That was all the invitation Tad needed! He started blowing furiously with puckered lips, which was enough to send the rest of us scattering. Pretty soon we were all occupied with looking over our new things, and I didn't even notice when Almeda came back in. I happened to glance up from my book about ten minutes later and there she and Pa were over against one wall trying to find the best place for Pa to nail up her new shelves.

The rest of the morning we spent cooking—Almeda checking on the ham from time to time, the rest of us cutting up vegetables and peeling potatoes. Becky and I mixed up the biscuit dough. Katie and Uncle Nick went back to their place for the morning, until all the others came for dinner in the afternoon.

Alkali Jones was the first to arrive, and as always he kept things pretty lively the rest of the day. Then Rev. Rutledge and Harriet and Hermon Stansberry came, all together, Hermon riding his horse behind the carriage. When the minister helped

Miss Stansberry down, I'd never seen him so gentle with anyone. Of course with her crippled leg, she needed assistance getting in and out of carriages and climbing steps. But he took hold of her arm so firmly, yet with such a kind look in his eye, I could tell she felt really safe. It was easy to see that he cared a great deal for her.

About half an hour later Little Wolf rode up with Mr. Lame Pony, each of them on beautiful horses. Little Wolf always seemed to be riding a different animal, always spirited but well behaved, always groomed and shining. It was obvious the Indian father and son took great pride in their animals, and loved them as if they were part of their family.

Pa and Lame Pony shook hands, and Pa made every effort to make him feel welcome and at home with us. After tying up his horse, Little Wolf walked over to see me and Zack. We chatted a while, then he said, "This is a hard thing for my father. But the more he knows your father, the more he will trust him."

"Look," I said, "it won't take long." I pointed to Pa, already leading Lame Pony toward the stables to show him our horses. Pa had his arm slung around the Indian's shoulder and was talking good-naturedly. I knew he would win Lame Pony over and make him a friend in no time. Pa was like that with people nowadays.

When Katie and Uncle Nick came back down from their place not too long after that, however, I wondered if the spirit of Christmas was going to be spoiled. Little Wolf had been around enough that Katie had gotten used to him, although she never spoke to him or was very friendly. But now when Pa introduced her to Little Wolf's father, she was noticeably hostile.

"Nick, you know our neighbor from over the ridge," said Pa as he and Lame Pony walked toward them as they approached from the bridge over the creek.

"Best horses in California," replied Uncle Nick, giving him a shake of his hand. "Nice to see you here, Jack."

"Katie," Pa went on, turning to her, "this is Jack Lame

Pony, Little Wolf's father. Jack, this is—''

Lame Pony nodded his head in acknowledgment toward Katie as Pa spoke, but before Pa could complete the introduction, Katie turned toward Uncle Nick and abruptly said, loud enough for everyone to hear, "What's *he* doing here?"

"He's our friend and neighbor, that's what," answered Uncle Nick hastily, obviously embarrassed by her rude comment, and a little riled at her at the same time.

"Well, neither of them are *my* friends," shot back Katie, and then marched off toward the house, leaving the three men standing there, Pa and Uncle Nick mortified at her behavior. And poor Lame Pony! What was *he* supposed to think after such an outburst?

But Pa didn't wait for the dust to settle around Katie's words. He said something about wanting to show Lame Pony something at the mine, and then I heard Uncle Nick trying to apologize for Katie, and adding something about women doing funny things when they're carrying young'uns. By dinnertime everything seemed to be smoothed over, although Katie was pretty sullen all day.

None of the rest of us could understand why she was so prejudiced against Indians, especially with what a good friend Little Wolf had been to our whole family. But we had learned to accept that Katie didn't think like the rest of us. She'd never been very friendly toward Rev. Rutledge either, as much as she knew he meant to the rest of us all. And although she was usually pretty tolerant, every once in a while she'd make some comment that let everyone know how ridiculous she thought trying to live like a Christian was.

"Going to church is one thing," she said once. "And though I don't have much use for it myself, I don't mind folks going themselves. But all this talking about God in between times, and praying, and trying to act religious about everything else you do—that's just taking it too far. Church is one thing, but you've got to live life without trying to bring God into every little thing. I've got no use for that kind of thinking. It's just not natural."

Almeda had been praying for her and hoping to find opportunities to share with her how she felt. I didn't know what Uncle Nick thought of it all. He never said much.

Mr. Royce was the last one to arrive, all alone in his expensive black buggy. Pa and Almeda greeted him as if he were an old family friend, and the look on his face made it clear he didn't know *what* to make of it. What he thought of getting the invitation in the first place I don't know, but being greeted and welcomed as a friend was altogether too much! Maybe he was so used to folks being suspicious of him that courtesy and friendliness made him uncomfortable. He was pretty reserved the whole day, yet entered into the spirit of the occasion as much as he was able to.

Once everybody had arrived, we went inside the house. The whole place was filled with delicious smells! The table was set as fancy as we had been able to make it, but Pa asked everyone to sit around in the big room where the chairs were rather than at the table.

"Almeda says the ham still has about half an hour," he said, "so that's why I arranged the chairs out here. There's some things I want us to talk about before we get down to the business of the dinner."

Everyone took a seat and it got quiet. Pa stood up in front and everybody waited for him to continue.

"Ever since me and the kids got together four years back," Pa began when everyone was situated, "we've kept up the tradition of reading the Christmas story together, kind of in memory of our Aggie, the kids' ma, and in memory of what this day's supposed to be all about."

Pa turned behind him and took down Ma's white Bible and flipped through the pages.

"This is our fifth Christmas together in California," he went on. "And, Avery, with all respect to you being our preacher, I think I'm going to keep this privilege all to myself today."

"Wonderful, Drummond!" said Rev. Rutledge with a smile. "It is a great blessing for me to be able to listen to you."

"So I'd like to invite all the rest of you to listen, though I guess I'm mostly reading this to the five of you kids. And you be sure to remember your Ma when I read, 'cause she got us going with this tradition, and I don't doubt for a minute that it's on account of her prayers that we're all together like this, doing our best to walk with the Lord like she did."

He drew in a sigh. I looked at Almeda out of the corner of my eye as he spoke. The radiant smile on her face was full of such love! I knew there was no confusion in her mind—or in any one else's—over the love Pa had for both her *and* Ma, and the special place both the women God had given him held in different corners of his heart.

"*And it came to pass in those days,*" began Pa with the familiar words out of Luke, "*That there went out a decree from Ceasar Augustus, that all the world should be taxed. And this taxing was first made when Cyrenius was governor of Syria. And all went to be taxed, every one into his own city. And Joseph also went up from Galilee, out of the city of Nazareth, into Judaea, unto the city of David, which is called Bethlehem; (because he was of the house and lineage of David:) To be taxed with Mary his espoused wife, being great with child. And so it was, that, while they were there, the days were accomplished that she should be delivered. And she brought forth her firstborn son, and wrapped him in swaddling clothes, and laid him in a manger; because there was no room for them in the inn. And there were in the same country shepherds abiding in the field, keeping watch over their flock by night. And, lo, an angel of the Lord came upon them . . .*"

As he read the story, Pa's voice filled the room. Everyone sat quiet, not just listening, but *absorbing* his words. It was a different voice than the one who had read the Christmas story four years earlier, just after we had arrived in California. This was the voice of a man of confidence, afraid of nothing—not even afraid to stand up and talk to other people about his God and the birth of His Son. Just listening to him read—well, it was no wonder that the people around here had come to respect and admire him. Now it was *Pa* reading from the Scriptures, and Rev. Rutledge sitting and listening with a smile on his face, as if he was proud of Pa and what he was becoming. Pa's voice seemed to have a *power* in it, even though he was reading softly.

As we sat there listening, I looked at the faces around me. What did Mr. Lame Pony and Little Wolf think of our Christmas religious practices? Franklin Royce's eyes were fixed on Pa as if he was trying to make sense of this man who was extending forgiveness toward someone who had done his best to destroy him. I saw something in that lonely banker's face, and a little spark of love for the man stirred in my heart.

Alkali Jones sat there more still than I'd ever seen him. He was staring down at the floor, so deep in thought he looked like he was a thousand miles and forty years away. I wondered what memories he was re-living as Pa read. Had *his* mother read him this passage as a child? What *was* going through that old mind? And Katie—she sat there, still looking solemn. I couldn't read a thing in her eyes. But I knew she was thinking.

Pa's voice pervaded the room, and the very sound was weaving a mood upon us. I don't think I've ever been so aware of what it might be like for God to be speaking through a man as I was that day. I felt as if God himself was telling us the story of Jesus' birth, and using Pa's voice to do it. It was hard to imagine that Katie had a hard time believing, or that Mr. Royce had ever been Pa and Almeda's enemy, or that there could possibly be enmity between Indians and white people. There was such a good feeling in the room, a sense of oneness. The story of Jesus' birth was so alive that we were all sitting on the edge of our seats to hear how it would all turn out.

". . . *And when eight days were accomplished for the circumcising of the child, his name was called JESUS, which was so named of the angel before he was conceived in the womb.*"

Pa stopped, and the room remained silent. Pa closed the Bible, and then after a short pause started talking again.

"I don't aim to start infringing on our good Reverend's territory. That'd be just a different kind of claim jumping, wouldn't you say, Avery? But it strikes me that a few more words might be in order on a day like this. Since this is my house and you all are our guests, then I reckon nobody'll mind if I take the liberty of delivering them myself."

A few people chuckled, and everybody relaxed in their seats. "You go right ahead, Drummond," said Rev. Rutledge. "I'm sure these good folks are sick of my preaching and will welcome the change!"

"Well, I thank you," replied Pa, "but I ain't gonna preach, and I don't aim to keep them as long as *you* do on Sundays!"

More laughter followed.

"I guess I just figured this was a good time for me to say a thing or two about what Christmas means to me," said Pa. "And what my family means. Somehow you need to say these kinds of things to other people once in a while for it to get all the way down to where it's supposed to go. So I'm going to tell you who're here with us today."

He paused, took a breath, then continued.

"Christmas is a time for giving and good food and friends," Pa said. "And for the youngsters there's always some toys and gifts and candy. So now and then we can get our eyes off what's the *true* meaning of this day. On this day God's Son, the little baby Jesus, was born. We need to remember that, because without his coming to the earth when he did, and living his life and then giving it up for us, there wouldn't be any life for the rest of us.

"But then I've been thinking, there really *is* something special about families at Christmas. So I just want to say how thankful I am that God gave me this family of mine—every one of these kids that Aggie gave me, God bless her. And for Almeda and the one that she's bearing right now, and for Nick and Katie and their family. I just feel about as full and blessed as any man ought to have a right to feel. And I'm thankful for the rest of you too, because you're what you might call a part of our bigger family.

"So, God bless you all—thank you for sharing Christmas with us. Let's not forget that Jesus was born on this day a long time ago. And let's never forget that good friends and family are what makes this world a pretty special place."

Pa stopped and sat down. In earlier years he might have shown a little embarrassment at making a speech like that. But not this time.

"Amen to every word, Drummond!" said Rev. Rutledge. "We are blessed to be part of your family, and that you are part of all of us too."

Pa nodded while a few other comments filtered around.

"And now, might I be permitted a word or two also?" the minister added, glancing first at Pa and then at Almeda.

"Of course, Avery," said Almeda.

"This won't take long," said Rev. Rutledge, standing up and then clearing his throat. He sent a glance and smile in Miss Stansberry's direction.

"I have a little announcement to make," he went on, "and I—that is, we—thought it would be nice to wait and tell you all about it all at once. And what more fitting time and place than here on Christmas day?"

He took in a big gulp of air, then plunged ahead. "And what I've got to tell you is this: Harriet and I are engaged to be married. . . ."

I think he was going to say something more, but before he could get another word out of his mouth, Almeda was on her feet nearly shrieking with delight.

"Oh, that's wonderful!" she exclaimed, hurrying over to Miss Stansberry and taking both her hands in a tight clasp.

In the meantime Pa and Uncle Nick had joined the minister and were shaking his hand and slapping him on the shoulder. In another minute everyone else was on their feet joining the hubbub and well-wishing.

"Couldn't keep from stealing the show, eh, Reverend?" laughed Uncle Nick.

Rev. Rutledge knew he was being kidded only because of how happy everyone was for him, and joined in another loud round of laughter with the men. His boisterous laugh could even be heard above Alkali Jones' *hee, hee, hee*! The fact that Pa and Uncle Nick and Avery Rutledge were laughing and joking and talking together like they were showed how much things had changed in those four years since our first Christmas together. Who could have foreseen it all?

I glanced over at Almeda. She'd been talking with Miss

Stansberry, but then looked over across the room at the men. For once she wasn't looking at Pa, but at Rev. Rutledge. She had tears in her eyes. She had cared for him, in a different way from Pa. And I knew his happiness meant a lot to her.

But she only watched the celebrating men a moment, then clapped her hands a few times and raised her voice above the din.

"Enough everyone!" she cried. "You can do the rest of your visiting and carrying on at the table. It's time to eat, and the food's hot! Come now, find your places!"

CHAPTER 31

THE FEAST

What a group that was!

Pa stood up by his chair at the head of the table and raised his hands to quiet everyone down for the prayer.

"Before you take your seats," said Pa, "let's all bow our heads and give thanks to God."

Everyone calmed down. A quiet settled over the room.

"God, we thank you for this day," said Pa solemnly. "Help us all never to forget what it means. And help us every day of the year to remember how much you loved us, and the whole world, to give us your Son. And thank you for family and friends, and the good food and fellowship you give us together. Amen."

"Okay, everyone," said Almeda, walking toward the stove while everyone got into their seats, "we've got ham and sweet potatoes, biscuits, stew, vegetables, and a special treat that Lame Pony and Little Wolf fixed for us—what did you call them, Jack?"

"*Pozoles*," answered Little Wolf's father. "That is Mexican word. Little Wolf and me, we just say pig's feet."

"So all of you try one of Jack's *pozoles*," added Almeda—handing two large pewter platters, one to Pa, one to Mr. Royce—"while we start this food around the table. But save room for the pies!"

It didn't take long for everyone's plate to be piled high, and within five minutes the sounds of eating and conversation and laughter echoed around the table. There was a harmony in it, almost like music. I sat with Becky on one side and Little Wolf on the other, trying to listen to Mr. Jones on the other side of Becky and Rev. Rutledge a little further away. I was especially curious about what Pa and the banker were talking about. So the whole meal for me was a mixed-together jumble of half-conversations, laugher that I didn't know the cause of, words, smiles, and always passing food and exhortations from Almeda to eat up on the one hand but to save place for dessert on the other.

Alkali Jones was in good form, as always, and must have told two or three of his famous "totally" unbelievable stories. But as interesting as they always were, on this day I found myself most eager to hear what was going on across the table, and I strained to listen whenever I could.

"Glad you could be with us today, Franklin," Almeda had said.

"I must say your invitation came as a surprise."

"Why's that?" said Pa. But when the banker turned toward him to answer, I couldn't hear what he said.

". . . put it in the past," I heard Pa say next. "Learn to live like neighbors and brothers. . . ."

"What my husband is talking about, Franklin, is forgiveness," put in Almeda. "Don't you think it's time to let bygones be bygones?"

Mr. Royce said something, but I couldn't hear it. He didn't seem altogether comfortable with the direction of the conversation. It was as if he didn't know how to react to it being so personal.

"That's exactly what I was trying to say," added Pa. "I figure if I'm gonna be mayor, even though you wanted to be when this whole thing started, then I've got to be your mayor too. And that means doing the best I can for you just like everyone else. And so we figured the best place to start was to invite you to our home and shake your hand like a friend and neighbor, and say, 'Merry Christmas, let's put the past behind us.' "

". . . kind of you—kind of you both," Mr. Royce said, "certainly more hospitality than anyone else in this town has ever shown me."

"We want to be your friend, Franklin," said Almeda, and although I was too far away to see into her eyes, I knew from her tone what kind of look was on her face.

"Even though I tried to put you out of business and have opened a store to compete against you? A Christmas meal may be one thing, but do you seriously think I can believe you want to be my friend?"

"Believe what you want, Royce," answered Pa, and now it was quieting down a bit around the table as more of us were listening to this most interesting conversation. "Whether you can understand it or not, we're supposed to be your neighbor and to try to do good to you and to love you. That's what the Lord God tells his folks to do, and it don't matter what they do back to you in return. So Almeda and I've been praying for you, and we want to do good for you however we can. I don't reckon I've been too neighborly to you in the past, and I hope you will find it in your heart to forgive me for that. In the mean time, I aim to change. I aim to forgive you for what you've done, to keep praying for you, and to do my best for you however I can."

He stopped, and the table was silent for just a moment. Mr. Royce just shook his head and muttered something at the same time as Alkali Jones let out with a cackle, "Hee, hee, hee! If that don't beat all! Mayor and preacher all rolled up into one!"

Then Tad asked for another biscuit and Almeda started passing food again, and pretty soon the conversation was once more at a loud pitch, although I never heard any more serious goings-on between Pa and Mr. Royce.

The only person who didn't enter much into the lively talk was Katie. She hardly said a word, and didn't seem to be enjoying the Christmas celebration at all. She was either feeling mighty poorly, or else had something brewing in her mind.

When the meal was done, the men went outside to light pipes and talk about horses and weather and whatever else men talk about. We girls and Miss Stansberry and Almeda got busy cleaning everything up, talking and chatting away, mostly about Rev. Rutledge's and Miss Stansberry's surprise news, and when they were planning the wedding and what kind of dress she would wear. Katie still didn't participate much. Claiming to be tired, she left and went back up to their place.

An hour or so later, when we had the place looking tidy again, the men came back in and we cut into the huckleberry and pumpkin pies. Uncle Nick had a piece of pie, then took little Erich and went to check on Katie.

By this time even Jack Lame Pony seemed to be feeling real comfortable and he and Pa and Rev. Rutledge were talking freely. Hermon was asking lots of questions about the horse-breaking work they did and was even planning to go up to their place in a day or two to look for a new horse. Zack and Little Wolf and Tad were off shooting their guns. Franklin Royce was even entering in a little to the conversation, though I still don't think I'd seen him smile the whole day. But at least the scowl that I'd always associated with him was gone from his face, and every once in a while I'd hear him say something to one of the other men. He seemed a little out of his element, however, with the others talking about such man-things as working and mining and shooting and horse-taming, and him there with his suit and white hands that hardly looked like they'd seen a day of work. But you almost had to admire him for entering in as much as he did.

Mr. Royce was the first to leave, late in the afternoon, but the others stayed a while longer, drinking coffee and nibbling now and then at the ham or one of the pies.

Around dusk, Uncle Nick and Katie and little Erich came back down the path, holding a lantern. The most memorable part of that Christmas was about to begin.

CHAPTER 32

KATIE'S OUTBURST

Katie was still quiet and sober. Everyone greeted her kindly, but she didn't say much. Uncle Nick looked a little nervous, and would glance at her now and then, although he entered into the spirit of the evening with everyone. I wondered if they had an argument, because they didn't say much to each other.

Everyone but Mr. Royce was still there. The day cooled off quickly. Pa stoked up the fire, and we sat around the hearth talking and chatting. I don't think I'd ever seen Rev. Rutledge so jovial and in such high spirits. Even he and Alkali Jones laughed together more than once about something one or the other said. Mr. Lame Pony was a little more reserved when Katie got back, and every once in a while I'd catch a glimpse of him glancing over at her, probably wondering what she thought. But he stuck around, visiting with the men, and I was glad of that. I hoped he and Pa might become friends!

As the evening progressed, the talk got more subdued and quiet, even serious at times. How different Pa was! He talked with Rev. Rutledge about spiritual things on equal footing, not as a miner talking to a preacher.

"What do you think, Avery," Pa was saying, "about how God lets folks know what he wants them to do?"

"Do you mean how he speaks, how he guides in our lives?"

"Yeah. How can you tell if God's telling you something or if it's just your own thoughts? Like me being mayor. I figure something ought to be different about my mayoring if I say I'm

160

trying to follow God in what I do. It ought to be different than me just following my own nose like most folks do, and like I spent most of my life doing."

"That's exactly what being a Christian is, Drummond, bringing God into all you do."

"It's easier for you, because religion's your business, ain't it, Reverend?" piped in Uncle Nick.

"Just the opposite, Nick," replied Rev. Rutledge, turning toward him. "Maybe you're right in one way," he added slowly. "It is easier for me to *talk* about things of God because people expect it of me. But it's no easier for me to have God's attitudes inside than anyone else. And, you know, I sometimes think being a preacher is a handicap."

"How's that?"

"Because my very presence gets it into people's minds that there is a difference between religious and non-religious people. Like I said, they expect me to be religious. After all, I'm a preacher, I get paid to talk about God. I can never go into any situation, any discussion, any group of people and just be myself—Avery Rutledge, a man with feelings and thoughts like everyone else."

The others were silent for a minute. Even the quiet showed that what Rev. Rutledge said was true, and that they *hadn't* thought of him as anything but a preacher. I knew that was true about me. The only ones among us who had really seen him as a *person* beneath the minister were probably Almeda and Miss Stansberry.

"I reckon you're right, Avery," said Pa after a minute. "That is how folks see you, and that's me too. I reckon maybe I owe you an apology."

"Think nothing of it, Drum," laughed Rev. Rutledge. "I wasn't looking for sympathy, only telling you how it is with me."

"Still, I aim to take your words to heart. So if I ever forget and start talking to you like you're only a preacher, and you need me to be a friend just as one man to another, then you stop me and say something. I want you to do that, you hear, Avery?"

"Agreed," smiled Rev. Rutledge, and I could tell Pa's words meant more to him that he was letting on.

"That goes for me too, Reverend," added Uncle Nick. "You can count on the two of us as your friends, whether it's preacher-business or not."

"I thank you too, Nick."

Alkali Jones and Mr. Lame Pony and all the rest of us were watching and listening to this exchange with a sense of wonder. Men rarely talk honestly and about their feelings with one another, and we'd never heard these three men talk like that. I knew what Almeda was feeling. I didn't even have to look at her. And I suppose something of the same mood was upon all of us. Christmas had brought a gift nobody had been looking for, the realization that these men weren't just "acquaintances" who got together for dinner, but *friends*.

"Okay then, well *I* got a question fer ye," piped in Mr. Jones, to everyone's surprise. I'd never heard a single word even hinting at religion from his mouth. Heads turned toward him. "How *do* you figure to bring God into yer mayoring, Drum? Sounds like a kinda crazy notion if ye ask me."

"I don't know, Alkali," Pa answered. "That's why I was asking the Reverend here. But there *oughta* be a way to do things different if you're trying to walk with God."

"So whatcha got in mind, Drum?" Mr. Jones asked again. Still he hadn't let out one of his cackling laughs. He seemed genuinely interested in the answer.

"I don't know. I figured maybe if there was something I had to do, or some decision to make that affected the town, I ought to pray about it, or maybe get together with some of the rest of you and Avery here, and try to find out what the Lord wants to happen. It seems like that'd be a better way to go about things than just barging ahead and doing whatever I think of to do. Nick and I did that for a lot of years, and I can't say as it always turned out so good. Maybe it's time I tried to learn a new way of going about things. The idea's just a little new to me. It'll take some getting used to. I don't know my way around too well yet with thinking like this."

"None of us do," said Almeda, speaking now for the first time. "Look at how long I've been trying to live as a Christian, and yet only a few months ago there I was out chasing my dream of being mayor without ever stopping to ask what God or my husband might have to say in the matter."

"It is easy to hitch our own horse to the wagon instead of letting God be the horse and us being the wagon."

"That's a good one, Reverend," laughed Mr. Jones. "Hee, hee, hee!"

"You could put that in your next sermon, Avery," added Pa.

Now it was Zack's turn to get into the discussion. "I'm not sure I see what you mean about the horses and wagon, Rev. Rutledge," he said. The serious expression on his face showed he was really trying to grasp the deeper meaning.

"I was only saying that sometimes we've got to stop and take a look at who's doing the leading and who's doing the following," replied the minister.

The puzzled look on Zack's face didn't disappear.

"Come on, Avery," said Pa good-naturedly. "If the boy takes after his Pa, he's likely a little thick-headed." As Pa said it he shot a wink in Zack's direction to show he meant only fun. "He's gonna need more explanation than that."

"You don't want me to preach a sermon, do you, Drum? You've got to be careful what kind of openings you give a preacher, you know."

Pa and the rest of us laughed.

"Don't try to fool us, Reverend," laughed Uncle Nick. "You'll take any chance you can get to convert us sinners! Remember that first Christmas in town at Almeda's?"

A huge roar of laughter followed. Now that they *were* friends, they all remembered that awkward discussion around the dinner table with affection for each other.

"I *did* do some preaching at you that day, didn't I!"

"I never wanted to see your face again," said Pa, still laughing.

"I figured it'd be up to me to save the new minister's life, hee, hee, hee!" said Mr. Jones. "I'd never seen ol' Drum so riled up!"

"Well, those times are all over now," said Pa, "and I for one am thankful for that. I was a plumb fool about a lot of things back then, and I don't want to remember it any more than I have to. So on with your sermon, Avery. Tell us about horses and wagons. We're all waiting."

"Are you sure? You know what I'm like on Sundays. Once you get me going, I can't stop!"

"Course we're sure. You still wondering about your question, son?"

"Yeah," answered Zack. "I'd like to know what you have to say, Rev. Rutledge."

"You listen to these men, Avery," said Almeda almost sternly. "They are all your friends, and they *want* the benefit of your experience and insights."

Rev. Rutledge took in a long breath. "All right," he said. "I suppose you asked for it. But I'll try to make it a *short* sermon."

"Agreed," said Pa. He looked at me with a quick smile and wink, as if to say, *Bet me, eh, Corrie! He'll never keep it short!*

"I've always thought the horse and wagon picture perfectly illustrated our relationship with God," Rev. Rutledge began. "It's easy to talk about what we call 'following the Lord,' but how we actually go about living through the day is much different. In practice, we try to be the horse, and we drag God along behind us as if he were the wagon. When it comes to deciding where to go and how fast to go and which forks in the road to take, *we* lead the way, just like a horse pulling a wagon.

"What God wants, of course, is that we allow him to take the lead and let *him* be the horse. He can do a better job of leading than we can. He knows how fast to go, which roads to take. Our responsibility as Christians is to follow."

"How do you follow horse you not see?" said Mr. Lame Pony, speaking up for the first time in a long while. He had been listening to everything intently.

"That is both the difficulty and challenge of life as a Christian," replied Rev. Rutledge. "It is no easy task. We have to unlearn a lot of habits because our natural inclination is to just gallop off, like Drummond said a while ago, following our *own* nose. That's the way we're made—independent. When Drummond says to himself, 'I want to find out what *God* wants me to do about this instead of what *I* might have thought to do,' he changes the whole order of his life around. He says, 'I'm going to become a wagon now, and stop being the horse.' And it takes a great deal of practice because we're not used to thinking that way. At least most adults aren't. I suppose children follow their parents when they are young. But then once they get out on their own, they take charge of their own lives. The way God really intended it, however, is for adulthood just to mean that we change horses—from letting our parents do the leading in our lives to letting God lead. It's a hard thing to do— especially because, as Jack says, we often cannot see the horse. We don't know what God might be saying to us about which path to take here or there. It takes a lot of practice, many new habits. It's a challenge that lasts a lifetime."

He fell silent and nobody spoke for a few seconds.

"Do you see what I mean, Zack?" Rev. Rutledge added. "I don't suppose I was real specific about *how* it all works. That's something God has to show every person individually, because he leads all of us on different paths and in different ways. But do you see what I mean about the principle of the horse leading the wagon?"

"Yes, sir," replied Zack.

"So in answer to my original question," said Pa, "about how God lets us know what we're to do, you're telling me that you don't exactly know what he's gonna be saying to me, but that I have to keep listening anyway so I don't accidentally get out in front of the horse, is that it?"

"Like I did before the election," added Almeda.

"I suppose that's about it," answered Rev. Rutledge with a smile. "An answer that maybe isn't an answer you can do much with until the time comes when you have to ask God for yourself what he's saying to you."

I found myself thinking back to the words of his sermon about how God speaks to us through our thoughts, and about pointing our thoughts and prayers toward God so that he could point his toward us. But before I had a chance to think too much about it, Tad's voice broke the silence.

"Who's driving the wagon?" he said.

Everyone laughed.

"That's the trouble with any illustration," said Rev. Rutledge. "There's always someplace where the parallel doesn't work. Maybe God is driving the wagon, and the horses are Jesus or the Holy Spirit. They're who we're supposed to be following, while our heavenly Father directs everything. It's difficult for it to make exact sense. But I think we all see the principle involved in trying to apply Proverbs 3:6: 'In all thy ways acknowledge him'—that's the part of letting him be the horse, the driver, the guide of our lives—'and he shall direct thy paths.' But thank you for your question, Tad. We need young fellows like you to keep us on our toes."

The whole conversation had been lively and warm. Just from the looks on their faces, I could tell everyone felt involved and felt the same thing I did, that it was all the more special this time since the men were open and talking freely with each other. Everyone except Katie, that is. She had been sitting the whole time a little ways off from the rest. I didn't want to look at her, but out of the corner of my eye I could see that she wasn't enjoying it. I couldn't tell if she was sick or angry. She'd had a sour look on her face all day. I felt bad for her not feeling well on Christmas.

Pretty soon Almeda got up and made some fresh coffee, and the conversation picked up again in other directions.

Little Erich was waddling around talking to himself. I listened more closely and heard the words, "God drive wagon . . . God make horse go." Just then Uncle Nick walked by and scooped his son up and tossed him up into the air.

"What's that you're saying, boy?" he said, catching him and burying his face in the plump little belly.

Erich just giggled.

"He was talking about God driving the wagon," I said. "He must have heard what Rev. Rutledge said."

"A little preacher in the making, that's what you've got, Nick," said Almeda with a smile as she held out a cup of coffee for him.

"That'd be a mighty hard one for my father to imagine!" laughed Nick. "Why the very thought of it—"

He never finished his sentence. Katie had had enough, and was suddenly on her feet.

"The thought of it's enough to make me completely sick!" she yelled. "You stay away from my son with any more of your talk of making him a preacher, do you hear, Almeda! And as for you," she added, spinning around and glaring at me, "you mind your own business, Corrie!"

In an instant there was silence in the whole house.

"Now wait a minute, Katie," said Uncle Nick, trying to calm her down. "They didn't mean no harm. There's no call to go yelling at—"

"You stay out of it, you big lout!" she snapped back at him. "You're the worst of the lot, talking about horses and wagons and God and the Bible like there was anything to any of it. It's all such ridiculous trash, you talking away with that minister and that Indian like you're some saint! You big hypocrite! I know you better than anyone here, and I daresay *you're* not holy!"

"Just you quiet down a minute! Just because you're not feeling so good doesn't give you the right—"

"I'm feeling fine!" Katie retorted, shouting louder now. All the rest of us were shocked silent. It was terrible to be in the middle of such an argument, especially with her having just yelled at me and Almeda, and now pouring out all her anger on Uncle Nick. "I'm not going to quiet down. I've been quiet too long! All this talk about God and religion—I hate it! I can't stand it one second more! Hypocrites, that's what you all are, and you're the biggest fool of them all, Nick, if you believe one word of all that! I'm getting out of here!"

She grabbed little Erich out of Uncle Nick's arms, and

turned around for the door before anyone could say a word.

"Katie, you just wait," said Uncle Nick, going after her. "You may be able to say what you want to me. But you ain't got no right to go shouting at Corrie and Almeda, or calling the minister or anyone else names. If you're bound and determined to go, then you owe them an apology."

"An apology! The only thing I'll apologize for is coming back down here at all. I should have stayed home! You and this family of yours are nothing but a pack of religious do-gooders, and I hate every bit of it!"

She was out the door with the final words trailing behind her. The door slammed in Uncle Nick's face with a loud crash. He opened it and went after her, leaving the rest of us in stunned silence. The only sounds in the whole room were the faint noise of the fire and the boiling water on the stove.

CHAPTER 33

A TALK ABOUT GOD'S TIMING

Almeda was still standing there holding the cup of coffee she had meant for Uncle Nick. Her face was deathly white. I suppose mine was too, after what Katie had said to both of us. But neither of us felt anger, only hurt and sadness to find out what Katie had been keeping inside all this time.

Slowly Pa got up, walked over, took the cup from Almeda's hand, and led her to a chair. "Don't think anything of it," he said. "It wasn't you she was upset at."

Almeda nodded and sat down. "I know," she said. She took in a breath and let out a long sigh. "Poor Katie," she said softly. "She's got so much turmoil inside, and so many mixed up ideas. She thinks God is her enemy, when really he's the only source of life she's ever going to find."

"Why don't you tell her that?" I suggested.

"Now?" replied Almeda, looking over at me. "Oh no, Corrie. She's in no frame of mind to hear it now—especially from me. Right now she needs some time to cool off and settle her mind down. And I'm sure she and Nick will have to work some things through after this, and he needs to be the one standing beside her."

"But she needs to know God's not at all like what she thinks."

"All in good time, Corrie," said Pa. "God can't be rushed in what he's about with people. Look at me. Sometimes it takes a good long while for him to break through the outer layers people have got up all around them. And from what I know about Katie, I reckon she's got a few for him to break."

"That doesn't sound too pleasant," I said.

Rev. Rutledge went to stand next to Pa. A look of deep concern filled his face.

"Pleasantness isn't always what the Lord is after, Corrie," he said. "His purposes are beyond what someone feels— whether they're happy or sad on a given day. He's after hearts and lives he can get inside of and possess more than he's after making a person happy."

Almeda let out a sigh. "I think we need to pray for our dear Katie," she said softly, then looked up at Pa.

He nodded, then sat down and immediately started to pray. I'd never heard Pa pray for another person like that. He seemed totally unconcerned about everybody else in the room listening. And everybody joined in silently, I could tell, even though only Pa and Almeda and Rev. Rutledge actually prayed out loud.

"Lord, we ask you to take care of Nick and Katie, and to calm Katie down so she can see how it really is with all of us."

"Oh, yes, God," Almeda went on. "And let her see how it is with our Father. Let her see that you love her, and that our lives are deeper and richer because we live them with you."

A short silence followed, then the minister prayed.

"Heavenly Father, we join together in asking for your touch to be upon Nick and Katie and their small family—right now, even as we pray. Give Nick the words to say to soothe and comfort his dear wife. And we pray that in your own way and time, you would draw Katie and open her heart to the influences of your life and love."

"Give us opportunities to show her that love, Lord," added Almeda. "Let your Spirit flow out from us to her. Help Katie to know that we do love her."

"Amen," said Rev. Rutledge.

As the room fell silent, gradually some of the others began getting ready to go. The mood of the wonderful Christmas we'd spent together was broken, and no one seemed inclined to try to be jovial any longer.

Hermon Stansberry got up and slowly put on his coat. Little Wolf and Lame Pony got up also and gathered their hats and coats.

"I suppose we ought to be heading back to town as well," said Rev. Rutledge, smiling toward Miss Stansberry. "But we will be in prayer for the situation here."

"Thank you, Avery," said Pa, shaking his hand. "And thanks for being part of our Christmas."

"*Thank you*, Drummond," rejoined Miss Stansberry.

"Oh, and we are so happy for the two of you!" added Almeda.

The minister and schoolteacher smiled. Almeda gave them each a big hug, and Pa led them to the door. In another few moments only our family was left inside, and everything was quiet. It had been a wonderful Christmas, but suddenly none of us felt very much of the Christmas spirit. Nobody said anything as we slowly gathered around the fire. Katie was weighing heavily on our hearts.

A few minutes later, Uncle Nick came back through the door.

"Well, I apologize to you all for what happened," he said with a sigh, taking off his hat and plopping down in a chair.

"Think nothing of it, Nick," said Pa. "It wasn't your fault. Just one of those things."

"I didn't make it any better by trying to shush her up. I shoulda just kept my mouth shut. But it's done now. I just wish I coulda said something to the others, though I did see the minister and Harriet outside."

"I'll go talk to Little Wolf and his father tomorrow if you'd like," said Zack.

"Would you, boy?" said Uncle Nick. "I'd be obliged to you if you did. You give them my apologies. That'd mean a lot to me."

"Sure, Uncle Nick."

Uncle Nick sighed again. He was really looking sad and downcast, more than I'd ever seen him.

"It's going to work itself right in the end, Nick," said Almeda after a bit, reaching out and laying a hand on his arm. "This is often the way God works. The storm has to come to clear the sky, and the rain falls to bring life. God is at work in your wife, Nick."

"I don't know how you can figure that, Almeda. She hates any mention of God. Didn't you hear what she said—she was sitting here stewing and fretting and getting more and more annoyed at all our talk."

"Those are only surface reactions, Nick. Down inside, God's Spirit is moving, making her think, and—I believe with all my heart—drawing her. The more people resist and argue against God, and the more they dislike hearing Christians talk about the way their lives are *with* God, the more they are actually being drawn by God. The resistance is a natural human tendency when we feel change in the wind blowing toward us."

"Hmm, I reckon I see what you mean," replied Uncle Nick slowly. "Though I can't say as I could picture Katie *ever* having anything good to say about religion. She can't stand any mention of it. I sure ain't no religious kind of guy, but I got my beliefs like anyone else, though my father'd probably be surprised to hear me say so! But alongside Katie you'd think I was a preacher. Why, just last week she got mad 'cause I tried to teach little Erich to pray before we ate. It was just a harmless little prayer, but she wouldn't have a bit of it."

"Her time will come, Nick. Everyone's time comes eventually. We all have to face God personally and decide what we're going to do with him. I don't think that time's come yet for your wife. She sounds so much like I was before I gave my life to the Lord."

"You?" said Uncle Nick, glancing over at Almeda with a surprised look on his face.

Almeda laughed. "You should have heard me back then! You wouldn't have even known me. I was pretty bitter about God myself."

"Bitter?" I said. I couldn't imagine Almeda being bitter about anything.

"I had plenty to be bitter about—in my thinking, at least.

My life hadn't been easy, and I took it out on God. So I know what Katie's going through."

"That's what I asked before," I said. "Don't you think it would help Katie if she knew that?"

"And your father's answer shows what a wise man he is, Corrie," replied Almeda with an affectionate smile. "It's all about time, Corrie—*God's* time. God wants *every* single person to know about him. But he's got to get a person ready so that he can hear the good news properly when that time does come. Some people's ears are so plugged up with wrong and distorted notions about God that even if Jesus himself were to appear to them and tell them about his Father, they *still* wouldn't hear, wouldn't be able to receive it. They would hear the words, but their minds and hearts would be so mixed up they might turn and walk away from the very Giver of Life himself."

"I know that's right," said Uncle Nick, " 'cause I was like that when I was young. Such a fool hothead I was! And now things are making more sense to me than they ever did, things I recollect my father telling me, and my Ma, things I learned in church. But I don't understand why it's gotta be that way. Is it just growing older?"

Almeda glanced in Pa's direction, seeing if he wanted to reply.

"Don't look at me, woman," he said laughing. "I'm still too new at this myself to know what to tell him. You're the philosopher here. You've been at this Christian life longer than any of the rest of us. So since Avery's on his way back to town with his wife-to-be, I reckon you're the most qualified. You just speak on!"

Almeda laughed.

"You married a long-winded woman, is that what you're trying to say, Drummond Hollister? Who, if she can't be a politician, will keep on being a woman-preacher!"

"You said it, not me!"

We all laughed, and it felt good after the tension and uneasiness following Katie's outburst.

After the laughter settled down, Almeda became serious again.

"Growing older's part of it, Nick," she said after a moment. "But not the most important part. Circumstances have a great deal to do with it. Through circumstances God gets us to a place where we're ready to listen and really *hear* his voice. You see, we hear with our hearts, not our ears. And our hearts have to be ready. It's exactly what Drummond said when you were gone with Katie. It takes a long time for God to break through the outer layers so he can get inside us. He uses the events of our lives to break down the layers of our resistance. Then, when the time is right, he comes and shows himself. If we have been listening and paying attention, and if our heart is open at that time, then we are able to receive his love, and say yes to him."

"Like you and me chasing around the country, getting into trouble, making fools of ourselves," said Pa. "Who knows but that God was using all that to get us ready for this time now when we're listening to him a mite better than back then."

"Sometimes it takes a crisis, a real moment of heartbreak, before our inner ears—our hearts I should say—are unplugged enough to hear God's voice. For you, Drummond, I suppose it was that moment when you learned your wife was dead and you were standing staring at your five children. Suddenly all you'd run away from came back upon you in an instant."

"You're right there," said Pa. He had a faraway, thoughtful gaze in his eyes. "All the layers of toughness I had tried to surround myself with all those years just started to break and crumble away in that moment."

"So that God's life could begin to come in," added Almeda. "Do you see what I mean, Nick? Circumstances. For Corrie," she went on, glancing at me with a smile, "there was her mother dying in the desert and her feeling of aloneness. Out of that pain, God was able to enter into her life in a greater way."

"What about me? There ain't been no great big thing like that for me. You saying I've still gotta face some awful thing before God's gonna be able to do anything with me?"

"Not at all. It doesn't work that way for everyone. God can also come into lives slowly, a little at a time. The more a person listens to him, the more he or she becomes open to God's influences. It's different with everyone. But *sometimes* it takes a crisis, some major change in outward circumstances, to open a person's heart to be able to listen. And judging from Katie's agitation and hostility right now toward spiritual things, I have the feeling God is speaking more and more loudly to her. I hope she will listen. I hope and pray she doesn't have to be broken by circumstances any more than she already has been. But I do have the sense that God is speaking to her and that she is trying to resist."

"Well I hope it don't take too long for him to get through," sighed Uncle Nick. "I don't know how much more I can take of her being so irritable."

"Have patience. Besides, she's carrying your child."

"I know, and I do all I can for her. But sometimes she can be the most ornery woman!"

Almeda laughed softly, then became very thoughtful. "I will talk to her, Nick. I've been praying for an opportunity. Perhaps this is it."

"I'd be mighty obliged, Almeda," said Nick.

"All in God's time. You just join me in prayer for the right opportunity."

CHAPTER 34

PRAYING FOR KATIE

We didn't see Katie or Uncle Nick much the whole week after Christmas. Katie kept to herself in their house up across the creek. No more was said by anyone about what had happened, but it was obvious she was avoiding us. From Uncle Nick's behavior it was clear he still felt mighty bad about what had happened. And from the look on his face it didn't seem that things were so well between him and Katie either. He'd walk down to our place most evenings, and although he didn't say much, his face said plenty. He loved Katie, I could tell that, but when she got in one of her moods, he didn't know how to help. Eventually it started to bother him that she wouldn't pay any attention to what he tried to say or do. And of course none of the rest of us were too anxious to get involved. Katie had made it plenty clear what she thought.

After a week and a half, one afternoon Almeda finally said, "Well, it's been long enough. I'm going up to see Katie. If she's not ready to see me yet, she ought to be. This isn't doing anybody any good."

She packed up some food, asked Becky to carry it up for her, and took a small pot of soup she'd made. The two of them headed for the bridge. We'd been sending things up with Nick, but this was the first visit any of us had paid in person. They were back about in about fifteen minutes. Almeda's face wore a smile.

"How is she?" I asked.

176

"The same," she answered. "Sullen, quiet. I didn't get a single smile and hardly two words out of her. But it's an open door, Corrie. Before long, when the time is right, I'm going to sit her down and have a long talk with her. And by then I think she'll be ready to listen."

"With the heart?" I said with a smile, recalling our conversation of the other evening.

"Yes," she smiled back in return. "Katie's heart is nearer the surface than she lets on. I saw something in her today, Corrie, for the first time since I've known her—hunger. Something in her eyes tells me she knows she isn't as self-sufficient as she wants everybody to think. She *is* being broken and made ready. I can see it! It's exciting. The Lord is tilling her soil, making her ready for the moment when he comes to her and says, 'Katie, it's time to let me in.' "

"But what about everything she said about God?" asked Becky, who was still standing beside Almeda. "She said she hates it when anybody even mentions him."

"Oh, but Becky, that's the best part of all!" replied Almeda. "The closer the Lord gets to a person's heart, sometimes the more that person resists and shouts and complains. That can take many forms, like Katie's outburst the other night. It's just a sign that God is getting ready to take hold of her heart. It's a sign that circumstances are pressing in closer and closer around her, that thoughts and ideas about God are on her mind, that she is watching and observing all the rest of us, seeing the part God plays in our lives. You see, Katie is aware of all that, aware that we are trying to live in a certain way. She says she hates it because way down deep inside she actually *wants* God living with her too. She wants him but she doesn't want him at the same time."

"How can that be?" said Emily, joining the discussion. The two boys were off with Pa at the mine, and it was special, just the three of us girls talking with Almeda.

"The human heart is a complicated thing, Emily," said Almeda with a smile. "It finds no difficulty at all in wanting and not wanting the same thing at once. That is especially true of a woman!

She chuckled, obviously thinking something to herself, then laughed outright. "If you doubt that, girls, just ask your Pa!" she said, still laughing. Gradually she got serious again, and then went on.

"It's also especially true in spiritual things, because just like love, our spiritual beings live in our hearts, not our heads. We both want God and don't want him. He created us to need him, to hunger for him. Life can never be complete unless we are living in a relationship with God. That's the only way we can be fulfilled as human beings. The *only* way. But at the same time, we've all got a stubborn streak. And that part of us wants to keep hold of our independence. We want to *think* we don't need anyone—God included. We want to think we're self-sufficient and strong.

"That's the great conflict down inside all of us—every man or woman, every boy or girl—until the time comes in our lives when we realize we need to walk *with* God, not independently from him. It's just like the minister was saying about horses and wagons. And I think Katie's time is coming, and so the independent part of her is fighting and resisting and complaining and yelling inside."

"Inside *and* outside," added Becky.

We all laughed.

"Yes, Becky," said Almeda. "But it's not any of us she's angry at. She's not really even angry at God. It's just her independence fighting to keep control, while all the time her Father in heaven is drawing her heart closer and closer to his, so that he can pour out his love to her and give her his life."

"But what if she doesn't want his life, doesn't want to be a Christian?" asked Emily.

"Then God may keep bringing circumstances to her that are harder and more painful, until one day she finally comes to the point of realizing happiness and freedom and contentment are not qualities she can have without him."

"So it's just a matter of time?" I asked.

Almeda shook her head. "Maybe. But God never forces people to accept him. Katie still has a choice—we must pray that she chooses to accept God instead of rejecting him."

We were all silent again, thinking about Almeda's words.

"Can we pray for her now?" said Becky.

"I think that's a wonderful idea."

We all bowed our heads and closed our eyes, and softly we prayed for Uncle Nick's wife. Almeda prayed for an opportunity to speak with her, the rest of us prayed that she would be open to God's voice and that we'd have chances to do things for her and show her how much we cared about her.

Praying with other people you love always makes you feel closer to them—especially when you are joining together to pray for someone else you love just as much. The rest of the day I found myself thinking about people praying together. I wondered if that was one of the reasons Jesus told us to pray in groups of two or three. In addition to the answers to the prayers, maybe praying itself brings those two or three people closer together.

Our prayers did get answered, although we sure couldn't have seen ahead of time how it was going to happen. It's a good thing Almeda told us about God sometimes using painful circumstances. That way, when the time came, at least we were a little more prepared for it.

CHAPTER 35

DEEP PAIN SURFACES

Several days later, out of the blue, Almeda said to me, "Come on, Corrie, we're going to see Katie."

She began gathering up some things in the kitchen, then to my questioning look added, "It's time, Corrie. From the moment I woke up this morning, I had the strong sense that today was the day."

"The day for what?" I asked.

"For doors to open."

The puzzled look on my face didn't go away with her answer.

"I can't even say that I'm sure myself what that means. But sometimes God puts within you a sense of purpose, a sense of urgency, a sense that it's time to *do* something, say something, take some action that will move things in his kingdom."

"Are you saying you think Katie will be open to God today?"

"I don't know. That's something I have no way of knowing. God holds the keys to our hearts, and nothing we do can open or close *those* doors without there first being nudgings and promptings and openings from his Spirit. I don't know what's going on in the deepest regions of Katie's heart. That's God's domain, not mine. Our responsibility is to obey his promptings *in us*, not concern ourselves with what he is saying to others."

"So what is it you think will happen today?"

"I have no way of knowing that. I wouldn't even want to.

God is in control of Katie's destiny, and her heart, not me. Yet sometimes God will place inside us an urge to do or say something that fits in with the groundwork he is doing inside someone else. The result is that a door opens. It's impossible to say what exactly that means, how it will come about, or what will be the eventual outcome."

"What will you say?"

"I won't try to plan that. To speak of holy things at the wrong time, before someone is truly ready to receive them, can do more harm than good. We must rely on God's guidance to provide the fit opportunity, and we must move slowly. I don't know what Katie needs to hear. God knows that. So I just want to be available."

We packed up some food, and two knitting projects we had been working on, and then set out for Uncle Nick and Aunt Katie's—just the two of us. All the way there Almeda said nothing. From the intense look on her face, I knew she was praying.

When we arrived, Katie was alone with Erich. Uncle Nick was at the mine with Pa and Zack. All the other kids were in town at school. It was the middle of the morning, and the men would be working for another two or three hours before lunchtime.

Katie did not seem particularly overjoyed to see us, but she went through the motions of being hospitable.

"How are you feeling?" Almeda asked.

"Well enough, I suppose," Katie answered.

"We brought you some fresh bread. I know sometimes it's difficult to keep up with baking when you're not feeling so well."

"I tell you, I'm feeling fine," replied Katie, a little crossly. "I don't need your help, Almeda. I'll get through this fine on my own. Just quit worrying about me so much."

Almeda looked away for a moment. "I'm sorry," she said after a bit. "I'm only trying to be a good sister-in-law to you, and a good neighbor, and I know how it feels to be alone and far away from—"

"Look Almeda," Katie interrupted. She turned and faced Almeda. Her face did not seem to be angry, but there was no trace of a smile to be found anywhere on it. She was cool, distant, reserved, and obviously not interested in returning Almeda's friendliness. "I know what you're trying to do. I know you feel sorry for me. But just don't bother. I can get along fine without you or anybody else's sympathy. Keep your bread and all your religious notions about neighborliness to yourself, and just leave me alone!"

The words stung Almeda; and the slight wince that flitted across her face showed that they had stabbed her right in the heart. I would have done anything to disappear right then and not be in the room with them.

How thankful I was for Erich. Little children are so innocent, and sometimes they can stumble right into the middle of a hornet's nest without realizing it. On this particular morning he toddled in and rescued us from any further embarrassment.

"Look, Aunt Corrie," he said, holding something up to me, "Papa make me wood bear."

I stooped down to look at the piece of wood he was holding, so relieved for *something* to do. After I'd seen it, he marched over to show it to Almeda. She had looked away after Katie's rebuke, but now she stooped down, put an arm around his shoulder. Though her face was still a little pale she flashed him a bright smile and asked two or three questions about his toy "bear," which looked like a stick that had been whittled on. Katie went about something on her stove without another word, and Almeda and I talked for a few more minutes with Erich.

When he finally waddled off to another part of the house, Almeda threw me a glance which was followed by a deep sigh. This did not seem to be turning out to be much of a visit.

Slowly we rose, still holding the things we brought. Almeda walked over toward Katie, whose back was still turned toward us.

"I brought the stockings I've been making for Erich," Almeda said quietly, "and the sweater for your husband. I thought you might like to see them."

Katie did not reply for a moment. Then, still not facing us, she said, "You can leave them on the table if you wish."

"They're not finished. I thought you might like to see how I'm planning to—"

"Then take them with you and finish them any way you like. Leave them if you like, or take them. I don't care."

Almeda winced again, as if she had been struck across the cheek.

Almeda stood still, facing Katie's back, looking helpless. She wanted so badly to be Katie's friend.

Finally she drew in a breath and said, "I suppose we'll be going now. I'm so sorry, Katie. I didn't mean to cause you any pain, or to intrude where I don't belong. Please, if you can find it in your heart to forgive me, I would appreciate—"

"Forgive you!" repeated Katie, spinning around. Her face was red and her eyes flashing. "Forgive you for what?"

"I don't know," stammered Almeda. "For upsetting you, for intruding when you wanted to be alone." I'd never seen Almeda so flustered and unsettled. "I'm just sorry to have caused you any more grief."

"The only grief you cause me is by trying to be so good and self-righteous all the time!"

"Oh, Katie, I'm so sorry," said Almeda in a quavering voice.

"Sorry . . . forgive . . . don't you ever get sick of being so *good*? Do you ever stop, Almeda? Don't you ever want just to be normal and let people live their own lives, without always being nice, always smiling, always doing things for them, always preaching to them with all your holier-than-thou notions of God? Sometimes you make me sick with all your talk of God and forgiveness, and that happy smile on your face—always with a kind word, always doing somebody a good turn, never getting upset, never getting angry!"

I sat shocked at what I was hearing, my eyes glued to Katie as she poured out her fury. Poor Almeda just stood standing in front of her, defenseless, tears pouring down her cheeks.

"Do you know what it feels like to be around someone like you who's always so good?" Katie went on. "It makes me resent every word I ever hear about God! What about the rest of us, Almeda, who can't be as good as you? What does God have for people like us? I'm sick of it, do you hear? I hate God, I hate you, I hate California, I hate this stinking house, I hate the whole rotten business, and I never want to hear another word about God as long as I live!"

I don't know if she was going to say anything else. Before her outburst was finished, Almeda ran out the door, one hand held over her face. The bread and knitting lay on the floor where she had dropped them.

The sound of her footsteps and sobs woke me from my trance. I looked hard at Katie and saw tears in her eyes too. The next instant I ran out the door after Almeda.

She was hurrying away from the house, but not down the path to our place. She stopped on the edge of the woods, and I caught up with her leaning against a tree.

She was sobbing harder than I'd ever seen before, from the depths of her heart. I walked up to her slowly and laid my hand on the back of her shoulder. It was hot and wet. She kept crying but reached up and grasped my hand with one of hers, clutching it tightly.

We stood there, alone and quiet next to that tree, for several minutes. Gradually her weeping calmed down, then finally stopped.

Slowly she turned around, looked deeply into my eyes, and attempted a smile.

"I am so thankful for you, Corrie," she said softly. "I don't know what I'd do right now if I didn't have you here to share this with me."

I had no words to say. I just put my arms around her and held her.

"Do you know what's the hardest thing of all, Corrie?" she said at last.

"What?"

"Being so misunderstood . . . having your motives—which

you thought were good—questioned as if you had some selfish end you were trying to gain."

"She didn't mean to hurt you," I said.

"Oh, I know. She has no idea what she's done. But to have love turned back on you as if you were trying to injure rather than help and minister . . . that's such a painful thing."

We were silent another minute.

"But of course she didn't mean it," Almeda went on. "I have no doubt she's hurting more right now than I am. And it must be especially bitter for her in that she has no place to turn, no source of help. I do. But she is alone with her anger and her frustrations. So of course I don't blame her for lashing out at me." Her voice was soft and clean, as if the tears had washed it.

"It's not you anyway, is it?"

"No. Katie's not angry with me. She just doesn't know where to turn for help."

By this time we had stepped back, and Almeda was leaning against the tree again. I could tell she was thinking about the last words she had said.

It was quiet a long time. Then Almeda took a deep breath, looked at me, and smiled.

"We do know where to turn for help, don't we?" she said. "Maybe this is the door I had the feeling the Lord was going to open. It just might be time I told Katie some things. As painful as it will be, I think the time has finally come. Let's go back to the house, Corrie."

She turned and led the way back toward the cabin.

I followed Almeda through the door. She didn't knock or wait to be invited in. Katie was sitting in a chair staring straight ahead, her face white.

"Katie, I know you and I haven't always seen eye to eye on some things," Almeda said. "And I know our views on religion are very different. I'm sorry if I've hurt you or done things to bother you. I've honestly tried to be a good neighbor and friend to you. I'm sorry if it's seemed otherwise to you."

Katie just sat there saying nothing. She looked spent, like

the storm of her anger had left her weak and with no more words to say.

"But there's one thing you've got wrong, Katie," Almeda continued. "And that's about me being good. When you said 'someone like me who's always so good,' your words felt like a knife piercing right through my heart. And so whether you like it or not, Katie, unless you actually demand that I leave your house, I want to tell you what I used to be. You've got to know some things about God that you have all mixed up in your mind. After you've heard what I have to say, then if you still think faith is ridiculous and want to hate it, that will be your choice. But I intend to tell you what I have to say."

She paused for a breath. She was still standing, looking straight down at Katie. Katie sat with her eyes focused on the floor. But she said nothing.

Almeda sat down in front of her, took another deep breath, and began to speak.

CHAPTER 36

ALMEDA'S STORY

"The person I was many years ago in Boston," she began, "was a different person than you have ever known me to be. Completely different, Katie. Do you understand what I mean—black and white, night and day different?"

Almeda paused momentarily, but apparently she wasn't waiting for any answer, because she went right on.

"My father was a wealthy Boston merchant. I was one of three daughters—I hesitate to say it, but three *beautiful* daughters. I was the eldest. My father was a conniving man who would do anything—including sacrifice his own daughters—to turn a profit or to make a deal that would pad his bank account."

A painful look passed across Almeda's face as she said the words. Then she took in a deep breath, as if she was trying to gather courage to continue.

"I have to tell you that even after all the years I have been a Christian and have been trying to forgive him deep in my heart, the very thought of what he did to us still causes resentments to rise up within me. He was not a good man. For many years I despised him. At least now I can say that is no longer true. I have learned to accept what happened, and his part in it, and to know that through it I discovered what I might not have discovered otherwise. To say that I am thankful for my past would not really be truthful. But I do accept it, and have come to terms with it.

187

"What my father did was to flaunt us before his important clients. From the time I was fourteen or fifteen he would make me put on scanty dresses and alluring silk stockings, then he would pour perfume on me and take me out in the evening with him. There he would meet men I always assumed he was doing business with. I was too young at first to have any idea what was happening to me. I just went along obediently. There I would sit or stand beside my father while he would talk or drink. Sometimes it would be for dinner, other times we would go to saloons or taverns. Soon enough I realized that he was talking to the men about *me*. They would look me over, and there would be laughing and winking and whispered comments, then more laughing, all with a lewd, suggestive tone to it. My own father was hinting to his various associates that he would let me be available to them in exchange for their business.

"At first it wasn't so awful. The men would try to joke with me or take me alone over to the bar to buy me a sparkling water to drink while they had their whiskey. But it got worse the older I grew. They wanted to touch me and put their arms around me and feel my hair, always leering at me through toothy grins and evil eyes.

"I hated it. I hated the men, and I hated my father. But there was nothing I could do except go along with it. If my father thought that I wasn't being 'friendly' enough, or wasn't doing enough to please his associates, he would yell at me and hit me when we got home, and say horrible and abusive things to me. Sometimes he beat me even when I had done my best to be agreeable, just because a certain client decided to take his business elsewhere. One time—"

Even as Almeda spoke, the memory made her shut her eyes and a momentary shudder passed through her. She took a deep breath and continued.

"One time, he stopped the wagon on the way home, shoved me down from my seat, jumped down after me, and struck me over and over, knocking me to the ground until my nose was bleeding and my dress was torn and I was covered with dirt and mud, then threw me in a heap in the back of the wagon. I had learned years before not to cry aloud in his presence. He hated it when I cried, and he would beat me all the more. So I had to learn to stifle my whimpered sobs, and bury the agony of pain from his beatings.

"That night riding home in the back of the wagon, blood and dirt on my face, my ear and shoulder splitting with pain from his blows, I realized, perhaps for the first time, that my father was not a good man, and that I hated him. And from that moment, something began to rise up from inside me, a determination to escape from his clutches whenever and however I could.

"But it wasn't as if I could just leave home. I was only sixteen, and I was still completely dependent upon my parents. They never gave any of us any money. What could I do, where could I go? We had no relatives, no friends I could turn to. My mother knew what he was doing to us, but she was just as afraid of him as we were. I could never understand why she didn't stand up for us and protect us from him. But as I grew older I saw that she felt just as helpless as we. I tried to confide in her about what he did when he took us out in the evenings, but she would only suffer with us in silence. I don't doubt that she had more than her share of beatings from his hand as well. Probably if she had tried to say or do anything, he would have punished us all ruthlessly—all of us. So she just must have figured it best to keep silent and hope we could endure it.

"Once I even tried to talk to my father. It was late in the afternoon, around dusk. He was out in the barn working on a new saddle he'd bought. How naive I must have been to think he would listen, that he would care. But something had come over me that day with more clarity than ever before that what he was doing was just *wrong*. It was so plain to me all of a sudden, with my little girl's trusting heart, that if I could just say it to him he would see it too. I was wrong.

"I walked up to him slowly. He had his back turned. I don't even know if he heard me approaching. I stopped a few feet from him, terrified. I mustered all my courage and blurted out, 'Daddy, I want you to stop doing what you're doing to me. It's wrong. I don't want to go out with you again to see any more men.'

"That was all I said. I stood there trembling, just looking at his back in the quiet of the barn. He said nothing, and what seemed like a long time passed, though it was probably only a minute. Then he slowly turned around and bore his eyes into me. His face was blank. It was not even a look of anger, just a total lack of feeling, an emptiness, a void. Then slowly a cruel smile spread over his lips. He just looked at me with that horrid half-smile. It was the same kind of expression I'd seen in the men he made me be friendly to. Then slowly he turned back to his saddle, never uttering a word.

"I don't even remember when or how I left the barn, or how I spent the rest of the afternoon. But I remember the night distinctly enough. He took me into town again, and it was an absolutely horrible evening. My father joined with the men in saying things about me—half of them I didn't even understand, but I felt ugly and small and dirty just from the looks and laughs and winks that went along with their words. And that night he made me go to a man's room alone. Nothing much happened; I suppose once he got me alone the man felt sorry for me because of how young I was, and he was almost nice to me when he saw how terrified I was.

"So he took me back downstairs to my father a little later. And then on our way home, out somewhere desolate where even if I did scream no one would hear me, my father gave me the worst beating of my life. He never said a word. He didn't have to. The message was clear enough: I must never speak boldly to him again like I had that afternoon in the barn. I had to stay in bed for two days. My mother hardly even came into my room except to give me something to eat. I knew she felt guilty, but powerless at the same time. So she did the worst thing of all—she did nothing. She didn't even offer me so much as a look or a smile of consolation, not even a glance to say, 'I understand . . . I'm sorry.' "

Almeda stopped. Her voice had grown quiet, and now she

looked down, took a handkerchief from her pocket and dabbed her eyes.

"You know," she went on in a moment, her voice soft and husky, "during all the years I was growing up, I never once remember hearing the words *I love you*. Not even from my mother. Love was nonexistent in our family. I don't know what my two sisters felt. But all my life I felt unwanted, that my parents would have gotten rid of me the moment I was born if they could have."

She paused again, crying now.

"Do you have any idea what it's like," she said through her tears, "never once all your life to be told that you are loved—by *anybody*? Not once. Never to be touched except in anger. Never to be held . . . never to feel arms wrapping themselves around your shoulders in tenderness . . . never to—"

She couldn't continue, but finally broke down and sobbed, her face in her hands.

I don't know what Katie was thinking. Part of me didn't want to look at her. Besides, I was far too occupied with my *own* thoughts and feelings. I was shocked, of course, but that was only part of my response. I could feel the hurt, the ache, in her voice. And because I *did* love her—oh, so much!—it made what she'd gone through so much harder to hear. I just wanted to go back and take that girl she had once been in my arms and wrap her up and protect her from any more hurt and any more unkindness.

On another level, as I listened I could hardly believe what I was hearing. From the very day I had first seen her, Almeda had been to me the absolute picture of strength, and Christian virtue, and maturity. I had never seen her "weak." There was never a time when I didn't know she could be depended on, no matter if everyone around her fell or faltered or even ran away. To hear her describe her past was like looking into a window inside of someone else. And I couldn't manage to make the two images come together into the single person I had always known. Suddenly there were two pictures of Almeda—the stately, solid lady, full of grace, capable and mature, and the young girl, frightened, alone, and unloved.

How could the two be the same person? Yet there sat Almeda, the same loving woman I had always known, my stepmother now, opening up this window into her soul.

Slowly I got up from where I was sitting and walked over to Almeda. I knelt down in front of her, took one of her hands in mine, and looked into her face, red with tears and the anguish of reliving the ugly memories of the past.

"Almeda," I said softly, "*I* love you . . . I love you more than I can ever tell you!"

At the words a fresh torrent of weeping burst out from Almeda. I put my hand around her waist and tried to comfort her, but she had to go on crying for another minute or two.

"Oh, Corrie," she whispered at length, "you'll never know how precious those words are to me! Your love is such a priceless treasure to me . . . words cannot express the joy you give me."

She blew her nose, then looked down at me with a radiant smile. I guess it's true that pain makes a person more capable of love. Almeda's face at that moment was more filled with love than any face I'd ever seen. Our eyes met and held. I felt I was looking right through her, not into her heart or into her past life, but into the deepest parts of *her*—the whole person she was, the person she had always been, the person she was still becoming. Maybe in those few seconds I had a tiny glimpse of what God sees when *he* looks deep into us—a glimpse into the *real* person, the *whole* person—apart from age or appearance or past or upbringing.

All these feelings passed through me in just a second or two. Then Almeda gave me a squeeze and took a deep breath.

"I want to finish," she went on, "or I might never get this far with it again. And I want both of you to hear what I have to say. I care about the two of you, and I want you to know me—to know *all* about me."

I stood up and went back to where I had been sitting.

"It's difficult for me to describe what I was feeling back then," she continued, "because I suppose I didn't even know myself. I was terrified, and yet at the same time I was growing more and more determined to escape from that awful life. I suppose there was a part of me that was a fighter. I've been called headstrong more than once, as you know, Corrie, from the very first day when we saw each other."

She looked over at me with a smile.

"You weren't afraid of anybody when you went into the saloon looking for Uncle Nick, that's for sure," I said.

"No, I don't suppose I was," she replied. "And as afraid as I was of my father, by the time I was sixteen a part of me inside was biding my time until I saw an opportunity. And after he'd done it once, my father started trying to make me go upstairs alone with men again. The next time it happened, knowing what I was in for, I refused to go. 'I just won't do it,' I said, which silenced the joviality around the table where we were sitting. And the look of daggers my father threw at me told me there was a beating waiting for me, the likes of which I'd never felt.

"And of course after that, nothing my father could say would make the man he'd been talking to take me away anyway, even if I'd given in. So I just sat there in silence, trembling about the ride home.

"Luckily my father had an appointment the next night with another man, a whiskey distributor I'd met before. I had never liked him one bit. The smiles he would give me, and the pinches and little jabs, were so horrible. It never took long in that man's company to know what kind of man he was. My next younger sister still had a black eye from the hand of my father, and he wanted to make sure I was presentable because whiskey was one of my father's main sources of income. So he didn't beat me that night, although he made sure I knew full well that as soon as the *next* night was over, I was going to be so black and blue I would be in bed for a week and would never refuse to do anything he asked of me again.

"All the next day I plotted my escape. I stole what money I could find in the house, packed a few clothes in a bag, and hid it in a field nearby. Then I waited for evening to come, filled with fear and anticipation all at once.

"This time I was as nice as I could be, and I just smiled when the men called me 'Honey,' as if I enjoyed it, and I went right upstairs with that awful man. But on the landing I managed to get ahead of him, and since I knew what room we were going to, I ran in and locked the door behind me, then climbed out the window onto the landing and scrambled down to the alley.

"I ran away from there as fast as I could, hardly even knowing what direction I was going. I ran and ran, through alleys and streets, but always with the vague intent of moving in the direction of our home, which was on the edge of the city.

"After that it all becomes a blur. I can't even say how I spent the rest of that night or the next few days and nights. I managed to retrieve my bag of things, but where I went and what I did after that I honestly can't even recall. There are just images that sometimes flash into my mind—a face, a place, or a set of surroundings.

"Actually that's all I remember for the whole next year. How I survived I don't know. Now I can say that the hand of God was upon me, but then I knew nothing of God, and certainly cared even less. If I thought it had been bad at home with my father, now my life turned black indeed. I don't even want to remember all the things I did, or what I got myself mixed up in. I lived on the streets, sometimes in the countryside, in saloons and cheap hotels, getting what jobs I could find. I stole, I drank, I used people if I thought it might get me a free meal.

"I knew my father probably hated me all the more for making him look foolish, and that he was no doubt looking for me. But I didn't care. I told people who I was and exactly what I thought of him. Over the next several years, as I got older and more capable, I was able to hold jobs for longer, and even to do a man's work when I had to. Living like I did made me tough and independent. I could take care of myself, and I wasn't afraid of my father finding me. I knew he'd never be able to get a hold on me again. I suppose I even had something of a reputation as a pretty hard, tough young lady—which no doubt is how Franklin found out about my past last year.

"To make a long story short, when I was about nineteen or twenty I fell in with a man who more or less took me under his wing. He was a confidence man, a card shark, a high-stakes swindler, but he lived a fast life, and I found that appealing. I didn't love him, and I know he didn't love me either. I was just a pretty girl for him to have around. I had no idea what love was and at that point in my life never stopped to even ask if such a thing as love existed. Life was survival. To survive you had to be tough, you had to take advantage of what opportunities came along, and you had to put yourself first. If other people got hurt in the process, that wasn't my concern. Life had dealt me a pretty bad hand, and I wasn't about to start getting pangs of conscience over anyone else.

"So I lived with him for a while, stole for him, set people up for him, and in the process lived better than I had for several years. At least I knew I was going to have a roof over my head, a warm bed, and a good meal. It was the closest thing to stability I had known in a long time. How much longer it might have gone on like this, or what might have become of us in the end I don't know. Because then something happened which changed everything."

Again Almeda stopped, and again I knew from her face and the tone of her voice that she was struggling within herself for the courage to say something that was painful.

The room was silent for a minute or two. I chanced a quick glance in Katie's direction. She was looking intently at Almeda, listening to every word. Every trace of anger was gone from her face.

"There was a child," Almeda said at last. She stopped again and hid her face in her hands.

I saw Katie gasp slightly, and I felt myself take in a quick breath. I couldn't believe what I'd just heard!

"I'm so ashamed to tell you what I have to say next," she went on, crying a little again. "The minute he learned I was pregnant, I was nothing to him but baggage. I woke up one morning in the hotel we'd been staying in to find myself alone with nothing but my carpetbag and a few clothes left in the room. I never saw him again. He left me ten dollars, and I was back on the street.

"I was too angry even to cry. It just drove my bitterness toward men—toward the whole world, and I suppose toward God too—deeper. The old hard determination rose up in me again, and I struck out after that day all the more mistrusting, all the more independent. I was a different person, I tell you— selfish, hateful, caring for no one but myself.

"When the baby was born—God forgive me!—I took it to an orphanage. I didn't want to—"

Almeda broke down and wept. I wanted to comfort her, but I was so stunned by what she'd said that I couldn't move.

"Oh, how many times I've relived it in my memory, wondering where I might have changed this course I was on, wondering if I did right or wrong. I was so unprepared to be a mother. Yet something in me has often wished—"

Again she stopped to collect herself, then continued.

"The birth of my baby sent me lower still. By now I was in my early twenties and something in that hard independent spirit slowly began to break. Guilt over what I had done began to set in. Gradually it ate away at me, burrowing deeper and deeper into my heart. I didn't realize it at the time, but now I see that all the hard, determined independence was only my young way of covering up my desperate hunger to be loved. The more I tried to assert my strength, the more my soul was being torn apart. I didn't have any idea who I was. My whole identity had come from my father. To him I was just an object to be used. No one had ever loved me. How could I do anything but despise myself? And even the most precious thing a woman has—that purity which is the only thing she has to offer her husband—I let slip away. And I gave away the child that should have been the wonderful outcome of love between a man and a woman. I was no better than my father! I didn't even want my own baby! Oh God . . . how could I have been so shameful . . . how could—"

Again she broke down and sobbed quietly.

"There is no way I can tell you what that time was like for me," she finally said after a while. "I felt so guilty, yet I tried to hide it. Inside I was slowly dying to all that life should be, sinking into a pit of despair, yet making it worse by the obstinate hard-bitten image I tried to keep up.

"I started drifting, caught trains to New York and Philadelphia. I worked here and there, stealing what I needed, living among some really rough men and women. I even got to be pretty handy with my fists when I had to be. It was a dreadful life! It wasn't life at all, it was a living death."

She paused once more. By now her tears had stopped. She breathed in deeply, and looked out the window off into the distance. As if she had suddenly become unaware that Katie and I were in the room with her, she seemed miles and years away. I'd seen that look before, a look of mingled pain and remembrance. Now at last I knew why those clouds had passed across her face.

She continued staring out the window for a long time, then suddenly came back to the present and turned and focused her gaze onto Katie.

"So you see, Katie," she said, "when you spoke of me as someone who's always so good, as if God was somebody I could understand but you couldn't, do you see why your words bit so deep? I *wasn't* good, Katie! I was about as despicable a person as they come. For the first twenty-five years of my life, I did everything wrong! I did not know love. I was miserable. I was mean and bitter and vengeful. I hurt people, I did more horrible things than I could count.

"If you're going to think of Christianity as something that's only for a certain kind of person, then you'd better leave me out altogether. If you think God reserves his life for churchy 'good' people, where does that leave me? All those things you said about me—nice, always smiling, holier-than-thou, forgiving, doing good turns, never getting upset, never getting angry . . . don't you understand, Katie—none of that was me at all! The person you think you see, the person you have known these last couple of years, wasn't me at all not so very long ago. I don't say that to be critical, Katie. But if you're going to criticize me for how I am now, then I think you should know the whole story. And that's why I wanted to tell you."

Still Katie just sat numbly, not saying anything.

"So what happened?" I asked finally. "How did you . . . I mean, how could everything have changed so much?"

Almeda turned toward me and smiled. Her eyes were a little red still, but the radiance that was normally on her countenance had returned. Having told us everything, reliving it as she did, she was ready for the sun to come back out.

"That," she sighed, "is almost an equally long story."

CHAPTER 37

ENCOUNTER WITH A SHOPKEEPER

"One day," Almeda began again, "when I was back in Boston, I was walking in one of the better sections of town. I don't even remember why I happened to be on that particular street because it really wasn't a part of town I went to very often. Fate, I suppose I would have called it back then. I would call it something else now.

"In any case, I walked into a shop that sold a mixture of many things—dry goods, some fine linens, with one glass case of some very expensive jewelry. I wandered in, probably looking every bit the street-tramp that I was. I must have stood out like a sore thumb, but I didn't really think of that myself.

"As you might imagine, my eyes immediately focused on the case of jewelry. I sauntered toward it, saw that it was filled with expensive gold and silver rings and necklaces and pendants. The proprietor of the shop was occupied along one of the far walls with a lady who was picking out some fabric, and the jewelry cabinet was out of the man's direct line of vision. All I would need would be a second or two. If I could get my hand inside the case and snatch three or four pieces, I'd be able to dash out the door and all he'd see was the back of my heels. I'd done the same sort of thing a hundred times and had the utmost confidence in my cunning and my speed once I lit out. The only question was whether the case was locked.

"I moved up to the case and searched quickly for a lock but

199

didn't see one. The back seemed to be open. I eyed the pieces I thought I could nab. Then with one motion I stretched over the top of the case and reached into the back. My fingers grabbed two or three rings. I hurriedly put them in my other hand, then stretched out again and reached for two pearl necklaces that were close by. Just as I'd laid hold of them and pulled my arm back, ready to make a dash for the door, I felt the grip of a strong hand seize my shoulder.

"The store owner had sneaked up behind me and now he had me redhanded. I winced from the pain because he'd grabbed me tight. His only words were, 'Drop them on the counter, Miss.' There was no anger in his voice, only a calm tone of command. I instantly did what he said. I had no choice.

"He relaxed his grip slightly, but still held on. The other lady had left the store and now we were alone. Still holding on to me, he walked me over toward the door and locked it. I was too feisty and stubborn to be scared. I squirmed a little, but he was strong and it did no good. I couldn't have escaped if I'd tried, and now with the door locked I settled down and decided just to wait and see what would happen next.

"The man was younger than I'd first realized, only a few years older than I was—in his mid-thirties. He led me, still with a strong hand, back behind the counter of the shop and into another room, which was his home, attached to the store. He sat me down in a chair, then finally let go of my arm and shoulder. He took a chair himself and sat down opposite me. He must have seen my eyes darting about already plotting my escape.

" 'There's no way out, young lady,' he said. 'All the doors are locked, and even if you did manage to find a key to one of them and get out, I'm quite a fast runner and I'd catch you before you were halfway down the street. And the sheriff's office is only two blocks away. So if I were you I'd just sit still for a moment or two.'

"His voice still had that calm, deep tone of authority. I couldn't help but find myself arrested by it. And though I slouched back in my chair with a look of angry resignation on my face, already I found myself wondering why he hadn't yelled at me or wasn't already on his way to the sheriff's with me.

"The longer I sat there, the more confused I became, although I wouldn't have shown the man a bit of what I was thinking. He just sat there for the longest time and stared into my eyes. I found his gaze annoying and looked away. I kept looking all over the room, but still he kept focusing in on my eyes and my face. It was very disconcerting. Yet at the same time I couldn't help thinking that there was something in his expression that I had never seen before, though I had no idea what it was.

"Finally he spoke again.

" 'Why did you try to steal from me?' he asked.

"I shrugged.

" 'If you were hungry, why didn't you just ask me for some food? I would have given it to you.'

"I still had nothing to say.

" 'If you needed money, why didn't you come in and tell me about it? Perhaps I could have helped.'

"*What is this?* I wondered to myself. *If you're going to have me thrown in jail, then get it over with.*

"Yet inside curiosity was already starting to well up in me about this strange man who didn't seem bent on condemning me but instead sounded as if he was interested in me.

"Well, I sat there for the next hour while he continued to question me and talk to me, always in the same calm voice, with his eyes probing into me in a way no one ever had before, and gradually he began to coax some words and then some whole sentences out of me. By the end of the hour, we were actually carrying on a conversation. Over and over he kept saying, 'I don't think you really want to be a thief. I think you want to be a lady, but you just don't know how.'

"I hardly knew what he meant. But the compassion and caring in his voice was real enough, and the commanding tone and the purposefulness of his eyes, slowly began to speak to me. I found myself listening with more than just my ears. I found myself *wanting* to listen, wanting to hear more of this strange man's words . . . wanting to *believe* that he was right, wanting to believe that perhaps he really did see something of worth and value as he looked into my face, saw something that maybe I didn't see, and had never seen myself."

Almeda paused and took a breath, but quickly kept right on going.

"After a while he offered me something to eat. I took it eagerly. I hadn't had much to eat all day and was famished. He heated me some soup on his stove, and poured me a cup of coffee.

" 'How about a slice of bread to go with it?' he asked. 'I made it just yesterday.'

"I nodded between spoonfuls of soup, half glancing up now and then with one of my eyebrows raised in puzzlement over this strange man who was treating me so nicely.

"I must have looked like a ravaged animal sitting there!"

She chuckled and the faraway gaze came into her eyes again.

"When I said earlier that my father had three beautiful daughters, I meant no boast in any way. Our faces were a curse, if anything, because they made men look upon us differently than they would have otherwise. A plain face is a young girl's greatest gift and greatest protection against many of the cruelties of this world, though most never discover that fact for forty or fifty years. But as I sat there in that man's kitchen, I can tell you I was anything but beautiful. My face had grown bitter, hard, calculating. There was a perpetual scowl on my brow. My cheeks were sunken, my hair ratted and messy, my clothes dirty, even torn in places. It was not an attractive sight. That man had absolutely nothing to gain by befriending me. I hadn't bathed in two weeks, and the plain fact of the matter is that I was foul. I looked and smelled ugly, inside and out.

"But he—"

Almeda paused and looked away, suddenly overcome again with emotion. I saw her handkerchief go to her eyes once more.

"But he saw something in me. Why . . . how . . . I hadn't any idea. I know now it was because God's love resided in him, but I didn't know it then. He *saw* something in me! Something that he considered of *value*. And you just can't understand what that did to my starved, confused, lonely, encrusted heart. It was as though he took hold of my eyes, looked deeply into them, and then said, 'Look, young lady. Look here—into my eyes. Gaze deeply into them, and you will find someone who has compassion on you, someone who cares about you as a person.'

"As I ate his food, he just kept watching me, quietly talking, and I'm sure praying too, though I was oblivious to that. And that same message kept coming through, even in his silence: *Here is someone who cares about you.*

"And then another strange and unexpected thing happened. As I was finishing up my second bowl of soup and starting to think about being on my way—that is, if he was going to let me go instead of having me thrown in jail—the man got up, pulled a book from a shelf nearby, sat back down, and said, 'Did you know there's a description of you in the Bible?'

"No," I answered.

" 'Well there is,' he replied, 'and I want to read it to you.'

"*No harm in that,* I thought as I kept eating.

"He flipped through the pages, stopped, and then began to read: *Who can find a virtuous woman? for her price is far above rubies. The heart of her husband doth safely trust in her, so that he shall have no need of spoil. She will do him good and not evil all the days of her life. . . .*

"I found myself listening more than I let on. Was this the man's idea of a cruel joke, calling me *virtuous*? *Me!* Couldn't he see that I was anything but good? I didn't even have a husband, but if I did I'd be the last person on earth anyone would say such things about! I had just tried to rob this storekeeper, and now he was reading words like, *She will do him good and not evil,* and saying it was a description of *me!*

"But when he got to the end, he paused a moment, then looked intently into my eyes with a piercing gaze and said: *Many daughters have done virtuously, but thou excellest them all. Favor is deceitful, and beauty is vain: but a woman that feareth the Lord, she shall be praised*. That's when I suddenly knew beyond any doubt that I'd landed in the house of a man whose wits had left him. There was that word *virtue* again! I knew how black I was inside! That hidden part of me that I tried so hard to keep anyone from seeing—I knew that part was selfish and horrid through and through!

"But even if he was a madman, he had been nice to me, after all. So I simply finished up my soup, then stood and asked if I was free to go.

" 'If you want to,' he replied. " 'But the day's almost over. It's going to be cold tonight. Do you need a place to stay?'

"*So that's it*, I thought to myself. *All this just to lure me into his lair! He's no different from everyone else!*

"Then he added, 'I have a guest room. I'd be happy to put you up for the night. You could take a hot bath, have breakfast with me in the morning, and then be on your way.'

"I eyed him carefully, squinting to see if I could detect some motive. But try as I might, I could see nothing. I don't think the man would have been capable of taking advantage of another. And even if he did try something, I thought, I could take care of myself.

"So I shrugged, and said, 'Sure, I suppose a bath and clean bed would feel good for a change.'

"That night changed everything, and altered the whole course of my life. The man could not have been a more perfect gentleman. He treated me like a queen, heated water for my bath, gave me clean clothes to sleep in, fixed me tea and brought it with some crackers to my room before I went to bed. I didn't know it at the time, but when I was bathing he took my clothes out to be cleaned by a lady around the corner.

"You can imagine the changes I was going through in my mind as I lay there that night. One part of me was laughing inside that anyone could be such a sap. I would sneak down in the middle of the night, find my way into the store again, and make off not with just three or four pieces of jewelry, but with everything in the case. My head was resting on a nice clean pillow cover that would hold everything.

"But somehow another part of me was feeling things I had never felt in my life. This storekeeper—madman or sap or religious nut, whatever he was!—had treated me with courtesy and respect and kindness and graciousness like no other human being in the world ever had. So the deeper part of me was hardly anxious to leave! It felt good to have someone care and treat me kindly. I was not consciously aware of these feelings at the time. Inside I was still pretending it was all ridiculous.

"But he had shown me my first real glimpse of love. He had reached out, looked into my face, and said, 'I see a person of value and worth inside there.' He'd even used that silly word *virtue* and said the passage he read was a description of me. No matter how I might rave and bluster on the outside about it all being syrupy and stupid, I couldn't help feeling cared about and loved.

"So even though I lay there plotting and scheming my escape and all the loot I would make off with, the deeper part of me gradually went contentedly to sleep. And I slept like a baby and didn't wake until I heard the man's familiar voice. I opened my eyes. Sunlight was streaming in through the window, and there he stood with a tray in his hands and a cup of steaming coffee on it, and saying with a bright expression, 'Good morning, young lady. I hope you slept well!'

"In just a few short hours, this place—a place I had walked into to rob, run by this man standing there whose name I didn't even know yet—had become more like a true home to me than any I had ever known. And as I lay there, suddenly the most unexpected thing happened. I felt tears in my eyes. I looked up at him, blinking them back as best I could, and then another unexpected thing happened. A smile came across my lips, and I said, 'Yes, I did. Thank you.'

"He left the coffee, and I lay back in the bed and cried. But they were like no tears that had ever come from my eyes before."

Almeda glanced over at me and smiled. Her eyes were glistening.

"Needless to say," she went on, "I didn't leave immediately, or rob him, or anything like that. I stayed for breakfast and for all that day, then for another night, and before I knew it I had been there a week. He gave me new clothes from his shop, he fed me, I had a bath every day and a room completely to myself. Within a couple of weeks he moved me into a boarding house just down the street and offered me a job in his store.

"The long and the short of it is—I became a new person. Life such as I had never known began to come up out of me. I began to notice things that had been dead to me before. People took on a whole new meaning, and I found within myself a desire to reach into them and find out about them.

"Well . . . if you haven't guessed it by now, the man who took me under his wing and helped me to believe in my own worth was none other than Mr. Parrish. The year after I first wandered into his shop I became his wife.

"What a transformation took place within me during that year! That wonderful man simply reclaimed me from Boston's gutters, pulled me up, gave me a place to stand, loved me, believed in me, spoke encouragement and worth into me, and showed me how to *live*. He was God's provision for me. I was dead to all that life was, and he rescued me. I became a new person, thanks to him—completely new, the person the two of you know today.

"Do you know what he did?" Almeda smiled tenderly at the memory.

"After that first day, he read that passage from Proverbs 31 to me every day until we were married. He kept reading it to me, over and over, and kept saying to me, 'You *are* that woman of virtue, Almeda. You are virtuous and pure and capable.' He kept telling me that, and kept reading those words to me, until they began to sink into my soul. God began to wash me clean with those words, and with many other passages from the Bible. Washed me clean from my past, at the same time as he was implanting within me a new picture of the person I could become. It was really quite a wonderful process, nothing short of a full transformation. The old fell away under the influences of this man's love and God's love, leaving the new free to emerge and then eventually to spill out onto others. All my life I had lived under a dark cloud—first from feeling unwanted, then from the awful things my father did, and then finally the cloud of my own blackness of heart that I had been carrying for many years. The clouds were swept away. Someone *did* want me and *did* love me. The horrible memories of my father were replaced by the present reality of a man who was caring and compassionate, a man who loved me and would never hurt me. And the blackness in my heart was cleansed and healed by his belief in me, and by his gentle and tender and encouraging words. The sun came out for the first time in my life. He gave me a place to stand in life, a place of warmth and smiles, and a contented feeling when I went to sleep at night.

"Of course, on a deeper level what was really happening was that he was giving me my first glimpse of God's nature and character. For what he did was exactly what Jesus did when he encountered people—he looked into their eyes and reached down inside them to touch the *real* person down at the core. That is what God is always trying to do in people's lives, in a million ways, sometimes using other people, sometimes on his own. He has a million ways to love us, a million ways to try to get through to us, if we're only able to hear that voice that is sometimes so hard to hear. We are locked away in the cocoons that life surrounds us with. Yet all the while the freedom of the butterfly lies hidden deep inside, and God is constantly trying to find ways to loose our wings and let us soar and be happy in the flight of his life.

"That's what Mr. Parrish did. He looked inside me and said, 'You are someone special. You are a gem that can shine—all we have to do is polish it a bit.' And he went to work polishing.

"At first it was just his words, his kindness, his caring, his love. He made me believe in myself, and believe that he loved me. I listened to him read the Scriptures, and I listened to everything he said about God, but the Lord was still distant. God was not someone who had yet touched my life in a real way. I listened and I probably absorbed more than I realized.

But it was still some time later when I awoke to the immediacy of God's relation to *me*—me personally! It took some time for God to steal closer and closer, until that moment when I was ready to surrender my heart to Him, as well as to Mr. Parrish."

CHAPTER 38

ENCOUNTER WITH THE FATHER

"How influences from our Father in heaven begin to penetrate our consciousness," Almeda continued, "is one of life's great mysteries. I know ever since the moment I met Mr. Parrish, God began speaking more directly to me. But for a long while, as I said, I was not aware of it.

"We worked together in the store, then expanded the business a little, and by and by built a pretty good life there in Boston. I was obviously not what you would call a 'society lady,' yet in a way my husband did succeed in making a lady of me. He would take me to the theater and sometimes to social gatherings, without the least shame in the kind of person I had once been. He knew everything about my past—about my father, about the men who had been in my life, about the baby. Yet nothing could stop him from continually saying to me, 'You, Almeda, are a woman of virtue and uprightness and righteousness. God made you in *his* image. He loves you, and I love you. Yesterday's gone. Your past has been washed clean.'

"All that couldn't help but make all of life new to me. The sun was brighter. The raindrops sparkled with a new radiance. Flowers took on such a wonderful new meaning. One day a little bee flew against our window and stunned himself and fell to the ground. I scooped him carefully into my palm, and just gazed upon him with a tenderness I didn't even know was in my heart. When he began to come to, I lifted him into the wind and blew him off my palm. And as I watched him fly away, tears came to my eyes, although I didn't even know why.

"Life was happening all around me, but it wasn't an *impersonal* life. Somehow everything was very personal. It all seemed to touch my heart so. To breath in deeply of the fragrance of an orange or yellow rose touched chords in my being I can't even describe. The smell itself was holy, as if it went back to the very foundation of the world itself, and then had come into being just for me, that I might smell that rose on that particular day. There are no words to convey what I felt. The smell was almost sad in a way, calling forth a yearning for something more than just the aroma of the rose's perfume, but a longing for something that could never be had, never be found. I think that's what it was with the bee too, a longing after something, a hunger—oh, I don't know!—to somehow be a sister, a friend, to that bee in the shared life of the creation we were both in. Yet the bee was just a bee, without the capacity to let me share his life, without even the capacity to know that such a thing as people existed. And somehow as a result I found tears in my eyes.

"Birds in flight held my gaze, something about their seeming freedom called out to me to join them. Sunrises, sunsets . . . even tiny green blades of grass—*everything* began to speak to me. Not speak in words, but speak in feelings. Just to see the intricacies of creation was to find feelings of love rising up in me for those things—for the rose, the bee, the bird, the blade of grass—each unique and so beautiful in its own way.

"Yet there always were tears to go along with the love. For a long time I didn't know why. But then a day came when at last I did.

"The moment came when we were on our way here to California. My husband got a business scheme in his head, and we sold everything and booked passage to join the rush to California.

"One night I was standing along the rail, gazing out across the expanse of the Pacific. It was late, and I was alone. There was a bright moon out, and its light spread glistening out across the water as far as I could see. A few clouds now and then slowly went across it, dulling the reflection for a few moments, and then it would return.

"All these things I have been telling you were filtering through my mind, images out of my past, the changes that had come, how alive and full I felt, such a great thankfulness that the downward path of my former existence had been stopped and that I'd been turned around. And I was thinking of the bee too, and wondering why it had caused me to weep. All the time I was gazing out upon the glow of the moon on the water. The ocean . . . the moon . . . the water . . . the clouds . . . the mystery of the silence . . . it all began to have a saddening, yearning effect on me and as I stood there, I found tears welling up in my eyes.

"But it only lasted a moment. The next instant a voice spoke to me. I don't mean out loud, but it was so clear in my heart it might as well have been an audible voice. It said: 'It's *me* your tears are meant for. *I'm* the one who put my life into the things I have made, and it's that life which calls out to you. All along I have been calling out to you through the fragrance of the pine tree and the buzz of the honey bee and the winged freedom of the butterfly . . . and this very moment I am calling out to you through the moon's light on the sea.'

"And I knew it was the voice of God speaking to me. And suddenly I knew that he had been there all along, all my life, speaking, calling out to me, trying to love me and touch me and heal me—and care for me. I knew that he knew all about my father and everything that had happened to me. And I knew that he had sent my husband to help pull me up and make a woman of me.

"Yet somehow, even in knowing these things, I continued to weep. I was filled with a sense of remorse because I hadn't seen God before this moment, even though he had been beside me, so close beside me since the day I was born. I had smelled the roses and picked the blades of grass, but I had never seen the *life* that was in them, the life that was God, so close as to be in my very hand, yet unseen.

"In that moment, in a sense, my whole life swept through my memory, and I saw for the first time my own responsibility in what I had allowed myself to become. Even as awful as my father had been, I saw that if I had seen that God *was* with me even then, and had listened to his voice, I could have shared that time with him, and that he could have protected me and kept me from what followed in my life. But my independence kept my eyes on myself, and until Mr. Parrish came along I just looked at nothing else but *me*.

"Right there on the ship, I dropped down onto my knees. And still clinging with one hand to the railing, I began to pray to God from the depths of my heart.

" 'Oh God,' I prayed, 'I want to live! And I want to live with you. I want you to be my Father. I said I'd never let anybody near me . . . I didn't think I could trust anyone, not even you! All those painful years growing up, people were so cruel . . . they only wanted me for what they could get out of me. I learned to be tough, and when anyone tried to come close, I'd just push them away . . . but inside I was truly afraid . . . I only wanted someone to love me. But there's been no one . . . until this dear man you sent me to . . . and *you* Lord! Please forgive me . . . it just hurt *so* bad. But now I see how much I've always needed you. Be the Father to me I never had. Oh Lord, forgive me for my stubbornness and independence when I was younger. I'm so sorry I didn't know you were there, didn't pay attention. Help me now to live, and to live for you! Help me to get my eyes off myself and onto others. Let me be a help to those who may not know love, just as I didn't. Oh God, please help me. I want to be your daughter. I want to be your woman. Do whatever you want with me, Lord, whatever it takes to transform me into the person you want me to be.'

"When I was through praying I got up and went back to our cabin. I knew there had been a change. And from the moment we got to California I was a new woman. Mr. Parrish had begun the process by picking me up off the ground. Now the Lord continued the transformation deep in my being, all the way through every part of me.

"And it goes on every day. I still have to struggle with my independence, as you both know from the events of the election campaign. But as I said when I began, even though the work God has to do in me goes on every moment, the difference between fifteen years ago and now is like night and day. You, Corrie, are very fortunate to have begun so early in your life to make the Lord part of your life. I hope and pray that you will one day give your heart to him too, Katie. Because there is no abiding contentment in life apart from him. I can tell you that, not because I am a good Christian lady, but because I've known life without him too, and I know how empty it is."

Almeda stopped. We had been sitting for nearly an hour and a half. It was the most moving story I had ever heard anyone tell, and I still could hardly believe Almeda was telling about her *own* life! She was visibly drained.

"What about all those rumors Mr. Royce was spreading around town last fall?" I asked finally.

Almeda smiled—a sad smile, yet without bitterness.

"There were elements of truth in everything that was said, Corrie, as you can now see for yourself. But like all rumors, it was half fact, half fiction, with usually the fiction parts being those aspects of it people are most eager to believe. All that ridiculous talk about meeting Mr. Parrish on the ship and marrying him practically the next day—I don't know where some of that was dredged up from."

"Does Pa know all this?"

"Everything," she answered. "I wouldn't have let him marry me without making sure he knew what he was getting. I told him every detail. And do you know what he said? He said, 'Everything you tell me just makes me love you more, not less.' He's quite a man, Corrie, that father of yours!"

I nodded and smiled.

"I suppose there's no disrespect in saying this," she went on. "But I'm just now seeing just how much I really do love your father. Mr. Parrish taught me that I could *be* loved. He showed me love. He gave me love. He opened up so much of himself to me. But once I came to know your father, Corrie, I found hundreds of new things opening in *me* that weren't there before. Or at least if they were there, I hadn't noticed. In knowing him, suddenly love began to pour out of me in a new way. Of course I loved Mr. Parrish, but—well, I suppose I just wanted you to know that your Pa is special to me in a completely unique way. There is a part of my heart that is only for him and no one else."

Again she was quiet. Still Katie sat without moving.

Almeda rose. "I suppose it's time we were going home," she said.

Then Katie rose and finally spoke. "Almeda," she said, "I am sorry for the things I said. I had no right."

Almeda smiled. "Think nothing of it, Katie. I just wanted you to understand." She gave Katie a hug, which Katie only half-heartedly returned, and then we left.

"What do you think she thought?" I asked as we walked home.

"That's something only God can know," Almeda answered. "He does everything in his own time, especially in the matter of the human heart. Katie's time will come just as surely as mine did on the ship. But what did you think, Corrie?" she added.

"I guess I'd agree with Pa," I said.

"How so?"

"That your story makes me love you more, not less."

She slipped her hand through my arm and we walked the rest of the way in silence.

CHAPTER 39

THE TOWN COUNCIL

Almost the moment we got back to our place, exhaustion came over Almeda from all the energy it had taken to pour herself out like she had. She slept for two or three hours that afternoon, and I went into the office in town. When I came back that evening and our eyes first met, she smiled at me, and there was something new in her look. I suppose I saw for the first time how much depth there had always been in that smile. And I could tell she was glad that I knew everything. It was like a smile exchanged between sisters who know each other completely.

Nothing much changed otherwise. Things returned to normal with Katie. No more sullenness, no more outbursts, but neither was there any exuberance or special friendliness. I was sure Katie had been touched by Almeda's story, but you could see nothing of it on her face or in her actions. I hoped something was going on inside her.

Meanwhile, business at the Mine and Freight hardly seemed to suffer at all on account of Mr. Royce's competition up the street. Now and then we'd hear of some sale he made to someone, or of something he was doing. But most of our customers remained loyal to Almeda. And of course the way the election turned out and what Pa and Almeda had done for Shaw and Douglas and had promised to do for the others—all that just deepened people's allegiance to them.

I thought that after Christmas dinner Mr. Royce might

eventually close down his store. But he kept it open, although he was pretty subdued about promoting it. He probably knew it wouldn't do much good anyway, and I think he was starting to realize that maybe Pa and Almeda weren't the adversaries he had always imagined them to be. He also stopped making so much noise about making trouble for Pa and his claim. Maybe getting beat in the election sobered him into recognizing that he wasn't quite as all-powerful in the community as he had thought. He made good on his promise to call no more notes due. In fact, just shortly after the first of the year he lowered the interest rate on a few of the larger ones, not wanting folks to be mad at him for what they'd heard about Pa and Almeda's arrangements with Mr. Shaw.

Mr. Shaw kept paying them, and they kept paying the fellow in Sacramento, and so in the long run it actually worked out better for the Shaws than it had been before.

As it turned out, I didn't get the chance to visit again soon with Ankelita Carter. She wrote saying that she was sending some men to Sacramento for supplies, so Zack and Little Wolf and I arranged to go to the capital and meet them and return Rayo Rojo without having to ride all the way down to Mariposa. But I still hoped to meet the Fremonts some day!

Even with Christmas and the beginning of the new year behind us, I still couldn't get myself in a frame of mind to do much writing. Somehow the motivation was missing after the events leading up to the election and disappointments about my article and Mr. Fremont's loss. I tried to write a few articles throughout the first months of the year, but they were nothing I wanted to send in to Mr. Kemble. I found myself wondering if I'd ever write much again. I drew lots of pictures and kept writing in my journal, and otherwise spent most of the daytime in town at the Mine and Freight. Almeda kept working too, although by the beginning of March her pregnancy was far enough along that she had to slow down and take most afternoons off.

Several interesting things happened in town during those early months of 1857. Some meetings were held in Sacramento about town planning. Now that the gold rush was gradually giving way to the growth of California and the concerns of statehood and settlement, the state's leaders in the capital seemed to think communities like Miracle Springs needed some help figuring out what to do with themselves. Because of my articles, someone there had actually heard about the election and knew of the outcome. And so Pa received a personal invitation to come to the meetings. They asked if he'd be willing to make a short talk about the problems and difficulties he felt *he* had in being a leader in a former gold-boom town that was now growing into a more diverse community.

When the letter first came, everyone was excited about it, and Alkali Jones was laughing and cackling about Pa running for president himself next. Everyone was excited, except Pa. His response was just what you might have expected—casual and disinterested.

"I can't see what you're all making such a fuss about," he said. "They most likely sent this same letter to a hundred other men just hoping that *one* of them would show up with something to say."

But inside I could tell Pa was mighty proud, and a time or two I caught sight of him alone re-reading the letter, so I know he was thinking about it more than he was willing to let on.

He did go to Sacramento, and he did speak a little to the meeting of town leaders who were there, although he downplayed that when he got back, too. But it was obvious that he was different after that—more serious about being mayor, talking more about problems that needed solving in the community, thinking about the impact of things on the people he served as well as his own life and family.

One of the results of Pa's going to Sacramento was a town council.

"It's the way a town ought to be run," Pa told us, "so no one man can tell everybody else what to do. They can vote on things, and that way it doesn't all just rest on the mayor's shoulders. And besides that, the council gives the mayor someplace to go for advice, other men to talk to—"

"Other *men?*" repeated Almeda with a sly smile. "Are only men allowed on the council?" The rest of us laughed.

"You're dang right, woman!" said Pa with a grin. "You don't think after what you put this community through last year that anyone's going to stand for a woman on the town council!"

"They just might! And I suppose you're going to tell me that only men can vote for the council too?"

Pa smiled, drawing it out a long time, waiting until everyone quieted down and was watching for what he would say next.

"Well, actually what they recommended," he answered finally, "is that the mayor himself pick the people to be on the first council, instead of trying to call an election."

"And so no women will get selected?" persisted Almeda.

"I think you've just about got the gist of how California politics works at last," said Pa.

We all laughed again, Almeda louder than anyone.

"Seriously, Drummond," she went on, "are you really going to pick the council yourself? How will you choose?"

"I don't know yet. But I gotta have some folks I can talk to besides just you and Nick and Corrie and Alkali and the rest of you. That was all right for trying to decide about the election last year, when we all just got together and discussed everything. But what would folks think if that's how I did my mayoring, just getting my advice from my family? One thing's for sure, I'd never get re-elected! No, folks want to know their voice is being heard somehow. That's what they called 'representative government' in Sacramento. We all know that everybody votes for president, but they said the same thing's important in a town too, that the mayor and council represent all the people, not just their own interests."

Pa was starting to sound like a politician!

"They said those towns without a council yet ought to get one appointed so they can get it working and get the bugs worked out of how town government's supposed to function. Then in two years—that'd be in fifty-eight, when the next state elections are held—they can have people run for town council and mayor, and make it all more official."

"How many are on a council?" asked Zack.

"Oh, depends, son. In big cities, maybe ten or twelve. But for a little place like Miracle Springs, four or five, maybe six, is plenty."

"What does a town council do, Pa?" asked Becky.

"I reckon they just help the mayor decide things."

"But who says what the mayor decides and what the council decides?" I asked.

"Well, another thing they talked about in Sacramento is a town drawing up a set of what they call bylaws. That's like a set of instructions of who does what and how rules and laws are made. So that's something we got to do too, after we get a council. They've got some from other places we'll be able to look at and work from."

"What if the council votes and it's a tie?" said Zack.

"That's why you have to have a wise mayor who knows what he's about," replied Pa with a smile. "In cases where they can't make a decision, the mayor casts the deciding vote and they do what he says."

As it turned out, Pa wasted no time in getting together the first Miracle Springs town council. He went around and talked to folks, got lots of opinions and suggestions of who people'd trust to sort of be their community spokesmen and leaders. The first man he selected was Mr. Bosely, the owner of the General Store, and then Simon Rafferty, the sheriff. Those two surprised no one because they were men most folks knew and respected. Next there was Matthew Hooper, a rancher who lived about five miles from town. Pa said he wasn't sure if him being on the council was exactly legal, since he didn't actually live in town. But that could all be straightened out later, he said, and if it wasn't, then a change could be made at the next election. For now he and most folks around thought Mr. Hooper would be a real good help for speaking up for ranching interests. And to represent the miners, there was Hollings Shannahan, who had been in Miracle since 1850. But the last two—Pa had decided on six for the council—shocked everybody. The first was Almeda, and she was the most surprised of all!

"What will people say, Drummond?" she said. "Picking a woman's bad enough . . . but your own wife!"

"I don't care what they say, woman. You're one of the most qualified people around here, and everyone knows it. You ran for mayor. And what anyone thinks is their own business—I want you on my town council."

But his final selection made everyone for miles throw their hands up in the air wondering if Drummond Hollister had finally gone loco once and for all. He wouldn't say anything to any of us ahead of time, and on the day when he made the announcement of the council members to a gathering of people in town, he saved the surprise name for last.

"As the sixth and final person to help look over this town," Pa said, "I name a fellow I've had a difference or two with, but who I reckon has just about as much a say in the things that go on around here as anyone—Franklin Royce."

So that was Miracle Springs' first town council—Bosely, Rafferty, Hooper, Shannahan, Parrish-Hollister, and Royce— with Drummond Hollister mayor over them. As time went on, everyone saw Pa's wisdom in picking the people he did. Everyone came to have a real confidence in the council to make decisions that were for the whole community's good. Even Mr. Royce began to be seen in a new light. I think it meant a lot to him that Pa had picked him, although he wouldn't do much to show it.

The first meeting of the town council was a celebrated affair that was held, of all places, in a back room of the Gold Nugget, which they cleaned up for the occasion. Lots of people were there, curious to see what was going to happen. But for the meeting itself, Pa wouldn't let any spectators in.

"There may be time enough one day for all you gawkers to see us do some of our town counciling. But for this first time together, we aim to just talk among ourselves, and get a few matters of business settled."

Then he shut the door and disappeared inside, leaving all

the onlookers in the saloon to drink and talk and wonder out loud what there could possibly be for a Miracle Springs town council to talk about, anyway.

When Uncle Nick was telling us about it afterwards, he said, "There was more than one of the men that said, 'What in tarnation's got into Drum, anyhow? He's done got hisself so blamed official about everything since the election! He ain't no fun no more!' "

But mostly Uncle Nick said the men had a lot of respect for how Pa was handling the whole thing.

When Pa and Almeda got back later that evening it was already pretty late, but we were dying of curiosity. Pa didn't say much, but Almeda went on and on about it.

"You should have seen him!" she exclaimed. "Your father ran that meeting like he was the Governor himself! Why, he even had to shut me up once or twice."

"You told me to treat you like all the others and not to give you preferential treatment on account of us being married," said Pa in defense.

"I didn't mean you had to silence me in mid-sentence."

"You were carrying on, Almeda," said Pa, "and I didn't see anything else to do but shut you down before you made a fool of yourself by what you were saying."

"A fool of myself!"

"You were talking like a woman, not like a town councilman. And maybe you are a council*woman*, not a council*man*, but you still gotta act like a councilman. I'm just trying to protect you from getting criticized by any of the others."

Almeda didn't say anything for a minute, then added, "Well, even if I am still vexed with you for what you did, I still think you ran that meeting like the best mayor in the world, and I'm proud of you."

"What did you talk about, Pa?" asked Emily.

"Oh, not too much, I reckon. A town this size hasn't got all that much that anyone needs to decide. We just looked at a copy of some bylaws I brought from Sacramento and talked about some of the stuff, trying to decide how *we* ought to do things here in Miracle."

One of the things they decided over the course of the next few meetings had to do with growth and new businesses that might come to Miracle Springs in the future. With the way the state was growing so fast—and this was something Pa said they talked a lot about at the meetings in Sacramento—communities like ours had to make some decisions early about how much they wanted to grow and in what ways. Pa and the council members decided that the council would vote on any new businesses that wanted to come and start up in Miracle, so that they'd have the chance to determine if they thought it was a good idea or not.

As it turned out, this decision was one of the first ones to be tested, and the results were different than anyone had expected.

CHAPTER 40

PA'S FIRST BIG DECISION

As a result of all the ruckus the previous autumn about money and foreclosures and all the threats Mr. Royce had made about calling notes due, an unexpected turn of events landed Pa and the rest of the council in the middle of a controversy. Pa and Almeda were even more in the middle of it than anyone else.

When Almeda's friend from Sacramento, Mr. Denver, had helped to arrange with his boss, Mr. Finch, for them to borrow the money to help Patrick Shaw, the incident had apparently stirred up Mr. Finch's old antagonism toward Franklin Royce. Mr. Denver told Almeda that there was a time when his boss had thought about expanding their financial holdings into the northlands, and now it seemed that uncovering his old grievances had brought that desire to life again.

One day out of nowhere Carl Denver rode into town to see Almeda. Almeda's first thought was that something had gone sour on their arrangement with Mr. Finch and that he was about to call Pa and Almeda's money with *him* due. But that wasn't it at all, Mr. Denver assured her.

"Finch couldn't be more pleased to be involved with you people up here," he went on with a smile. "In fact, he's hoping this is but the beginning. Which brings me to the reason for my trip."

He reached into his coat pocket and pulled out several papers. From where I was standing in another part of the office, they looked like legal documents of some kind.

"Mr. Finch wants to open a branch of Finchwood Ltd. right here in Miracle Springs!" he announced. "He's already had all the documents drawn up, and he sent me up to find a site and begin making specific preparations."

"That's wonderful," replied Almeda. "But I can't imagine . . . why Miracle Springs? Finchwood is a sizeable investment firm. What can there possibly be here to interest you?"

"All of California is growing at an explosive rate. Mr. Finch is a shrewd businessman, and loses no opportunity to get in on the ground floor, as he calls it. He's convinced that Miracle Springs will one day become a sort of hub for this region north of Sacramento. And I have to tell you, Almeda," he went on, "no small part of that has to do with your impact upon him. He was quite taken with you—with your resolve, your determination. He's watched what went on here, followed the election, and then saw your husband at the recent town-leader meetings down in Sacramento."

"Mr. Finch met Drummond?"

"No, they didn't actually meet. But Mr. Finch has been considering a move of this kind for some time, so he went to the meetings to explore possibilities. He heard your husband address the meeting, and was duly impressed with him as well. Out of all the growing communities represented at those meetings, he came away thinking more strongly than ever that Miracle Springs was the town he wanted to invest in—with a new bank, with investment opportunities for the miners who happen to be doing well and need a place for their funds, and perhaps with other businesses as well."

"I must say, Carl, I'm . . . I'm rather speechless. It's so unexpected—to think that Miracle Springs could one day grow into an actual city."

"There's no *could* to it, Almeda. If Mr. Finch has his way—and he usually does—there will be no way to stop Miracle Springs from growing by leaps and bounds. A population of 10,000 or more within three to five years would not be out of the question. And you know what that means?"

"I imagine it would mean a great number of things," replied Almeda slowly, her expression turning very serious. "But what do you think it means, Carl?"

"It means money, Almeda, opportunity, jobs. Your business, even if no changes were made, would positively explode. But as I said, Mr. Finch is very taken with you and your husband. He would lose no chance to make some very attractive and lucrative opportunities available to you. He would like to help you expand your business. He told me to convey that to you personally. He would invest money in your husband's re-election campaign when the time comes. He even hopes to persuade one of you to join him in Finchwood in some capacity or other—perhaps with a stock option—in order that you and your husband might be influential in securing Finchwood access into the community, so that we would be able to gain people's trust, as it were."

"I see," responded Almeda, thinking heavily.

"It's a once-in-a-lifetime opportunity, Almeda. If the growth happens as Mr. Finch is convinced it can with his money pouring into the area, in five years you and your husband could wind up in a very secure position—even wealthy, by the standards of most people. Your husband would be mayor of one of California's leading small and growing cities. And who knows what opportunities can open up politically, with your being so close to Sacramento. Not to mention the vast influence you would both have right here in your own community. You would become its first man and first woman, with the prestige and wealth to accompany it!"

Almeda was silent a moment. It was clear Mr. Denver didn't understand her hesitancy.

"There is one thing you have perhaps not considered in all this," said Almeda at length.

"What is that?"

"The town council."

"Oh, not to worry. A mere formality," said Mr. Denver buoyantly. "It's money that runs politics, not politics that runs money, Almeda. Once the people of this community realize all the good to come of the kinds of investments and growth Finchwood will bring, they'll be begging us to come."

"A recent town ordinance was passed which says the town council must authorize any new business within Miracle Springs."

"Yes—and aren't both you and your husband on the council?"

"I am. Not Drummond."

"But he's the mayor. Why, with the two of you behind this thing, it can't lose!"

"There is one person who *will* lose from it, that much is certain," said Almeda."

"Who's that?" asked Denver.

"Franklin Royce," she answered. "His bank won't survive six months once a new one opens its doors."

"Mr. Finch *did* think of that," Mr. Denver observed with a sly smile. "He's been waiting for a chance to put him out of business for years. And ever since you came to us for help last year, he's been slowly hatching this scheme in that clever brain of his."

"Seems a little too bad."

"Too bad! Royce is a no-good crook! You as much as said so yourself. I thought the two of you hated him as much as Mr. Finch does. Hasn't he tried to put *you* out of business?"

"Yes, there's no denying he has . . . several times."

"Then here's your chance to get even and rid Miracle Springs of him forever."

Again, Almeda was silent.

"And from what I understand, he's opened a supplies outlet in direct competition with you," Mr. Denver added.

She nodded.

"Well, now do you see how well this will work out for everybody? Kill two birds with one stone, as the saying goes— drive Royce out of business, and his bank and store with him! And all the while Miracle Springs will be growing and you and your husband will be making money and gaining power. What more could anyone hope for!"

"What more, indeed," repeated Almeda, her voice filled with reservation in spite of Mr. Denver's enthusiasm. "But you do know that Franklin is on the council too?"

"Of course. I've done my background work before coming here. One vote won't hurt us. Five to one is just as good as six to zero. Besides, everyone in the whole community hates Royce too. We'll be performing a service to the whole area by getting rid of him! And just to make sure, I'll be contacting the other council members to outline the advantages to them personally for voting with Finchwood."

Almeda did not reply, and then the conversation moved off in other directions. Finally Mr. Denver left to go to the boarding house where he would be staying.

Miracle always seemed to be in the middle of *something* or another that had people stirred up and talking and taking sides. And no sooner had all the election hullabaloo settled down than we were smack in the midst of another upheaval. Carl Denver saw to that! He started right off talking to the members of the town council—all except one. Within a few days it was all over town about Finchwood's plans and all the growth and prosperity that would come to Miracle Springs and how good it would be for all its people.

Folks talked about it a lot, and almost everyone seemed to think it was a good thing. You can't stop progress, Mr. Denver had been telling them, and no one seemed inclined to try. Besides, they said, new businesses and new money and new investments in the community couldn't help but be good for everybody. And if California was going to grow, why shouldn't Miracle Springs get right in and grow as fast as anyplace else?

Undoubtedly the change would do damage to the Royce Miners' Bank, especially because Mr. Denver let it be known that Finchwood would probably lend money for land and homes at lower interest than Mr. Royce. I don't think most people wanted to hurt Mr. Royce, but at the same time they weren't all that worried about him, either. "If he can't keep up with the times, that's his own fault," Mr. Shaw commented to Almeda when he was over visiting. "Wouldn't bother me none at all to see him run out of here for good!"

Of course, Mr. Shaw had good reason to dislike Franklin Royce, but a lot of other people would probably have agreed with Alkali Jones assessment of the situation: "Serves the dang varmint right, hee, hee, hee!" he cackled. "He ain't been out fer nobody but his blame self for years, an' now it'll just be givin' him a dose o' his own medicine!"

Pa and Almeda were surprisingly quiet through the whole thing. I knew they were talking and praying together, but they didn't tell anyone what they were thinking. Almeda had remained somber ever since the day when Mr. Denver had come into the Freight office. I didn't understand her hesitation, if that's what was making her quiet about it. It seemed to me that it couldn't help but be good for her and Pa and the business. And in a way they'd already thrown in with Finchwood months before with their dealings over the Shaw and Douglas notes. I'd heard them talk once or twice about the possibility of getting even more money to lend to people if Mr. Royce got troublesome again. Pa had even jokingly said something about the new Hollister-Parrish "bank," and then laughed. So it seemed that what Mr. Finch was proposing fit right in with what they'd been thinking of themselves.

A special town council meeting was planned to vote on it, so that Mr. Denver could get the papers signed and finalize everything before he went back to report to Mr. Finch. During the week he was here, he had a sign painted, and the day before the meeting it went up in the window of an empty building two doors down from Mr. Bosely's. It read, *Future Home of Finchwood Ltd.*, with the words, *Investments, Banking, Securities* underneath in smaller letters. No one saw much of Mr. Royce all week.

On the morning of the meeting, I said to Pa at breakfast, "How are you going to vote, Pa?"

"Don't you know, girl, it's the council's decision to make, not mine."

"Then how's Almeda going to vote?"

"You're asking me? She doesn't tell me ahead of time.

When it comes to the council, she's not my wife. She's representing the town, not me. And I don't want to know what she's thinking, because then one of us might try to do some convincing for our own side, and that wouldn't be right for the town, now would it?"

"I guess not," I answered.

Just then Almeda walked in from the other room.

"Corrie asked me how you're going to vote," Pa told her.

"And what did you tell her?"

"That I didn't know, which I don't."

"When we're representing Miracle Springs, Corrie," Almeda went on, "we've got to do our best to lay our personal feelings aside. If we're going to be faithful to the town and its people, we've got to vote our conscience, even if it sometimes means being on the opposite side of a certain issue. Both of us have spoken to a lot of people, and we've prayed together for wisdom, but that's as far as our communication on the subject goes."

The meeting of the council was scheduled for six o'clock that evening. Because so many people were interested, Pa had arranged for the tables and chairs in the Gold Nugget to be moved aside and organized so that the meeting could take place in the main part of the saloon—the biggest single room in all of Miracle Springs.

When the time came, the place was full, with another twenty or thirty people milling around in the street outside. The council members sat up in front at a long rectangular table with Pa in the middle. Mr. Denver was full of smiles and greetings for everyone, and sat down in the front row of chairs. It was the first time our whole family had been in the Gold Nugget together since that first church service when Rev. Rutledge was new in town. There were chairs for us and for all the women who came, but most of the men had to stand.

Pa called the meeting to order by banging his fist down on the table two or three times.

"Quiet down!" he called out. "Hey, quiet . . . we have to get this meeting called to order!"

Everybody gradually stopped talking and buzzing. "This is a meeting of the Miracle Springs town council for the purpose of deciding whether to grant this petition—" Pa held up Mr. Denver's papers which had been sitting on the table in front of him. "This petition is from Finchwood Limited in Sacramento to set up a bank here in Miracle Springs."

You could still hear quite a bit of noise coming from the men standing around outside, but Pa ignored it and kept right on going.

"So before we decide, I need to ask if anybody's got anything to say. You've all got a right to speak to the council before we vote if you think there's anything we need to hear before making the decision."

Pa waited. The room was silent for a moment. Then Mr. Denver rose to his feet. He talked for about ten minutes, half toward Pa and the others up in front, but turning around into the saloon a lot too, saying mostly the same kinds of things he'd been saying all week about all the good Mr. Finch wanted to do for the people of Miracle Springs.

When he sat down, Pa said. "Any of the rest of you got anything to say?"

Mr. Shaw came forward.

"All right, Pat. What do you have to tell us?"

"Only this—that I think it's an opportunity we might not get again. And as for the folks of Finchwood, it seems to me we can trust them just as far, if not even further, than some of the people we've been having our financial dealings with up till now."

A small buzz went around at his pointed words. Mr. Royce sat in front not moving a muscle, but everyone knew what Mr. Shaw was talking about. Since Patrick Shaw had almost been thrown off his land by Mr. Royce, if anyone had a right to be saying what he was, it seemed that Mr. Shaw did.

"So I say we give them all the approval they want," he added, then went back to where he'd been standing.

From the nods and expressions of agreement, it was clear that most of the men present felt the same way.

"Anyone else?" said Pa over the hubbub.

"Get on with the votin', Drum!" called out someone. "We all know well enough what's gonna happen without no one talkin' 'bout it no more."

"Do yer mayorin', Drum!" cackled Alkali Jones. "Hee, hee, hee!"

"Okay, that's enough from you ol' coots," said Pa. "But I reckon you're right. It's time to get this thing decided and over with. So if there's nothing more to be said, I'm going to call the vote."

Immediately there was silence, and Pa called on the council members one at a time.

"Hooper," said Pa. "How do you vote—yea or nay about Finchwood's petition?"

"Yea," said Mr. Hooper. Another round of chatter spread through the room.

"Bosely?" said Pa.

"Yea."

"Rafferty?"

"I vote against it," said the sheriff. At his words the noise got immediately louder.

"What you got against 'em, Simon?" called out someone.

"Quiet down," said Pa. "You can't interrupt the voting like that. You all will just have to keep your opinions to yourself till we're done."

"I just got a feeling about it, that's all," said the sheriff, not paying any attention to Pa but answering the man anyway. "I just can't see all the good it'll do for Miracle to grow so big as they're saying. It'll make my job all the harder, that's for sure. And that's why I'm voting no."

"Royce?" said Pa.

"Nay," replied the banker. Everyone had expected that.

"Shannahan?"

"Yea."

Now it *did* get quiet. Everybody had figured the vote to be five-to-one, with Mr. Royce being the only person to be against it. Now suddenly it was three-to-two, with one vote left. No one had expected it to be close. And they sure hadn't expected what came next.

"Almeda," said Pa. "Looks like you're the one who's going to decide this thing."

"I wish you'd have remembered to let ladies go first, Drummond," said Almeda with a smile. "Then all this pressure would have fallen on one of the other men."

"Couldn't be helped," replied Pa. "It's just the way you were all sitting around the table. Besides, on a town council everyone's equal."

"Well, I'd still feel more comfortable not being last because I'm afraid I'm not going to clarify matters much. I vote no."

The silence instantly erupted into gasps and oohs and ahs and comments all filling up the room. The certain outcome was suddenly three-to-three—a tie vote on the first major decision the town council of Miracle Springs had to make!

"What you gonna do now, Drum?" someone called out.

"He's gonna vote himself," said Uncle Nick loudly. "That's what we got a mayor for!"

"Well, I reckon now we're about t' see what kind o' stuff our mayor's made of, ain't we?" said someone else.

"What's it gonna be, Drum—yea or nay?"

"Yeah, Drum, don't keep us in suspense! How you gonna vote?"

"Well, maybe I'd tell you if you baboons'd shut up long enough to let a mayor get a word in edgeways!" shouted Pa into the middle of all their hollering and talking.

Gradually the noise subsided, and within another minute the place was dead silent, with every eye in the room fixed on Pa, who was standing up behind the table where the other council members were sitting. He waited a moment longer. I don't know what he was thinking about, but everyone was listening for him to say just a single word—yea or nay. When he finally spoke, he said neither.

"I aim to say a few words before I cast my vote," he said. "You all know I'm no speechmaker. But I reckon a mayor's gotta get used to making a speech now and then, and so maybe now's as good a time as any for me to have a start at it. I didn't plan this out, because I didn't figure I'd have to do any voting today. But since it looks like I have to cast the deciding vote, I suppose I ought to tell you what I've been thinking about this week."

He stopped and took a breath, as if he was getting ready to jump into an icy river and wasn't too pleased at the prospect. Then he plunged ahead. And if I didn't know it was my own Pa, I would have taken him for a downright politician! It was just about one of the finest speeches I'd ever heard!

"We've got a lot of things to consider," Pa finally went on, "if it's gonna fall on our shoulders to say what should be the future of this town of ours. Now I've been talking to a bunch of you this past week, and doing a lot of thinking. Most of you say you figure change and new business and more money would be good for everybody, and so we ought to just let it go ahead and happen. And I guess we all figured that's how the vote would go, too. Probably most of you are a mite surprised that we've got a tie on our hands. And I'm as surprised as anyone. But even as little as I know about it, because I take my mayoring seriously, I did a bit of thinking these last days about what I thought too, and what I'd do just in case I did have to vote. And a couple of things stuck in my mind."

He stopped for a couple of seconds, just sort of looking around the room at all the eyes on him, then went ahead.

"The first thing I found myself wondering is this—if all this change and growth that Mr. Denver's predicting *does* happen, what kind of place is Miracle Springs going to be five or ten years from now? I'm sure he's right, because he knows more than a man like me about bringing in lots of money and new people. And maybe we'd all get rich. But that's what they said about the gold too, and not too many of us in *this* room are getting fat from having so much money stashed in Mr. Royce's bank."

A ripple of laughter spread through the room.

"Maybe we would get rich," Pa went on. "But it still strikes me that we'd have to ask what kind of place Miracle would be with five or ten thousand people here. Speaking just for myself, I'm not at all sure I'd want to be mayor of a place like that, or would even want to live here. Can you imagine Miracle with ten thousand people? Why, tarnation, the place'd spread so far in every direction, the Hollister place would be in the middle of town! We'd have no woods, no creek, no mine! Even half of Hooper's spread would have streets running through it!"

He paused for a minute while everyone laughed.

"Why Miracle would be a dad-blamed city! There'd be no room for mines anymore. Every inch for miles would be taken up with buildings and people! And I guess I'm just not at all sure I like the idea of that. I don't know about you, but I kind of like Miracle Springs the way it is."

Suddenly everyone quieted down as Pa's words sank in. It was obvious nobody had thought about the question quite like that, and Pa's questions got everyone sobered up in a hurry.

"The second thing that bothered me is gonna surprise a few of you. It surprises me to find myself thinking like this too! But you all know that besides my mayoring, I've been trying to take living as a Christian seriously too, so I'm not afraid to tell you that I pray about things a lot more than I used to. And I've been praying about this vote too. When you pray, every once in a while you find an answer from God coming your way that you didn't expect. And this is one of those times.

"What I got to thinking about was loyalty, and what it means. Loyalty to other folks—not just to friends and family, but to all sorts of others we owe something to. Seems to me loyalty's in short supply these days. Everyone's out to get all he can, and we don't stop too much to consider what we should be doing about those people Jesus calls our neighbors. But he tells us in the Good Book that we're supposed to do as we'd like to be done by. And that means standing by our neighbor whether he stands by us or not. It means being loyal whether someone's been loyal to us or not. It means trying to do good wherever you can, no matter what anyone else has done to you.

"So I found myself thinking a lot about a certain individual in this town of ours by the name of Franklin Royce—"

Another buzz of whispers and movement went around, then quickly settled down. Everyone was anxious to hear what Pa was gonna say.

"Now, you all know that Royce hasn't been a particular friend of mine, or anyone else's around here. He's pulled some pretty lowdown stuff, and he's hurt more than one upstanding man with his greed."

I glanced over at Mr. Royce. His face had a scowl on it, but he didn't dare move a muscle. I could almost feel the anger rising up from his reddening neck into his cheeks!

"He's tried to take my place a time or two, and would've taken Shaw's and Douglas's if Almeda and I hadn't stopped him. So I'd have to say that Mr. Royce has been a mean man, and maybe some of you'd just as soon be rid of him and his bank altogether.

"But you know, if it hadn't been for his bank, half of you in this room wouldn't have your houses and farms and ranches. Almeda's store used money from Royce's bank a time or two, and so did I. Much as we don't want to admit it, Franklin Royce has done a lot for this community. Even if we don't always see eye to eye, he's just as much a part of Miracle Springs as I am or as you are. Why, he was almost your mayor! And it was money from Royce's bank that saved the life of my Becky.

"Maybe Mr. Royce, for all his faults of the past, deserves a little of our loyalty too. He's put five or six years of his life into this place, and I'm not so sure I can be party to watching his business get ruined because he hasn't treated me so kindly. Seems like when times get rough, folks have to stick together and show their loyalty to one another. Maybe this is the time when we need to show Mr. Royce that the folks of Miracle Springs can be loyal too."

There was another pause, this time a long one, while people shifted around in their chairs or shuffled their feet.

"So here's what I figure to do," Pa continued finally. "I think we ought to think a little more about what kind of future we want for this place we call our home. Do we want it to stay the nice little town it is, or do we want it to become a city that's growing faster than we can keep up with? Then I want to go have a talk with Mr. Royce. And I want to tell him I'm willing to give him my hand and be a friend to him, and show my loyalty to him, even if he does try to put my wife's store out of business!"

More laughter erupted, and people shifted about nervously.

"What I aim to say to him is this: 'Now look, Franklin, it's no secret that you're charging more interest than some of the big banks in Sacramento. Why don't you be neighborly, and show *your* loyalty to the folks of Miracle Springs, by lowering the rates on everybody's loans to match what Finchwood would give them? They'll like you all the more for it, and then there won't be any reason for a new bank to open up. What do you say, Franklin?'

"That's what I'm going to say to our friend and banker, Mr. Royce, first chance I get," said Pa, glancing around the table where the council sat. Everyone chuckled when he looked straight at Mr. Royce.

"And in the meantime, since we've got town business to conduct right now, I'm going to cast my vote. I vote no."

He was immediately interrupted by sounds throughout the room. I had been looking at Mr. Royce, and my eyes drifted to Almeda, who was sitting right next to him. She was crying. She was so proud of Pa—we all were!

"So, Mr. Denver," Pa was trying to say, "I'm afraid you're going to have to tell your Mr. Finch that the petition's denied for right now. But you tell him how much we appreciate his interest in Miracle Springs. And you can tell him for me, that if he is still interested in Finchwood coming up this way, try us again a year from now. That'll give us a chance to think about all this a little more slowly. And it'll also give us a year to decide whether we think Miracle Springs is in need of some more competition in the banking business, or if the bank we've got seems to be operating to everyone's satisfaction."

Again Pa glanced in Mr. Royce's direction. The banker's face had a look of stunned joy on it, realizing that the man he styled his arch enemy had just saved his bank from another enemy.

I think Pa's final words were lost on Mr. Royce for the moment. But there would be plenty of people to remind the banker of their significance in the coming months!

People began moving around the room, and lots of men were already walking up to the bar to start ordering drinks. The women and children who had been there made haste to leave. The members of the council stood up, and some talking and hand-shaking followed.

Then almost as an afterthought, Pa shouted out: "This meeting of the town council is adjourned!"

CHAPTER 41

UNCLE NICK LEARNS TO PRAY

Pa's speech and vote sure did show what the new mayor was made of! Pa had shown his mettle in front of the whole town, and there couldn't have been a prouder, happier bunch of kids and a wife than we were riding home in the wagon that night after the meeting! It didn't even matter about the vote— it was what Pa'd done. He'd been a leader, a mayor. And it felt good to see him strong like that, and courageous to speak out.

Things seemed to change after that. The mayor and town council were more than just formalities now. They had made a real decision that changed something that would have happened without them. And if Mr. Royce did lower interest rates like Pa hoped he would, then as mayor Pa would have done everybody a lot of good. Miracle Springs might not grow as fast as some of California's new towns and cities. But at least from now on, folks around here knew they had people they could trust looking out for them.

One of the other events that happened early that spring before the babies were born was a big town picnic. But first I want to tell you about a conversation Pa and Uncle Nick had. I didn't actually hear it. Pa came in late one evening, got me and Almeda and Zack together by ourselves after the others were in bed, and told us about it.

"Nick's worried about Katie," he said quietly. We all waited for him to explain further.

"She's still quiet and moody. Of course, that's no surprise

238

to any of us," he went on, "because we can see it well enough. But he thinks it's his fault in some way, that he must have done something, or that he isn't being all to her he ought to be."

"Bless his dear heart," said Almeda tenderly.

"I told him it's not his doing—"

"Of course not," added Almeda. "He's a fine husband and father."

"That's exactly what I said," Pa went on. "Why, nobody from the old days would even recognize Nick! He's that different."

"So what did he say?"

"Aw, he just kept going on about how Katie wouldn't talk to him and was sullen and quiet and how he didn't know what to do. He was frustrated, I could tell that much. Seemed like he was ready to get angry with her one minute, but then the next remembered her condition and felt bad for not having more patience. He just doesn't know what to do, that's all."

"What did he say?"

"He said, 'She's been downright impossible lately. When I married her I didn't bargain for no wife that's moody all the time. What kind of marriage is it when you can't even talk together? But she ain't saying nothing no more, and I wind up talking just about the weather and the mine.' He'd go on like that, but then suddenly stop himself and feel bad just for saying it."

"It could be the pregnancy, you know, Drummond. It's harder on some women than others, and she's a good seven months along."

"So are you," said Pa.

"Are you saying I'm fat?"

"Just good and plump," replied Pa with a smile. "And you aren't moping around like you're mad at the world."

"But then I have you for a husband," said Almeda with a loving smile.

"Yeah, I guess you do at that!"

"But it's not really the pregnancy," Almeda mused. "That probably is wearing her out some, especially with little Erich to keep up with. But there's more than that—it's down deep. She's a troubled woman, Drummond. It's her spirit that's in turmoil, not her body."

Pa sighed. "Yeah, I know you're right. That much is plain from one look in her face. She's just not at peace with life."

"Does Nick know that?" she asked.

"I think so. I asked him when it all started. He said that it had been growing gradually for a long time, but it seemed to start getting worse a while back after he'd gotten her to go to church with us one Sunday. Avery preached a sermon about how we've all got to make God a regular part of our life every day, not just here and there."

"I remember the day very well. And now that you mention it, she was particularly quiet that afternoon."

"Nick said he had a feeling she was thinking about it. 'You remember when she first came' I asked him, 'when she said her aunt used to go to church every Sunday and prayed and did all kinds of religious stuff, but then didn't really live by it much the rest of the week?' Then I told him that she was more than likely watching all the rest of us mighty close, and especially him, to see if our religion was something we lived by. 'I don't mean no offense to you, Nick,' I said, 'but you gotta make sure you live by what you believe.'

" 'What do you mean?' he asked. 'I'm doing the best I can. But it ain't easy, Drum, tryin' to be helpful with her grumpy all the time and ignorin' me.'

" 'Calm down,' I said, 'I know what kind of man you are. I'm just saying you can't go on with your business like maybe you done in the past. You gotta go out of your way to help her.'

"I kept reminding him that she most likely had lots of things brewing down deep inside that had nothing to do with him, but with what she thought about God, and other memories out of her past like her aunt. I told him that all those things and attitudes were probably coming back at her now.

" 'Why won't she tell me about it then?' he asked me.

" 'Can't tell you that, Nick,' I said. 'It's not easy to talk about the past sometimes, especially for a woman like Katie who's used to being independent and in control of things. She probably doesn't want to admit to having any kind of trouble inside herself. That's just the way some folks are.' "

"Sounds to me like you gave him pretty good advice," said Almeda.

Pa shrugged, then continued his story. " 'Well what am I supposed to do?' Nick asked me.

" 'You just be as nice and as gentle to her as you can be,' I said. 'And keep remembering that she's carrying your little son or daughter inside her.'

" 'I'll do it, Drum,' he said.

" 'Then you pray for her, Nick,' I told him. 'You pray for her real hard, and you pray for her all the time.'

" 'What am I supposed to pray? I ain't no praying sort like you and Almeda.'

" 'Well then it's high time you became a praying man,' I told him. 'You look here, Nick—that wife of yours needs you now more than she's ever needed anyone in her life. And she needs more than just you being nice—even though she needs that too. She's got something going on down inside her, and she needs God to be her friend. And that probably isn't going to happen without lots of prayer, because Katie's mighty headstrong when it comes to God. And you being her husband, your prayers mean more than anybody else's because you know what her needs are. We'll all be praying too, but you being the man of that house, and Katie being your wife, you're the one who can take charge of the situation with your prayers. So you gotta do it, you hear me? You gotta pray for her.'

"Well, he shrugged and didn't say much for a long time. He wasn't used to thinking of himself like that. He's like most folks with that fool notion that praying's something you hire the preacher to do, and that living like a Christian's something you do on Sunday and forget the rest of the time. But I told him he's got to get to the business of being God's man in that family of his if he wants to pull his wife through this.

" 'But I don't know how to pray, Drum,' he said again.

" 'You can't have forgotten all your ma and pa taught you,'

I said. 'Even I knew them well enough to know they taught you and Aggie better than that. You know how to pray well enough. You just got out of practice because you haven't done it all these years. And now it's time you got at it again!'

" 'But what do I *say?*'

" 'There's nothing special you have to say. Just talk to God, that's all.'

" 'Out loud?'

" 'God doesn't care if it's out loud or not, Nick. Just talk to him, like he was right there in the room with you. You don't have to say a lot of words to get his attention. He's there. He's waiting for you to make him part of what you're about. He's not like us, Nick, who can only talk to a few folks at a time. He can be with all his children at once. So just tell him what you're thinking and feeling. And pray for Katie. Pray that he would open up Katie's heart.'

"He was quiet again. He was thinking pretty hard on what I was saying. I think it was like lots of things coming back to him from when he was just a kid, things he hadn't stopped to think about for a long time.

" 'But I don't know what's supposed to happen, Drum.' he said.

" 'Well, if you're praying for God to open up Katie's heart, then that's what's gonna happen,' I told him. 'That's the way it works. That's the kind of prayer God wants real bad to answer.' "

Pa looked around at the rest of us with a smile. " 'Look at me,' I said. 'That wife of mine—before she was even my wife, I don't doubt—and my daughter, and maybe even my son, for all I know—they were all praying for *me*. And lo and behold if some places down inside me didn't eventually open up and I begin to remember things and think about how I ought to be living and how I ought to be listening to God more. And pretty soon, Drum Hollister's praying out loud and trying to live his life as a Christian, and even some of his old friends are calling him *Reverend*.'

" 'So you see, Nick,' I said, 'that's just the way it works. If you pray for somebody, one way or another there's gonna be a change in their life. You remember what kind of man I used to be! It ain't gonna be all that tough for God to get through to a woman like Katie, just so long as you keep praying.'

" 'She can be a mighty headstrong woman,' said Nick. When he said it he sighed, and I could tell he wasn't being critical. It was just that frustration coming out again.

" 'Well, maybe that's so. But we'll all be praying with you, Nick,' I told him. 'And some time or another, something down inside her is going to tell her she's not as in control of life as she's always figured. That time comes sooner or later to everyone. For me it was Aggie's dying and the kids showing up. All of a sudden, my whole world changed and a little door somewhere inside me opened a crack. And that's when God started poking his head through, and for the first time in my life, I was ready to listen.

" 'Well, that time will come for Katie too. So when I say you have to wait, that's what you're waiting for—that time when the little door inside of her heart opens up a crack and she looks out and says, "Maybe I do need to know God more than I've always thought." Then you can pray with her.'

" 'I'm not sure how,' Nick said.

" 'You're the man,' I told him. 'You gotta take the lead and show her that you can pray. Just ask for God to be in both of you and to show himself to you, and pray that you'll be open to let him do what he wants to do in your hearts. And then if she's willing,' I said, 'then you encourage her to pray that same thing, that God would show himself to her and that he'd live in her heart and help her to understand things better and be a friend to him like she hadn't been up until then. If she'd pray that, I think you'd have yourself a new woman, Nick—one with a smile on her face.'

"He was real quiet again. This was all pretty new to him. I'm not sure he even liked it much. But I could tell he knew it was true, and knew what he had to do."

The cabin got real quiet. From the look in Almeda's eyes I could tell she was far away. But this time it wasn't the look of pain that came from memories of Boston. It was a contented, peaceful look. I knew she was reflecting on the changes that had come to us all, to her, and especially to Pa. Even though no one said anything right then, we all *felt* so complete—a genuine *family*, talking and praying together about the deep and important things in life.

The late-night silence was broken by footsteps as Emily walked out from her room.

"I'm sorry, Pa," she said. "I wasn't asleep, and I couldn't help listening. I was concerned about Katie."

"Come over here, girl," said Pa. Emily walked over to him, and he stretched out his arm around her waist and pulled her close to him. "I'm glad you came out to join us. We're gonna pray for Katie, and I want you to pray with us."

"Thank you, Pa," she said, then sat down on the floor at his feet. Pa kept one of his great strong hands resting on her shoulder.

"After Nick and I were done talking," Pa went on in a moment, "I asked him if he wanted to pray right then with me. I think it took him by surprise, the thought of two grown men praying together like that. But he just nodded. Then he waited to see what I was gonna do. So I bowed my head and reached across and put my hand on his arm, and then I closed my eyes and started praying for him and Katie. Afterward he told me he was surprised to hear me pray in just normal words, without trying to use a bunch of church-words like the Reverend does on Sundays. But I told him, 'Nick, the Lord's not much concerned with a batch of big words that sound like they come out of the Bible. He only wants us to talk to him, that's all, like the people we *really* are, not like someone we're pretending to be. That's what I told him afterwards. But right then I just closed my eyes and prayed for him and Katie, and especially that Katie would come to see that God wasn't her enemy and that he wanted to be her friend. Then I prayed that Nick would find the courage to pray for her and to be the man he was supposed to be. He hardly moved a muscle, and when I finished it was quiet a long time.

"I kept waiting with my eyes closed, 'cause I wanted him to pray, so he could see it wasn't such a fearsome thing after all. It seemed to take him forever to get up the gumption, but finally he said, 'God, I ain't much practiced in this kind of thing. But if you'd give me a hand now and then, I'll try to pray more. So I ask you to help me do what Drum says and pray for Katie. Help me to know what to say to her. And I ask you to make her be able to listen when people talk about you without getting her dander up. Help me to know what to say and do. And help me to be able to listen to you too.'

"Anyhow, that's something like what he prayed," Pa added.

"Good for him," said Almeda softly. "What a wonderful beginning! I know many doors will begin to open for the two of them very soon."

"And now let's us pray for them both," said Pa. "Five of us praying, especially five of us who love Nick and Katie— why, that's a powerful lot of prayer for God to be able to use!"

He took his hand off Emily's shoulder and placed it around her little white hand. Then he reached out with his other and took hold of Zack's. Almeda and I joined hands to complete the circle. We all bowed our heads and one at a time prayed for Uncle Nick and Aunt Katie.

CHAPTER 42

SPRING PICNIC

One of the next decisions Pa made as mayor was to announce that there was going to be another town picnic on the first day of spring that year. He told us that he'd been thinking about the gathering we'd had three-and-a-half years earlier at the church's dedication, and thinking it had been too long since we'd done something like that as a community together. So he figured that if he was mayor, he ought to be able to do something about it.

He announced it in church one Sunday early in March.

"On the twenty-first of March," he said, "that's on the Saturday two weeks from today, we're gonna bring in spring with a picnic right out here in the meadow between the church and the town. I want you all to come, and we'll celebrate the day together. That's on orders from your mayor!"

Everyone chuckled, and Pa moved to sit down. For the next two weeks, the whole town looked forward to the chance to get together again. Most of the women—and there were a lot more of them now than there had been in 1853!—spent the time cooking and baking. It was almost like getting ready for a fair!

When the day came, it couldn't have been prettier. There had been rain through the week, and Pa was wondering what to do if it rained on Saturday. But the storm passed on into the mountains and the sun came out Friday afternoon. It was a bit chilly on Saturday, and still a little wet, but *so* fresh and clean!

As I walked into the meadow that afternoon, there was still

moisture and dew all about in the shady places, and where the sun shone the grass sparkled. It looked as if the whole area was covered with thousands of tiny glass prisms, all reflecting the sunlight like diamonds.

We were the first to arrive, and as I walked through the meadow, in the distance by the edge of the woods I saw a deer calmly nibbling on the fresh wet grass. She lifted her head and looked around, her tan coat gleaming when the sun hit it as she moved through the shadows. With each movement her velvet-like body shone with the essence of freedom I had always dreamed about.

I looked up and breathed the crisp air with pleasure. The sky was blue with clouds billowing gently across the sky. A whisper of cool wind blew by me, and I smelled again the fragrance of clean, fresh, springtime air.

Gradually more people began to arrive. The women were dressed brightly in colorful spring apparel, the men wearing dark trousers and flannel shirts. A few of the women were carrying parasols and twirling them around—some red, some pink. As the people slowly came and the meadow filled, all the colors and sounds and sights reflected the joy that was felt by everyone.

The men got tables set up and then we arranged food as it arrived and got everything ready. As the crowd enlarged, most of the younger kids went running off, some playing tag and other games.

"What can I do?" asked Becky, as Almeda was preparing one table.

"Hmm . . . let's see," replied Almeda, "why don't you go see if you can pick me some nice wildflowers to use here on the table."

Becky was off in a second, glad to be of some help. "But don't get near those woods again!" yelled Emily after her. Almeda and I both laughed.

After a while we were ready to begin eating. As the men were gathering around the table and the women were spreading out the last of the food, Rev. Rutledge asked if he could say a few words before we began.

"Ye mean we's gonna have t' listen to another one o' yer sermons?" said Alkali Jones, loud enough that everybody could hear.

A great laugh went up from those nearby.

"I will try to make this one as short as possible," said Rev. Rutledge, laughing himself and joining in the fun.

"You know preachers, Alkali," said Pa. "Whenever they see a crowd of people, they immediately start thinking of something to say!"

"And if they don't think of something right off, then they pass the collection plate!" added Rev. Rutledge. His joke got another good laugh out of everybody.

"When I was a child," the minister began as the laughter died away, "my parents always had a celebration like this to start off the season of spring. Most of our friends remembered the coming of spring on Easter, and in the church we went to, Easter was always a busy day. But my parents wanted to preserve Easter as a day spent thinking only of the resurrection and the true meaning of the day. Thus our family celebrated the first day of spring separately, as we are doing now."

The minister paused a moment to look around at the townspeople gathered in the meadow.

"Spring is the season of new life," he went on, "when new things begin to grow and new life bursts forth out of the earth. During springtime we witness the cycles of life and nature emerging in their newness, and all about us we see God's creation alive in the earth. But spring is also the time of year when Jesus Christ rose from the grave. And so the resurrection is the true basis for what spring means. We can let ourselves be reminded of the life that Jesus gave us when we see the new life that nature gives us during this wonderful green, growing, fragrant time of the year.

"So I would like to give a special thank you to our mayor, Drummond Hollister, for arranging this picnic today. As you can see, it is especially meaningful for me. And I would like to thank you all for being here."

Then Rev. Rutledge prayed, and immediately everyone began to eat. I don't know if I'd ever seen so much food before. There was every kind of meat and salad and fruit and bread imaginable. Afterward, people gradually began getting up and going about, visiting, the children playing, men smoking their pipes or chatting and playing horseshoes or discussing their claims and the latest gold prices, while the women worked on clearing up the tables and leftover food.

When no one else was around him for a minute, Mr. Royce walked up to Pa.

"Hollister," the banker said, "I think the time has come for me to acknowledge what you did for me at the town council meeting."

"I meant what I said," replied Pa.

"Nevertheless, I want you to know that I'm extremely appreciative."

"It was for the good of the town."

"*And* for me," said Mr. Royce. "Your vote more than likely saved my bank, and my whole future. And I want to say thank you."

He extended his hand. Pa took it and gave it a firm shake. Then the eyes of the two men met. Pa still held on to Mr. Royce's hand.

"I meant what I said about loyalty, Royce," said Pa. "And about being a friend and neighbor to you."

"I know you meant it, Hollister. You've proved yourself a man of your word. I didn't think I could admit this several months ago, but I have to say now that the best man won last November. Miracle Springs is better off with you as its mayor than it would have been with me."

"Well, I'm just glad you're on the council," said Pa, "and that we can start working together on the same side from now on." He relaxed his grip and let the banker's hand go.

"Well, thank you again, Hollister. And as for the question

on interest rates, I'm looking into all that. I want to be fair to the people. If you'll just give me some time to get the details worked out—"

"Certainly, Royce," answered Pa, then added with a smile, "just don't wait too long. The people are all anxious to know what you're going to do."

"I'll move along as quickly as I can, believe me. Just tell the people they can count on me."

"Done!" said Pa. "They will appreciate it, Franklin."

The picnic that day gave us our first sight of someone who would be part of the Hollister future, though we had no idea of it at the time. There were quite a few people at the picnic that I didn't know. New families were coming to Miracle Springs regularly.

After we were through eating, I saw Zack over on the other side of the field throwing a ball back and forth with someone I didn't know, a boy who looked about Zack's own age. Then a while later, when I looked at them again, there were four or five others who had joined them scattered about. The stranger was hitting the little ball with a stick and the others were chasing after it. A few minutes later Zack brought the new boy over to where Pa and Almeda and Emily and I were seated on the grass. He was every bit as tall as Zack, and wearing a straw hat with a white shirt and blue knickers (which I found out later to be of some significance). He had light brown eyes and curly red hair with lots of freckles on his face.

"This here's Mike, Pa," said Zack. "His family just got here from the east."

Pa stood up and shook his hand. "Mike what?" he said in a friendly voice.

"McGee's the name, and baseball's the game," the boy replied. The instant he let go of Pa's hand, he reached into his pocket and pulled out a little white ball, the same one they had been playing with earlier.

"Baseball . . . what's that?" asked Emily.

"What's baseball!" exclaimed Mike McGee. "Why it's just

the newest, most exciting game there is. They call me 'Lefty.' "

"Well none of us have ever heard of it," said Pa. "Why don't you tell us about it? Is that stick you got there something to do with it?"

"This stick," said McGee, holding up the rounded piece of wood, "has *everything* to do with it! This is called a bat, and you've gotta hit the ball with the bat."

He took a few steps away from us, then tossed the ball up into the air, slung the bat up over his shoulder as he grabbed it with both hands down near one end. As the ball came back down, he swung the wood around fast. It hit the ball with a loud cracking sound, and the ball went sailing out across the meadow in a big arch, landing over next to the woods.

"Just like that!" he said. Tad, who had just walked up to join us, was off like a flash to retrieve the ball and bring it back to Mike. By now a few more people were gathering around, but something told me young McGee was paying more attention to my sister Emily than all the other people put together.

"You hit it a long ways!" exclaimed Tad, running up puffing with the ball.

"That's nothing. You should see how far they hit it in a real game. My older brother Doug took me to see the first baseball game played between two regular teams. He played for the New Jersey Knickerbockers himself. That was back in '46. I was just eight then. They played against a team from New York."

"How'd it turn out?" asked Zack.

"I was nine before the game ended," replied Mike. "That first game took almost a year because they'd stop and then start again later. Nobody really knew how to play, so there were arguments and disputes through the whole game. My brother was so sick of the arguing, on top of losing the game 23 to 1—"

"Tarnation, boy!" exclaimed Uncle Nick, "that ain't no game, however you play it. That's more like a slaughter!"

"That was the score, all right. And my brother said he'd never play baseball again. So he gave me this here bat and ball and uniform. Now, do any of you want to get up a game?"

"But how do you play?" asked Zack.

"I plumb forgot—none of you know how to play!" he said. "Well, one team hits the ball and tries to run around the diamond and score an ace."

"What's an ace?" asked Emily, looking up into Mike's face.

"That's what it's called when you score a point by running in from third and touching home plate."

"Home plate . . . diamond . . . third? You're not makin' sense!" said Zack.

"And in the meantime," Mike went on without paying any attention to Zack, "the other team tries to catch the ball and throw it ahead of the runner so one of his teammates can tag him out before he gets to the base."

"It sounds mighty confusing," said Pa laughing. "I doubt if you're gonna get many around here to play. We can't understand a word you're saying! How many does it take to play?"

"Eighteen—nine on each team."

"Eighteen! You'll *never* get eighteen people in all of California to make heads or tails of what you're talking about!"

"If nobody knew how to play for that first game, how did anybody know what to do?" asked Emily.

"It sure sounds like one side knew how to play, judging from the score," Uncle Nick said.

"To answer your question, Miss," said McGee, "all the fellers who were there knew how to play, but everybody had their own brand of the game, coming from different places. You see, it was already played a bit before that, but not in an organized way or anything. That's why the game took so long. The arguments got so fierce they had to keep stopping it and figure out a way to agree on the rules before continuing on. The one game had three different sessions to it, like I said, stretching for almost a year."

"Well that's about the dad-blamdest kind o' game I ever heard of!" piped up Alkali Jones. "Weren't no *game* at all, from the sound of it, but more like a war. Hee, hee, hee!"

Everybody had a good laugh, and after a little more talk,

Mike managed to get half a dozen or so of the boys to join him. They walked over to the far end of the field where he began explaining the game to them. Emily followed to watch.

I got up and walked toward the hillside overlooking the meadow, where over three years ago I had looked down on the gathering we'd had to celebrate the completion of the building of the church. That other day seemed so long ago and much had happened since. Yet up there on the sloping hillside, everything still looked the same. It reminded me of how God had watched over us during the years since then.

Wild lilies were in bloom, and the birch trees were just beginning to get their fresh growths of new bark and tiny green leaves. The wildflowers brought back to my mind Rev. Rutledge's words, *"We can let ourselves be reminded of the life that Jesus gave us when we see the new life that nature gives . . ."*

I walked up the hill, turned around, and looked down on the meadow just at the same spot I had that day three years before. When I was alone, questions about my future always seemed to nag at me. I wanted God to have complete control over my life in whatever I did, but I couldn't keep the fears and anxieties from bothering me from time to time.

Down on the field I watched the group of boys playing with "Lefty" Mike McGee. Every once in a while I heard his voice yelling out some kind of instruction to them, or pointing to get them to go stand someplace else. He didn't seem to be having much success explaining the game of baseball to them. I couldn't help laughing a time or two as I watched.

Zack and Tad were in the middle of it. My eyes followed Zack around. I knew that occasionally he struggled with the same kinds of questions that I did, although being a boy I don't suppose his anxieties went as deep. Boys have a way of being able to take things more as they come, while girls have to think everything out on a dozen levels.

"What are you going to do, Zack?" I asked him once.

"What do you mean?"

"Well, we can't just stay at home and live with Pa and Almeda forever, you know."

"There's the mine," he said. "I figured I'd work the mine with Pa and Uncle Nick."

"No mine lasts forever. Then what?"

"I don't know."

"Don't you find yourself wondering about things, about other places you might go, things to see, people to meet?"

"Not much. I like it here in Miracle. But I reckon you're right, we can't just live with Pa when we get to be adults."

"Hey, I've got an idea, Zack!" I said. "We could go live in Almeda's house in town. It's been empty all this time. Then we could stay in Miracle and do whatever we'd be doing, but it'd sorta be like being on our own."

"You think she'd let us?"

"Sure. She's said once or twice what a shame it is for the house not to be used."

"But what if one of us gets married?" suggested Zack.

"Well *I'm* not worried," I answered. "There's no fear of that about me! *You're* the one some girl will come along and want to grab."

"Nah, not me! I ain't gonna get married."

"Then what are you gonna do if the mine plays out?"

"I don't know. Maybe Little Wolf and I will raise horses like his Pa. And we've talked about going riding together, but I don't know where. I reckon you're right—there is a heap of world to see.

"What about you, Corrie?" Zack asked. "You got plans? What're you gonna do?"

"I don't know. I want to keep writing. But it's hard to say if something is always going to be what God wants for you. I'd like to travel."

This conversation was the most I'd ever gotten Zack to talk personally about himself, and I hoped we'd have the chance to talk like that again.

I didn't stay up on the hillside for too long, just long enough to quiet myself down. I got up from the base of my favorite old oak tree, gave its gnarled trunk an affectionate pat with my hand, and then started back down the slope to rejoin the picnic.

In fact, I thought to myself, maybe I'd go join in whatever Lefty McGee was trying to teach the others about his new game. I'd like to see if I could hit that little ball with that stick!

CHAPTER 43

UNEXPECTED LABOR

Doc Shoemaker figured Katie would be due to give birth around the last of April or first of May. He said Almeda would probably follow about two weeks later. So both of them were mighty big around the middle by now and were moving slow, with Pa and Uncle Nick worrying and fussing over them every minute. At the picnic it seemed the women talked about nothing else to Almeda. Katie stayed home. Almeda was still spry enough and went into town every other day or so, but she also stayed in bed longer and took lots of rests. Pa saw to that.

Tuesday night in the second week of April, the doctor had been out that afternoon, had seen both Almeda and Katie, and had left with a smile on his face. "Won't be long now, Drummond," he'd said from his buggy. "Everything looks good. Both your wife and sister-in-law are healthy and coming along just fine."

In the middle of the night I was awakened by a loud banging on the door and shouts outside. I bolted awake and knew in an instant it was Uncle Nick. And from the sound of his voice I knew something was wrong.

I jumped out of bed and put on my robe, but by the time I got out of my bedroom Pa and Almeda were already at the door and talking to Uncle Nick.

"It's Katie!" he said frantically. "Something's wrong, Drum—she's yelling and carrying on—"

"I'll go right up there," Almeda said as she started to throw a coat around her robe, then sat down to put on her boots.

"You ain't in no condition to—" Pa began.

"Don't even say it, Drummond," she interrupted. "This is a woman's finest hour, and the hour of greatest need."

"But you gotta take care of—"

"I will take complete care of myself," she said. "Katie needs me now, and I am not going to sit here and do nothing. Are you ready, Nick?" she added, standing up and pulling her coat tightly around her. The door was still open and a cold wind was blowing right into the cabin.

Uncle Nick just turned around and hurried back outside into the night. "She's in terrible pain, Almeda!" he said.

"Then you go on ahead, Nick! Tell her I'm coming. And put water on the stove!" Uncle Nick had already disappeared toward the bridge across the creek.

"I'll need the good lantern, Drummond," Almeda said, "so the wind won't blow it out."

"I'll get it lit," replied Pa as he went toward the fireplace. "Then I'll take you up there."

"You must go for Doctor Shoemaker," objected Almeda.

"I ain't gonna let you walk up there at night alone. You fall, and we'd have two women in trouble in their beds! Corrie," Pa said turning to me. "Go see if Zack's awake, and get him in here pronto."

By the time I got back into the room with Zack, who was still half asleep, Pa had the lantern burning bright.

"Zack, you gotta ride over and get the Doc, you hear me, boy!"

"Yes, Pa."

"We need him fast!"

"I'll bring him, Pa."

"Corrie, you get out there and saddle up—let's see, who's fastest in the dark, Raspberry or Dandy?"

"At night, probably Dandy, Pa," said Zack.

"Then Corrie, you get to saddling Dandy. Zack, you get dressed and get going!"

Then he turned to the open door, holding the lantern in his

left hand while Almeda took hold of his right, and the two of them walked out as quickly as they could to follow Uncle Nick.

In another five minutes, Zack was off, and the sound of Dandy's hoofbeats died in a moment. Suddenly I was left alone. I stoked up the fire with a couple of fresh logs, and lit another lantern. Then I went into the girls' room and woke up Emily, who was already stirring from the noise.

"Emily," I said, "Katie's in trouble. Pa and Almeda are up there already, and Zack's gone for the doctor. I'm going too."

"Should I come, Corrie?" she asked.

"I don't know, Emily," I said. "There probably isn't anything we can do to help, but I've gotta know if Katie's all right. You stay here with the others, and if they need us, I'll come and get you."

I was glad Pa had gone with Almeda! A storm had blown in while we'd been sleeping, and the wind was howling fiercely. I had trouble keeping my lantern from blowing out.

By the time I arrived at Uncle Nick's cabin, it seemed like an hour had already passed! Things were happening fast and I could feel the tension the minute I walked in. Pa stood at the pot-bellied stove watching a kettle of water that was nearly boiling. Alongside, a pot of coffee was brewing. Uncle Nick paced around with a horrified look on his face. I'd never seen him like that before—so helpless, so concerned, wanting to help yet looking like a lost little boy who didn't know what to do. Even though it was his house and his baby being born, it looked like he felt out of place.

Both of them glanced at me as I came in but hardly took any other notice. Just as I closed the door I heard a scream from the other room. Uncle Nick spun around. "Oh God!" he cried. He took a couple of quick steps toward the bedroom, then stopped. Pa went over and put an arm around Uncle Nick's shoulder, and from the slight movement of his lips, I knew he was praying hard.

Oh God, I breathed silently, *whatever's going on, I ask you to be close to Katie and take care of her. And Uncle Nick too.*

"Anything I can do, Pa?" I said.

He gave me a wan smile that showed he appreciated my being there. "Could you check on Erich? He's sleeping in the other room," he answered. "And pray that the Doc'll get here in a hurry."

Almeda came in from the bedroom. She was so obviously pregnant, walking with a bit of a waddle, and her face was a little pale. But otherwise you'd have thought *she* was the doctor! Still wearing her robe, she had her sleeves rolled up. Her hair was loose and hanging all out of place. And you could see the perspiration on her forehead. She looked like she'd been on the job working with Katie for an hour already.

She came up to Uncle Nick and attempted a smile. "You have nothing to worry about, Nick," she said. "The baby's just a few weeks early, that's all."

"Why's she crying out and screaming then?" said Uncle Nick, still looking frantic.

"That's what labor is like, Nick," she answered. "You weren't here when Erich was born, were you?"

"No, you and the Doc made me and Drum get outta here."

"And this is exactly why," said Almeda, smiling again. "It can be harder on the husband, who's fretting and stewing in the other room, than for the woman herself."

"But is Katie . . . is she all right?"

"Of course. She is fine. Labor is a long and painful process, Nick. It hurts, and sometimes we can't help crying out. It might not be a bad idea again for you and Drum to go down—"

Before she could finish another shriek came from the other room. A horrified look filled Uncle Nick's eyes. You could tell the sound pierced right through to his heart.

"It's another contraction!" said Almeda, turning to return to Katie. "Drummond, why don't you take Nick down to our place. And take little Erich with you."

"We oughta at least wait till the Doc's here."

"We'll be fine. Corrie, come with me."

Nick bundled up little Erich, still half-asleep despite all the commotion, and he and Pa took the lantern and started down the hill to our house.

I followed Almeda into the bedroom. Katie lay there with only a sheet over her. She yelled out again just as we came in. I was frightened, but Almeda walked straight over to the bed and took Katie's hand.

"Go around the bed, Corrie," she said to me. "Take her other hand so she has something to squeeze. It helps with the pain."

I did as she said.

Katie was breathing hard, her face wet and white. Her eyes were closed and a look of excruciating agony filled her face. Just as I took hold of her, she cried out again and lurched up in the bed. She grabbed on to my hand like a vise and held it hard as she pulled herself forward. The pain lasted ten or fifteen seconds, then she began to relax and lay back down, her face calming, her lungs breathing deeply. Still she held my hand, but not as hard. Slowly she opened her eyes a crack, glanced feebly at the two of us, managed a thin smile, then closed her eyes again. It was the first smile either of us had had from her in a long time.

Almeda left the bedside and wrung out a towel that had been soaking in a bowl of hot water. She pulled back the sheet and laid it over Katie's stomach just below where the baby was.

"Corrie," she said, "we need some more hot water. Go in the other room and fill this bowl from the kettle on the stove."

"That feels good," I heard Katie murmur as I left the room. "Thank you, Almeda," she added, and then all was quiet.

I got the hot water and went back into the bedroom. Katie was resting peacefully for the moment. Almeda sat by the bedside holding her hand. The look on my face must have been one of anxiety, because Almeda spoke to me as if she were answering a question I hadn't voiced.

"Don't worry, Corrie. This is just going to take some time, and Katie's not done hurting and crying out. She needs us to be strong for her."

Just then another contraction came. Katie winced and held her breath for a minute, then suddenly let it out in a long wail of pain. She lurched forward, holding her breath. I hurried over to the other side of the bed and took her hand. She grabbed on to it for dear life until the pain began to subside a minute or two later.

It went on like this for a while. In between contractions Almeda changed the hot towel while I wiped off Katie's face with a cool cloth, went to get water, or did whatever else Almeda said. It must have been a half an hour or forty minutes before we heard the outside door open.

"It's Doc Shoemaker," a voice called out. Doc walked into the room, carrying his black leather case. "How is she?" he asked.

"The contractions are coming about every two or three minutes now, Doctor," Almeda replied.

"She's getting close then," he said with a sigh that didn't sound too enthusiastic. "Three weeks early," he mumbled to himself as he approached the bed. "Hmm . . . don't suppose that's too worrisome in itself."

I stood aside and the Doc spoke softly to Katie, then put his hand on her stomach where the baby was. He held it there a long time with a real serious expression on his face. He didn't say anything.

Another contraction came. Katie winced and cried out. The doctor kept one hand on the baby and with the other took hers. I stood on the other side of the room watching. The Doc's face was expressionless.

When the contraction finished and Katie fell back on her pillow, the Doc let go of her hand and again felt the baby, this time with both hands. Still I couldn't tell a thing from his face. Almeda, too had her eyes fixed on him, looking for any sign that might betray what he was thinking.

He looked over at Almeda, then back down at Katie, then glanced up in my direction.

"Corrie, do you mind if I have a few words with Almeda," he said, "alone?"

"Sure," I said. "I'll go put some more water on the stove."

I left the bedroom, wondering what the matter was. I scooped out some water from the big bucket Uncle Nick had

pumped up from the stream and added it to the kettle sitting
steaming on the stove. Just as I was putting another log or two
on the fire, I heard Katie cry out again. It wasn't quite as loud
as before, but the tone sounded so painful, more like a wail
than a scream. It shot straight into my heart and a shiver went
through me. I heard the Doc's voice too, though I couldn't
make out anything being said. I hurried and shoved the wood
into the stove. Then I tried to find something else to keep me
busy, but there wasn't anything to do but pace around the floor.

Another scream came from the bedroom. It had been less
than a minute since the last one! I was getting worried, and I
wished they'd call me back in instead of making me wait outside.

Almost the instant the cries and sounds stopped, the bedroom door opened. It was Almeda. Her face was pale.

"Corrie, go get your uncle."

"Is everything—"

"Just get Nick, Corrie," she said. "Get him now!"

I didn't wait for any more explanations. I turned around
and ran from the house, hearing another mournful cry from
Katie just as I shut the door. I was halfway back to our place
and stumbling along the path beside the stream before I realized
I'd forgotten both a lantern and my coat. I would have known
the way blindfolded—and I might as well have been because
of the dark! The wind was still howling. Finally I saw the faint
glimmer of light from one of our windows. I crossed the bridge,
still running, and ran straight up to the house, tore the door
open, and ran inside.

"They want you, Uncle Nick!" I said, all out of breath.

"Is the baby born?" he asked, jumping up and throwing
on his coat.

"I don't know. They just said to get you quick."

He was already out the door at a run.

"What is it, Corrie?" Pa asked.

"I don't know, Pa. They made me leave the bedroom, then
Almeda told me to go fetch Uncle Nick."

He had his coat on now too, then grabbed the lantern and

headed out the door after Uncle Nick. I followed, running after him, although the bobbing light ahead of me got farther and farther away as we made our way up the trail along the creek.

By the time I reached Uncle Nick and Aunt Katie's place, I was breathing hard. The door to the cabin was open, and Doc Shoemaker was standing in the doorway. Nick was trying to get by into the house but the Doc was holding on to him trying to talk to him.

"Not yet, Nick!" he said. "Give her a few minutes."

I didn't see Almeda. Pa was standing beside Uncle Nick. He saw me coming and stretched out his arm to put around me. I came up close and he drew me to him tight, but just kept looking at Uncle Nick.

"I gotta go to her!" said Uncle Nick frantically. "I gotta know if she's—"

"She's fine, I tell you, Nick. But she's just been through something awful, and you must let her—"

"Get outta my way, Doc!"

"Please, Nick, just wait for two or three minutes until you calm—"

"I ain't waiting for nothing!" said Uncle Nick. He pushed the doctor aside and ran inside.

"Nick, please!" Doc Shoemaker called after him. But it was too late. Uncle Nick was through the door and the tromping of his heavy boots thudded across the floor toward the bedroom.

The doctor sighed, looked at Pa with a helpless expression, then followed slowly after Uncle Nick.

"What is it, Pa?" I said finally, feeling a great fear rising up inside me.

"The baby's dead, Corrie," he answered. I'd never heard such a sound of grief in his voice in my life. He squeezed me tight with his arm again. I felt the sobs tugging at my breast even before the tears came to my eyes. Pa knew what I was feeling. I knew he had tears in his eyes too, even in the darkness, even without looking up into his face. I just knew.

Slowly we walked inside. Pa closed the door. The next moment Almeda emerged from the bedroom. Before she got the door shut behind her, I heard the sound of the doctor's voice again, and Nick's. Uncle Nick was crying.

Almeda walked toward us. She was very pale, her face covered with sweat, with splotches of blood on her robe. Her eyes met Pa's and they looked at each other for a few seconds, almost as if they were wondering in the silence whether something like this was in store for them in the near future.

Then Almeda glanced at me, and gave me a thin smile. Pa put his arm around her and Almeda embraced us both. The three of us held on to each other for a long time. I knew Almeda was crying, too.

"God, oh God!" Pa said after about a minute. "They need your help now more than they ever have. Be a strength to them."

"Yes, Lord!" Almeda breathed in barely more than a whisper.

Again they were silent. Slowly Pa released me and led Almeda to a chair and made her sit down. He turned toward the kitchen and found a towel, dipped it in the bucket of cold water, then gently began wiping Almeda's face and forehead with it.

She sat back, closed her eyes, and breathed in deeply.

In another minute Doc Shoemaker came back from the bedroom. He walked over to Pa.

"Drum," he said softly. "You've got yourself a mighty brave woman there. But she's in no condition for all this. This has taxed her more than I like. You get her home and into some fresh things and to bed."

"Yes, Doc."

"Then you send one of your kids—Zack or Corrie, or if you want you can go yourself—but one of you go into town and get Mrs. Gianini. You'll have to rouse her, but she'll come right out when you tell her I need her. She'll spend the night with Katie and help me clean up and get the baby ready for burying."

"You need any more help, Doc?" Pa asked.

"She'll know what we need, Drummond. Don't you worry

about anything but that wife of yours. She's put in a hard night's work. If we need anything, I'll get one of your girls. As soon as things are in order here, I'll come down and check on Almeda."

"I'll be fine, Doc Shoemaker," said Almeda softly.

"I will check on you anyway. And, Drummond," he added, again to Pa, "fix me some place to spend the night. The barn will be fine. I want to stay close."

"You can have my bed," I said.

"Doesn't matter to me," replied the Doc. "I appreciate it, Corrie. But I'm sure I'll be able to catch a little sleep anywhere!"

Pa helped Almeda get slowly to her feet. Then we began our way home, both of us helping her so she wouldn't stumble in the dark. It was a slow walk, but within half an hour Almeda was in her own bed and sleeping peacefully.

CHAPTER 44

BITTER WORDS

Almeda was tired the next day, but otherwise fine. She stayed in bed the whole day except for about an hour when we had the funeral for Uncle Nick and Aunt Katie's little stillborn daughter.

Mrs. Gianini helped get everything cleaned up and tended to Katie through the night. Then in the morning she got the baby ready. Once the new day came Uncle Nick showed what a strong man he had become. His tears were now past and he did everything he could for Katie, being tender and serving her when he could, being brave and in charge when that was necessary too.

Doc had spent the night getting what sleep he could, but checking on both Katie and Almeda every hour or two to make sure they were all right. Katie was weak and stayed in bed all the next day, although Doc Shoemaker said she would recover and be fine in a week or two. She didn't even get out of bed for the burial.

A few people came out to pay their respects to Nick and to stand with him at the graveside—the Shaws and Miss Stansberry and a few others. Rev. Rutledge, of course, took care of things, read from the Bible, and prayed before the tiny box was lowered into the ground. Pa had dug a grave not far from the apple trees Katie had planted from Virginia. The little cross marker on the grave, so near the trees that were a symbol of hope and new life, became a poignant reminder that things

266

don't always go the way we expect or want them to, and that frontier life in this new state sometimes brought hardship along with it.

I cried. So did the other women—Becky, Emily, Almeda, and the others. Pa and Uncle Nick were pretty straight-faced and serious. Afterward people shook Uncle Nick's hand and tried to say encouraging things to him. They wanted to go in and pay their respects to Katie too, but she wouldn't see anybody.

Doctor Shoemaker went home after the funeral, got some fresh clothes, and came right back out. He wanted to spend the rest of the day near both ladies. They were all right, so he managed to get a good bit of sleep during the afternoon. After checking on them early in the evening, he went home. He kept coming out every day for a while.

Almeda stayed in bed for another day or so. She said she felt fine, but the doctor had told her to rest, and she complied with his wishes. Katie hardly got out of bed except when she had to for two weeks. We all admired the way Uncle Nick tended her. But through it all Katie was sullen and cross, hardly speaking, even to him. She just lay there in her bed, either sleeping or staring straight ahead across the room, not even noticing when people came and went.

Pa and I tried to help Uncle Nick, and after a few days Almeda went up to visit Katie. I went with her. We took a pot of soup and some bread we'd made. Little Erich was glad to see us, but the look on Uncle Nick's face made it clear he was feeling awkward about Katie's moodiness. We went in to see her. Almeda tried to be as cheerful as she could, but sensitive too.

"I'm so sorry, Katie," she said, sitting down beside the bed and taking Katie's hand. Katie continued to stare straight ahead. Her hand just lay limp in Almeda's. She didn't act as if she was even aware that anyone was in the room. She didn't move a muscle to acknowledge us.

"Is there anything I can do for you?" Almeda asked. "Anything you need or would like to eat or drink?"

Katie said nothing. There was a long silence.

"Would you mind if I prayed for you?" Almeda asked at length. Suddenly Katie's eyes shot wide open and her nostril's flared. She yanked her hand from Almeda's and turned on her with red face.

"How dare you talk to me about prayer!" she shouted angrily, as loud as her condition would allow. "After God's just taken my baby, and you want to pray to him?"

"It's impossible for us to understand his ways," said Almeda softly, smiling sadly down on Katie.

"I suppose you're going to tell me next that I ought to thank him for what he's done!"

"We just can't know what's in God's heart, Katie. All we can know is that he loves us more than we can imagine, and that everything he does can work for *good* if we allow it."

"Good! Ha!" she shot back, seething now. "I suppose if he takes *your* baby, you will smile and give him thanks—is that what you're telling me?"

"I would try to have a heart of gratitude, in spite of the pain I'm sure I would feel."

"Well, you're a foolish woman, Almeda!" said Katie bitingly. "You're more of a dimwit than I took you for! Don't you even know what it's like to feel a woman's worst grief? I don't think you have any feelings at all, Almeda!"

Almeda turned away. The words stung her to the heart. Her cheeks reddened, and hot tears rose to her eyes.

"Katie," she said, looking back toward the bed, "I'm so sorry. I didn't mean to sound unfeeling. I understand the pain you must feel, and I want you to know—"

"*Understand*! What could you understand about what I feel? Spare me your sympathy, Almeda. I don't need you feeling sorry for me any more than I need your idiotic prayers! Just leave me alone!"

"Oh, Katie, please let us—"

"Get out, Almeda! You and Corrie just go. I don't want to see you . . . or anybody!"

Again Almeda turned quickly away, fighting back emotion.

Slowly she rose and without any further words the two of us
left the room.

We closed the door behind us. I think Uncle Nick had heard
everything because he was standing close by. The look that
passed between him and Almeda was enough. They both
seemed to understand what the other was thinking and feeling.

"You come get us if there's *anything* any of us can do, Nick,"
said Almeda. "Fixing something to eat, cleaning up, taking
Erich for a while . . . anything."

Uncle Nick nodded, then went into the bedroom. We left
and started the walk home in silence, going slowly on account
of Almeda's condition. I kept hold of her arm. We were barely
out of the clearing toward the creek when we heard Uncle Nick
running up from behind. We stopped.

"She's crying," he said. "She won't say a word, she's just
sobbing."

"Did she ask for us?" said Almeda.

"Not exactly," replied Uncle Nick. "But I can tell she's
sorry for how she treated you. Won't you come back and try
to talk to her?"

"It's got to be in her time, Nick."

"But she's hurtin' something terrible, Almeda."

"I know. Anybody can see that, Nick. But she's so angry
and bitter toward God that she can't hear anything we try to
say, and she can't receive any love we try to offer her."

"But won't you just try?" His voice sounded almost desperate.

"Of course we'll try. We'll be back every day. We'll do all
we can. And yes, I'll come back and try to talk to her. But right
now, Nick, I just don't think she's open to anything I have to
give or to say. Come down this evening and let us know how
she is. If you think she would like to see me, you know I'll be
on my way that very minute. Corrie too—any of us. We'll stand
with you through this, Nick, whatever comes."

"But what do I do for her in the meantime?"

"Pray for her, Nick. She is fighting against some things that
have been with her for a long time. God is moving closer and

closer to her heart, but she is resisting him. She needs your prayers now more than ever."

"I'll try," sighed Uncle Nick, turning back toward his cabin.

"You pray, and then you serve her and love her every minute," added Almeda. "When she finally breaks, it will be your love that will see her across that unknown gulf she's so afraid of."

"I'll try," repeated Uncle Nick. He walked back to the cabin, frustration showing in the slump of his shoulders. We turned and continued our way back down the slope toward the creek.

CHAPTER 45

REMORSE AND CONFUSION

Almeda was quiet the rest of the day. It was hard to hear the kinds of things Katie had said to her. She had done so much for Katie, only to be spoken to so rudely because of it. I have to admit, as sorry as I was about the baby and for the grief Katie was feeling, her angry words toward Almeda got me more than a little riled. But Almeda kept saying, "It's not me she's angry at, Corrie. She needs our patience and our love now more than ever. The Lord is pushing aside her outer shell, and she needs us to stand with her until he breaks through to her."

She asked me to go back up that evening to ask about Katie. Emily and I went. Uncle Nick came outside with us.

"She's calmed down and is feeling better," he said. "She slept most of the afternoon."

"That's good," I said. "Almeda said to tell you that if you think she wants to talk again, to come get her."

"I wish she would," he replied. "I don't ever know what to say when she's feeling down and upset like she gets."

We took Erich back down to our place with us for the night so Uncle Nick would be free to look after Katie and get some sleep. He looked tired.

Nothing much happened for another day or two. Uncle Nick was still downcast from worrying about Katie. Doc Shoemaker came out again. He pronounced Katie fit and said she could get up and about for a few hours a day if she wanted. But she remained glum, and stayed in bed.

271

He told Almeda to take care of herself. "Only three or four weeks for you now, Almeda," he said. "Don't you go getting any ideas about going back into town or doing anything around this house. You've got three daughters for all that. You just keep yourself rested, you hear?"

"Of course, Doctor," she laughed.

The next day, early in the afternoon, Uncle Nick came running down to our place. His face looked more full of life as he came through the door than I'd seen it in weeks. Pa was outside, but he came straight to me.

"She asked to see you!" he said out of breath.

"Katie?" I said.

He nodded.

"Me?"

"You and Almeda."

In an instant I was off to tell Almeda in her room. She was dressed but lying in bed. She got right up and came out to where Uncle Nick was still standing. The look on his face was bright and excited.

"Did she really ask to see us, Nick?" Almeda asked.

A sheepish expression crossed his face. "Well, we were talking," he said, "and I happened to say as how I thought she'd been a mite hard on the two of you last time. She was pretty quiet, you know how she's been of late. Then she just kinda nodded and said, 'I suppose I was at that.'

"So after a minute I said, 'What'll you do if Almeda or Corrie comes calling again? You gonna send 'em away like you never want to see them again?' I reckon it was a hard thing to ask her, but doggone if she wasn't beginnin' to try my patience with all her surly scowls and irritable talk."

"She can't help it, Nick," said Almeda softly.

"I figured that," replied Uncle Nick. "Well, anyhow I said it, and she didn't say nothin' for a while, then she said, 'No I wouldn't send them away.' I figured that was about as good an invitation as you was gonna get, so I came down when she fell asleep to tell you."

Almeda looked at him for a moment with a blank expression. Then her face broke into a laugh. "You are something, Nicholas Belle! You really love that wife of yours, don't you?"

"I reckon so. I just can't cotton to you and her being apart and for her to be angry with my own kin. Will you come?"

"Of course we'll come," she replied with a smile. "You go on home. We'll come up for a visit sometime this afternoon."

A couple of hours later we walked up. I had made some shortbread to take, which I knew was one of Katie's favorites.

Uncle Nick met us at the door and took us straight into the bedroom. Katie was awake. I told her I'd made her some shortbread. She tried to smile, but it was one of those smiles that showed there was something on her mind behind it. I think she was embarrassed about what had happened before.

"How are you feeling, Katie?" Almeda asked.

"Oh, better, I suppose. You?"

"Very well."

"How much longer?"

"The doctor said probably three weeks."

"I hope . . . I hope it goes well for you," said Katie. It was hard for her to say.

"Is there anything you need?" Almeda asked after a minute. Her voice was so full of tenderness and compassion, and her eyes so full of love as she stood beside Katie's bed. Katie looked up at her and her eyes filled with tears.

"Almeda, I'm sorry for the things I said before," she said.

"Oh, Katie, dear, think nothing of it." Almeda sat down on the chair at the bedside and took Katie's hand.

"It's just that I was so afraid of dying," Katie went on, trying to maintain her composure. "When I was lying here having the baby, it hurt so bad! I was more worried about myself than . . . than my little daughter! Every time I screamed out, I was sure it was going to be the last breath I breathed. It was so much worse than with Erich!"

"There, there," said Almeda, running her hand gently along Katie's head and smoothing down her hair. "It's all right, dear."

"And then when she came out, and the doctor told me she

was dead," Katie said, sobbing now, "I felt . . . I just felt so guilty! All I had been thinking about was myself! And all the time, even while she was inside me . . . my poor little daughter was—"

She couldn't even finish the sentence, but let out a mournful wail of such bitter remorse that it went straight into my heart and my eyes filled with tears. Poor Katie!

"She was dead!" sobbed Katie. "Dead, and the whole time I was worried about *myself!* I can hardly bear the thought of how selfish I was! Oh God, why couldn't you have taken me instead of her?"

I could hardly keep from crying. I wondered if I should leave and let Katie and Almeda be alone. But when I looked at Almeda as she stared down into Katie's forlorn face, I could tell she was praying even though her eyes were open. I had seen her pray for others like that and I always knew when she was talking to the Lord. Then I thought maybe it would be best for me to keep sitting right where I was.

I closed my eyes and began praying for Katie myself.

"He wanted you to live," said Almeda softly.

"But why? Why should he want me to live, instead of my baby?"

"I don't know, Katie. He loves you, Katie. I know that. He loves you, and your baby."

"Oh God!" Katie wailed again as if she hadn't even heard. "How could I think of myself at a time like that!"

Almeda didn't reply. Katie was sobbing.

"I've always thought more of myself than anyone else," she said. "Nick's so considerate to me, but I don't show him half the love he does me! I've acted dreadfully to you . . . to both of you! I'm so selfish! I hate the person I've become! I'd rather it *had* been me that had died! You'd all be better off without me!"

"Don't say such things, Katie. Don't you know that we love you?"

"Love me! How could you love me? Look at me! There's nothing to love!"

"God wouldn't have made you if you weren't special to him."

"That's ridiculous! Why should God care about me? I've never given him a thought! Why should he love me?"

"He loves us all."

"You, maybe. But I've always told him to keep away from me."

"Don't you remember all I told you, Katie? I used to be further from him than you could ever be."

"I don't know if I believe half what you told me, Almeda." I opened my eyes. One look into Katie's face told me the old anger was coming back. Her voice had changed, too.

"Oh, Katie, I would *never* tell you something that wasn't true."

"Well, I don't care anyway. I never had any use for God, and I certainly don't mean to start now."

"Oh, but Katie . . . dear! You need him now more than ever."

"I won't need him! I refuse to need him," she snapped back. "If he's going to take my baby, then he's not going to have me! He took my parents from me! He's taken everything I ever cared about. I've had to make my own way. It's little enough he's ever done for me! And now he's taken my daughter! I won't need him, I tell you!"

"Perhaps he took your little girl because he loved her so much he wanted to have her near him," said Almeda after a moment, still speaking calmly.

"That's absurd, Almeda!" said Katie angrily. "If there's a God at all, which I doubt, then what right has he got to toy with our lives like that?"

"He doesn't toy with us, Katie. We just can't see how much he loves us. But everything works for good if we will only let—"

"There you go again, saying it's good that my baby died!" interrupted Katie. "I suppose you'll tell me next that it's good I'm such a hateful and selfish person! If that's your God, Almeda, then curse him! I hate him, too . . . I hate you all . . .

I hate myself . . . God . . . just go . . . leave me alone . . . just let me die!"

She turned over in her bed, sobbing bitterly.

Almeda looked over at me, sick at heart. She closed her eyes again. Then after a moment she sighed deeply, rose from the chair, and together we left the room. Katie was still weeping.

"Your dear wife really needs you, Nick," Almeda said to Uncle Nick. "Love her, Nick. Give her all the love you can. She's more alone right now than she's ever felt in her life. God is right at the threshold, but she doesn't know it. That tough self-sufficient outer layer is nearly broken. And when it does break, she's going to need you there to help her."

Uncle Nick nodded. We left the cabin and started home.

We had nearly reached the bridge over the creek when Uncle Nick overtook us. This time he had a message directly from Katie's lips.

"She told me to get you," he said. Almeda looked him intently in the eyes. "She *wants* to see you," he said.

We turned around at once and walked back up the trail. Almeda took Uncle Nick's arm, and I followed behind them.

CHAPTER 46

THE ANGELS SINGING

Once again we walked into the bedroom. This time Uncle Nick went in with us.

Katie was sitting upright, propped up by several pillows. Her face was red and her eyes puffy, but she wasn't crying any more, and there was a look of determination on her face.

"Please forgive me, Almeda . . . Corrie," she said. "Please have patience with me for my rudeness."

"You are forgiven," said Almeda softly, smiling at Katie. I walked over to the bedside, leaned down, and gave Katie a hug. She put her arms around me and squeezed me in return. The feel of her arms around my shoulders filled me with such happiness I started to cry again. I pulled back and sat down across the room. Almeda again sat down next to the bed.

There was a long silence. Finally Katie spoke again.

"Do you *really* believe that God intends everything for our good?" she asked. For the first time her voice sounded as if she genuinely wanted to know.

"Oh yes, Katie," smiled Almeda. "He is more wonderfully good, and his ways are more wonderfully good than we have the faintest notion of."

"Then why did my parents die . . . why did he take my baby?" said Katie, starting to cry.

Almeda took her hand. "I don't know, Katie," she replied with tenderness. "There's so much we *can't* understand about life. Corrie lost her mother also. I have had to struggle with all of the *whys* my past life. There are hurts every man and woman has to face and wonder about. There are disappointments. We can be lonely. We lose things and people who are precious to us. But there is one thing I've learned in the years since I gave my heart to the Lord, and I think it's just about the most important lesson our life in this world has to teach us. Do you know what that lesson is?"

Almeda stopped and waited. Finally Katie spoke up. "I don't suppose I do," she said.

"It's just this, Katie," Almeda continued, "that when life's heartaches and hurts and disappointments come, running *to* God, not *away* from him, is our only hope, our only refuge."

"Is that what I've been doing—running away?"

"I'm not sure, Katie. I don't know that it's my business to say. Only you would know for certain. But you haven't been running *to* him." There could be no mistaking the love in Almeda's voice, in spite of the directness of her words. I knew that at last Katie realized Almeda loved her and wanted to help her. She began to weep softly.

"I know you've suffered hurts and losses, Katie," Almeda went on. "But they've made you bitter and resentful toward God, when actually he was the one you should have gone to for help. He would have borne the pain *for* you. But by keeping him away, you had to bear it all alone.

"Katie, I'm so sorry about your daughter! I grieve with you! But don't you see, the only place for the pain to go is into the hands of Jesus. Otherwise it will tear you apart inside. Instead of turning *from* him, and blaming him, and crying out *against* him, he is the one you must go *to*. He did not take your daughter to inflict hurt. He loves that precious little girl, who is now radiantly alive in his presence, more than any of us ever could! And he loves you, Katie! His arms are wide open, waiting for you to run into his embrace. He is waiting to enfold you in his arms and draw you into himself, waiting to pour out his love in your heart, waiting to fill you with his peace."

Still Katie wept softly.

"I'm ready to listen to what you want to tell me," she said

finally, her voice barely above a whisper. "But I don't know what to do, how to do what you say, even if I want to."

"There's nothing to do, Katie, except to receive the love he offers, the love his arms are waiting to wrap around you."

"How do you receive his love?"

"Just by telling him you want to be his."

"You mean . . . praying?"

"It doesn't matter what you call it, Katie," said Almeda. "God is a friend we can talk to. He is also our Father. We can crawl into his lap and let his arms wrap us up tight, and we can tell him we're tired of being wayward children and we want to stay close to him from now on. Whatever you say, however you say it, he understands. And once you open up your heart to him like that, he will be with you from that moment on, for the rest of your life. With you, and *inside* you! The Bible says that he actually takes up residence inside our hearts and lives with us forever. It's what Jesus calls being born again. That's what it means to give your heart to God. It's what Mr. Parrish helped me to do, and it changed the whole course of my life forever."

A long silence followed.

Without another word, very softly Almeda rose from her chair. With the slightest gesture of one hand she motioned for Uncle Nick to take her place beside Katie's bed. Uncle Nick got up, a momentary look of confusion on his face, not exactly sure what she meant. As he approached Katie and sat down in the seat where Almeda had been, Almeda and I quietly left the bedroom and closed the door. Then we left the cabin and started toward home.

"I'm glad Erich is down at our place," Almeda said after we were a ways along the path. "The two of them need to be alone for a while."

"Why did you get up so abruptly to leave?" I asked.

"Was it abrupt? I didn't mean it to be. I just knew there was nothing else for me to say right then. The next step was Katie's to make, and I felt it was best she have some time to reflect on everything I'd said. God's timing cannot be rushed."

"I know," I said with a smile. "You've taught me that."

"Katie has finally stopped fighting against God. That is a good beginning. How far she goes now, and at what pace—that will be up to her. But I would never want to push someone too fast. We do great harm when we impose our own timetable on the work of the Spirit."

We walked on to the creek and alongside it in silence.

"What do you think will become of Katie and Uncle Nick?" I asked finally.

"Oh, Corrie," said Almeda excitedly, "life is just beginning for them! Everything that's happened up till now has just been preparing them for this time, getting them ready to walk with God in a new way. I truly believe that!"

"And the baby?"

"Sometimes I don't understand God's ways anymore than Katie does. But he turns all for good—when we let him. The two of them losing their daughter is no exception. If they allow him to use it in their lives, it will draw them both closer to him . . . and to each other."

We walked the rest of the way without talking again. When we got home, Almeda lay down.

About an hour later I saw Uncle Nick coming toward the house. Pa was out in the barn. I'd been talking to him and was just coming out when Uncle Nick came up. He had a great big grin on his face and his step was lighter than I'd seen it for several days.

"Where's Almeda?" he said.

"In bed."

"And your Pa?"

"In the barn."

"Well, get Almeda up and I'll go fetch Drum. We'll be inside in a minute."

"What for?" I asked, dying of curiosity.

"Never you mind! I'll tell you all at once," said Uncle Nick, heading off in the direction of the barn. "I got news, that's all I'll say." He was still smiling.

A few minutes later Pa and Uncle Nick walked into the

house, Pa's arm around Uncle Nick's shoulder.

Uncle Nick scooped his son up in his arms. "Well son, your ma did it!"

"Did what, Nick?" asked Pa. "Come on, out with it!"

Uncle Nick was beaming, both from embarrassment and pride all at once. "She prayed, just like you said she ought to, Almeda," he said. "Dad blame if she didn't grab my hand the minute you two left and say, 'Nick, will you pray for me? I want the life that Almeda and Corrie and Drum and the others have. I don't want to be like this any more!' Then she started crying, and I didn't know what to do. 'Please, Nick,' she said, 'you've got to help me! I don't know what to do, but I want to live with God. I don't want to live alone in my heart any more.'

"So I just got up what courage I could muster. Except for that one time with you, Drum, I've never prayed out loud before, but I just said, 'God, you gotta help us, 'cause I don't know what to do. So I ask you to just help Katie, like she said, and show her how to let your arms go around her.' "

"Well, at that, she starting bawling as if she couldn't stop, and I just sat there wondering if I'd said something wrong, getting kinda worried. She just kept crying. But then all of a sudden she burst out praying herself, and she prayed on and on, asking God to forgive her for being so ornery all this time, and for being angry and resentful and for treating people rude and for being selfish. She was crying out how she had hurt so deep inside, saying things I never thought I'd ever hear her say. It was like she was a different person once the shell around her broke apart. There was a look of pain on her face worse than when she was having the baby. She seemed far away in a place all alone—it was a place even I couldn't reach her, though I was sitting beside her holding on to her hand. She was talking to God like I'd never imagined anyone doing, as if he was sitting on the other side of the bed from me—saying . . . all kinds of things."

He stopped and took a deep breath.

"And. . . ?" said Almeda expectantly.

"I guess you could say she and God were having their own

private time together. She said, 'God, I've been so lonely, my heart has felt so cold . . . but now I feel like a little girl again . . . Oh God, why did you take my mother and father from me . . . why did you leave me all alone? I felt so unloved, God . . . no one needed me or wanted me. And now my baby's gone! Was it because of me that you didn't let me keep her . . . wasn't I good enough? Oh, God!' And then she really started to wail— stammering out stuff about being mad at him and getting angry when people would talk about him, and resenting people who went to church. She cried, 'Nobody ever really understood me, Lord . . . no one wanted to be near me, and I took it out on you . . . oh, forgive me—please, Lord! I don't hate you . . . I'm not angry at you any more . . . I *need* you . . . I want so much to trust you . . . so much to feel your love, to know that your arms are wrapped around me like Almeda said. Oh God, I want you to hold me like my daddy never could!' "

Again, Uncle Nick stopped. All the rest of us were silent, hanging on his every word. It was such a moving story, there was nothing to say!

"That was about it," he said, but then a sheepish expression came over his face. "After she was done praying," he continued, "she opened her eyes and looked over at me with a smile, just about the happiest look I'd ever seen on her face. Then she said, 'Oh, Nick, you've been standing with me a long time, and putting up with a lot from me. How can I possibly thank you?' "

"Well . . . what did you say?" asked Pa when Uncle Nick stopped.

"Aw, not much. I just told her I loved her and that it weren't no big thing I done. Then she opened up her arms to me, still smiling, and I sat over on the edge of her bed and leaned over and gave her a hug. And, tarnation if she didn't nearly squeeze the insides out of me! That's when I knew she'd got back most of her strength!"

"Hallelujah!" said Almeda quietly. "God *is* good!" She closed her eyes, and I knew that inwardly she was giving praise to God.

We were all awestruck at what we'd heard.

"God bless her!" said Pa. "I told you if you prayed for her, everything would come out right in the end, Nick."

"What happened to Aunt Katie?" asked Tad, not quite understanding all that was being said.

"The angels in heaven are singing, boy," said Pa, "that's what."

"Your Aunt Katie just gave her life to Jesus, Tad," said Almeda.

"What did you two say to each other after that, Uncle Nick?" I asked. Another sheepish look came over his face.

"Well, if you wanna know," he said, "I prayed again. You see, I'd been sitting there listening to everything you said, Almeda, and it was going down mighty deep into me too. Now you all know I went to church when I was a kid, and that was fine as far as it went. But then I went my own way for a lot of years, as you know better than anyone, Drum. And now I been trying to live my life a mite different, now that I'm married and got myself a family. And I been praying like you said, and trying to remember what I used to know about being a Christian.

"But while you was talking, Almeda, it just sorta dawned on me all of a sudden that I didn't know if I'd ever actually done what you was talking about—prayed, you know, and told God all that about wanting to be different and have him live in my heart. I reckon what I'm saying is that I didn't know if I'd been what you called born again *myself*. I just couldn't say for sure. So I figured it couldn't do no harm to pray all that again, even if I was already on my way to heaven.

"So I did. I prayed it just like Katie'd done. I was still holding her hand, and I closed my eyes and told God I wanted him to live with me too, just like Katie, and I asked him to help me, and to help us both do what he wanted us to, and to be the kind of people he wanted us to be for a change. And when I was all done I stopped, and then I heard Katie whisper a real soft *Amen*. I looked down at her and her eyes were closed again, and the most peaceful look was on her face. I just sat there a long time, her hand in mine. And pretty soon she was asleep, with just a faint smile still on her lips. So I slipped my hand out from hers and came straight down here to tell you what we done."

Our house was so quiet! The only dry eyes in the place were Tad's and little Erich's.

Pa's hand was on Uncle Nick's shoulder again. "You done good, Nick," he said. "You done what you needed to do. It takes a real man to do what you did, to stand up in prayer for himself and his wife. Aggie and your ma and pa'd all be proud of you." He paused just a second or two, then added, "And I'm right proud of you too!"

"Amen!" said Almeda.

I was so happy! We all were. And even though nobody said anything for another spell, all I could think of were Pa's words. And I knew he was right—there was rejoicing going on right then in heaven!

CHAPTER 47

GOD'S LITTLE COMMUNITY

The next few days were a joyous time. Uncle Nick's and Almeda's faces showed that a weight of concern had been lifted from them. And among all of us there was a sense of calm and peace, a good feeling, that would erupt every so often in laughter. Pa played with Tad like I hadn't seen him do in a long time, and Emily asked if she could invite Mike McGee to the house for dinner the next Sunday afternoon. Uncle Nick could be seen bounding all over the property and up and down between the two houses with Erich on his shoulders, laughing and carrying on like they were two little kids. There was really a change in him. How much had to do with Katie, and how much had to do with what he'd done himself, I didn't know.

It didn't matter. A new spirit was suddenly alive among us all because Katie had opened up her heart—and it was wonderful!

Almeda remained quiet. I knew she had to take it slow on account of the pregnancy, and every time Doc Shoemaker came to the house he would say, "Now you just don't let yourself get excited about anything, you hear me, Almeda?" But I think her joy went deeper than it did for anyone else. She probably knew in a more personal way how hard it had been for Katie, and knew more of what Katie was feeling because she had felt the exact same things herself. She had shared her own life with Katie, painful as all the recollections were, and endured the emotional pain over what Katie had said. After all that, and the loss of Katie's child, to have Katie finally say that she wanted to know God's love for herself meant more to Almeda than she could have expressed.

She went up to see Katie the next morning. I asked her if she wanted me to go with her.

"Walk me up to the creek, Corrie," she answered. "But then you can come back down here. I want to talk to Katie alone."

She was there a long time. When she got back home she was clearly tired but there was a peaceful smile on her face. Pa asked her what had happened.

"We had a long talk," Almeda said. "A more personal time than we've ever had. She opened up whole new areas of her life to me. She's really a changed woman! I think we're at last ready to be sisters. And then we prayed together, for the first time, and when I left *she* hugged *me*."

There were tears in Almeda's eyes even before she was through telling about it. She turned and went inside and straight to her bed. Pa just put his arm around my shoulder and gave me a squeeze, and said nothing for a minute.

"The Lord's really up to some unexpected things around here, ain't he, Corrie?" he said finally.

"You can say that again!" I said.

"Nick's just as changed inside as Katie," he said. "And I aim to sit him down like Almeda's done with Katie, and talk about some things and get him to praying too. It's time all ten of us—well, at least the nine of us except for little Erich—it's time we all started praying together and bringing God into *everything* we do around this little community of ours."

"Community, Pa?"

"Yeah, Corrie. Don't you see—we got two houses, two families, nine or ten people, however you count them—"

"Soon to be eleven," I put in.

"Yeah, well I reckon you're right—eleven. But you see, here we are a little community within the bigger community. And if all of us—this nine or ten or eleven of us dedicate ourselves to live in what we do by what God tells his folks to do, then it just seems to me that other folks around might sooner or later stand up and take notice, and say, 'Hey, I want to be part of living that kind of life too.' You see, Corrie, it's gotta start someplace, people joining themselves to live together like God's people. I've been thinking a lot about this, and now with Katie and Nick doing what they've done, I figure God might be about to do some new things among us that we haven't seen before."

"That sounds exciting, Pa," I said. My mind flashed back to my talk with Zack at the picnic, and I wondered if I *wanted* to leave this little "community," as Pa called it, of the Hollister-Belle families. Pa made it sound like there couldn't be a better place to be than right here in the middle of where God was at work. "What do you think he's going to do now?"

"How could I know that?" he answered. "I'm not about to start trying to figure God's ways out ahead of time. I'd have never figured a bunch of people like us would be all together like this. Almeda's from Boston, and Katie's from Virginia! But God's got a way of bringing folks together from places about as far apart as we can imagine, and then, *boom*—there they are together and he starts working among them. So how could I try to figure what he's gonna do *next*?"

"I see what you mean, Pa."

"But I'm sure of one thing."

"What's that?"

"When God sets about knittin' folks together—just like weaving threads to make a piece of cloth—when God starts doing that, then good things happen. Just like all of us here—good things are gonna happen, Corrie, I can just feel it. Other folks besides Katie and Nick are gonna find out what it really means to live like God's people."

"How will they find out?"

"Who can tell? They just will. I don't doubt my being mayor's got something to do with what the Lord's up to. It's no accident I got elected when nothing could have been further from my mind. And your writing, Corrie. People read the things you write."

"But I don't write anything about God or what's happened here in our family."

"You might someday. And when you do, people are gonna pay attention to what you say. They're gonna listen, and they're gonna say, 'Hey, I want to live the kind of life Corrie Belle Hollister talks about . . . I want to be a Christian like that . . . I want to pray and know God's love.' You see, Corrie, there's all kinds of stuff God's gonna do with all of us, and with lots of other people too. We've only just seen the beginning!''

CHAPTER 48

NEW LIFE

Katie was up and out of bed within two days. Everything about her was changed. You'd have never known she just lost a baby. It was as if she had made a decision to be different from now on—which she had!—and was determined to act accordingly. And of course, God living inside her made the biggest difference of all!

All of a sudden, she was down at our place all the time. It reminded me of the time before Pa and Almeda had been married. There was Katie again in our house, bustling about the kitchen, helping with everything. Now Almeda was being pampered and cared for—with Katie and the three of us girls all taking care of her. I usually went into town to handle the business at the freight office. Doc Shoemaker came out every day. Pa wandered about, not able to get much work done for nervousness, but hardly able to get near Almeda—as much as he wanted to help—for all the women tending to her!

After all that had happened, the birth of Pa and Almeda's baby came almost as a routine event in our lives. It was, of course, one of the greatest things that had ever happened, but there was no huge crisis like there'd been with Katie. One morning about two and a half weeks later, Almeda calmly said to Katie, "I think my labor's begun. You'd better send Drummond for the doctor."

The birthing wasn't routine for Pa! He scurried around like a nervous old lady! He sent Zack for Doc Shoemaker. He didn't leave Almeda's side for a second until the Doc came and shooed everyone out of the bedroom.

Almeda's labor lasted about five hours. I don't know whether it was as painful as Katie's, but she didn't cry out like Katie had. About the middle of the afternoon, all of us except Doc and Katie were gathered in the big room. Suddenly we heard some shouts and exclamations, followed by the cry of a baby.

Pa jumped out of his chair and was off to the bedroom like a shot! The doctor tried to keep him out for a few more minutes, but it was no use.

For the next hour the whole house was like a beehive—nobody could sit or stand still for a second. There were kids and men and women, the doctor and Katie and Uncle Nick—everyone moving to and fro, cleaning and congratulating and laughing and talking. Mrs. Gianini was there too—there was hardly a birthing for miles around Miracle Springs that she didn't attend.

Late in the afternoon, after things were more or less back to normal, Doc Shoemaker let us go into the bedroom one at a time and have a visit with Almeda and to see her and Pa's little daughter. Almeda gave me such a smile when I walked in! For the first time in my life, I found myself wondering what it would be like to become a mother.

"What do you think of your new baby sister, Corrie?" she said.

"She's wonderful." What else could I say? She truly was!

They named her Ruth. "Ruth has long been one of my favorite Bible women," said Almeda. "God took a foreigner from a strange land and grafted her into the royal line of his people. That's just how I feel to be married to your father," she told me. "So blessed of God beyond what I deserve. Our daughter's name will always remind me of God's goodness in bringing me, like Ruth, from a distant place to give me a new life here."

There was a bit of a dispute over little Ruth's middle name, with both Pa and Almeda showing that they wanted to honor the *other* above themselves.

"*Parrish* has gotta be her middle name," said Pa.

"But I was only a Parrish for a few years," objected Almeda. "How can we name *our* daughter after my first husband?"

"Ain't no different than naming her after my first wife." Almeda wanted to use the name *Agatha* in honor of Ma.

"That's completely different," said Almeda. "Your Aggie is the mother of *my* children now. I love her because of them."

"That may be," said Pa. "But I'm still mighty grateful for what Mr. Parrish did for you. If it hadn't been for him, you wouldn't be walking with God now, and wouldn't be my wife. I owe the man plenty, and some day I'm gonna shake his hand and tell him so. Besides, I first knew you as a Parrish, and I kinda like the name!"

In the end they compromised and used both names. She became Ruth Agatha Parrish Hollister.

CHAPTER 49

TWENTY-ONE

The rest of the spring and then the summer passed quickly. What a difference a little baby made to life in our little community! There was new life all around—on Katie's face, in little Ruth's crib, in Uncle Nick's walk, and in Pa's stature as a leader in town and among his acquaintances. I could see what Pa had said to me happening—that people would be taking notice of the life that was flowing out on the Hollister-Belle claims.

I had done a lot of thinking about what he'd said about my writing too. And so later that summer I started devoting myself to it again. I didn't write any major articles, but I started spending more time thinking about stories I could write, and dusting off some of my old ideas. I sent some stories to Mr. Kemble and he printed them all in the paper, and was always encouraging me to write more. As I did, I found myself thinking more and more about how I could work God into what I wrote in a way that Mr. Kemble would still find newsworthy. I wanted people who read my articles to know that I was living my life as a daughter of God, not as a person who never thought about him.

I also kept writing in my journal. I wrote about Rev. Rutledge's and Miss Stansberry's wedding. Rev. Rutledge asked Pa to perform the ceremony, and then the men in town *really* started teasing Pa about being a preacher! But he didn't mind. And pretty soon Harriet was expecting a baby too!

I also filled several pages of my journal with the story about Emily and Mike McGee. He didn't just come for dinner that Sunday. He started coming out to the cabin nearly every day. And just before Christmas later that year, he came to see Pa and asked if he could marry Emily. Pa was shocked! Everybody liked Mike, even though he always talked about that new game he liked to play. But *marry* him! "The girl's only just seventeen!" Pa must've exclaimed three dozen times.

But the most important entry in my journal came in March of 1858. It was my twenty-first birthday, and in a lot of ways it was a day when something inside me said, "Well, I suppose I'm getting close to being grown up now."

I wanted to do something special, something I would always remember. For several weeks I'd been considering the idea of taking a ride up into the high hills east of Miracle Springs, maybe even as far as the lake region by Grouse Ridge or Fall Creek Mountain. I didn't really have any definite plans—I just wanted to get high up so I could see the sunrise over the Sierras further east.

It was still dark when I got up, and for the first hour of riding I had to make my way slowly until the faint gray light of dawn gradually began sending the darkness away. In the distance, as I climbed higher and higher over the rugged terrain, gnarled weathered oak trees sat on the horizon, silhouetted against the clear early morning sky that was gradually brightening in the east. Everything was so still and quiet—just a horse and rider moving as one through a smooth grassy meadow of the foothills, dotted sparsely with massive trees, then suddenly encountering the steep rockiness of the mountain region.

Of all the horses I had known and ridden, Raspberry remained my special friend. He was a golden brown color, except for his white stockings and the blaze of white running from between his ears forward to his nostrils. His bulging muscles glistened with sweat. *What a magnificent beast he is,* I thought as he glided with liquid ease, responsive to my every change of the reins, alert to everything around him. I think he enjoyed the morning's ride as much as I did! We galloped across the gently sloping meadows, then slowed to ascend steeper paths upward, and I almost felt Raspberry knew what I was thinking ahead of time!

For an hour we rode, many thoughts passing through my mind, the beauty of the surroundings giving way to reflections on what this day symbolized. What was it that made this, my twenty-first birthday, different from all the ones that had come before? I didn't *feel* any different . . . or did I?

Perhaps it was a deeper sense of accountability—accountability toward others . . . toward God . . . an accountability for my *own* life, my own self.

Even though there were still areas of my life where I felt like a little girl—tentative, unsure of certain things—people would look at me from now on as a "grown up" adult. I was no longer a young girl, but a woman. On this day I was stepping over a threshold into being totally responsible for my own actions, my own thoughts, my own attitudes—accountable for my own decisions, and responsible for making good and right decisions.

God had brought me so far!

Such a short time ago, it seemed, I hadn't known much of anything about what life truly was. I didn't know about God and how he was involved in people's lives, how he wanted to be intimate with us. I hadn't known much about who I was or where I was going, or even who I wanted to be and where I wanted to go.

Yet God had given me such a sense of purpose, so many desires of who and what I wanted to be and become as a person, as his daughter. I wanted to be pure before him. I wanted to love God with my whole being. I wanted to be able to love others with his love. I wanted to be able to tell people about him, about my life with him, about the thoughts and feelings that were in my heart toward him. I wanted to meet and know people who shared that same commitment, those same desires—people who were also on that same road of life.

When I found my thoughts drifting toward marriage, I surprised myself. I didn't think such things very often, and usually figured I'd never marry. But on the occasions when it did cross my mind, I wondered what kind of man God might have for me to share my life with. I'd even fall to imagining about it sometimes. And then I'd realize that in spite of what I'd said to Zack, I did have certain feelings and ideas about the man I would marry, *if* I did. He would be strong and sensitive and loving. But strong in an inward way, not strong the way boys and men talked about strength. *Strong* to me was the quality of character that made someone willing to stand up for what they believed, even to make sacrifices to do it. Almeda was strong in that way. So was Pa. And *sensitive* to me meant the kind of man who could tell what another person, especially a woman, was thinking. Sensitivity meant respecting the thoughts and feelings of others, a gentleness, and especially the ability to talk and share and be open with feelings. Women didn't have much trouble doing that kind of thing, but men usually did. I wanted to marry a man who knew how to talk and share and feel—a man who knew how to cry and wasn't ashamed to be an emotional, open, tender man. That was sensitivity to me. I wondered if such men even existed! As hard as it had been for him at first, Pa was learning to be that kind of man, and I loved him so much for it!

And of course *first* of all, such a man would have to be a Christian, sharing with me the desire to follow God with all his heart in *everything*. How could a man and woman be friends for a lifetime if they didn't share that most important thing of all? And if marriage was something God had for me, I didn't want to just be a wife, and have a husband. I wanted to have a best friend to live the rest of my life with!

Raspberry stumbled momentarily on a rock in our path, and suddenly my thoughts were jolted back from marriage to the present. We were climbing pretty steeply now. It was completely light, and over the mountains ahead of us hues of pink were starting to spread upward from the horizon. The summit up ahead looked like a good place to stop. From there I'd be able to see the sun rise over the peaks in the distance. I urged Raspberry on.

But in spite of the difficult climb, I couldn't keep my thoughts on the ride itself. I found myself thinking about myself and what kind of person I was—the kind of thoughts you usually keep to yourself and don't tell anyone, even your parents or closest friends.

God had given me certain talents and strengths, although sometimes it was hard to admit good things, even to myself. But I knew I had done a lot of growing up in the five-and-a-half years since we had come to California. I'd been fifteen-and-a-half then, and so young. Now here I was looking at life as an adult would. And I wanted so badly to put to good use all that God had given me. I wanted to use the gifts and abilities and strengths he had put inside me to help other people, to grow still closer to him, and to glorify him.

"Oh Lord," I found myself praying, "help me to cultivate what you've given me. Don't let me waste anything. Help me to grow to the fullest, so that I can be the person you want me to be!"

Even as I prayed I realized how much he had already done within me. The growth hadn't all been easy. I'd cried a lot of tears since Ma's death out on the desert. I'd cried with Almeda. I'd cried with Pa. And I'd cried alone. Yet I had grown and matured so much through it all!

And I wasn't the only one who had changed. I'd seen so many other relationships develop and deepen, from Pa and Mr. Royce to Uncle Nick and Katie, Little Wolf and Zack. Mr. Lame Pony was having more to do with people in the community. Rev. Rutledge had changed and become a friend to our family. I saw so much growth in so many people.

I thought about what it was like to toss a pebble into a pond. The rock starts a motion of ripples that spread outward in concentric circles, which eventually goes the entire length of the water in every direction. I was reminded of Almeda, one woman, left alone at her husband's death, yet with faith alive and growing inside her heart, like a rock thrown into the middle of this community.

Then we had come. And through Almeda's walk and life with God I saw something I desired to share, something I wanted and knew I needed. As I searched for the truth, with Almeda helping and guiding and teaching me, our friendship developed and deepened, as did my faith. I became a daughter to her in many ways.

Then Pa was gradually drawn by the same thing I had felt. His faith in God began to grow deeper too, not just from Almeda, but maybe even from me and seeing Rev. Rutledge reach out to him. God was already spreading his life out into the community through more than just one or two.

After Pa and Almeda were married, the circles of deeper faith continued to widen. As Zack and Emily and Becky grew, we all started praying more together as a family. Then things began changing for Uncle Nick. And then God, in his mysterious ways, worked through tragedy to bring Katie into the ever-widening circle.

God, O God, I thought, *you have transformed me and the people around me in so many extraordinary ways! Where will it go from here? What are you going to do next? Whose life will you change . . . whose heart will you get inside of next?*

As we crested the peak, Raspberry struggled up the final bit of the steep climb. Then the path leveled out and continued along for some distance over the high ridge.

I reined him in and sat still in the saddle for another moment or two, glancing around in all directions. What a beautiful view! The long ride, the climb . . . it had all been worth it for this one moment!

Slowly I dismounted, taking the reins in my hand, and walked to a lone tree, growing by itself on the high plateau. I tethered Raspberry to its trunk and patted the red splotch in the middle of his white forehead, the reason for his name.

I walked on farther, climbed onto a big boulder, and sat down on top of it. The sky in the east was now full of vivid colors, all melting into each other as the brightening flame on the horizon gathered in intensity.

Suddenly, from behind a snow-capped peak in the distance, a sliver of the sun shot into view. The intense ray pierced my eyes like a blinding arrow. In a second the whole eastern horizon was changed as brilliant, flashing rays spread out in all directions. All other colors instantly vanished in the core of blinding orange fire.

I turned around and looked in the direction from which I had come. Down in the distance the early morning haze still clung to the trees and ridges and hollows, some of which wouldn't see the sun for several more hours. And then, still farther off, I could just glimpse the big valley into which all the rivers of these mountains poured.

I am twenty-one, I thought to myself. *Twenty-one*! It hardly seemed possible! What would my future hold? I wanted so much to do what God wanted me to. I wanted always to be growing in my knowledge of him, growing in what the Bible called righteousness. I never wanted to let myself relax in my faith and take the easy way. I wanted to hold on to the standards that God had established, the way he wanted his people to walk.

"God," I prayed as I sat there, "I want my whole self to belong to you. I give my all to you. Show me how to do it. I know I can only do it with you beside me and in me."

I could feel the warmth of the sun's rays on my back. I sat still for a long time. Everything was still and quiet. The only sounds to meet my ears were the songs of birds celebrating the sun and the springtime.

Seized by a great surge of joy, I wished I could soar like those birds. I had grown in the years since coming to California from a timid and uncertain young girl into a confident, though occasionally still struggling—could I actually *say* the word?—into an—*adult*.

As I sat there basking in the sunrise, the dawn reminded

me of the day Almeda shared her story and her feelings with Katie. Almeda had said that Mr. Parrish gave her a place to stand. I remembered her words, and I could almost hear her voice when she said, *"Not only was he giving me a place to stand, it was a place of warmth and smiles."*

I got down off the boulder and walked back to the tree where Raspberry was waiting patiently for me. I mounted and we moved on for a short distance in the other direction, gazing toward the mountains, then back westward toward the valley below, where the sun's rays were now probing the hollows and caressing the ridges above them.

Suddenly the overpowering radiance of the sun became a revelation to me. *I have been given a place to stand, too,* I thought. *A place right here, a place in this new state, "the sunshine state." God has given me a place in the sun!*

A sense of calm and peace and assurance flooded over my being. Even as I felt the sun's warmth on my arms and back, I felt God's presence wrapping around me.

I sank to my knees on a patch of nearby grass. Lifting my face toward heaven, I was filled with a heart of gratefulness.

"Thank you, God, for being so near to me, so present with me. Thank you that I am here. Thank you for bringing me to California. Thank you for the place you have given me to stand . . . and to walk. And thank you for everything my future holds . . . whatever it may be."

I lingered a while longer on the grass, soaking in everything I was feeling. Then I slowly stood.

The sun was already climbing into the sky, its fiery beams waking up every inch of the sleepy earth. I walked back toward Raspberry, gave his nose a pat, untied him, and remounted.

"It's time we headed back, my old friend," I said.

Down the way we had come, we made our way toward home. I knew my family would all be up by now and wondering where I was. I smiled at the thought. I probably should have told someone where I was going. But I had wanted to be completely alone, even in the knowledge of where I was!

My heart was still welling up within me, full of God's peace and love. My thoughts and prayers seemed to take up where they had left off on the ride up.

"God," I prayed again, "help me take care of the good things you are doing inside me. Never let me take for granted all you've given, and the life you've put within me. I give my life to you, Lord, and place into your hands whatever my future holds."

People Making A Difference

Family Bookshelf offers the finest in good wholesome Christian literature, written by best-selling authors. All books are recommended by an Advisory Board of distinguished writers and editors.

We are also a vital part of a compassionate outreach called **Bowery Mission Ministries**. Our evangelical mission is devoted to helping the destitute of the inner city.

Our ministries date back more than a century and began by aiding homeless men lost in alcoholism. Now we also offer hope and Gospel strength to homeless, inner-city women and children. Our goal, in fact, is to end homelessness by teaching these deprived people how to be independent with the Lord by their side.

Downtrodden, homeless men are fed and clothed and may enter a discipleship program of one-on-one professional counseling, nutrition therapy and Bible study. This same Christian care is provided at our women and children's shelter.

We also welcome nearly 1,000 underprivileged children each summer at our Mont Lawn Camp located in Pennsylvania's beautiful Poconos. Here, impoverished youngsters enjoy the serenity of nature and an opportunity to receive the teachings of Jesus Christ. We also provide year-round assistance through teen activities, tutoring in reading and writing, Bible study, family counseling, college scholarships and vocational training.

During the spring, fall and winter months, our children's camp becomes a lovely retreat for religious gatherings of up to 200. Excellent accommodations include heated cabins, chapel, country-style meals and recreational facilities. Write to Paradise Lake Retreat Center, Box 252, Bushkill, PA 18324 or call: (717) 588-6067.

Still another vital part of our ministry is **Christian Herald magazine**. Our dynamic, bimonthly publication focuses on the true personal stories of men and women who, as "doers of the Word," are making a difference in their lives and the lives of others.

Bowery Mission Ministries are supported by voluntary contributions of individuals and bequests. Contributions are tax deductible. Checks should be made payable to Bowery Mission.

 Fully accredited Member of the Evangelical Council for Financial Accountability

Every Monday morning, our ministries staff joins together in prayer. If you have a prayer request for yourself or a loved one, simply write to us.

Administrative Office:
40 Overlook Drive, Chappaqua,
New York 10514 Telephone: (914) 769-9000